Russia and Europe
1789-1825

Russia and Europe 1789-1825

By

Andrei A. Lobanov-Rostovsky

GREENWOOD PRESS, PUBLISHERS
NEW YORK 1968

Reprinted with the permission of the

DUKE UNIVERSITY PRESS

First Greenwood reprinting, 1968

LIBRARY OF CONGRESS catalogue card number: 68-30825

Printed in the United States of America

Foreword

Up to very recent times Russian historians have shown little interest in the field of Russia's foreign relations, preferring to concentrate on the internal problems of their country. Russia's role in Europe has been dealt with mainly within the framework of general European histories. French historians have done exceedingly valuable work on the period covered in this volume, and the writer acknowledges his indebtedness to the monumental works of A. Sorel and A. Vandal. But the Russian factor is presented in Sorel's great work as a fractional part of the European scene; whereas Vandal, who devotes himself more exclusively to Russia, covers merely five momentous years (1807-1812). Moreover, both historians necessarily leave out many side issues not immediately related to their subject but still relevant to a complete understanding of Russia's foreign policy. It is to fill this gap that the present work has been written. It aims at presenting an over-all picture of the role of Russia during a crisis in European history which is strikingly similar to the great storm out of which the world is now emerging, particularly with reference to Russia. The writer is fully cognizant both of the magnitude of the task which he set himself and of his own limitations. He hopes nevertheless that the present work, however inadequate, will stimulate further interest in a field the importance of which cannot be overestimated.

In conclusion the writer wishes to express his sincerest appreciation to Professor F. J. Klingberg, of the University of California, Los Angles, for his encouragement and valuable advice, to Mrs. Marjorie D. Kern for assistance in matters of idiom and style, and to his wife for much necessary work in connection with the preparation of the manuscript.

Andrei A. Lobanov-Rostovsky

Ann Arbor, Michigan
January 5, 1946

Contents

Introduction

ON JUNE 27, 1709, while Western Europe was in the throes of the War of the Spanish Succession, in a second war fought over the vast expanse of Eastern Europe the Russian Army under the leadership of Peter the Great inflicted at Poltava a crushing defeat on the Swedish Army of Charles XII. This battle, one of the decisive battles of history, marked the emergence of Russia as a great power in Europe, a fact which was symbolized in 1721 at the time of the celebration of the Peace of Nystadt, which ended this war, by the change of the name of the Czardom of Muscovy to that of the Empire of Russia, and the title of its ruler from Czar to Emperor of All the Russias. This event was hailed in Europe somewhat presumptuously as the birth of a new nation which, previously "Asiatic" and "barbarous," had overnight and by the genius of its great reformer been brought into the fold of European civilization with the concomitant blessings of the light cast by that civilization. In so judging this event, Western Europe overlooked the important fact that the reforms of Peter the Great on the one hand, and his military victories on the other, marked the culmination of eight hundred years of Russian history, and hence that only in the light of this past can the events of his reign be judged in their proper perspective.

Three factors have to be taken into account to explain the optical illusion which affected Western European judgment of Russia at the turn of the eighteenth century, and which has vitiated this judgment even to the present day. The first factor was the adherence of Russia to the Greek Orthodox faith, introduced into that country in the tenth century from Byzantium, which segregated it from the Roman Catholic Church and the Germano-Latin civilizations of the West. The second factor was the Mongol invasion which swept over Russia in the thirteenth century and caused the subsequent Tartar domination, lasting two centuries, and the third factor was the relative isolation of Muscovy from contacts with Western Europe, an isolation maintained from the time of the overthrow of the Tartar domination to the reign of Peter the Great.

To get the correct perspective, we must recall that the Russians did not come from Asia, as commonly believed, but that as members of the Slav subdivision of the Caucasian race they were to be found, as recorded history opens, in the western part of their present home —the original area of Slav habitation extending over Central Eastern Europe from the Elbe River to the Carpathians and the Danube, and thence through Eastern Germany and Poland to Western Russia and the Ukraine. In the course of the subsequent unfolding of centuries the destiny of the Russian people imposed upon them the task of conquest of the vast plain stretching from the Baltic to the Pacific, upon which present Russia is superimposed—a process not unlike the colonization of the United States, only in reverse direction, going from west to east. In the course of this gigantic undertaking, which absorbed the energies of the nation and took nearly a thousand years to accomplish, however, the Russians were faced with problems which do not find a counterpart in American history: They had to overcome the impact of counterinvasions coming westward from inner Asia and challenging the Russian domination of the plain. The Russians succumbed to the most formidable of these invasions, the Mongol invasion of Genghis Khan and Batu, but two centuries later they were strong enough to resume unhindered their eastward drive toward the Pacific. In the course of their struggle against the Mongols the Russians were forced to yield to their western neighbors, Poland and Lithuania, and later to Sweden and Turkey, much of the territory which had been their original home, including the area west of the Dnieper River with Kiev, the capital of the first Russian state. This fact imposed upon the Czars of Moscow the double problem of expanding eastward and at the same time regaining this lost territory to the west and, with the tenacity of purpose shown by Russian diplomacy, led to a struggle extending over two centuries with Poland and Sweden, culminating ultimately in the defeat of Sweden and the destruction of Poland. It was this quest for lost territories which brought Russia out of the complete isolation of the period of the Tartar domination, an isolation as complete as though a curtain had been drawn between her western border and Europe. It is true that even then the Russian republic of Novgorod maintained close trading and diplomatic relations with the Baltic powers, particularly with Sweden and the Hanseatic cities of Germany, but Europe well-nigh forgot the existence of the rest of Russia. But behind that curtain Muscovy was growing strong, reasserting her authority over the whole of the territory of Russia; and after freeing herself from the Tartar yoke, she dramatically emerged once more on the European horizon. Cultural and diplomatic relations with the Italian states were established in the reign of the first "Czar," Ivan III (1462-1505), who also at the turn of the century made an alliance with the Holy Roman Empire directed against Poland. Fifty years later his grandson Ivan IV (Ivan the Terrible) took the offensive against the Livonian Order—the now decadent but once powerful Order of the Teutonic Knights, which had given the Germans the possession of the Baltic coast along the present territory of Estonia and Latvia. This war developed into an international struggle involving Poland, Sweden, and Denmark, and paved the way for the repeated later Russian drives toward the Baltic Sea. When the neighbors of Russia, thus endangered, attempted with the connivance of the Pope and Holy Roman Emperor to establish a *cordon sanitaire* to isolate Russia once more, Ivan succeeded in outflanking his enemies by securing close trading relations with England by way of the White Sea and the Atlantic.

The struggle thus initiated lasted without interruption for over a century, and by a dramatic recoil in the first decade of the seventeenth century brought on a double invasion of Russia, the Poles taking possession of Moscow and the Swedes of Novgorod. However, not only were the Russians able to expel the invaders, but in the second half of the century they succeeded in recapturing the greater portion of the Ukraine, with the ancient capital city of Kiev. Also by this time the Russian Court had established regular diplomatic relations with all the major European countries. However, so far the Russian factor had weighed only in the settlement of border problems directly concerning Russia, and she took no part in the great European conflicts of the century such as the Thirty Years' War and the wars of Louis XIV. The game of balance of power was played in Europe without Russia, and European diplomacy ignored her existence. But when Peter the Great, in coalition with

Denmark, Poland, Saxony, and later Brandenburg, attacked Sweden, the picture changed; and Russia could no longer be ignored in the settlement of European affairs. Not only did Russia capture from Sweden the Baltic coast, which had passed from the Livonian Order under Swedish domination, but the Russian Army made its first and effective appearance on the soil of Germany proper, by occupying Pomerania, Mecklenburg, and Holstein, and pushing as far as Hamburg.

II

The emergence of Russia at this point as the new great power in Europe upset the European balance of power and was anything but welcome to European chancelleries. Timid attempts were made to block the rise of Russia's power, but the time was now past when these could succeed. Not only Russia had changed as a result of the reforms of Peter the Great, but also Europe itself was undergoing an equally momentous change. Indeed, the times were propitious for the emergence of Russia. Of the six great powers then existing in Europe, two, Spain and Sweden, had dropped out, the second through the instrumentality of Russia. Poland was so much on the decline that, although an ally of Russia in the war against Sweden, she had become a pawn in the conflict between Peter the Great and Charles XII, both parties putting on the throne of Poland their respective candidates—Augustus of Saxony and Stanislas Lesczynsky—as the ebb and flow of the struggle gave them the upper hand. It may here be parenthetically observed that just as an expanding physical mass displaces the objects around it, so Russia in the course of her growth to power destroyed or reduced to impotence all her immediate neighbors: first Livonia, then Sweden, then Poland, and lastly the Ottoman Empire, the latter then at the zenith of its power but soon to be reduced by the strength of the Russian arms to the position of the "sick man of Europe." Of the powers not immediately bordering Russia, France had been ruined by the disastrous War of the Spanish Succession, and the first rumblings of the not-too-distant French Revolution were soon to be heard. Moreover, she was in the midst of her death struggle with England over the mastery of the seas and the domination of the colonial world. England, engaged in building up her empire at the expense of France and Spain, was playing in Europe the game of maintaining the balance of power, and was not averse to backing Russia when circumstances demanded it. Lastly, within the Holy Roman Empire, exhausted by the Thirty Years' War and the wars of Louis XIV, the rise of Prussia was challenging dangerously the predominant position of Austria. Austria, faced with this threat on one side, and with the continuing great dynastic struggles of the Hapsburgs and the French Bourbons which had lasted for centuries, was one of the first to see the advantages of a Russian alliance, which was to be continued in one form or another throughout the greater part of the coming century. Thus the new Russian Empire faced in Europe only one really dangerous and implacable enemy, and that enemy was France. In her titantic struggle against the House of Austria, France had relied for over two centuries on an alliance with the three powers bordering upon the Holy Empire from the east—namely, Sweden, Poland, and Turkey—in order to place Austria (and the Holy Roman Empire she dominated) between two fires. But as we have seen, the sudden rise of Russia had endangered the very existence of France's eastern allies. Faced with this situation, French diplomacy not only remained bitterly hostile to Russia, rejecting every offer of friendship made by the Court of St. Petersburg, but at the same time pursued unrelenting efforts to use Sweden, Poland, and Turkey against Russia in an effort to establish once more a *cordon sanitaire* segregating Russia from Western Europe. Two centuries later, after the first World War, France reverted to the same policy in the modified form of the Little Entente, and with as little success.

Such was the diplomatic pattern which existed in Europe at the time of the death of Peter the Great, and it explains why henceforth the struggle of Russia with her western neighbors became an issue which shook the whole fabric of European diplomacy. Notwithstanding the dark days of confusion and constant palace revolutions which followed the death of the great Czar, the power and weight of Russia, from the standpoint of her international position, kept on steadily growing. In the War of the Polish Succession (1733-1735) not only did Russia impose upon the unwilling Polish nation her candidate for the throne of Poland, Augustus III, as against the French-supported Stanislas Lesczynsky, but the Russian Army overran Poland, captured Danzig, and forced the capitulation of a sizable

French force sent to the aid of the Poles, this being the first instance in history of French and Russians meeting on the battlefield. Following this, at the request of Austria, a Russian army twenty thousand strong was sent through Bohemia and Germany to the Rhine in 1736 to bolster up the Austrian campaign against France, this again being the first of the four times the Russians were to reach that historic river. Having knocked out Poland, the Russians conjointly with the Austrians attacked Turkey and inflicted upon that country the first of the many defeats to follow, which was made the more significant by the humiliating defeat suffered at the hands of the Turks by the Austrian Army. France, seeing her whole political system going to pieces, retaliated by putting pressure on Sweden to attack Russia. The move was carefully planned and timed by French diplomacy. The Swedish attack was to be co-ordinated with a revolution in Russia staged by French agents, which aimed at putting on the throne the pro-French Empress Elizabeth, the daughter of Peter the Great. The plan miscarried, for although the French-engineered revolution in Russia was a success, Elizabeth refused to pay off France by the cession to Sweden of territories conquered by her father, and inflicted a crushing defeat upon the Swedes. Undaunted, the French proceeded to rebuild once more their shattered diplomatic system and half a century later staged another co-ordinated military attack on Russia, only to find their schemes irremediably wrecked by the formidable military and diplomatic power of Catherine the Great.

In the meantime, following close upon the three wars just mentioned, a much greater storm was brewing over Europe, which did not directly affect Russia but which by the very nature of the position achieved by Russia was to involve that country for the first time in an all-European issue. The growing rivalry between Austria and Prussia for the domination of the Holy Roman Empire came to a head in 1740 with the simultaneous accessions of Empress Maria Theresa and King Frederick the Great to the thrones of their respective countries. Frederick opened the attack by his totally unwarranted invasion of Austrian Silesia, and in the ensuing hostilities the various powers were forced, through the interplay of the balance of power, to take sides. Since France sided with Prussia as a result of her traditional enmity for Austria, France's great maritime and colonial rival, England, in turn sided with Austria. Russia, too, sided with Austria, partly because of her alliance with that country, partly because of the fear of rising Prussian power, and partly because of Empress Elizabeth's personal dislike for Germans and particularly for Prussians—a feeling that she had developed as a young girl. The Russian armies moved to the assistance of Austria, but had no real share in the fighting, because they came late into the war; the hostilities were over by the time they took up their battle positions on the Rhine. Nevertheless, Russia's contribution to Austria's cause was not entirely negligible. But here a resounding snub awaited Russia. She was not invited to be a member of the Congress of Aix-la-Chapelle, which negotiated the terms of peace—a fact which showed that she was still deemed not important enough to participate in the councils of Europe. Another issue made this fact plain: The powers of Europe, with the exception of the King of Prussia, whose own title dated officially only from 1713, obstinately refused to acknowledge the imperial title of the Czarina. Even Austria, Russia's ally, attempted to stave off this recognition as long as possible, with the result that a tragicomic incident nearly brought on a rupture between the two countries. At the time when the Russian Army was marching to the assistance of Austria on the Rhine in 1736, the Austrian general who welcomed the Russian troops in Bohemia pointedly drank a toast to the Czarina of Muscovy. This brought a stinging rebuke from the Russian commander, who in his reply referred to the Holy Roman Emperors as Archdukes of Austria. The matter created a sensation, and the Austrian government deemed it wise in subsequent communications to acknowledge the new title. Thus it may be said that up to the middle of the eighteenth century Russia was still suppressed and refused her rightful place as a great power. But the dramatic events of the next decade which revealed to a stunned Europe her tremendous power were rapidly to change this estimate, just as in our own day the sudden revelation of Soviet Russia's might in her war with Germany was to produce the same result.

The Peace of Aix-la-Chapelle had been a mere truce, and a second European war flared up in 1756 over the same issue. This was the Seven Years' War. In the interval, however, there had occurred the famous shift of alliances known as the Diplomatic Revolution:

France and England had changed sides, followed by the smaller European powers. Russia alone remained faithful to Austria, and therefore found herself fighting alongside of France. But though both had their alliances with Austria, they were not allied to each other, and the hostility of France toward Russia did not diminish. In this war, however, the Russian Army played a decisive role. Whereas the French made a very poor showing and were badly beaten, and the Austrians—though winning some victories which were offset by heavy defeats—played a cautious game and showed little initiative, the Russians conquered East Prussia, which they held for four years, and boldly attacked the forces of Frederick the Great. They fought four major battles in this campaign, and the score was one draw and three victories. Particularly spectacular was their victory at Kunersdorf, where, with the aid of a small Austrian force, they all but annihilated the Prussian Army. With only three thousand men remaining, Frederick considered everything lost and wanted to commit suicide. The road to Berlin was open, and the following year the Russians seized the Prussian capital. Just as Frederick appeared to have lost the war, the death of Empress Elizabeth saved him. She had selected as her successor her nephew Peter III, the German Duke of Holstein-Gottorp. The latter was a personal friend and admirer of Frederick the Great, and was more interested in the fate of his native duchy of Holstein than in the country of his adoption. Hence he withdrew from the war, throwing away the fruits of a hard-won victory, and involved Russia in a totally unnecessary war with Denmark. The antagonism in Russia produced by this and by his inept internal policy brought him to an untimely end in 1763.

Curiously, though Russia appeared to have wasted her great effort in this war, fate seems to have meted out to her a compensatory historic justice by bringing to the throne, in Catherine the Great, Peter III's wife, a political genius of the first magnitude. Furthermore, though Russia had gained nothing from the treaties of peace, her victories had given her such prestige that nobody any longer thought of challenging her position as a great power. Rather it was the reverse: All the powers of Europe were now courting her friendship, and Catherine II was in a position to pick her alliances. But of all the great powers of Europe, Russia was the only one not to possess stable or natural frontiers along her western and southern borders. Peter the Great had achieved these along the Baltic coast, but farther to the south, although the Ukraine had been regained, Volhynia, Podolia, and White Russia were still in Polish hands. Still worse was the situation in the steppe area north of the coast of the Black Sea. The Ottoman Empire, after extending its sway over the Balkans, had brought under its subjection the Khanate of the Crimean Tartars. Thus the whole vast territory stretching north of the Black Sea from the Danube to the Don and the Caucasus had come under the domination of the Turks. As late as the 1730's the Russian government had to build an extended and heavily garrisoned line of fortifications to protect the border cities of the Ukraine and Central Southern Russia from constant Tartar incursions. This situation had, as we have seen, existed for five hundred years, but Catherine was now in a position to settle it definitively, and she did so through the combination of her driving energy and astute, cynical policy backed by brilliant military victories. Only broad outlines need be given here since the subject is discussed in more detail in subsequent pages. She began with Poland, where, upon the death of Augustus III, she got her candidate, Stanislas Poniatovski, on the throne of Warsaw. Backed by Russian bayonets and the support of the pro-Russian great landed aristocracy of Poland, he became a mere puppet in the hands of Russia. But the more patriotic elements of the small nobility and middle class formed the "Confederacy of Bar" and declared war on Russia (1768), appealing to France for aid. France at this time could not give much aid, but she sent one of her best generals, Dumouriez, of later Revolutionary fame, to command the Confederate army. Her diplomacy also induced Turkey, worried at the extension of Russian power menacing her northern flank, to attack Russia. Thus Catherine faced two wars at the same time, and when the Confederates were easily beaten by Catherine's best general, Suvorov, Frederick the Great proposed the first partition of Poland. In the meanwhile the Turks had been driven back to the Danube, and their fleet had been destroyed in Greek waters by the Russian Baltic fleet, which had sailed around Europe. The Treaty of Kuchuk-Kainardji (1774), which ended the war, gave Catherine full control of the coastline of the Black Sea, with the subsequent annexation of the Crimea. It brought Russian influence on a major scale into the Balkans; and Turkey, definitely set on the road to ruin, was henceforth to be the sick man of Europe. The prestige gained by Catherine was such that in the bloodless War of the Bavarian Succession fought between Prussia and Austria both parties appealed to Catherine to mediate the quarrel, together with France, whose participation in the negotiations was merely nominal. It was Catherine's arbitration which settled the quarrel, and as a result of the Treaty of Teschen Catherine was made the coguarantor of the *status quo* in the Holy Roman Empire.

Thus Russia's power was reaching its zenith, and, Russia having obtained her natural frontiers, a thousand years of history were coming to an end. The house built by the Russian people throughout these centuries, with storm and stress and occasional setbacks, was now completed, and merely a few architectural changes and additions, mostly in Asia, were made during the following century. This task finished, the forces molding Russian history were to be henceforth canalized in two directions: The emphasis shifted in internal affairs to the furnishing of the house, that is to say, to cultural, economic, and social developments; and in the field of foreign relations, after the solution of immediate border problems, Russia was able to devote full attention to matters of general European policy. This development occurred just as another tremendous storm was about to break—the French Revolution with the chain of wars it engendered. In this great historical drama Russia was not only to be one of the active personages, but at times was to play the leading role.

Russia and Europe
1789-1825

Chapter I

Catherine II and Paul I

The outbreak of the French Revolution in 1789 produced a wave of enthusiasm in Russia. The ground had been well prepared by the influence of the French philosophers in educated Russian circles, the Russian nobility of the period being educated by French tutors and speaking French freely. Referring to the all-pervading influence of Voltaire among Russian intellectuals, Joseph de Maistre wrote, "The first lessons in French that Russians learned were lessons in blasphemy."[1] But Voltaire was losing ground in Russia to Rousseau, with his appeal to sentimentalism, even though censorship forbade the publication of Rousseau's works, while the works of the other philosophers were circulated freely. A number of educated Russians had had personal contacts with the philosophers during their travels to France, and Paris harbored quite a large Russian colony.

Of these, Kargavin, a rich Moscow merchant, went to Paris because it was "the most propitious place in the world for the study of philosophy," and he educated his children in the atheistic spirit of the new teachings. It was rumored that a Prince Golitzin had participated in the attack on the Bastille; and, under the assumed name of Paul Otcher, the young, aristocratic, and extremely wealthy Count Paul Stroganov joined the Jacobin Club, where he made ardent revolutionary speeches. "It will be the finest day of my life when I see Russia renovated by a similar revolution," he declared. He became the archivist of the club, and on August 7, 1790, was given a diploma of honor signed by Barnave, having twice been sent by the club to make speeches before the Assembly.

In Russia itself similar enthusiasm greeted the news of the fall of the Bastille, and Ségur, the French minister in St. Petersburg, noted in his memoirs that people stopped in the streets, excitedly and joyfully congratulating and kissing each other. He was dum-

[1] Emile Haumant, *La Culture française en Russie (1700-1900)* (Paris, 1910), p. 152.

founded, while walking down the Nevsky-Prospekt, to have two young men come up to him to express exuberantly their pleasure at the news, and to recognize in them the heir to the throne, Grand Duke Alexander, and his brother Constantine. At the Military School of Aspirant Officers the director, Prince Anhalt, ordered the establishment of a special reading room for the reading of French newspapers,[2] and manifestations occurred in theaters and other public places.

Catherine did not share this enthusiasm, which indeed soon waned. In its place arose apprehension and horror at the excesses committed in France. Catherine had recanted her liberal views, and her friendship and correspondence with the philosophers which had given her wide publicity as the most enlightened ruler of her day were a thing of the past. She took an intense dislike to the Revolution from the outset because it upset all her schemes. The rise of popular passions in France horrified her; writing to Grimm, she called the Assembly "a hydra with twelve hundred heads," and acted swiftly. In October, 1789, she broke off diplomatic relations with France, and Ségur departed from St. Petersburg, leaving a chargé d'affaires, Genêt, to represent him.

But with two wars on hand, one with Sweden and the other with Turkey, Catherine was not prepared to go further, merely contenting herself with repressive measures at home to stop the inflow of revolutionary ideas. Moreover, both Prussia and England were assuming a menacing attitude toward Russia. Indeed, the policy of Prussia was to bolster up the resistance of Turkey against Russia and her ally, Austria; in a convention signed between the Porte and Dietz, the Prussian envoy in Constantinople, on January 30, 1790, Prussia went so far as to promise armed assistance for the reconquest of the Crimea and of the regions lost by Turkey to Russia in the Treaty of Kuchuk-Kainardji. It is true that the convention remained a dead letter, King Friedrich Wilhelm showing himself reluctant to take the risk of open hostilities with Russia. Nevertheless, Prussia signed on March 22, 1790, a treaty of alliance with Poland, obviously directed against Russia, whereby Prussia was to guarantee both the territory and the constitution of the Polish Republic in exchange for the cession of Danzig and Thorn.

[2] *Ibid.*, p. 177.

As for England, Catherine had always been pro-British. She openly expressed her dislike for the French, and wrote, "Love for the English is natural to me."[3] She had eagerly subscribed to the scheme promulgated by her chancellor, Count Panin, for the so-called "Northern System," an alliance to include Russia, Sweden, Denmark, England, and Poland, the aim of which was to counterbalance the alliance of the Latin countries. Although it fell short of this goal, Catherine had signed a treaty with England on June 26, 1766, giving British commerce some important advantages; later she made a second attempt to obtain a definite alliance with England by renewing and enlarging the treaty, stating explicitly that such an alliance would prove to be the foundation on which the Northern System could be established.

But with the outbreak of the American Revolution, Russian vessels were subjected to seizure by British privateers, and a serious conflict developed between the two countries. Indeed, Catherine retaliated by conceiving the League of Neutrals, which amounted to a modification of the idea of the Northern System with special relation to the situation on the high seas, specifically challenging the British policies.

A declaration made to all governments and dated April 20, 1780, established five basic principles with regard to the rights of neutrals on the high seas: (1) Neutral vessels were to be free to navigate from port to port and along the coast of belligerent powers; (2) except for contraband of war, all merchandise on neutral vessels, even that belonging to belligerent powers, was to remain safe from seizure; (3) Articles X and XI of the treaty of commerce with England were to be extended to all belligerent powers; (4) a definition was given of ports which could be blockaded; and (5) these principles were to serve as basis for the legality of prizes of war.

This declaration, to which the northern powers adhered and which was strengthened by the appearance of Russian squadrons in the North Sea and along the coast of Portugal, caused strong indignation in England. In Parliament, Lord Camden declared that the Empress of Russia intended "to dictate her own law to the maritime powers," and called for a declaration of war against Russia.[4] But

[3] *Sbornik, Imperatorskago Russkago Istoricheskago Obchestva* (St. Petersburg, 1864-1916), XXXIII, 302.

[4] Nicolai Notovich, *La Russie et l'alliance anglaise . . .* (Paris, 1906), p. 163.

after signing the Treaty of Versailles, England returned the Russian and Danish vessels seized, and the more liberal cabinet of Fox accepted the principles of the declaration in a letter addressed to the Russian ambassador, Simolin, on May 4, 1782.

But after the fall of Fox, England once more refused to accept the declaration; and with the coming to power of William Pitt, British hostility toward Russia increased. When the Second Russo-Turkish War started, Pitt openly supported Turkey, foreshadowing the role to be played by Disraeli nearly a century later. Britain made military and naval preparations against Russia, followed by an embargo on privateering and the seizure of Russian vessels. It was only when the French Revolution, reaching the terror stage, began to alarm the governments that they decided to forego their mutual hostility; but this was still in the future.

In the meanwhile the military alliance of Russia and Austria in the war against Turkey had been of doubtful value to the Russians. It is true that at Fokshani General Suvorov had won a signal victory (August 9, 1789) in co-operation with the Austrians under Prince Coburg. But two months later the Austrian Army found itself in a critical position and was rescued only by the arrival of Suvorov, who brought up his army by forced marches and, attacking the enemy with greatly inferior forces, routed him completely at Rymnik. The Austrians succeeded in capturing Belgrade, Semendria, and Passarowitz, but the Russians captured Benderi and Akkerman, and Suvorov accomplished what probably will remain a unique feat in military history—the capture of Ismail. A first-class fortress, one of the strongest in Europe, Ismail was defended by an army thirty-five thousand strong and was captured by storm by an army of twenty-two thousand men, given an irresistible impetus by the driving power and genius of Suvorov. Demoralized by the fall of Ismail as well as by the approach toward Constantinople of the Russian Admiral Ushakov, the Turks sued for peace (December 29, 1791).

By the Treaty of Yassy not only was the previous Treaty of Kuchuk-Kainardji reconfirmed, but Russia further obtained the fortress of Ochakov and the territory between the Bug and Dniester.

Even though her armies had not made so brilliant a showing, and though after the death of Joseph II in 1790 she had retired from this war, Austria rendered one very signal service to Russia.

She helped to neutralize Prussia, and thus left Russia free not only to dispose of the Turks but to turn her attention toward the Swedes as well.

At this time the Swedish war had reached a crisis. Gustavus III was advancing on the Russian capital with his army just when the Russian Army was almost wholly engaged against the Turks and in watching Poland; at the same time the Swedish fleet made its appearance in the Gulf of Finland. Prince Nassau Siegen, in command of the Russian fleet, succeeded in driving the Swedish fleet away from the vicinity of Viborg on June 24, but got himself badly beaten two weeks later. In this crisis Catherine showed herself the strong woman she was and, undaunted, prepared to defend the capital. In contrast Gustavus III vacillated, fearing internal agitation in Sweden and dreaming, too, of organizing a crusade against the French Revolution. In this frame of mind, and also fearing for his crown in the event of defeat, Gustavus signed the Treaty of Verela (August 14, 1790), re-establishing between Russia and Sweden the *status quo ante bellum.* Thus both attacks on Russia, from the north and from the south, had failed, and both wars which had been thrust upon Catherine had been brought by her to a successful conclusion before the French Revolution developed into a European conflict.

Having thus cleared the decks for action, Catherine was now free to turn her attention to one of the major problems of her diplomacy—the Polish question. She began to see that the French Revolution, in that it absorbed the attention of Europe elsewhere and left her free to come to grips with the question of Poland, had a direct bearing on this problem. Before attempting to settle the Polish question, however, she had to be sure that there would be no obstruction to her policies on the part of Austria and Prussia, both copartners in the first partition of Poland. "I am breaking my head," said she, "to find a way to drive the courts of Vienna and Berlin to meddle in the affairs of France. I want to have them involved in these affairs so as to have my elbows free."[5] She skilfully connected the events in Paris with those in Warsaw, and tried to prove that they formed two aspects of the same revolution. She was determined to put an end to the new Polish constitution, which

[5] Fedor Fedorovitch de Martens, *Recueil des traités et conventions conclus par la Russie avec les puissances étrangères* (St. Petersburg, 1874-1909), II, 196.

might have saved the country, by declaring that, whereas the National Assembly was destroying royal authority in Paris, the Diet in Warsaw was a menace to true freedom.

Thus Catherine's policy was shaping itself under guise of participation in the great European league which was forming itself against the French Revolution; she was allocating Poland to herself as her field of action.

To Gustavus III of Sweden, who sent his ambassador, Baron Stedingk, to Russia to work out a plan of joint action against the French Revolution, Catherine virtually promised eight thousand Russian troops to co-operate with sixteen thousand to be sent by the Swedes. The King of Sweden, elated, rushed to Aix-la-Chapelle to promise the French *émigré* leaders—the Count of Provence and the Count of Artois, brothers of Louis XVI—a joint Swedish-Russian army which was to land in Normandy and march up the Seine to Paris. In humble and obsequious tones the future kings Louis XVIII and Charles X wrote to the Czarina, asking the fulfilment of this promise. But Catherine was in no hurry to act, and vaguely stated that the season was too advanced and that she had first to obtain the co-operation of the other courts of Europe. But at the time the Austrian and Prussian armies were actually starting the invasion of France, the Russian Army was entering Poland, where the new constitution of May 3, 1791, was to have abolished the evils which had brought that country to virtual ruin. An hereditary monarchy in the hands of the House of Saxony was to replace the election of kings, the *liberum veto* was to be suppressed, the Diet was to become bicameral, and the king's powers as chief executive were to be more clearly defined and increased.

But a large portion of the conservative aristocracy rebelled against these reforms and appealed to Russia for aid in restoring the traditional privileges, particularly the *liberum veto*, and the right to a "confederation," or organized revolt. This right which the nobles so zealously guarded served Catherine's aims, for a delegation of Polish aristocrats came to St. Petersburg for the specific purpose of working out with the Czarina a joint plan of revolt. The Russian armies were to enter Poland—one coming from the Danube, sixty-four thousand strong, and one from the north, thirty-two thousand strong.

The advance of these forces started on April 18, 1792, and it will be noticed that this was coincidental with the beginning of the war between France and the Holy Roman Empire (April 22, 1792). The Confederates met on May 14 at Targovice and declared that the King had usurped the traditional privileges of Poland which were to be safeguarded by the action of Russia; at the same time the Russian ambassador in Warsaw, Bulgakov, in a strongly worded note accused the Diet of having violated the laws of the country, usurped rights, and established illegally an hereditary monarchy in place of the republic. Thus both agencies, the pro-Russian Confederacy and the Russian military forces, were operating according to a well synchronized and carefully worked out plan. In the meanwhile, under her treaty of alliance with Austria, Russia was obligated to send military aid to Austria should the latter be attacked by France. The declaration of war by France on Austria put this *casus foederis* into effect, and both Vienna and Berlin appealed to Russia to join the coalition against France. But Catherine, not without cynical irony, pointed out that the danger of revolution in Poland was of greater concern to the neighboring powers than the revolution in France, and that accordingly it was she who had the right under the alliance to ask for aid from Austria, instead of the other way around; but that in view of Austria's difficulties she was willing to forego any such claims. Writing to Grimm, she declared that her mission was to fight Jacobinism in Warsaw, for it was affiliated with the Jacobin Club in Paris.[6] In the meanwhile the Russian armies had crushed the resistance of the Poles, and King Stanislas Augustus surrendered on July 24 to the Confederacy in accordance with the orders of Catherine, after making an offer to turn the throne of Poland over to Grand Duke Constantine upon condition that the new constitution should remain in effect. This offer Catherine contemptuously turned down. The Russians then occupied Warsaw, and the constitution was abolished.

The clue to Catherine's policy at this stage may be found in a declaration made earlier (February, 1792) by Vice-Chancellor Ostermann to the Prussian minister in St. Petersburg, Goltz: "If the constitution of May 3 survives, Poland united with Saxony will

[6] Albert Sorel, *L'Europe et la révolution française* (Paris, 1885-1904), II, 464.

become a first-class power and will hamper Prussia even more than she will hamper us."[7]

But since Catherine was not strong enough to dispose of Poland without the assent of her neighbors, she was forced to maintain the illusion of active co-operation in the European antirevolutionary coalition on the one hand, and to negotiate with both Austria and Prussia on the other. A gift of two hundred thousand rubles for the furtherance of the *émigré* cause so kindled the enthusiasm of the French princes that they wrote enthusiastically, "Crossing the Rhine with only ten thousand, we will soon have one hundred thousand; the genius of Catherine II will march ahead of us." The Count of Provence compared her to Prometheus stealing the rays of the sun, and Calonne, writing from London, spoke of the "sublime and decisive letter of the magnanimous sovereign of Russia."[8] But aside from recognizing the Count of Provence as Regent of France and receiving his ambassadors, Russia gave no effective military aid throughout the year; the Russian Army was busy elsewhere.

On October 5, however, Russian warships put into the port of Leghorn in Italy. The French Admiral Truguet was ordered by the Executive Council of the Convention in Paris to demand that the Tuscan Government should turn these vessels over to the French. The Tuscan Government protested, and the Convention decided to avoid any overt act of hostility against Russia until the naval forces of the French Republic were of sufficient strength to attack her openly with some hope of success.[9] In the meanwhile the negotiations between Russia and Austria resulted in the conclusion of a new treaty of alliance on July 14, 1792, whereby mutual military aid was pledged and the integrity of Poland as of 1773 was guaranteed. Similarly, an alliance was signed with Prussia on August 7, renewing the treaty of 1764, pledging the nondismemberment of Poland but specifying that Prussia was to receive an acquisition of territory elsewhere, the issue to be decided by direct negotiation between Austria and Prussia. This treaty permitted Russia to become an ally of both powers, whose rivalries and jealousies over territories to be acquired at the expense of France, or in Belgium and Bavaria, had hindered mutual co-operation in Poland.

In signing this treaty, however, the Prussian Government had

[7] *Ibid.*, II, 376. [8] *Ibid.*, II, 250. [9] *Ibid.*, II, 157.

interpreted the vague clause concerning territorial compensation as referring to Poland; accordingly, when Russian victory had forced the restoration of the old and chaotic conditions in that state, the Prussians became more explicit: King Friedrich Wilhelm demanded the cession of Thorn, Danzig, the regions of Posnan, Kalish, and Plock. Catherine was not pleased at these exorbitant demands, but fearing that her refusal might alienate Prussia, agreed to negotiate; and on January 23, 1793 (rather significantly two days after the execution of Louis XVI in Paris), the Treaty of St. Petersburg was signed between Russia and Prussia and the second partition of Poland became an accomplished fact. Prussia received the aforementioned territories, or 1,065 square miles; Russia, the palatinate of Kiev, Volhynia, Podolia, and Vilna, or 4,500 square miles. Austria had been left out in the cold.

The death of Louis XVI, in the meanwhile, gave Catherine a reason for more pronounced gestures against the French Revolution. She decreed an official court mourning for the King, and ordered all Frenchmen residing in Russia to give their oath not to return to France during the Revolution, and publicly to disavow Jacobin ideas.

British diplomacy used this occasion to attempt to moderate Catherine's action in Poland by declaring that all monarchs had to remain united in the face of the revolutionary danger in Europe and that Russian aggression in Poland was endangering Anglo-Russian relations. But Catherine paid no heed to the warning. She was, however, prepared to abandon her stand on the problem of the neutrality of the seas, and even pledged herself to put pressure on Denmark and Sweden to follow suit. This made possible the signing on March 25, 1793, of a treaty of friendship between England and Russia, whereby both powers pledged each other mutual assistance during the war against France and promised not to sign any peace with France until the territories conquered by the French should be returned to their rightful owners. Furthermore, Russia was to close her ports to French ships, stop French vessels on the seas, and hinder the giving of aid to France and to French trade.

Thus, without actually engaging in hostilities, Catherine had gone a step further toward war with France. The treaty of 1793 was followed, in the next twenty-two years, by a series of similar treaties with England, all devised to promote Anglo-Russian cooperation against France.

Encouraged by the results obtained through this treaty, the British Government approached Russia to ask that an expeditionary corps be sent to the Rhine, but was met with a polite refusal which stated that the Czarina was too jealous of the glory of her armies to risk sending a small force, the success of which would depend entirely on the measures taken by England. As for Austria, she made one more attempt to invoke the *casus foederis* of her treaty of alliance with Russia, this time astutely demanding, not aid against France, but joint action against Turkey, a move calculated to give her a better hold over her wavering ally. Catherine responded by declaring that her fleet would be ready for action against Turkey in the spring, and furthermore declared herself ready to support any Austrian claims for territorial compensation, provided they were for areas outside of Poland. Thus she gained a respite for facing once more the Polish issue, which was now rapidly moving toward a climax; in addition she obtained a voice as an arbiter in the wider field of Austro-Prussian litigations over the territorial redistribution along the French border, and in Germany as well. This came about through the occupation by the Prussians of the Polish cities of Thorn and Danzig, which were Prussia's share of the Polish territory allotted by the Treaty of St. Petersburg. In support of the Prussian move, Russia imposed upon a puppet Polish diet assembled at Grodno the acceptance of the treaty of dismemberment.

At the same time Count Razumovsky, the Russian minister in Vienna, approached the Austrian Government to obtain ratification of the treaty between Prussia and Russia. But the fury of Emperor Francis at being left out of the bargain was such that it resulted in the replacement of Chancellor Cobenzl by Thugut, who refused to accept the treaty, declaring that Austria should get an adequate compensation in Poland, and not—as suggested—in the Netherlands. Prussia thereupon threatened to leave the coalition, and the matter was put squarely up to Catherine for decision. Thugut further asked the Czarina to make a military demonstration against Prussia, but finally agreed to relinquish his claim on Polish territories if given the Netherlands as far as the line of the Somme, and thence a rectification of the frontier down to Sedan and Mézières. Not content with these results, Catherine bolstered up her carefully thought-out diplomatic schemes by swift military action. As a result of the acceptance of the second partition of Poland by the Diet of Grodno, a treaty of alliance was signed by Poland with Russia. By this treaty a Russian army 40,000 strong entered the country under the command of General Igelstrom, who acted as if he were in a conquered country and ordered the Polish Army to be reduced from 30,000 men to 9,000 in Poland and 6,000 in Lithuania. This resulted in the revolt of a Polish brigade which refused to be demobilized, and the revolt turned into a national insurrection under the leadership of the great Polish patriot, Kosciuzko.

In the meanwhile the Prussians had entered Poland proper on May 14, 1794, with an army of 50,000 men and marched on Warsaw, where they rallied the remnants of the Russian Army of Occupation, which the insurrection had placed in a perilous position.

To have her hands free to act, Catherine approached Austria and was informed that the Viennese Government demanded two compensations: one for the partition of 1793, and one for the partition to come. "If it is necessary to partition, better partition the whole," observed Markov to Cobenzl.

In the meanwhile Kosciuzko had been successfully holding out against the Prussians in Warsaw, and in September had actually forced them to retreat. To prevent a Prussian defeat which would have had perilous repercussions, Catherine ordered her best general, Suvorov, to go to the rescue with an army of 20,000 men. Kosciuzko marched against Suvorov, but was no match for the Russian general; and after being badly defeated on October 1, he was taken prisoner by the Russians. Suvorov now marched against Warsaw, storming the suburb of Praha. In this attack 13,000 Poles perished, 1,500 were made prisoners, including 3 generals, 5 colonels, and 438 officers,[10] while 2,000 men were drowned in the Vistula.

The next day after the fall of Praha the capital surrendered, and on October 8 the Russians made a solemn entry into Warsaw. The small bodies of Polish troops scattered over the country were easily disposed of, and resistance came to an end.

On January 3, 1795, once more in St. Petersburg, the treaties for the final partition of Poland were signed. By these Austria

[10] William Richard Morfill, *Poland* (London, 1893), p. 246.

acceded to the treaty of 1793, receiving in compensation for that partition an exchange of Bavaria for the Netherlands, and by the present partition the country between the Pilica, the Vistula, and the Bug, and the city of Cracow; Prussia received Warsaw and the territory up to the Nieman, or the main part of Poland; to Russia went the rest. King Stanislas resigned his crown and went to St. Petersburg to live on a pension.

During the negotiations preceding the signing of the treaty Austria made one more effort to involve Russia in the war against France, asking that Russia join Austria in a secret convention directed against Prussia and that a force of thirty thousand men under Suvorov join the Austrian armies on the Rhine to operate with Prince Condé's French *émigré* corps in Pfalz. Catherine, as might have been expected, refused, although she intimated her willingness to discuss a renewal of the Austro-Russian alliance for a partition of Turkey, and expressed her consent that Austria should take Venice, if she so desired.

Thus far the astute if cynical policy of Catherine had paid handsome dividends. In the words of the French historian Sorel:

> There exists on the Continent and on the side of the coalition but one political figure of outstanding stature, capable of seeing the whole field, of setting a goal and pursuing it without faltering, and that is Catherine II. There is also but one war leader, sufficiently intrepid, daring . . . to fanaticize his troops and compete in audacity with the Republican generals, and that is Suvorov.[11]

No phase of Catherine's policy has been more bitterly assailed by both Russian and foreign historians than "the crime" of Poland. In this connection the following facts should be noted: First, Catherine did not take any Polish territories proper, leaving that to her allies; the territories she annexed had belonged to Russia and Lithuania prior to their passing into Polish hands. Second, the initiative of the partition did not come from her but from Prussia. And third, the very idea of partitions was the stock in trade of the diplomacy of the century; schemes of partition had been worked out for Spain, Austria, Prussia, Sweden, Russia, Turkey, and France, and the only difference was that Catherine succeeded where the

[11] Sorel, *op. cit.*, II, 557.

others had failed. The wisdom of settling the Polish question in such a drastic and unethical way is a different question, but that was a matter for the future to decide.

The Polish issue thus settled and Russia's hands freed, both Austrian and British diplomacy lost no time in trying to get Russia actively involved in the great European struggle. Thugut openly declared that the only way to defeat the rising star of Napoleon was to obtain the aid of the Russian Army and particularly of Suvorov. The French Directory, seeing the danger, offered Austria two thirds of Bavaria and outlets on the Adriatic, in exchange for an alliance against Russia with the purpose of re-creating Poland to serve as a buffer state against "the devouring power of Russia" (November, 1795). While Thugut was thus conducting simultaneous negotiations with both sides, Pitt made an effort to convert into a triple alliance Russia's agreements with both Austria and England. Furthermore, he asked outright that Russia send her fleet to the coast of Spain. Napoleon's brilliant victories in his Italian campaign of 1796 so alarmed Catherine that she ceased to turn a deaf ear to these overtures. She began to think more seriously of armed intervention, particularly as a result of the threat of France to the status of Germany (guaranteed by her under the Treaty of Teschen), and she approached England with a demand for a subsidy of 200,000 pounds, ordering Suvorov with 60,000 men to be in readiness to proceed to the aid of Austria. In the meanwhile, through carefully conducted diplomatic negotiations, she succeeded in arranging a marriage between the new King of Sweden, Gustavus IV, and her granddaughter, Grand Duchess Anna Pavlovna.

The King arrived in St. Petersburg for the marriage, which was to take place on September 26; but at the very last moment Gustavus changed his mind, excusing himself on the grounds of religious differences. The ceremonies had to be canceled, and Catherine gave vent to a veritable tempest of fury. This may have had something to do with her death, which occurred without warning a few weeks later; she died suddenly from apoplexy on November 17.

II

With the death of Catherine the throne passed to her son, Paul I, who must be regarded as one of the least understood characters in history.

Coming to the throne in middle age, after being kept in virtual seclusion by his domineering mother, whom he hated, Paul had developed an erratic and unbalanced temperament which resulted in his being labeled a madman by many historians. But he was intelligent, had keen judgment in foreign affairs, and had a will and a mind of his own; his actions, if impulsive and erratic, were not devoid of common sense, or of a sense of the realities of the situation.

Upon his accession to the throne he reversed many of his mother's policies and thereby immediately created a conflict with most of his own ministers, including the two leading statesmen of the day, Chancellor Bezborodko and Vice-Chancellor Ostermann, who were faithful to Catherine's policy. Similarly, the ambassador to London, Count Vorontsov, upon his own initiative detained in British waters the vessels of a Russian squadron, which Paul had ordered back. True, these vessels did prove to be useful when the mutiny of Nore occurred in the British fleet, and Paul later boasted that he had saved "the greatest fleet in the world" and commended Vorontsov. But this incident, occurring as late as June, 1797, showed that the new Emperor had not yet obtained control of his own diplomatic machine.

Defining the new policy he was to inaugurate, Paul himself wrote to his envoy in Paris, Kolychev:

> The change which has taken place in the political system of the Russian Empire upon our coming to the throne, a system previously founded on views of aggrandizement, and now transformed into an absolute abandonment of any desire for conquest, has necessarily influenced our relations with the different courts.[12]

Accordingly, immediately after his accession Paul ordered the release of all Polish prisoners in St. Petersburg. On November 26, 1796, he visited Kosciuszko, kept in internment in the Marble Palace, and informed him that he was free. Upon the latter's expressed desire to go to the United States, Paul made him a grant of sixty thousand rubles. He similarly invited the former King of Poland, Stanislas Augustus, to come and reside in the Kamenny Ostrov Palace, and accorded him royal honors. In an interview with him

[12] Martens, *op. cit.*, II, 283.

Paul declared that the partition of Poland was both unjust and bad policy, and that had it not been for the interests of the neighboring powers, he would have restored the independence of that country.[13] Nevertheless, he pursued the negotiations with Austria concerning the frontier delimitations of partitioned Poland, and the agreement was duly signed the following year.

Much more important was the new Czar's decision not to send the expeditionary corps Catherine had prepared for action on the Rhine. The Austrian Government was notified of this decision. The disappointment was so keen in Vienna that Cobenzl attempted to persuade the Czar not to withdraw the promised aid. In a lengthy note addressed to St. Petersburg, he brought out all the arguments in favor of the plan, but Paul merely wrote sharply on the margin of the note: "I do not allow myself to be told what I should do."

Similarly, commenting on the passage in the note which asked Russia to put pressure on Prussia to keep her from assuming an antagonistic attitude in the war, Paul remarked: "I will say what is suitable for my interests."[14] Nevertheless, during the negotiations for the peace of Campo-Formio and the subsequent Congress of Rasstadt between Austria and France, Paul instructed his minister in Berlin to moderate Prussia's attitude and to inform the French minister that Russia could not countenance any act of hostility against "our ally, the Emperor of the Romans, or [leading to] the overthrow [of] the Germanic Empire."[15]

Very different had been his attitude toward Prussia, and in this one point he concurred with his mother. He could not forgive Prussia the signing of the Treaty of Basel with France, and he left unanswered a personal letter of King Friedrich Wilhelm II explaining the reasons why Prussia had made a separate treaty with France.

Nevertheless, at this stage Paul envisioned the creation of a four-power alliance which would align Austria, Prussia, England, and Russia against the French Revolution. Demands, coming from Vienna and London, that Russia should become a mediator of the differences between Prussia and Austria on the one side, and England

[13] Report of the Saxon minister to Russia, Felkersam, dated November 28, 1786 (Nikolai Karlovich Schilder, *Imperator Pavel Pervyi*, St. Petersburg, 1901, p. 321).

[14] Martens, *op. cit.*, II, 283.

[15] *Ibid.*, II, 359.

and Austria on the other, seemed to offer him the opportunity of ironing out such differences and of paving the way for this four-power alliance.

He appointed one of his most able diplomats, Prince Repnin, as special envoy to Berlin to handle the Austro-Prussian mediation, while the negotiations between England and Austria concerning a dispute over subsidies were carried out in St. Petersburg.

Both negotiations failed; the bitterness between Austria and Prussia was merely increased thereby, and the Austro-British quarrel was later settled directly by London and Vienna. Thus the project of the alliance had to be given up, but more than ever, Paul declared, it was necessary "to tame the French in the name of general security." He outlined in April, 1797, his ideas of a basis for the pacification of Europe: The French Republic was to be recognized with the frontiers of the Alps, and if need be, as an extreme concession, the frontiers of the Rhine; Belgium was to be given to France, but Holland was to remain under the rule of the House of Orange and under the protection of the King of Prussia; an international congress was to be convoked to decide the terms, either in Leipzig or in some other German city. These ideas, however, meeting with no response, the newly appointed Russian minister to Berlin, Count Panin, was ordered (June, 1798) to initiate very secret and direct negotiations with the French chargé d'affaires, Caillard, for a reconciliation between France and Russia. The two diplomats carried on these negotiations surreptitiously in a city park, while the Russian minister, having bought over one of Caillard's servants, was able to lay his hands on the secret correspondence of the French diplomat with his government. The perusal of these documents convinced the Czar that there was no hope of coming to an agreement with France, since the French Directory was aiming at the reconstitution of an independent Poland.

Thus step by step and in a relatively short period, Paul's mind was turning from nonintervention to active participation in a war with France—the same war (starting in 1792, between France and the Holy Roman Empire) from which Catherine had held aloof and in which England alone had until now remained a belligerent power. A grave incident which occurred on October 20 brought on the final rupture with France: The Russian consul at Zante was arrested by the French forces of occupation in the Ionian Islands. There appears to be a definite relation between this incident and the cessation of the secret negotiations between France and Russia.

With attention thus shifting to the Mediterranean, there had arisen a new issue which gained such importance as to be completely out of all proportion—the question of Malta.

In view of the political theories of Paul, tinged with romanticism and a special brand of idealism, this issue transcended its real importance and became the cornerstone of the Czar's policy.

III

During the reign of Catherine II, in April, 1795, there arrived in St. Petersburg a special envoy of the Grand Master of the Order of the Knights of St. John, who was accredited to the Russian Court as Ambassador of the Order. This diplomat, Count Litta, came to Russia with introductions from the Viennese Court for the purpose of settling the question of the fate of the Priory or chapter in Poland, affected by the partition of that country, and more specifically, the matter of the payment of arrears due to the Order by the chapter, which he hoped would be assumed by the Russian Government. The choice of Litta for these negotiations was an obvious one, for, having joined the Order in 1780, he had entered the Russian Navy in 1789 and had fought in the Swedish campaign, where he had sufficiently distinguished himself to be promoted to the rank of rear admiral and decorated with the Cross of St. George. Even more important, he had married the niece of the great Potëmkin. Although these qualifications made him *persona grata* at the Russian Court, he nevertheless failed in his mission, for Catherine paid no attention to the claims of the Order. But with the advent of Paul I, the picture suddenly changed.

However much the new Czar attempted to keep Russia out of foreign entanglements, in his heart he carried an undying hatred for the French Revolution and viewed the ideas propagated by France as poison, corroding the very essence of civilization and society. Paul, in this respect, represented the typical figure of post-Revolutionary storms. Thoroughly determined to keep the contagion out of Russia, he passed a series of repressive decrees, which oddly have been duplicated in our present day in totalitarian states, but which at the time were regarded as sheer tyranny. But he felt that repressive measures alone would not suffice; hence, as an antidote to the Revolution, he evolved the quixotic dream of developing an order of international chivalry which, as a military-religious association of European nobility, would fight the revolutionary disease with the same crusading zeal with which the medieval orders fought the infidel. Some such idea had been entertained in his youth by Frederick the Great; and Paul, a great admirer of the King of Prussia, may have taken over the idea from him.

Be that as it may, the presence of Litta at his Court turned the attention of the Czar to the Knights of Malta. The Order of St. John, on the other hand, had found itself in very stringent circumstances owing to the abolition in 1792 of the three French "tongues" (the Provençal, Auvergne, and French), as a result of the antireligious attitude of the French Convention. These three subdivisions of the Order had provided it with its main source of income; hence Litta's negotiations had assumed tremendous importance for the survival of the Order.

It is significant that the first treaty which Paul concluded in his reign was with the Order (January 15, 1797). Not only did Paul meet all the claims of the Order with regard to Poland, but he endowed it with special funds; thus Litta's mission, after its initial failure, proved to be a resounding success. The treaty was duly ratified by the Grand Master at Valletta in August, the delay being caused by the fact that the courier carrying the treaty had fallen into French hands.

A second ambassador, Ratchinsky, was thereupon dispatched to St. Petersburg by the Order, bringing not only the ratification of the treaty and the crosses and insignia of the Knights, but, more important, a request that Paul, in view of the menacing attitude of France in the Mediterranean, should assume the protectorate of the Order. But the French Directory, having obtained possession of the Russian treaty, got wind of these negotiations and did not intend to allow Russia to get virtual possession of such a strategically important island as Malta.

Hence, in June, 1798, Bonaparte on his way to Egypt occupied Malta and concluded with the last Grand Master of the Order, Ferdinand Hompesch, a convention which not only brought the

Order under the control of France, but virtually abolished it by establishing on the island the ways and laws of Revolutionary France. A force of six thousand French troops was left to hold Valletta, the capital.

The news of the occupation of Malta by the French produced the most violent indignation in St. Petersburg; and the Russian Grand Priory of the Order, even though Catholic and not Orthodox, declared that Hompesch had sold out to the French and requested the Czar to assume the dignity of Grand Master. Paul officially accepted and in a proclamation, issued in December, announced that he had assumed the Grand Mastership of the Knights of St. John, with the seat of the Order being transferred to St. Petersburg. Twenty-two chapters were opened in Russia, and the membership of the Order was extended to those of the Russian nobility who were members of the Orthodox Church, provided that their ancestors had distinguished themselves in wars not less than a century and a half earlier.

A second proclamation issued by Paul on January 1, 1799, invited the other chapters of the Order to join with the Russian Priory. Austria did not reply to this invitation, but the Elector of Bavaria, after first abolishing the Priory in his own territory to avoid an awkward situation, six months later not only reinstated it but recognized Paul as the new Grand Master. The Russian Priory, in accordance with a treaty which Bavaria signed with Russia, was to become a part of the Anglo-Bavarian tongue. The German and Bohemian Priories merely sent delegations to Russia, thereby half-acknowledging the claims of the Czar.

Such was the issue which was to become the main cause of the war.[16] It is true that romantic idealism alone was not the sole issue; underneath it were considerations of practical policy as well: Malta's geographical position was just as much a threat to Russia in the eastern Mediterranean as it was to France in the western half of that sea. Furthermore, the French showed no respect for vessels flying the Russian flag, particularly the Greek merchant vessels which sought the protection of the flag of the great Orthodox power. But basically it was Paul's dream of fighting the Revolution through chivalry that brought this otherwise secondary issue to the very

[16] The Second Coalition against France. See pp. 31 ff.

forefront of the causes of the war. The issue was finally settled by the seat of the Order finding a haven in Rome, where it had really belonged from the outset. As for Litta, he re-entered Russian service to become a member of the Council of State and a Chamberlain of the Court. He died in 1840.

Writing about this whole Maltese question, the Abbé Georgel, a member of one of the delegations of the Order sent to St. Petersburg, said: "The Emperor of Russia, separated from the Roman faith by the schism of Photeus, becoming the Grand Master of a religious and military order having the Pope as superior, appeared to the eyes of surprised Europe as a phenomenon."[17]

Once the Czar's mind was made up for war, he approached England, and a treaty was signed on December 29, 1798, in St. Petersburg, between the Chancellor Bezborodko and the British Minister Whitworth, whereby both powers pledged themselves to put pressure on Prussia to join the coalition. Should Prussia agree to do so, Russia was to place an army of 45,000 men at her disposal, and England was to pay for the upkeep of this army by a down payment of 225,000 pounds, and 75,000 pounds per month for the duration of the war.

At the same time, a treaty of alliance was signed with Turkey for joint naval action in the Mediterranean. But having achieved that much, Russian diplomacy was unable to move Prussia from a position of cautious neutrality, notwithstanding the bait offered—to restore the Stathouderat of Holland. Thus negotiations pursued in Berlin came to an end.

As for Austria, having so long demanded Russian military aid, now that she had been notified that the Russian corps of General Rosenberg had been placed at her disposal and in October had started crossing the Bug at Brest to proceed to Cracow and Brünn, she suddenly showed fear and extreme caution. Thugut told the Russian ambassador, Count Razumovsky, that he felt both countries should first make secret preparations before falling upon France. Exasperated, Paul instructed his ambassador (December 20, 1798) to demand outright from Austria an unequivocal answer, whether she had the intention of fighting France or not, and that should Austria fail to fight, Russia and her allies "would take such measures

[17] Schilder, *Imperator Pavel Pervyi,* p. 397.

against the French as [are] compatible with our dignity and security."[18]

Thus pressed for a clear-cut decision, Austria broke off relations with France early in 1799, and in a personal message Francis II requested that Suvorov should be appointed commander in chief of the allied forces.

According to the plan of action worked out, the triple alliance of England, Russia, and Austria was to drive the French out of Italy, and if possible reduce France to her pre-Revolutionary limits. The King of Prussia was to attack in Holland, and Belgium was to be united with Holland under a Prussian protectorate with the House of Orange restored. Austria was to get Venice and Lombardy.

The obstinate refusal of Prussia to be involved in the war necessitated a change of plans resulting in a joint British-Russian expedition into Holland. Paul had promised sixty thousand men to Austria (ten thousand men in Dalmatia, twelve vessels of the line, and, if necessary, an army to Turkey, and finally later an expeditionary force in Holland). Austria still vacillated, even though Naples had already declared war.

After Thugut had promised to start the campaign in the spring and to dissolve the Congress of Rasstadt, it was decided that the main effort would be pursued in Italy; Austria was to occupy Bavaria, a Russian army was to march to the Rhine, and the Russian army originally intended to aid Prussia was to remain on the border to watch and threaten Prussia if need be. A portion of the French *émigré* corps of Prince Condé was placed in Russian service, and the future Louis XVIII, who found himself in a precarious position in Italy, where he had taken refuge at the threat of hostilities, was invited to Russia and there was given a palace in Mittau and a pension of two hundred thousand rubles.

In April, 1799, Chancellor Bezborodko died, opening the way for new men who were to replace the statesmen of Catherine's period, and in July Russia formally declared war on France.

In the meanwhile for over a year the Russians and the French had been engaged in open hostilities in the Ionian Islands, at that time a remote corner of the Mediterranean, and although these

[18] Martens, *op. cit.*, II, 362.

operations eventually merged with the greater operations on the Continent, they form a picturesque and separate chapter of Paul's policy.

IV

The Ionian Archipelago, composed of three major islands—Corfu, Zante, and Cephalonia—and four smaller ones, was Greek in population, but had been under Venetian administration for centuries. With the decline of the Venetian republic the islands suffered from maladministration by a corrupt and impoverished Venetian bureaucracy, which looked upon the islands as a happy hunting ground for redeeming its fortunes at the expense of the native population. No wonder the Greek population looked upon the French and Russians as liberators, since from France was coming a call to liberty and equality, and from Russia, agents who were honeycombing the islands to stir up the Orthodox natives in the name of a common religion. Bonaparte, during his conquest of Italy in 1796, had had an eye on the strategic value of the Ionian Islands. "The islands of Corfu, Zante, and Cephalonia," he reported to the Directory, "are more interesting for us than the whole of Italy. The Turkish Empire is crumbling more and more every day; the possession by us of these islands will afford us the means of either bolstering up the Turkish Empire or of taking our share [of its territories]."[19] Conversely, Russia, having such vital interest in the fate of the Turkish Empire and the eastern Mediterranean, could not permit the growing imperialism of France to assert itself in defense of or at the expense of Turkey; hence the Ionian Islands appeared to Russia as the advance bulwark against French aspirations. When Bonaparte conquered Venice he immediately sent a naval force to occupy the islands (June 29, 1797) and established there a French republican administration. But while the municipality of Corfu was proclaiming liberty on the island and glorifying France (July 11, 1797), the inhabitants of the neighboring island of Zante were raising the Russian flag and acclaiming Czar Paul I (July 31), and this pro-Russian demonstration had to be suppressed by force by the French garrison. Very soon the inhabitants of Corfu, after placing such high hopes in their French liberators, turned against them because of the misbehavior of the French and their antireligious policy.

[19] Emmanuel-Pierre Rodocanachi, *Bonaparte et les îles Ioniennes . . .* (Paris, 1899), p. 33.

However, just then, as a result of the Treaty of Campo-Formio between France and Austria, the islands were annexed to France (October, 1797).

When Russia actively joined the Second Coalition against revolutionary France, she found herself in the curious position of having Turkey as her ally. Incensed over the occupation of Egypt by Napoleon, the Turks declared war on France and signed with Russia a military and naval convention on August 20, 1798. By this convention a squadron of thirteen Russian vessels under Admiral Ushakov entered the Bosporus from the Black Sea on September 5 and joined forces with the Turkish Navy. At the same time the Albanian governor of Janina, the notorious Ali Pasha, who had his own dreams of empire, was coming out openly against the French on the Ionian Islands. He attacked Preveza, on the mainland opposite the islands, captured the city, and massacred the inhabitants, forcing the weak French garrison which had surrendered to participate in this gruesome task. The French garrisons on the islands were now facing a critical situation when on September 27 the Russo-Turkish fleet arrived off the coast, attacking the secondary islands first. On October 7 Ushakov anchored in a bay off the island of Cerigo—Cythera of mythological fame—and summoned the French garrison to surrender. Upon its refusal, Ushakov, who had 2,500 men on board, proceeded to land his forces and artillery, while his ships kept up a running fire on the citadel. After ten hours of continuous fighting Russian and Turkish staff officers were admitted to the port, where they were courteously invited to dinner by the French officers, and where, after drinking to each others' health, they discussed the terms of the capitulation of the island. It was decided that the French should be sent back to France at the expense of the allies.

The next attack was against the island of Zante, where the population was openly pro-Russian. Proclamations were issued by Ushakov to the inhabitants of Zante stating that the Russians and Turks were coming to deliver them from the yoke of atheistic France. Ushakov further promised in the name of Russia to respect their independence and to leave them free to choose the form of government they wished, even if it were a republic—a curious concession on the part of the representative of the autocratic Paul I. These proclamations were strengthened by an appeal of the Greek

Patriarch in Constantinople to support the Russian cause in the struggle against the impious, blasphemous French, who looted churches and were "predestined to be the victims of the wrath of God." Excited by these words, the population turned against the conquerors and paved the way for the Russian attack, which started on October 24. The fleet approached the city, all the vessels including the Turkish unfurling the Russian flag, and the bombardment of the forts started. Bands of Greek peasants broke into the city, while a landing force of seven hundred men attacked the fortress, which surrendered on the following day, the French garrison being taken prisoner. Next came the great island of Cephalonia, where once more the peasants took to arms at the approach of the Russians, and the Greek clergy organized religious processions in favor of Russia. The island fell without great difficulty. Following a methodical plan, Ushakov turned next to Ithaca, but here the small French garrison succeeded in escaping in boats which passed through the line of the squadron by raising the Turkish flag. With the fall of Santa Maura, which came next, all the secondary islands had passed into the hands of the allies. Under the convention of August 20 half of the French prisoners were taken to Constantinople, where they were treated with great cruelty; the other half went to the Crimea, where the Russian authorities gave them humane treatment.

There remained Corfu, the main island. Corfu was defended by a French garrison of 1,800 men with 500 cannon; but once more the natives took the side of the invaders, and from the citadel the French could see the Russian flag being raised in one village after another. However, Ushakov did not feel strong enough to handle the situation with the crews from his vessels alone; but at this point he received unexpected reinforcements from the mainland: Ali Pasha, though he had been kept in check by the Russians, sent a few thousand Albanians to their aid. On the island itself the rebellion of the Greeks, which was headed by a lawyer, Capo d'Istria, who had been condemned to death by the French, became general. Thus began the career of one of the most formidable opponents of Napoleon, who was to make a name for himself on the vaster fields of Russian diplomacy. Supported by a small fleet composed of a frigate, a brig, a corvette, and some twenty smaller vessels, the

French put up a desperate resistance, and it became necessary to proceed to a regular siege, which lasted four months. The siege was at first conducted by Albanians, but their lack of discipline offset their courage; hence in January the Russians came into line. We have an interesting opinion concerning them expressed by one of the French defenders of Corfu and the historian of this siege, J. Bellaire:

> Russian infantry is one of the best in Europe. The Russian soldier either by superstition [i.e., religious belief] or obedience to the orders of his sovereign, is not afraid of death; ofttimes one sees him killing himself so as not to surrender, but he has the bravery of the stupid; he is incapable of doing anything without orders from his officers.[20]

At last on March 5 came the final surrender of the island, and Russian garrisons took over the French fortifications. While bells were ringing from all the churches and Russian flags were hanging from all the windows, the French paraded past their victors and deposed their arms. Then started an exchange of courtesies. Ushakov invited the French officers to dinner on his ship, while Russian bands played French marches. He accepted a return call of General Chabot, the French commander, and a Russian guard of honor was present at the burial of a French officer killed in action. The captured French garrison was sent back to France on condition that it would not participate in any further wars.

And now there arose the question of the future status of the conquered Seven Islands. The Turkish Government had proposed to Russia three solutions: (1) to give the islands to the Kingdom of Naples, (2) to establish a republic, or (3) to make of them an independent principality under the suzerainty of the Sultan. Not wanting to bring the archipelago under the influence of the Catholic Church as represented by the Court of Naples, on the one hand, or on the other to see the position of Turkey strengthened in the Adriatic, Paul I selected the second solution, and in an official note issued in February, 1799, it was stated that: "His Imperial Majesty has decided that the inhabitants of the Ionian Islands, having before their eyes the example of the Republic of Ragusa, happy and orderly for so many centuries, would prefer a form of government the advantages of which are known to them."[21] Russia conceded to Turkey

[20] *Ibid.*, p. 157.

[21] *Ibid.*, p. 176.

the right of protectorate of the Republic. The Sultan, however, did not find this enough, and attempted to extend a more complete domination over the islands; this drew a sharp rebuke from Russia, and Paul I declared to his ally (September, 1799) that his government would not permit the re-establishment of "odious principles dating from barbarous times." Turkey yielded, and, by a convention signed March 21, 1800, between Sultan Selim and Czar Paul, the Ionian Islands were constituted a republic, vassal to Turkey but guaranteed jointly by Russia and Turkey, and to be governed by native-born prominent citizens.

In the meanwhile the issue had already been settled by Ushakov, acting on his own authority. Faced with the disappearance of all constituted government even before the French troops had been evacuated from the islands, he formed a council of sixteen members which was to become the provisional government. The Council restored Greek as the official language and uprooted all remnants of French administration. Then it worked out a new constitution which was submitted to the Czar and obtained his approval, thanks to the support of Count Pahlen. This new constitution, put into effect in 1801, was to be federative: Each island was to be ruled by a local council composed of nobles, and the whole headed by a senate, which was the supreme executive and legislative body of the republic. Thus the new republic was definitely aristocratic. In the meanwhile Russian garrisons maintained peace and order, and it was because of Ushakov's enlightened administration that the cities were saved from looting and destruction at the hands of the Turks and Albanians. The peace which reigned on these islands through the presence of Russian garrisons made them a haven for refugees from more troubled parts of the Continent, particularly from Italy, such eminent Italians as Prince Borghese and Cardinal Pignatelli making their temporary homes at Corfu.

It was during the negotiations with Russia over the constitutional issue that Capo d'Istria went with a delegation to St. Petersburg, and thereby laid the foundation of his future brilliant career.

In July, 1801, under the clauses of the convention and with the constitution in working order, the Russian forces of occupation left the islands. Immediately trouble broke out. Cephalonia and Ithaca declared their independence, and Zante raised the British flag. A democratic movement against the senate resulted in the establishment of a popular assembly, the Onoranda, and unleashed such violent hatreds that terror and anarchy reigned. The islands were drifting toward civil war when a Russian squadron of five vessels once more entered Corfu, bringing a new force of 1,600 men, who re-established order. This force of occupation was placed under the command of Count Mocenigo, a native of Zante in Russian service, subsequently the Russian Resident Minister. Mocenigo immediately proceeded to work out a new constitution based on the liberal ideas of Ushakov. The constitution was in the main the work of the new Czar Alexander I, to whom Mocenigo had submitted the draft. Alexander was very proud of it, and later boasted of it to Napoleon. Indeed, a new principle was introduced which was not yet admitted outside republican France, namely, the giving of political power not only to the nobility, but also to the intelligentsia, which, together with the hereditary nobility, was to form a "constitutional nobility." This idea was taken up by King Louis Philippe of France thirty years later, when the latter gave special electoral priviliges to the *capacités*. A College of Regents elected from the members of this constitutional nobility was to govern every island, but the real power was vested in a senate divided into three chambers. Three censors were to be responsible for the execution of the law, the Greek Church was made the State Church, and the judiciary was reorganized. The constitution suffered from being too complex, and was redrawn in 1806. Russian control operated through the Resident Minister (Mocenigo), who reserved the right of appointing the high administrative and judiciary officers.

The subsequent story of this venture in Russian imperialism in the Mediterranean will be told later. It was necessary here, for the sake of continuity, to tell the story beyond the war of 1799 and the reign of Paul I; for the question of the Ionian Islands, though integrated with the operations of the Second Coalition against France on the mainland, formed at the same time a part of the Russian quest for the domination of the Eastern Mediterranean, and thus links up with the Near Eastern Question, so vital for Russia as well. We have now to return to the study of the military operations of the Russian Army against the French in the six months' campaign which followed the declaration of war by Russia on France. It will be recalled that the Russian Army was to co-operate with the Austrian Army in both Italy and Germany, and that the elderly Field Marshal Suvorov, now in his early seventies, was by special request of Emperor Francis to be put in supreme command. We therefore now have to examine the movements of the Austrian armies prior to the arrival of the Russians on the front.

CHAPTER II

The Campaign of 1799

I

IN JANUARY, 1799, 120,000 Austrians under Archduke Charles had occupied Bavaria and were marching toward the Rhine and Switzerland, while Field Marshal Kray and 75,000 men were assembled in nothern Italy beyond the Adige, and 47,000 men under Count Bellegarde were in readiness to support these forces from the Tyrol. The actual hostilities with the French started in March, when Masséna advanced into Switzerland. But the so-called French Army of Mainz under Jourdan having been beaten and forced back from the Rhine by Archduke Charles, the latter advanced in April toward Schaffhausen, and in May entered Switzerland, occupying Zurich the following month; at the same time in southern Switzerland, in the region of the St. Gotthard, the French were driven back to the shores of the Lake of Lucerne. In northern Italy in the meanwhile Kray's army, though much superior in size to the French army under Scherer holding the line of the Mincio, was merely engaged in protracted operations around Verona.

Such was the position on the various fronts when the Russians came into the war. The army of 60,000 men assigned by Paul to co-operate with the Austrians was divided roughly in two, with Suvorov's army marching through Austria into northern Italy, and the corps of Rimsky-Korsakov moving in May from Russian Poland through Bohemia to Schaffhausen to join Archduke Charles. A third and smaller corps under Rehbinder was originally scheduled to join Rimsky-Korsakov's forces at Teschen, but was diverted into Italy and joined Suvorov. The fate of Rimsky-Korsakov's forces will be told subsequently, and we will concern ourselves here only with Suvorov's campaign in Italy. As he passed through Vienna in his new capacity of Commander in Chief of the Allied Armies, Suvorov had his first clash with the Austrian *Hof-Kriegsrat*, or Aulic Council of War. He refused to communicate his plan of campaign to Thugut, and impatient, too, with the slowness, pedantry, and exceeding cautiousness of the war council, observed:

To know how to conquer well, but to be always beaten is not smart! The Emperor of Germany desires that, when I have to give battle the next day, I should first address myself to the Court of Vienna. The accidents of war change rapidly; one cannot be tied down to a fixed plan.[1]

Arriving in Italy in April, Suvorov immediately started training the Austrians, now under Melas, who had replaced Kray, in Russian methods of bayonet attacks and rapid marches. Suvorov had under his command 17,000 Russians and 35,000 Austrians, totaling 52,000 men. The French on April 12 abandoned the line of the Mincio and fell back, leaving garrisons in Peschiera and Mantua. Suvorov entered Verona in triumph, the cheering crowd unharnessing the horses and themselves pulling his carriage through streets bedecked with flags (April 14). The next day Suvorov ordered his troops to advance on an hour's notice: "The head does not wait for the tail, suddenly like snow on the head,"[2] said his order of the day, and he moved his headquarters to Valeggio. Scherer, faced with this advance and with a rising of the Italian population in his rear, retreated to Milan with Suvorov close upon his heels. On his way Suvorov captured Brescia, which surrendered with 1,246 men and officers and 46 guns. The Austrians could not keep up with the breath-taking pace of this advance, and when Melas halted his troops because of heavy rain, Suvorov wrote stingingly to him: "Complaints have come to my notice that the infantry have their feet wet. For that the weather is to blame. . . . If anyone is ill he can stay behind."[3] Kray having been left with 20,000 Austrians to watch the fortresses still held by the French and to garrison Verona, the rest of the army advanced in three columns toward the river Adda, where the French had set up a new defense line, reinforced by garrisons brought up from various cities in Lombardy. On the way the Cossacks of Denisov captured the city and citadel of Bergamo with 19 guns, and

[1] Alfred Nicolas Rambaud, *A Popular History of Russia, from the Earliest Times to 1880* (Boston, 1882), II, 132.

[2] Walter Lyon Blease, *Suvorof* (New York, 1920), p. 225. ("Snow on the head" in the Russian language signifies a sudden blow.)

[3] *Ibid.*, p. 226.

the Austrians took Crema with 30 guns. By the twenty-fifth both armies were facing each other on the Adda, strung out on a line 70 miles long. The river was wide and unfordable, and could be crossed by bridges only at Lecco, Cassano, Lodi, and Pizzighetone. The French were holding these points: Serrurier with 8,000 men at Lecco, Gregnet with 8,000 at Cassano, Victor with 8,000 at Lodi, and Laboisière with 4,000 at Pizzighetone, totaling therefore 28,000 in the first line. On the Austro-Russian side the three columns under Suvorov totaled 43,500 men, and thus had a tremendous numerical superiority, but these forces were scattered and had not yet come up. Suvorov established his headquarters at San Gervasio, facing approximately the center of the enemy line. The main Russian forces of the vanguard—Bagration and the corps of Rosenberg supported by the Austrian division of Vukassovich—moved to Lecco on the extreme northern end of the battle line, whereas Melas with the Austrian divisions of Fröhlich and Keim was opposite Cassano. At the last moment Suvorov held back Vukassovich at Caprino, halfway between Lecco and Cassano, so that he would be in a position to support either Bagration or Melas as the tide of battle should require. Melas was to attack first the following day, but Bagration, with only three battalions of infantry and a few hundred Cossacks, became engaged against superior French forces, and although he at first drove the French out of Lecco, he was later outflanked by the enemy and driven out in turn. The division of Miloradovich came to his aid, and Lecco was recaptured and the French driven back in full retreat, the Russian losses here for the day amounting to 385 killed and wounded.

On the French side the much more able General Moreau, the future victor of Hohenlinden, had replaced the inefficient Scherer on the evening of the twenty-sixth, and started concentrating his forces by ordering Gregnet and Victor to Cassano to support the French, now hard pressed by Melas's attack. He also ordered all available reserves up from Milan, but he was too late. By midnight Suvorov had established a pontoon bridge at San Gervasio and had thrown six Russian battalions across the river, while Ott's and Zopf's divisions and Bagration's three Cossack regiments hurried up from Lecco. Thus 11,500 men crossed here to find one French battalion. Moreau hurriedly brought up Gregnet's and Victor's divisions and blocked Ott's progress, but a charge of Denisov's Cossacks drove the French back, Moreau himself barely escaping capture at the hands of the Cossacks. Austrian infantry thereupon captured the villages of Pozzo and Vaprio, and Moreau began to fall back upon Cassano. But in the meanwhile Melas, who with 13,000 men had succeeded in crossing the river, threatened Moreau from the rear. With the road to Milan cut by Russian cavalry, Moreau's only thought now was to save his army by retreating southward toward the Appenines, closer to Macdonald's army, which was hurrying up from Naples. The day had cost the French 2,000 prisoners, 19 guns, and the loss of their last line of defense in Northern Italy.[4]

In the meanwhile Serrurier, who, after the loss of Lecco to Bagration had moved to Verderia, found himself cut off from the rest of the French army, and surrendered to Rosenberg with 3,000 men and 8 guns, the rest of his division escaping northward toward Lugano by scrambling over hills and vineyards. The total loss of the French in this defeat amounted to 2,500 killed and wounded, 5,000 prisoners, and 27 guns, while the allied losses did not exceed 2,000 men. Three days later, on Easter Sunday, April 29, Suvorov made a triumphant entry into Milan. The next day he attended a solemn thanksgiving service in the great cathedral and said to the archbishop, "I am sent to restore the ancient throne of the Popes and to bring the people to obedience to their sovereign."[5] He invited Serrurier to a great banquet in honor of the local magnates, and released the French general from captivity upon his word of honor. He further disarmed the National Guard which had been mobilized by the French, and abolished the Cisalpine Republic set up by Napoleon in 1796. Thereupon he worked out a plan for his next move in the campaign: The Russians were to cross the Po and defeat the next French army under Macdonald, while the Austrians were to clear the northern Alpine passes of remnants of French troops holding them; then Suvorov from the south and Archduke Charles from the north were to invade Switzerland and crush Masséna. This plan, however, was vetoed by the Austrians, under the absurd pretext that Archduke Charles could not move so long as the Elector of Bavaria with his army of eight thousand men had

[4] Miliyutin, *Istoria Voiny 1799 Goda* (St. Petersburg, 1852), p. 292, as quoted in Blease, *op. cit.*, p. 233.

[5] Blease, *op. cit.*, p. 235.

not made clear his position in the war. Hence the *Hof-Kriegsrat* in Vienna issued strict orders that Suvorov should not go beyond the Po. Thus the conflict between the Russian Commander in Chief and the Court of Vienna finally came out into the open; of this more will be said later. But by the time the order from Vienna reached Suvorov, he had already crossed the Po and was advancing against Macdonald, reaching Piacenza on May 13. As for Moreau, after leaving a garrison at Alexandria, he made for the Appenines, following a futile attempt to move into Suvorov's rear and to cover Turin. Hearing of Moreau's move, Suvorov marched rapidly on Turin and captured the city on May 25, blockading the garrison in the citadel, which nevertheless refused to surrender. In the arsenal of Turin, Suvorov found 382 cannon, 15 mortars, 20,000 muskets, and a much-needed siege train. Suvorov immediately appointed an executive council for the administration of the city and of the whole of Piedmont as well, with Piedmontese nobles, the Count of St. André and Baron de Latour, receiving full administrative and military powers. He also issued a proclamation stating: "The allied armies have come in the name of the legitimate sovereign, to place him again on the throne, to make for the final triumph of religion, to break the iron yoke of the oppressors of Piedmont . . . to guarantee property."[6] He further issued an invitation to the King of Sardinia to re-enter his capital, and proceeded to raise a national Italian militia. The city had offered little resistance, and the population had itself opened the gates to the Russians after disarming the French. The French historian Sorel gives the following graphic picture of Suvorov's entry into the city from eyewitness accounts: "The Turinese then saw with stupefaction twenty thousand admirable troops dash into their streets, in parade dress, the cavalary galloping and the infantry at rapid pace . . ."; and riding between the Austrian General Melas and the Grand Duke Constantine was Suvorov, "on a small Tartar horse, the harness and the Cossack saddle of which were worth not more than six francs."[7] When at night the republicans who were blockaded in the citadel opened fire on the city, Suvorov threatened to shoot the French prisoners, and the firing ceased. The citadel held out until June 7, when it capitulated,

[6] Sorel, *op. cit.*, V, 409.

[7] *Ibid.*, V, 410.

Suvorov having then already resumed his offensive against Macdonald.

In the meanwhile Suvorov's actions in Turin brought to a climax his conflict with the Austrian Government and Military Command in Vienna. It must be said, however, that the Austrian forces in Italy co-operated loyally with their allies and fought bravely. Even though serious friction arose over the question of supplies which the Austrians were to provide for the Russians, and the lack of efficiency in this respect was to become tragic later on when Suvorov was to move into Switzerland, still Suvorov was on friendly terms with Melas and liked his Austrian chief of staff, Chasteler, even though he derisively nicknamed him *Nicht Bestimmtsager* for his vagueness and indecision. But as his successes increased, his bitterness and his complaints against the Austrian Government increased also, and in Vienna they were repaid in kind. Suvorov had succeeded too well and too rapidly. The *Hof-Kriegsrat* in Vienna wanted a slow war which it could direct from Vienna with all due caution, not going further than the besieging of fortresses and long and intricate maneuvers, and Thugut after the capture of Turin openly spoke of having to restrain the "Russian fury." Similarly, politically Austria wanted to hold northern Italy and keep Piedmont under control, whereas Suvorov was playing upon the Italian national feeling and setting up an Italian administration wherever he went. Because of him the Pope was able to return to Rome and King Victor Emmanuel to Turin. And after the next battle—that of Trebbia—through the action of the guerilla leader Ruffo supported by Russian troops, Naples was delivered from the French (Suvorov having forced Macdonald to go north) and King Ferdinand as well was able to return to his capital.

In short, Suvorov's policy of restoring Italian sovereigns to their thrones and playing up Italian national feeling alarmed and infuriated Vienna. Hence the Austrian Cabinet ordered the rescinding of every one of the measures taken by Suvorov. By order of Vienna the Italian levies raised by Suvorov were placed in Austrian service, and an Austrian governor appointed in Turin. All proclamations to the Sardinian people were in the name of the Emperor of Austria and not of the King of Sardinia, and Austrian generals received orders directly from Vienna over the head of Suvorov, who in his anger wanted to resign. Furthermore, the inactivity of Archduke Charles in Switzerland endangered Suvorov's rear, since he was exposed to attacks from the north over the Alpine passes while he was planning his maneuvers southward toward the Appenines to crush Macdonald. Accordingly, by June 8, he had made the following dispositions: with 21,700 men Suvorov remained around Turin, while Bellegarde, Schweikovsky, Tchubarov, and Seckendorf were around Alessandria with 16,700 men; Ott with 7,400 covered the road to Bologna at Regio; Kray was still besieging Mantua too far away to be of use, while Haddik and Klenau, with 10,000 and 5,000 men respectively, were assigned to watch the Alpine passes; between Alessandria and Turin, Vukassovich with 8,000 men formed a liaison between the two forces. These 30,000 men could be rapidly assembled at any given point which might be threatened by a French advance from the south, the west, or the north.

On the French side what remained of Moreau's army had fallen back to the Genoese Riviera, except for Victor's division, which had crossed the Appenines and joined Macdonald. A concentric offensive was launched, with the aim of trapping Suvorov, and for this purpose Moreau was to advance on Alessandria, while Macdonald with 36,000 men was to cross the Appenines and turn west. Indeed, on the eleventh Macdonald's right wing occupied Bologna, and on the following day Modena, where he defeated the Austrians of Hohenzollern. But Moreau moved so slowly that by the nineteenth he had only reached Voghera near Genoa, and he thus gave Suvorov a chance to act in the interval. Indeed, foreseeing the coming attack, Suvorov left Turin on June 10 and covered the thirty-three miles to Asti in one day, over bad roads and in heavy rain, reaching Alessandria the following day and ordering Ott and Vukassovich to come up as well. Using Alessandria as base, Suvorov decided to crush Macdonald first. Thus, leaving the Austrians of Bellegarde at Alessandria, Suvorov with 25,000 men (of whom 15,000 were Russians) moved against Macdonald.

In the meanwhile Macdonald, leaving Ollivier's division at Modena and Montrichard to face Kray, with the rest of his forces marched swiftly toward Parma, to fall upon Ott, and also to come closer to Moreau. The position of Ott with 9,000 men facing 16,000 French became so critical that on the fifteenth he fell back to Piacenza, and Suvorov rushed to his assistance. Suvorov was held back by the necessity of putting a bridge over the Bormidas, but he made up the lost time by a phenomenal march covering fifty-three miles nonstop in thirty-six hours, an effort which he alone could demand from his troops. Melas, with nine battalions of infantry and twelve squadrons of cavalry had reached Ott on the seventeenth, but the combined Austrian forces had been completely defeated by the French and were fleeing in disorder. At 4:00 P.M. the Russian vanguard of Bagration arrived on the scene of battle, preceded by two hours by detachments of Cossacks who attacked immediately, routing Dombrovski's Polish cavalry. Notwithstanding the complete exhaustion of his men, Bagration, with only forty men to a company, on being ordered by Suvorov to attack the French immediately, made his way through columns of retreating Austrians and by a bayonet charge drove the French back across the river Trebbia. Only darkness stopped the Russian advance and gave a much-needed rest to the army.

This preliminary action made the river Trebbia the line between the two armies. Flowing through a plain some ten miles wide covered with vineyards, its shallow waters permitted easy crossing, and it was held by the French partly on one bank and partly on the other bank. Suvorov, who had with him twenty-two thousand men, decided to pursue the defeat of Macdonald before Moreau could come up, and hence ordered the attack for the next day. "The word *halt* not to be used," read his order. "It is neither for drill nor for battle. Attack, strike, cut down, hurray, drums, music."[8] Once more, as on the Adda, the French held the key points along the river: Salme at San Nicollo, Dombrovski at Casaligio, the divisions of Rusca and Victor on the right bank in the center at Grignano, and Watrin at Piacenza. Bagration attacked Dombrovski and drove him back in hand-to-hand fighting, the latter losing one flag, two guns, and six hundred prisoners. Rusca and Victor came to Dombrovski's rescue and turned Bagration's flank, while Schweikovsky in turn rushed to Bagration's assistance; then while Bagration cleared his right flank by a bayonet charge, Schweikovsky drove the enemy back on the left flank. Meanwhile Förster took Grignano, denuded of Rusca's infantry. The Austrians of Fröhlich and Ott, re-formed

[8] Blease, *op. cit.*, p. 258.

after their defeat of the previous day, attacked Salme and captured San Nicollo, the French losing seven hundred prisoners here. Again night put an end to the fighting. Thoroughly alarmed, Macdonald brought up the divisions of Ollivier and Montrichard, which, it will be recalled, had been left at Modena to watch Kray. Strengthened by the arrival of these forces, the French attacked Ott during the night, but were repulsed, and Rosenberg broke through their lines. The following morning Macdonald ordered a general attack—all his forces were to cross the river. Once more Bagration came to grips with Dombrovski and defeated him so severely that the latter's division had to be taken out of line; but in pursuing him Bagration opened a dangerous gap, and Victor and Rusca, profiting by this, cut off Schweikovsky and surrounded some of his forces. The rest of Schweikovsky's division fell back in a disorderly retreat, while Bagration made a desperate but unavailing flank attack to save his comrade. In this crisis Suvorov himself dashed into the fray in his shirt sleeves and, rallying Schweikovsky's fleeing battalions, threw the French back across the Trebbia. In the meanwhile Montrichard's attack against the Austrians of Förster had failed, and, with the battle once more coming to an end at nightfall, Macdonald ordered a general retreat. The French had lost in the three-day battle 17,000 men (of whom 12,000 were prisoners), 7 guns, and 8 flags; whereas the total Russian losses amounted to 2,768 and the total Austrian losses to 2,157 men. Thus another French army had been crushed.

In the meanwhile Moreau had made his way into the rear of Suvorov's army close to Alessandria at Novi, and had fallen upon the Austrians of Bellegarde while the battle of Trebbia was being fought. Bellegarde fought gallantly to stem this grave danger to the main allied armies, and drove Moreau back. But the latter, reinforced, counterattacked to cut Bellegarde's forces in two, but too late; Suvorov, after his victory, came up and routed Moreau.

Suvorov now gave his army a well-deserved rest, and proceeded with the sieges of the citadel of Turin and the various fortresses still holding out in northern Italy; the last of these, Mantua, capitulated on July 31. Much-needed reinforcements in the shape of Rehbinder's corps, originally scheduled to join Rimsky-Korsakov, came up from Russia and were stationed at Piacenza. Suvorov was also rewarded with the title of Prince of Italy, given to him by the

Czar. But his relations with the Austrian Court went from bad to worse. He was ordered by Emperor Francis to make no moves in the direction of Naples or Rome, not to allow the King of Sardinia to return to his kingdom, and not to use Sardinian levies; his Austrian chief of staff Chasteler was removed. In a state of blind fury Suvorov wrote of "the cowardice of the War Council, jealous of me as a foreigner, the double-faced sectional commanders in direct communication with the council. . . ."[9] The French had now lost control of the whole of Italy with the exception of Rome, Ancona, Perugia, Genoa, and the Riviera.

Suvorov next prepared an attack on Genoa, preliminary to an invasion of southern France. Of the 108,000 men under his command, he had 45,000 immediately available around Alessandria, and by ordering Kray to rejoin him after the fall of Mantua he brought this army up to 64,000 men. While persuading Nelson to cut the communications of the Riviera from the sea, he set his army in motion on August 2, capturing Serravallo five days later. But the French had not been idle in the meanwhile. Thoroughly alarmed by the loss of Italy, the Directory in Paris had put into the field a new army of 45,000 men, with the young and promising Joubert as commander and Moreau as his advisor. This army, advancing in three columns, was once more aiming at Alessandria with the object of getting into Suvorov's rear, and on the twelfth its right wing (Watrin) attacked Serravallo. Suvorov at first did not realize the seriousness of this threat, until advised by Bellegarde of the appearance of the enemy in the valley of the Bromida. Suvorov then canceled his offensive and ordered the concentration of all his forces around Novi. Joubert came up to Novi, effecting a junction of his various columns on the fifteenth, St. Cyr having previously captured the city.

The French now took up a good defensive position on a series of heights overlooking the plain of Novi where the Austro-Russians were camping between the rivers Serivia and Orba. The walled town of Novi formed a bastion in the right center of the line, and Suvorov could attack this position only by climbing the steep grade up the hill, which precluded the use of cavalry. But a disadvantage to the French lay in the fact that behind the French line, and paral-

[9] *Ibid.*, p. 271.

leling it, ran deep ravines with streams which flowed into the Orba; thus there was only one good line of retreat—on the left flank through the village of Pasturano, which line would have to be used by both the center and left flank, the right wing being able to retreat on Serravallo. Suvorov opened the attack on the sixteenth with 35,000 men, of whom 10,000 were Russians (Bagration and Miloradovich); the French had only one division in line (Lemoine) holding the dangerous sector ahead of Pasturano, and two other divisions (Clausel and Partouneaux) were still coming up. The Austrians of Seckendorff attacked up a gorge, threatening Pasturano, and the cavalry of Grouchy thrown into the gap failed to block the attack. Joubert himself in rushing to the danger point was killed.

In the meanwhile another Austrian attack was developing on the French left flank. For once the situation was reversed, the Austrians doing all the fighting and Suvorov holding back and not showing his customary energy. Moreau, who had taken command after Joubert's death, had summoned St. Cyr from Novi, and with reserves coming up had succeeded in driving the Austrians back. Kray, desperately pressed, asked support from Bagration; but Bagration refused, pending orders from Suvorov, who seemed to be taking vengeance on his allies by his immobility. Then suddenly his energy returned; he ordered Bagration and Miloradovich to attack, but only after the French had secured their hold on the whole crest of the heights. For this reason the Russian attack failed, although according to St. Cyr "the behavior of the Russian troops was beyond praise. Fired upon in front and in flank, they moved as if on parade."[10] Kray's second attack on Pasturano was also thrown back. By one o'clock no definite gains had been achieved, and both sides claimed victory. But whereas the French had all their forces engaged, the main Russian forces of Rosenberg and the Austrians of Melas did not come up until the afternoon, and the general attack which followed was so overwhelming that the French defenses were broken, and Miloradovich captured Novi. Now the French found themselves trapped along their single line of retreat, and their withdrawal became a rout. With the French divisions trying desperately to make their way through the gorge of the Riasco at Pasturano, they lost their whole artillery, all their baggage, 6,500 killed and

[10] *Ibid.*, p. 282.

wounded, and 4,500 prisoners—Moreau's army was dispersed. The allied losses had been unusually severe, with 7,000 killed and wounded and 1,000 prisoners. Suvorov's pursuit of the French resulted in another defeat of their rear guard at Monte Rosso on August 18, but, with the allied army running out of supplies and bread available for only two days, Suvorov put his army once more into camp around Asti.

The battle of Novi marks the highwater mark of Suvorov's fame and popularity. Czar Paul ordered that military honors given only to sovereigns should be granted by the army to the aged commander; medals were coined in his honor in England, ladies' fashions included Suvorov hats and Suvorov feathers, and portraits of Suvorov appeared in shop windows all over Europe (although in Vienna the one which was supposed to represent the features of the Russian general was actually a portrait of George Washington!). Meanwhile Suvorov's relations with his allies were becoming steadily worse. Melas, against his orders, proceeded to disarm Italian levies in Tuscany, declaring he was acting under direct orders from Vienna. A rescript of Emperor Francis forbade Suvorov to advance into France, and soon afterward the Austrian troops were removed from his command. These bickerings resulted at this time in a general shift of allied strategy, which opens a new chapter in the story of this campaign.

In London, Pitt, who had been watching the growing dissension between the allies with justifiable alarm, proposed a plan which received the warm approval of Austria. The idea originally suggested by Thugut was that as many Russians as possible should be grouped in Switzerland with the Russian corps of Rehbinder, at that time marching into Switzerland, while Archduke Charles should divide his army in two, one half to operate in Germany, and the other under Archduke Joseph to replace Rehbinder in Italy. Paul had assented to this plan; but, since Macdonald was at the time still a threat, it was the Austrian Government itself which asked that Rehbinder go to Italy. Then, with the threat of Macdonald removed, the Austrians changed their minds once more and asked that Rehbinder be sent to join Rimsky-Korsakov. Paul, exasperated, refused outright; and Rehbinder remained with Suvorov. Now, however, the plan proposed by Pitt was much more comprehensive: It suggested the complete removal of all Russian troops from Italy, with Suvorov going to Switzerland and the Austrians replacing him in Italy; thus concentrated in Switzerland, the Russians were to form the center of the front, while Archduke Charles on their right flank was to operate along the middle Rhine. But since at that time Archduke Charles was still in Switzerland and had been joined near Zurich by the Russian corps of Rimsky-Korsakov, it was well understood that he should not leave Switzerland until the arrival of Suvorov, in order not to leave Korsakov to face Masséna alone. Once concentrated in Switzerland, Suvorov was to destroy Masséna and invade France conjointly with Archduke Charles, while a combined Anglo-Russian fleet was to land a British-Russian expeditionary force in Holland to operate against Brune. Such was the outline of the plan endorsed by Paul and communicated to Suvorov on August 27 as an order, which Suvorov protested in vain as strategically unsound. Having no choice but to obey, he started preparing for the expedition. At the same time dramatic events were taking place in Switzerland, to which we now have to turn.

II

By the middle of June the Austrian army under Archduke Charles was holding a line in Switzerland extending from Airolo along the Limmat and the Aar to Zurich. This line, running roughly north-south, pivoted around the eastern side of the Lake of Lucerne and cut the country in two. The French were holding Lucerne, Thun, Brunig, the valley toward Altdorf, and Göshenen, while to the north a cordon of troops faced Zurich and extended as far as the Rhine at Basel. With 75,000 men under the command of Masséna, they had a decided preponderance over Archduke Charles, who had at his disposal merely 47,000 Austrian regulars, and some armed Swiss peasants whose military value was questionable. For this reason the Russian corps of Rimsky-Korsakov, which originally was destined for the Upper Rhine, was ordered to march into Switzerland to reinforce the Austrians. This corps was composed of 18,000 infantry, 7,000 cavalry including seven regiments of regular cavalry and four regiments of Cossacks, and 1,700 men of artillery with 110 guns, totaling 27,000 men.[11] Commanded by

[11] 1,002 officers, 26,355 men. See Captain Louis Hennequin, *Zurich. Masséna en Suisse . . .* (Paris, 1911), pp. 135-138.

the forty-six-year-old Rimsky-Korsakov, who had distinguished himself in the wars of Catherine, but who showed the utmost scorn for the French republican armies and was termed "imprudent and presumptuous," this corps was equipped with an artillery not suitable for mountain warfare, and was overburdened with transports. Nevertheless, it was well trained and showed endurance and excellent military spirit; in the words of the French General Bacher, who presented a secret report to the Minister of War in Paris, Bernadotte: "The regiments of this corps present themselves well under arms. . . ."[12] The Swiss observer, Colonel Rovera, speaks of the infantry as being redoubtable because of its stolidity in defense, the impetus of its bayonet charges, and the rapidity of its advances. The officers, he says, were brave but lacking in knowledge, the staff too sure of itself and negligent in taking elementary precautions for safety, the cavalry too heavy for mountainous country, and the transports defective and short of pontoons.[13] Its vanguard reached Schaffhausen on the Swiss border on August 14, then proceeded to Zurich, the rest of the corps following at intervals of a week.

The French had not been idle in the interval. Fearing a pincer movement by the Russians—Rimsky-Korsakov from Germany and Suvorov from Italy—they attacked and succeeded in driving the Austrians back all along the line, in order to obtain command of the vital passes and valleys. They thus gained control of the St. Gotthard Range, the valley of the Reuss, and both sides of the Lake of Lucerne by driving the Austrians from Schwytz into the Muothathal, and finally forced the Austrian garrisons holding Zurich to take shelter within the city walls (August 14–24). It will be recalled that according to plans worked out by the allies earlier in June Korsakov was intended to replace the Austrians in Switzerland, but only after Suvorov had rejoined him by successfully crossing the Alps. Furthermore, he was promised the Russian corps of Rehbinder, which had been diverted to Italy, though originally scheduled to join Korsakov's corps around Lake Constance. Under these circumstances, awaiting new orders, Korsakov, upon his arrival in Switzerland, followed the last orders he had received, namely, to reinforce Archduke Charles by taking over a

[12] Hennequin, *op. cit.*, p. 139.
[13] *Ibid.*, p. 140.

sector of the latter's left flank and working jointly with him. The Archduke, however, at the first meeting of the two commanders, tried to persuade Korsakov to take over the whole front in order to relieve the Austrians and permit them to effect their withdrawal from Switzerland. Korsakov objected violently, saying that Rehbinder with his 20,000 men had never reached him, nor had the 6,000 Bavarians promised to him, and that he would thus have to hold a front of some 200 kilometers against 80,000 French, quite alone and unaided until the arrival of Suvorov. Apparently impressed, the Archduke proceeded to carry out an important joint operation; since the French had been pressing his left flank particularly hard, he would in turn counterattack and drive back the French left flank. For this operation, which entailed the crossing of the Aar, Korsakov was to give him ten battalions of infantry and one regiment of Cossacks, or 6,700 men, out of the advance forces of his corps which had thus far come up. These forces duly reached the Aar on August 16 at Gross Dottingen, but the lack of technical preparations for the crossing delayed them and gave time for Ney to bring up 10,000 men and block the passage. Discouraged, the Archduke gave up the attempt and decided next to reinforce his badly battered left flank, in order to facilitate the approach of Suvorov. Hence on August 17 he sent nine battalions of infantry and six squadrons of cavalry toward Kapperswill to the south, just as the Russians, who were approaching Zurich in force, had made camp at Seebach, four miles from the city.

These movements of the Austrians, as well as the failure of the crossing of the Aar, instilled in the mind of the Russian commander a profound distrust of the Archduke. Whereupon the Archduke received a curt demand from Suvorov that 10,000 men of Korsakov's corps should march to Lake Como to meet him halfway. The Archduke, furious, refused, and complained to his brother, the Emperor Francis. At the same time he ordered Korsakov to send 5,000 men to the aid of the Austrian General Hotze, who was attempting to stem the French advance in the valley of the Reuss. It was then Korsakov's turn to refuse, considering that he still lacked his artillery and cavalry, which had not yet reached Schaffhausen. Finally, and as late as August 22, it was agreed that the whole of Korsakov's corps should march to the aid of Hotze's corps. Korsakov therefore started his march on August 24, only to learn that the Archduke had merely been anxious to get him out of the way in order to start evacuating Switzerland. Furious, Korsakov stopped his advance, but found that the Austrians were already on the march. Indeed, the Archduke had left his headquarters for Germany on August 26, taking with him 39,000 infantry and 18,000 cavalry, and thus leaving behind with Korsakov only the corps of Hotze, composed of 16,000 infantry and 5,000 cavalry.

What induced the Archduke to make this extraordinary decision remains a mystery. The official explanation—that the French had become a threat on the Upper Rhine and needed to be checked there—does not bear close examination. Indeed, when Charles went into Switzerland he left 20,000 men on the Rhine under General Starray. In July a French army began assembling around Mannheim, endangering the valley of the Upper Danube; but, owing to the absence of reinforcements, the French did not move until August, and with Charles advancing after leaving Switzerland, they not only fell back to Mannheim but speedily recrossed the Danube. To leave Korsakov and Hotze to face single-handed the real threat of Masséna's 80,000 men, in order to offset the much weaker threat on the Rhine, did not make sense. More plausibly, the explanation may be found in the friction between the Russian and Austrian commanders, and in the reluctance on the part of the Archduke to place himself under the orders of Suvorov. Still, by his speedy and unwarranted departure he placed both Korsakov and Hotze in an inextricable position and jeopardized the whole campaign. Korsakov's predicament thus suddenly became very grave: Not only did there now remain 48,000 Austro-Russians to face an army nearly double their number, but, whereas Korsakov's forces were near Zurich, the bulk of Hotze's forces were far to the south; the interval was only thinly held, and by his capture of the Gotthard Range Masséna had effectively closed the road from Italy over which Suvorov's army could come to Korsakov's aid.

Masséna was quick to see his chance and decided to strike at Zurich by crossing the Limmat at Dietikon, but failed (August 29–30); whereupon he concentrated upon the weaker opponent and drove Hotze farther into the mountains, consolidating his right flank. He was then in a position to try once more to capture Zurich, and this time he carefully prepared for the crossing of the Limmat, bringing up pontoons and bridge equipment. His plan was to cross with his main forces at Dietikon, while a demonstration and a feint of crossing were to be made by General Menard fifteen miles farther west at Brügg. Mortier was to advance on Zurich from the south by crossing the Linth between the Lake of Zurich and Lake Wallenstedt, and Soult was to attack the Austrians on the Linth proper. Thus the Russians had to hold a long semicircular front stretching due west from Zurich for about 45 miles, roughly parallel to the Limmat, and then curving from Zurich southward. The main Russian forces covering Zurich itself and holding the line along the Sihl south of the city (in other words, facing Soult) amounted to 10,000 men with 16 guns, under Prince Gorchakov. West-east along the Limmat, holding a front 25 miles long to Baden, was General Markov with 3,000 men and 6 guns; while beyond Baden, spread over another 20 miles to Brügg and beyond, was General Puschchin with 4,800 men and 16 guns. The forces on the Limmat formed a division under the general command of General Durassov. All told, in the line of battle were 19,500 men with 38 guns (5,600 men under General Koslov had been detached to go to the aid of General Hotze, and 3,200 men, including the bulk of the cavalry, were still at Schaffhausen). Against these 20,000 men Masséna had earmarked 34,000, the bulk of whom, or 27,000 men (Masséna with 14,000 men, Menard with 4,000 and 6,000 reserves) were to advance against Durassov's division holding the 45-mile front on the Limmat with 10,000 men.

The French began their offensive on September 25, and Masséna succeeded in bringing up his forces to the Limmat in such silence that the unsuspecting Russians got wind of the crossing at Dietikon only when it had actually started (4:00 A.M. the next morning). The small Russian forces fell back to a plateau where, supported by hurriedly brought up reserves, they held out for several hours, but the French were able to cut Durassov's line of communications. In the meanwhile Mortier attacked Gorchakov, but the latter not only succeeded in driving him back and recapturing the ground he had first lost, but actually, with the support of Tuchkov on his right, pushed back the French brigade of Brunet seven miles farther in the plain of Sihlfeld, and captured the strategically important plateau of Uetlisberg, which threatened the French line of communications. Seeing the danger, Masséna brought up his reserves and attacked the Russians from the flank, while the Russians carried out three successive attacks against the battered forces of Brunet. By noon, however, with the French reserves appearing on his right flank, Gorchakov ordered the Russians to abandon the plateau and to fall back to their original line. By this time the French forces which had crossed the Limmat at Dietikon had advanced on the highway running parallel to the river, and threatened not only Zurich from the north, but also Korsakov's line of retreat to Schaffhausen. By 10:00 A.M. they had captured the city of Hongg, advancing some ten miles. Sacken, defending this sector, fell back two miles farther east to Wipkingen, and vainly demanded reinforcements from Korsakov. His attempt to counterattack without these reinforcements failed, and he resolved to concentrate on the defense of Wipkingen. But by early afternoon Masséna succeeded in turning his position from the north and forced him back to within two miles of Zurich itself. But here Sacken counterattacked a second time, pushing Oudinot back and gaining some two miles.

In the meanwhile, caught in a pincer movement by this attack composed of some sixteen thousand men from the north, and by the main attack of Masséna himself from the south, Korsakov by evening ordered Gorchakov to enter Zurich proper, abandoning the plain of Sihlfeld. This gave Masséna the opportunity of bearing with all available forces upon Sacken, who was thereby also forced into the city. But Sacken, by his fire from the houses of the suburbs, after another counterattack, blocked French attempts to penetrate into the city. The battle came to an end with the darkness, and the Russians found themselves besieged in the city, where dreadful confusion reigned in the narrow streets jammed with transports, artillery, and wounded.. Korsakov during the day had been in such constant motion that his generals, unable at critical moments to get in touch with him, had been left to themselves; but he was to redeem somewhat his poor generalship by a show of courage and determination in the darkest hour. He called a council of war which, with only thirteen thousand men remaining, advised holding out in the city until the arrival of Suvorov. But the city was without food, and no news had been received of the whereabouts of Suvorov.

Moreover, intelligence had been received of a crushing defeat sustained by the corps of Hotze during the same day on the Linth at the hands of Soult. Hotze himself had been killed, and his successor, Prokash, was falling back eastward in an attempt to gain the valley of the Rhine, making his way virtually out of Switzerland. Even under these circumstances Korsakov refused an offer from Masséna to surrender, and decided to attempt to break through to Schaffhausen. For this, Sacken was to attack Oudinot frontally and clear the main road north to Eglisau, while Pribyshevsky with four battalions was to occupy the plateau of Zurichberg west of this road. Gorchakov with the whole artillery, cavalry, and four battalions of infantry, was to pass between Pribyshevsky and Sacken, while the transports were to take a road farther east; and General Koslov, forming the rear guard, was to hold the city until all were safely out.

The movement started early in the morning of the twenty-seventh with a vigorous attack by Sacken, who succeeded in driving the French as far back as Hongg, while Pribyshevsky occupied the plateau. Gorchakov succeeded in slipping by as arranged, only to be attacked by Masséna; but charges of his cavalry drove the French back, and he got through safely, joined later by Pribyshevsky. In the meanwhile Oudinot, having brought up fresh reserves, pushed Sacken back to the city, the latter receiving a serious head-wound. The remnants of his forces joined with Koslov's rear guard and held out until 2:00 P.M., when the French finally broke into Zurich; but by that time the main force was safe, and the rear guard, escaping eastward, eventually rejoined it. Less lucky were the transports, which, along with the cash of the army, fell into French hands. The two-day battle had cost the Russians three thousand dead and five thousand wounded and prisoners, among whom were three generals; twenty-six guns and nine colors were also lost. The French gave no estimate of their losses. The following day Korsakov reached Schaffhausen and crossed the Rhine, the French pursuing weakly. General Durassov came up, with the division on the Limmat as well as the Russian forces which had been sent to the aid of Hotze, and thus the corps was reassembled. It was at this point that Suvorov, having forced his way over the St. Gotthard, appeared in the valley of the Reuss—too late.

Suvorov had arrived at Taverno at the foot of the Alps on

September 15. He had marched from Alessandria with his customary speed, covering one hundred miles in six days over difficult roads. He had sent his heavy baggage and artillery by the roundabout way of Chiavenna and the Engadine, beyond the reach of the enemy, and had taken with him only twenty-five mountain guns. According to the arrangements made, the Austrian Staff was to provide the means of transportation over the mountains and 1,429 mules were to be awaiting him at Taverno; but upon Suvorov's arrival at Taverno he found no mules, and he lost five all-important days collecting them from the local inhabitants; he finally succeeded in getting less than half the number required, or 650 mules. He cut down on the rations; each man carried food for three days; the mules, for four; the remaining baggage was put on Cossack horses, the Cossacks themselves dismounting and proceeding on foot. He was thus able to start climbing the St. Gotthard Range only on September 21, his vanguard under General Rosenberg having started two days earlier on the nineteenth. Those five days lost at Taverno through the inefficiency of the Austrian Staff were to prove fatal, for the delay gave Masséna time to fight the Battle of Zurich.

The situation as it stood in Switzerland when Suvorov left Taverno, that is to say, five days before Korsakov's and Hotze's defeat, appeared encouraging. Korsakov was still holding the Limmat, whereas the Austrians were stretched out along the Linth south of Zurich. Of immediate importance for Suvorov's advance were the positions of the Austrian brigades of General Auffenberg (3,000 men) at Dissentis, Strauch (4,500 men) at Biasco, and Victor Rohan and Haddik, with 2,500 and 7,500 respectively, covering the roads over the Simplon and Great St. Bernard passes into Italy. On the French side, Lecourbe, with 12,000 men distributed between Glaris and Airolo in the immediate path of Suvorov's advance, was backed by Masséna's main forces, subsequently freed by the Battle of Zurich and spread from that city to the Lake of Lucerne. Thus the French had some 50,000 men to use against Suvorov, once Korsakov and Hotze were eliminated, whereas Suvorov on his side could draw upon only the smaller Austrian forces of Auffenberg, Strauch, and Förster, his whole army numbering some 24,000 men. Suvorov had two ways open to him in order to reach Zurich: the easy but long and roundabout way through Chiavenna and the Spluga Pass into the valley of the Upper Rhine and that of the Linth, and the shorter and more direct way over the St. Gotthard Range and thence around the Lake of Lucerne, which entailed the crossing of major Alpine ranges. He selected the second one, for, as he wrote to Hotze on September 13, "The true law of the art of war is to fall directly upon the enemy."[14]

The immediate problem facing Suvorov was the crossing of the St. Gotthard Range over a pass towering 7,000 feet above the valley. Lecourbe, having been informed of the coming of the Russians, not only occupied the summit with a brigade, but pushed his advance units down the slope on the Italian side; the French had thus 4,250 men defending the range, with some 2,000 holding the road above Airolo, at the foot of the pass on the Italian side. The Austrians, who were immediately facing Lecourbe and might have attempted to interfere with his movements, did not move. Suvorov's plan was to attack Lecourbe frontally by following the main road over the pass, which from Taverno followed the course of the Ticino to Airolo and thence wound its way to the summit; at the same time the corps of Rosenberg was to undertake a vast turning movement eastward by climbing over the neighboring Luckmaniers Pass (6,289 feet) to Dissentis and thence turning once more west through the Oberalp Pass (6,719 feet) to reach Andermatt at the foot of the St. Gotthard on the Swiss side, where Lecourbe had established his headquarters. Rosenberg had to cover some sixty miles as the crow flies, but actually much more along the winding road, and he had to negotiate two passes over roads which were merely goat trails. It was for this reason that Rosenberg had started two days earlier and was to meet Suvorov at Andermatt. The main army was in turn divided into three columns. The most difficult task was assigned to the vanguard under Bagration: This column was to turn right after reaching Airolo and climb the sheer slope of the mountains to the plateau of Bosco, and thence to the summits overlooking the pass itself. The second column—the Austrian brigade of Strauch and one Russian battalion—was to turn left from Airolo and follow up a lateral valley, the Val Bedretto, to cover the army from any French attack coming from the Valais and the Furka, where the French had more than a division. Lastly, the main column, led by

[14] Blease, *op. cit.*, p. 306.

Suvorov, was to follow the road from Airolo to the Hospice at the summit of the pass.

The attack started at 3:00 A.M. on September 24; heavy rain had been falling during the night, which meant snow in the mountains still capped by heavy storm clouds. To give time for Bagration to make headway, Suvorov delayed his own departure. By six in the morning Bagration's forces were in touch with the advance French units, which retreated up the slope of the mountain to the plateau of Bosco, where, hiding behind rocks, they opened a withering fire on the Russians climbing the steep slope and inflicted heavy casualties. Thereupon Bagration sent a regiment of infantry and some Cossacks clambering over the rocks to the summit overlooking the plateau, and this forced the French to evacuate it. In turn the appearance of Bagration on the plateau cleared the way for the main column, which, after passing Airolo, had to thread its way through a narrow gorge rendered dangerous by flood waters from the melting snow. Here two French battalions, still hidden securely behind rocks, held up the Russian column until they—the French—in turn saw the Russians of Bagration above their heads on the plateau. Then the French concentrated on the defense of the summit and, heavily reinforced, inflicted terrible casualties on the Russians crowded on the narrow, winding road. Two Russian attacks on the summit had been thrown back; while Suvorov was organizing his third attack and his men were becoming demoralized, Bagration succeeded in making his way to the top of the Alp della Sella overlooking the summit of the pass. The French then abandoned the defense and retreated in disorder down the Swiss side of the pass. The day had cost the Russians 1,200 killed, but it was the first Russian victory in a type of warfare with which they were unfamiliar—mountain warfare.

In the meanwhile Rosenberg, taxing the strength of his men to the utmost, pressed his major flanking movement with the greatest energy, crossing the passes and clearing the mountains of isolated French detachments. In so doing his vanguard under General Miloradovich had to climb directly over the peaks of the Piz Nurschallas, and two regiments under Mansurov, after engaging in difficult fighting in the narrows of a gorge, forced the French brigade of Gudin to fall back to Andermatt at the point of the bayonet; at the same time Suvorov, coming down the St. Gotthard, captured Hospenthal and forced the retreating French to abandon the line of the Reuss and to flee westward toward the Furka and Valais. Thus the road down the Reuss toward the Lake of Lucerne had been cleared; and the Russians at Andermatt captured, in addition to a large amount of ammunition, provisions enough to feed the army for one day. On September 25 Rosenberg and Suvorov joined forces, and the first operation was completed.

On this day Masséna was opening the Battle of Zurich against Rimsky-Korsakov. From Andermatt the road followed the course of the river to Göschenen, and thence to Fluelen, where the river falls into the Lake of Lucerne. Upon the fall of Andermatt, Lecourbe had been forced to throw the bulk of his artillery into the Reuss and had escaped by climbing over the Belsberg to Göschenen. Here he collected what forces he still had, the greater part of the French defenders of the Gotthard having been thrown back in a westerly direction by Suvorov and hence away from Lecourbe's line of retreat. Immediately below Andermatt, however, the Russians faced a natural obstacle extraordinarily difficult to negotiate, the so-called Unerloch, back of which was the famous Devil's Bridge, the place where the French rear guard under General Daumas could and did attempt to block the Russian advance. This led to the famous episode of the Devil's Bridge, as celebrated in the annals of the Russian Army as the Charge of the Light Brigade has become in England.

At this point the Reuss enters an extremely narrow gorge, the walls of which rise perpendicularly to a great height, presenting a slippery granite surface impossible to climb. As the river, here a tumultuous torrent, emerges from this gorge, it descends in a waterfall which winds its way through a mass of most picturesque rock formations, giving this stretch the name of the Devil's Circus. In making the road the Swiss engineers had been forced to blast a tunnel along the gorge beyond which the road, just over the waterfall and high above the torrent, crossed the Reuss on a stone bridge composed of two arches. This was the Devil's Bridge, built in 1707. General Daumas, passing through the Unerloch, took up a position on the far side of the bridge with two companies and one cannon between the tunnel and the bridge, the rest of the forces being scattered among the rocks on both banks of the river. French engineers had mined the bridge. When Rosenberg came up, advancing in the van, he immediately attacked, screening his advance by a charge of Cossacks, to be followed by the Grenadiers of Mansurov, who broke through the tunnel but were mowed down by the French cannon as they emerged.

In the meanwhile another column made its way over the mountain overlooking the gorge on the other side—the Teufelsberg—while a third column descended into the bed of the river and waded into the gorge in four feet of icy water, a number of men being carried to their death by the swift current. Not being able to find a footing on the tunnel side owing to the steepness of the bank, this column finally succeeded in crossing the river just above the waterfall. With the Russians finally breaking through the tunnel and climbing over it, while another battalion descended into the river by ladders which they had brought from Andermatt, the French, who had been firing at the hopelessly exposed Russians from their concealed position, finally fell back on the other bank and blew up the bridge. Whereupon the Russians brought up three beams, each twenty-six feet long, taken from a Swiss chalet which they had torn down. Tying them together with the belts of the officers, they threw the beams across the broken bridge, and, forming a chain, crossed under withering French fire. The French then gave up and retreated, the Russians pursuing them to Göschenen. The crossing had cost the Russians nine hundred killed, and the French lost some two hundred prisoners.

By the evening of the twenty-sixth Rosenberg made his entrance into Fluelen after another violent engagement with the French at Amsteg. The other columns were coming down the Reuss; and the Austrian brigade of Auffenberg, which Rosenberg had passed at Dissentis, had crossed the mountains over the Kreuzli Pass and now formed the reserve of the army. Thus the Lake of Lucerne had been reached and Lecourbe had been forced to retreat into the mountainous wilderness on the left side of the lake. Suvorov did not yet know what had happened to Korsakov and Hotze, and continued to send them peremptory orders to advance conjointly with his own advance. His plan was now to follow the eastern side of the lake to reach Schwytz and there link up with Hotze. He had the choice of two roads. One, along the lake itself, was not the fine scenic highway it is today, but a road in very poor condition; moreover, it had the disadvantage of revealing his movements to the boats of Masséna's flotilla which were sailing the lake. For these reasons he selected the longer and much more difficult second road. This road wound eastward through a lateral valley at right angles to the lake and came out into the valley of the Linth. About midway another road, merely a trail for mules, turned north and climbed over the Kinzig Pass (altitude 6,800 feet) and led out into the neighboring valley of the Muotha, or Muothathal, at the farther entrance of which was the city of Schwytz. The following day, September 27, at 5:00 A.M. the army started its march to Schwytz with Bagration in the vanguard, while Rosenberg, now in the rear guard, attacked the French positions beyond Fluelen to keep the enemy occupied. It had been raining in the valley, and as the Russians proceeded to climb the Kinzig Pass they ran into snow and heavy fog. The road became so narrow and slippery that men and horses lost their footing and rolled down the precipice. Lacking food, warm clothing, and shoes, the army suffered terrible hardships. The steep descent down the pass was more dangerous than the climb; nevertheless, after a twelve-hour march Bagration reached his destination and camped in the Muothathal in the outskirts of Schwytz, after destroying or capturing a small French force covering that city. The main body of the army passed the night shivering in the snow near the summit of the pass, and reached the valley the following day; Rosenberg did not come up until the thirtieth. Masséna, in the meanwhile having been informed by Lecourbe of the march of Suvorov and having disposed of both Korsakov and Hotze, was now in a position to set a trap for the exhausted Russians.

The Muothathal is a large valley stretching from northwest to southeast; its western end comes out on the Lake of Lucerne at Brünen, at a point where the lake itself turns sharply westward toward Lucerne. At the eastern end it narrows into the Klonthal, which links it with the valley of the Linth running northeast. Coming down from Zurich, Masséna was able to block both entrances into the valley; indeed he directed Mortier to bottle up the western entrance, and the latter moved up one brigade (Brunet) to Schwytz and a second brigade (Drouet) to Zug. The remnants of Lecourbe's division were transported by boat across the lake to serve as reserve. At the eastern end Soult proceeded down the Linth to the support of Molitor's brigade, which had been fighting the Austrians of Linken at Glaris. Just as the Russians arrived in the Muothathal, Molitor, having defeated Linken so heavily that the latter was in headlong flight southward, was thus able to move up the Klonthal and bottle up the narrow gorge which formed the eastern outlet of the Muothathal. Masséna himself had gone to take command of the whole operation at Schwytz. It was at this moment, as he arrived in the Muothathal, that Suvorov finally learned the true state of affairs—a courier brought him the news of the defeat and retreat of both Korsakov and Hotze; not only was he in a trap, but he had relied on Hotze to feed his army, for he had completely run out of provisions. Most commanders finding themselves in such a critical position would have surrendered; but Suvorov called a council of war wherein, in a most dramatic speech, he stressed the necessity of fighting to the bitter end. Since the road to Schwytz was barred by the presence of Masséna's overwhelming French forces, the Russians would break through the eastern end of the valley. Accordingly, Auffenberg, whose forces had thus far not been engaged, was to move on the twenty-ninth into the Klonthal, driving Molitor ahead of him, to be followed on the thirtieth by Bagration; and both, supported by Schweikovsky's division, were to push on to Glaris on the Linth. Meanwhile Rosenberg, aided by Förster, was to remain in the Muothathal to hold back Masséna, and if possible to drive him out of Schwytz; in any event he was to fight to the last man, to give time for the army to get out of the trap.

Auffenberg attacked Molitor and drove him back, but when the French counterattacked he was forced to retreat. Bagration came to his support, and during the night of the thirtieth his infantry scrambled over the rocks to the left of the road and made their way to the summits overlooking the French right flank. This gave a chance for Schweikovsky's division, which was following Bagration, to attack straight down the road and force Molitor to fall back four miles into the valley of the Linth. Here Molitor took up a position across the river slightly to the north, his line of retreat being on Zurich. The Russians attacked him again, and Molitor was driven back to Nafels, losing three hundred prisoners, one flag, and one gun. The battle now seesawed along the Linth between Nafels and Netsthal until Molitor, powerfully reinforced, finally drove back the sixth Russian attack and reoccupied Netsthal. But as this fighting was carried on by Bagration and Auffenberg north of the entrance into the Klonthal and the Muothathal, it permitted Suvorov and Schweikovsky's division to reach Glaris safely. Thus, except for Rosenberg, the army had successfully made its way out of the trap, and Suvorov hoped by reaching Glaris to rejoin the Austrians of Linken, not then knowing of the latter's precipitous retreat. We must now see what happened during this time to Rosenberg, who, it will be recalled, had been left behind near Schwytz to hold back Masséna.

Rosenberg had with him 5,500 men whom he had placed in several lines on both banks astride the River Muotha. Miloradovich, with three regiments of infantry, held the village of Mütten; Rehbinder with one regiment of infantry, one battalion of Jaegers, and two regiments of dismounted Cossacks was a mile farther down stream; and Major Sabaneev with one battalion of infantry was a mile closer to Schwytz at the entrance of a narrow gorge. Here Masséna attacked at 2:00 P.M. on the thirtieth with eight thousand men. Sabaneev was forced back on Rehbinder, who in turn, after making six bayonet counterattacks, was driven back, losing one gun and abandoning Mütten. But he regained the village in a last counterattack, while Miloradovich came up with his three regiments and, sending his Cossacks climbing over the mountains in hit-and-run attacks on the French rear, finally succeeded in driving the French back two miles. Thus not only had the Russians regained their lost positions, but, when nightfall put an end to the fighting, Rosenberg had moved up all his forces to Mütten.

The next day Masséna, now with fifteen thousand men, once more attacked the Russian advance guard at the entrance of the gorge. The French were advancing in three columns: one with artillery through the gorge on the road, which crossed the river on a stone bridge, and the two others at some distance from the stream, pressing out over the open ground to the right and left of the stream beyond the gorge. Once more the Russian advance guard fell back to the main lines, and the French were in possession of the gorge.

Then the whole of Rosenberg's corps charged vigorously in a bayonet attack and drove the French back into the gorge. Masséna brought up reserves and stopped the Russians, but the Cossacks climbed the rocks overhanging the gorge and attacked the French artillery in the rear, while the Russians once more succeeded in breaking into the gorge. Here in the narrows the French were driven back to the bridge in the utmost confusion; artillery and ammunition wagons scrambled for safety over the bridge, and the French retreat became a rout, with many wagons falling into the torrent. The French were pursued in the utmost disorder all the way into Schwytz; Masséna had sustained a major disaster. The Russians, whose losses did not exceed 1,000 men in the two-day battle, took 1,200 prisoners, including General Lacour, and captured a number of guns. They left 1,500 French wounded at the Franciscan monastery in the outskirts of the city. The total French losses amounted to about 4,000 men, and Masséna was forced to give up any further idea of attacking the Russians. But the victors, instead of enjoying the rest they had earned, passed the night after the battle in a desperate search for food. Nevertheless, on the following day, October 2, Rosenberg left the Muothathal and safely rejoined Suvorov at Glaris.

Now came the problem of what to do next: the obvious move would have been to turn north and go up the Linth, even though Molitor was barring the way with some eight thousand men. In so doing Suvorov could link up with the last remaining Austrian corps in Switzerland, that of Jellachich, and reach the Rhine near Schaffhausen. But Suvorov had run out of ammunition, and the feeling in the army against the Austrians was such that at the council of war (held on the fourth) it was decided not to co-operate with them any further, but to march on Chur (Coire). In doing this the army would cross the Panixer Pass into the valley of the Upper Rhine, running parallel and directly east of the valley of the Linth.

The march started immediately, all the severely wounded being left behind to the mercy of the French. The hard-fighting Bagration, who according to his own report had lost one third of his men in the engagements of the previous days, was to remain to hold Molitor back. The French made an attempt to cut the road of the Russian retreat by a flank movement, but Bagration, although without any artillery, managed to drive them away by bayonet attacks; then he fell back slowly to the village of Engi, where he held on until nightfall, throwing back French attacks until the main army was safely out of reach of the enemy. Following this, though he lost a great many prisoners and nearly all his mules and horses, he managed to extricate his forces and get away himself.

The crossing of the Panixer Pass (7,897 feet in elevation) was the most difficult operation of the campaign. It had been raining heavily below, and the pass itself was under deep snow; an icy wind was blowing, and a thick fog blanketed the mountains, making the trail all but invisible. The men's clothes were in rags and their boots had given way. The trail was so steep and dangerous that three hundred mules fell down the precipice. Suvorov's own horse had to be held by two Cossacks. No artillery could negotiate the trail; hence all the guns were rolled down the precipice. Only Miloradovich was able to give some shelter to his men for the night in the little village of Panix; the rest of the army had to sleep in the snow and piercing wind along the winding trail, without food and without fuel to light fires. On the eighth the army finally reached Chur, bringing with it 1,400 French prisoners. Here food and rest were given the men, who mended their clothes, cleaned their weapons, and sang and joked. Thus came to an end this famous campaign.

Suvorov still had fifteen thousand men, and he had written to Archduke Charles on October 7 from Panix that, if the latter could promise him food and ammunition, he would join him. He repeated this offer by a second courier before reaching Chur, but Charles refused. The final council of war was held on October 18, at which it was decided that nothing but treason could come from these allies, and four days later Czar Paul I wrote sharply to Emperor Francis:

> Seeing my troops abandoned and thus delivered to the enemy by the Ally on whom I counted most, his policy contrary to my views and the safety of Europe sacrificed to the plans of your monarchy for its own aggrandizement . . . I declare to you with the same loyalty which made me fly to your aid and co-operate in the success of your arms, that from this moment I abandon your interests, to occupy myself solely with my own and those of my other allies.[15]

[15] *Ibid.*, p. 338.

Accordingly Suvorov marched to join Korsakov, and thereafter the Russian armies marched via Prague back to Russia, thus ending their foreign adventure. In mentioning the other allies in his letter Paul had chiefly England in mind, but here also a bitter disappointment was awaiting him. In this connection the story of the joint Anglo-Russian expedition in Holland has to be told.

V

It will be recalled that, according to Pitt's plan, an Anglo-Russian landing force was to operate in Holland simultaneously with the march of Suvorov into Switzerland.

In accordance with this plan ten thousand British troops, under General Sir Ralph Abercromby, forming the vanguard of the expeditionary force, sailed from England July 13, 1799, and on August 27 were safely disembarked at Helder in Holland, at the south entrance to the Zuyder Zee. The Dutch troops holding the city fell back; and the Dutch Fleet, seeing the British vessels carrying the flag of the Prince of Orange, mutinied and surrendered. Thus the British were able to bring up without difficulty the rest of the expeditionary forces, while Abercromby was establishing a defensive line along the Zype Canal.

On September 13 the Duke of York, placed in supreme command of the expedition, landed with his staff; following him came two Russian divisions amounting to some twelve thousand men, which had been brought to Holland by a Russian squadron under Admiral Chichagov.

From the outset there was friction between the allies. General Essen, commanding the Second Russian Division, refused to land until conditions for the operation were more propitious. At a council of war, convened by the Duke of York, four British generals were invited to be present as against one Russian—General Hermann, the Commander in Chief of the Russian forces—who thereby found himself outvoted and resented it.

As for the quality of the troops themselves, according to a British eyewitness, the Russians were "formed altogether for service, and not for show"; they were not, however, accustomed to fight in broken country cut up by many canals.[16] Regarding the relative merits of

[16] Colonel Ramsey Weston Phipps, *The Armies of the First French Republic and the Rise of the Marshals of Napoleon I* (London, 1939), V, 197.

the leaders, it could be said that if the Duke of York seemed to lack the qualities of a commander, the Russian Commander seemed to be too sure of himself and to lack cautiousness.

Once the landing had been effected, at the very tip of the peninsula dividing the Zuyder Zee from the North Sea, the obvious procedure for the allies, in order to get out of the dangerous and narrow bottleneck, was to move south in the general direction of Amsterdam.

General Brune, who had arrived in June to organize the defense of the country, had under his command, in the Army of Batavia, 18,500 French scattered over the country, plus Dutch contingents. He could muster against the advance of the allies some 21,000 troops to cover the first objective of the allies, which was Alkmaar. He therefore took up a position at Bergen, north of the city. The plan worked out by the allied staff was that the Russians attack Bergen, with a British brigade to support them. Two more British columns totaling 9,000 men were to advance on the Russian left, and finally Abercromby's column was to operate a vast flanking movement following the coast of the Zuyder Zee as far down as Hoorn, then converging on Brune's left rear.

The plan was ill-conceived, for Abercromby had to cover some thirty miles, compared to the seven-mile advance of the direct attack. Abercromby reached Hoorn only at 3:00 P.M. and still had thirteen miles to go at the time the battle was over.

The Russians opened the attack early in the morning of September 19 and, advancing in mass formation, drove the French back and captured Bergen. Brune, upon seeing this, threw his major forces against the Russians, transferring Vandamme's division in an attempt to regain Bergen, and thus uncovered himself on the side of the British advance. Skilfully taking advantage of the terrain confronting the massed Russian columns, he spread out his infantry thinly and succeeded in enveloping the Russians with a formidable cross fire and, just as a Russian cavalry charge was developing, unmasked a battery of artillery which fired point blank. The Russian advance broke, and to quote General Moore, "Their retreat was as unsoldier-like as their advance."[17] In this retreat General Hermann and a number of prisoners were taken by the French, and the British columns fell back in turn. The day cost the French 836 killed;

[17] *Ibid.*, V, 201.

the Dutch 1,539 killed and 1,502 prisoners. On the allied side, the British lost 1,016 men and 12 guns; the Russians 2,975 men and 6 guns.

The command of the Russian forces now passed to General Essen, who showed anti-British feelings from the outset, and reported to the Czar that the defeat was due to the British not supporting the Russian attack, a point which is denied by Admiral Chichagov in his memoirs.

The Duke of York on his side "took up a violent contempt for, as well as dislike of, the Russians. He ridiculed them at his table and talked of them not wisely and too loudly."[18]

To avenge the defeat a second attack was carried out, once more in four columns, and the French were driven back. But this time it was Abercromby who complained that Essen did not support him. Brune, having lost 1,600 men and 7 guns as against the allied loss of 1,971 men, retreated to a very strong position covered by a lake at Beverwijk.

The allies followed and on October 6 attacked the approach to this position at Kastrikum. Brune was holding the line with 14,000 French and 3,220 Dutch as against 12,000 Anglo-Russians. The Russians advanced in the center with Dundas on their left and Abercromby on the right. Essen's attack was so successful that Brune's position became critical, but once more Brune was able to concentrate the major part of his forces to block Essen; hence, with night falling, although the allies had gained a slight advantage, the French had kept their line. The losses of the allies amounted to 3,439 men as compared with only 1,398 for the French. Writes Bunbury: "Our best troops were disheartened, our officers had lost all confidence; the Russians were angry, sullen, and scarcely to be counted as allies."[19]

At the council of war which followed this battle Essen complained bitterly that, notwithstanding 4,000 reinforcements he had received, his forces had dwindled to 9,800 men. The decision was taken to retreat to the line of the Zype; and, discouraged, the Duke of York informed Brune of his readiness to negotiate an armistice. By the convention signed ten days later at Alkmaar (October 18)

[18] *Ibid.*, V, 202.

[19] Sir Henry Edward Bunbury, *A Narrative of the Campaign in North Holland 1799* (London, 1849), at quoted in Phipps, *op. cit.*, p. 205.

the allied forces returned the French and Dutch prisoners and evacuated Holland, the Russian contingent being taken to the islands of Jersey and Guernsey.

This fiasco, synchronizing as it did with the news of the events in Switzerland, produced a decisive effect on Paul I. Whether or not the Russian contention that their defeat was due entirely to British non-co-operation was justified is beside the point. What is important is that it fell on fertile ground in the mind of Paul, already incensed at the behavior of the Austrians. "To our Russians," wrote Bunbury, "this disastrous intelligence [of the Battle of Zurich] afforded fresh food for discontent; they regarded their countrymen (and not without reason) as having been deserted and sacrificed by the Austrian government; and the bitter fancy that they themselves had been deserted by the British on the 19th of September became more deeply rooted in their minds."[20] And, one might add, more ominously, in the mind of the erratic Czar. Indeed on October 22, four days after the signing of the Alkmaar Convention, the Czar announced that he was withdrawing from the coalition and ordered his armies home.

This resulted not only in the breaking up of the coalition but, as far as Russia was concerned, in a veritable diplomatic revolution. As always in Russia, when sudden and violent change altered the direction of Russia's foreign policy, new men came to replace those whose policy had been discredited. Panin, who was watching with horror the trend toward friendship with France, was replaced by Count Rostopchin, who had written a memorandum outlining a new policy which received the fullest approval of the Czar.

According to this memorandum, Russia's real interests lay in Turkey and not in Western Europe; the partition of Turkey might be achieved through an alliance with France, for France would thus humble Britain. Austria and Prussia would be invited to join in the scheme and receive appropriate compensations: Austria to get Bosnia, Servia, and Wallachia; Prussia, territories in Northern Germany; and Russia to take the lion's share of Turkey—namely, Moldavia, Bulgaria, and Greece, which, Rostopchin naïvely said, would come of itself under Russian rule.

Thus, at the expense of Turkey, a Continental system of alliances

[20] Bunbury, *op. cit.*, as quoted in Phipps, *op. cit.*, p. 205.

was to be evolved, directed in the main against England and replacing the previous system, which, according to Rostopchin, was the result of English intrigue. England, the traditional enemy of France, had succeeded through the agency of "alternate threats, cunning, and money in arming the powers of Europe against France," to which words Paul added in the margin, "and against us sinners as well."[21]

This new orientation resulted in the clamping down of an embargo on British ships and merchandise in Russian ports and the freezing of all debts owed to British merchants, in reprisal for the occupation of Malta by the British (October–November, 1800).

VI

The withdrawal of the Russian armies broke up the coalition, and the fighting petered out. We have already seen how incensed Paul was at the "treachery" of the Austrians. The failure of the Anglo-Russian expedition in Holland, coupled with the tenacity shown by England in her endeavor to get possession of Malta, turned him against England. As for Prussia, she refused to participate in the reconstituted League of Neutrals, the creation of which Paul now had in mind for the end of the war. Thus Paul developed a bitterness against his erstwhile allies which was compensated for in his erratic mind by a sudden sympathy for his enemy. Bonaparte, upon his return from Egypt, was quick to sense this change and was eager to capitalize on it: he offered to send back seven thousand Russian prisoners captured in Switzerland, as well as the colors taken. Paul replied through his minister in Berlin, Baron Krüdener, that he was grateful for this offer and that he would send General Sprengporten to Paris to negotiate for the return of the prisoners. His state of mind is well illustrated in the instructions which were given to Sprengporten:

> The Emperor participated in the coalition with the aim of giving tranquillity to the whole of Europe. He withdrew when he saw that the powers were aiming at aggrandizements which his loyalty and disinterestedness could not allow, and as the two states of France and of the Empire of Russia are not in a position, owing to the distance [separating them], to do each other any harm, they could by uniting and

[21] Schilder, *Imperator Pavel Pervyi*, pp. 413-414.

maintaining harmonious relations between themselves, hinder the other powers from adversely affecting their interests through their envy or desire to aggrandize and dominate.[22]

In the mind of the Czar this new orientation of his policy was to be complemented by the creation of the League of Neutrals, which would be strong enough to keep order in the Baltic and in the North Sea, and at the same time the return of Malta to the Order of St. John would permit the policing of the Mediterranean. Indeed he had already suggested the following terms for a general peace in a note dated October 8, 1799: (1) restitution of Malta to the Knights and the re-establishment of the King of Sardinia in his domains; (2) integrity to be guaranteed for the frontiers of the kingdoms of Naples, Bavaria, Württemberg, and Prussia.[23] At this point there arrived the news of the fall of Malta to the British. Paul retaliated on December 16 and 18 by signing in St. Petersburg a treaty of neutrality on the seas with Denmark, Sweden, and Prussia, with the special object of annoying England—thus for once emulating his mother, Catherine II. Thereupon Bonaparte immediately declared that he would not sign peace with England unless she acknowledged the freedom of the seas, and further revealed his wish to co-operate with Russia when he told Sprengporten: "Your sovereign and I are called to change the face of the world."[24] As the Russian delegate was about to leave Paris he gave him a personal letter for the Czar, in which he declared that "the continents and seas will be peaceful" twenty-four hours after England, the Holy Roman Empire, and the other powers realize the strength of the union "of our great nations," and suggested that Russia send an ambassador to Paris. At the same time he sent his ambassador, Beurnonville, to Berlin with the object of negotiating with Russia the evacuation of the Russian troops on Jersey and Guernsey, and if possible to conclude a treaty of peace, coupled with an offer of an alliance against England. Beurnonville was to propose to Russia the following conditions: Russia to take the Straits of the Bosporus, the Dardanelles and Constantinople, as well as certain Greek islands; France to get Egypt, Cyprus, Crete, Sicily, and the Ionian Islands;

[22] Sorel, *op. cit.*, VI, 73.
[23] Martens, *op. cit.*, XIII, 254.
[24] Sorel, *op. cit.*, VI, 88.

Prussia to get back Silesia, Germany to be reorganized, Austria to be excluded from Italy; Poland to be reconstituted with one of Paul's sons as king; Russia to co-operate with France in an attack on British India by sending an army through Persia, while the French would march through Egypt. Beurnonville in Berlin persuaded the King of Prussia to offer his mediation for a peace along these lines, and the above-mentioned conditions were forwarded through Krüdener to the Czar.

Paul was at first favorably inclined and wrote to Krüdener on January 28, 1800, that he welcomed a *rapprochement* with France to offset the influence of Austria. But Panin's influence eventually prevailed; he insisted that the main object of Russia's policy should be the re-establishment of the thrones shattered by the French Revolution, and on February 12 Paul wrote to Krüdener declining the offer of mediation and declaring he would not listen to any offers coming from "the Corsican usurper." Nevertheless, he ordered the withdrawal of the troops from the Channel Islands. But his increasing bitterness against England got the better of his monarchist sentiments, and replying to Bonaparte's request in the letter he sent through Sprengporten, he appointed Kolychev as ambassador to Paris, with instructions to study with Bonaparte the possibilities of joint action against England "to make her repent her despotism and arrogance."[25] In a further gesture of conciliation toward France he ordered the immediate expulsion from Mittau of the future Louis XVIII and all the royalist *émigrés* who formed his court—the French pretender being forced thereby to seek refuge in Warsaw. The instructions given to Kolychev were specific: he was to arrange for the restitution of Malta to the Order and of Egypt to Turkey, and he was to work out a joint attack by Russia and France on the British coast. Bonaparte, in turn, was to close all revolutionary clubs in Paris, and in particular the Polish Club. Russia would recognize the frontiers of the Rhine for France and would not object to the First Consul's taking the title of king.

Arriving in Paris on March 6, Kolychev got in touch with Talleyrand and had no difficulty in arranging the terms of peace with Russia; but the issues concerning the general pacification of Europe were more difficult to settle. Bonaparte was willing to recognize

[25] *Ibid.*, VI, 108.

Paul as Grand Master of the Maltese Order, but objected to the island's coming under the sovereignty of Russia. He further insisted that the French should occupy a portion of the territory of the Kingdom of Naples as long as the British held Egypt, and that Russia should aid France in evicting the British from Egypt. Thus negotiations began to drag, and during the interval France signed peace directly with Naples, permitting a French force of 4,000 men to remain in occupation in that kingdom, and also signed a treaty with Spain. Whether or not a plan for a joint Franco-Russian invasion of India by two armies, each 35,000 strong, had been discussed, as rumored at the time, remains an open question. Nevertheless Paul issued an order on January 12, 1801, for a force of 22,000 Cossacks and 24 guns to start an advance on India, via Orenburg and Bokhara. The British retaliated by sending their fleet under Admiral Nelson into the Baltic. Bonaparte thereupon, with the French definitely evicted from Egypt by the British, became more amenable, and declared to Kolychev his readiness to accede to Russian terms concerning Naples, Bavaria, and Württemberg; to accept Russian mediation in regard to a peace with Sardinia; and to agree that Malta be returned to the Order with Paul I as Grand Master. Thus a new phase in Russia's foreign policy had shaped itself, with the prospect of a war with England and an alliance with France. But, whereas this policy was to become a reality six years later with the signing of the Treaty of Tilsit, it was now still premature; and the assassination of Paul I on March 23, 1801, put an end to the whole venture. With the accession of Czar Alexander I on the death of Paul, a new era opened in Russian history.

CHAPTER III

Czar Alexander I and the Third Coalition

I

ALEXANDER started his reign with a clean slate. Within a month after coming to power he had canceled all the tyrannical restrictions imposed by his father in an attempt to segregate Russia from Western Europe and its revolutionary menace: thus were restored the right to enter and depart from Russia, to import books and music, and to export grains and wines; trade restrictions concerning imports and exports of merchandise were removed. Count Nikita Panin, the statesman exiled by Paul, was recalled and put in charge of foreign affairs.

The first and most important issue confronting the new regime was to stop the impending hostilities with England and renew friendly relations with that country. Accordingly the British ambassador in St. Petersburg was notified of Alexander's advent to power in a letter signed by Count Pahlen, which, coming from the murderer of Paul, had all the elements of supreme irony:

ST. PETERSBURG, March 20, 1801.

MY LORD:

It was the will of God to call to him H. M. the Emperor Paul I, deceased on the night of the 11th and 12th instant[1] as result of an apoplectic stroke, and to realize the finest hopes of the Russian people by placing on the throne the August Alexander. The usual relations between our courts having been interrupted by unexpected events, the Emperor, My Master, has deemed it right to inform His Britannic Majesty of his accession, and has instructed me for this purpose to notify Your Excellency.

This bid for the restoration of good relations was followed five days later by an order to General Orlov, commander of the force of Cossacks who were then on the march to India, to return home.

[1] Old Style (Julian Calendar).

The British fleet, which had passed the Sund and was cruising off the coast of Reval, was withdrawn at the request of the Russian Government, and in May the embargo was lifted from British cargoes in Russian ports and sequestered British merchant vessels were freed. The negotiations thus initiated between the two countries led to the signing in St. Petersburg on June 17 of a convention which established broad principles of international law with regard to the vexed question of the freedom of the seas and rights of neutrals. Both sides compromised: England relented on the question of the closing of ports under blockade to neutral shipping, while Russia acknowledged that neutral flags do not cover the cargoes and that the inspection of merchant vessels should be permitted even when they are convoyed by men-of-war. Denmark and Sweden were to be invited by England to accede to this convention, and Russia was to approach Prussia for the same purpose. Thus the main issue dividing the two countries was settled.

Similarly was settled another issue which had gained much undue prominence in the preceding reign: the question of Malta. Alexander refused the Grand Mastership of the Order of the Knights of St. John, but by a decree issued on March 16, 1801 (Old Style) proclaimed himself protector of the Order. He further ordered that the Maltese cross should be eliminated from the Imperial crest, and also that Malta should not be listed as Russian territory in the calendar issued by the Russian Academy of Science. Thus the vexatious question ceased to play a dominant role in Russian history, though Malta by its geographical position was too important a factor not to take its place in the subsequent negotiations with France and England.

Next, normal relations with Austria were restored. Upon receiving a friendly letter from Emperor Francis, in which the Holy Roman Emperor expressed his desire to regain the old friendship with the Russian court, Alexander by decree of May 22, 1801, restored diplomatic relations with the Viennese court and appointed Count Andrei Razumovsky ambassador to Austria.

But the success of this new policy of all-round pacification depended on the relations of Russia and France, and these were more difficult to settle. In Paris the news of the assassination of Paul was regarded as a calamity. Indeed it was obvious that it meant the end of the League of Neutrals, of the blockade of England, and of Bonaparte's dreams of the conquest of Egypt and India. Napoleon saw in the assassination the hand of England. The *Moniteur* announced the news in the following terms: "Paul I died in the night of the 25th. The British squadron passed the Sund on the 31st. History will teach us the relation between these two events."[2] Left alone to face England, Bonaparte decided that it was in his interest to capitalize on the war fatigue existing in London by offering peace to England, but before doing this he wanted to place himself in the best possible military position on the Continent; hence the very next day after he learned of the death of the Czar, Bonaparte decided upon the annexation of Piedmont, though the decree regulating the administration of that occupied country was purposely antedated to the second of April to cover up the connection with the events in Russia.[3] At the same time he dispatched his aide-de-camp, Duroc, on a confidential mission to St. Petersburg with instructions to stress particularly Russia's advantage in having the British out of the Eastern Mediterranean and Turkey. In the meanwhile the Russian chargé d'affaires in Paris, Kolytchev, received instructions from the new Czar which foreshadowed Alexander's future policies and which permitted him to take a stronger stand. According to these instructions, dated April 28, Russia had no personal or outstanding claims but was to act solely in the interests of general peace, aiming at an equilibrium which would guarantee the peace of Europe. Basing his claim on the treaty of Teschen, the Czar asserted the right to mediate in Germany just as, on the basis of Russian guarantees given to the Kings of Sardinia and Naples, he also claimed the right to mediate in Italy.[4] Thus Russia was squarely opposing France clear across Europe from the North Sea to the Mediterranean.

At the same time Alexander, still in his near-Jacobin phase, professed such personal admiration for the French Revolution and for the First Consul that he received Duroc very cordially, and in an interview called him "citoyen," nonplussing the formal Duroc. "Tell the First Consul that I am attached to his glory. I do not want anything for myself; I only wish to contribute to the tranquillity of

[2] Sorel, *op. cit.*, VI, 140.
[3] *Ibid.*, VI, 142.
[4] *Ibid.*, VI, 144.

Europe," said the Czar.[5] The result of Duroc's mission was the reappointment of a full-fledged Russian ambassador to Paris, Count Morkov, an astute and hard-headed diplomat who had had a hand in the partition of Poland. With the arrival of Morkov in Paris, negotiations started with Talleyrand which led eventually to the signing of a peace convention on October 8, 1801, in which it was stipulated that France and Russia would act in concert with regard to the affairs of Germany, Sardinia, and the Holy See. France guaranteed the integrity of the territories of the King of Naples, and would occupy them only pending the settlement of the status of Egypt. Russia was to mediate in the peace negotiation between France and Turkey, and both parties would strive to assure a general peace on the basis of a just equilibrium in different parts of the world, and also to assure the liberty of the seas.

Following the Peace of Amiens with England a general peace seemed at last to have been reached. But as long as Italy and Germany remained battlegrounds in the conflict between Russian and French influences, this peace remained very precarious. Futhermore, when the following year Bonaparte was proclaimed Consul for life, thus paving the way toward the throne, the hero worship of the twenty-four-year-old Alexander vanished. Writing to his tutor, La Harpe, on July 7, 1802, Alexander stressed his disappointment and change of opinion. "Since his consulate for life the veil has fallen. He missed the glory reserved to a human being, that of proving that he had worked without personal aims for the happiness and glory of his country. Now he is one of the famous tyrants that history has produced."[6]

In this mood, acting spontaneously and on his own initiative, he turned to Prussia. Keeping his destination and the object of his journey secret even from his ministers, Alexander left for Memel, where he had an interview with King Friedrich Wilhelm of Prussia and his beautiful consort, Queen Louise. The Czar's own Minister of Foreign Affairs, the newly appointed Count Kochubey, complained bitterly that he was left in the dark with regard to the object of this journey; and, though Alexander had said that the trip had no political motives, Kochubey kept on suspecting the worst. The meeting of the two sovereigns, which took place at Memel on June 10,

[5] *Ibid.*, VI, 151.

[6] *Ibid.*, VI, 251.

was notable for the establishment of lifelong intimate relations between them. Friedrich Wilhelm was thirty-two years of age, Queen Louise twenty-six, and Alexander a year younger. Both the beautiful Queen and her insignificant husband fell completely under the spell of Alexander's charm. "I have not seen the Alps," wrote the Queen to her brother in a mood of romantic enthusiasm, "but I have seen men, or more exactly one man, in all the significance of the word. The meeting at Memel was divine. The two sovereigns love each other tenderly and sincerely."[7] The relations between the young Emperor and the beautiful Queen assumed a lasting and delicate shading of *coquetterie platonique* which appealed to their romantic natures. As for the King, he naturally took second place in the shadow of the brilliant young Czar and accepted, in the exchange of pledges of lifelong fidelity and confidence given at Memel, the position of near-vassal to Alexander. Even though Prussia did at times turn to France when her interests so directed, she was assuming the position of a satellite of Russia, and this was the most important result of the interview. Politics were studiously avoided between the sovereigns, but not between their ministers. Prussia had aspirations for Hanover which interested Russia a great deal; on the other hand, the future status of the Holy Roman Empire depended upon the negotiations being carried on between Morkov and Talleyrand in Paris, and Prussia was vitally interested in their outcome. On June 3, one week before the meeting at Memel, an agreement had finally been reached between the Russian ambassador and the French minister, and an act signed which was to be submitted to the approval of the Diet of Regensburg, and which later became the basis of the famous "Recess of February 25, 1803." A considerable change in the structure of the Holy Roman Empire was to take place under this act. Indeed, the number of electors was increased from six to ten, the ecclesiastical princes were reduced to three, and the number of free cities in Germany was cut from fifty-one to six.

More cautiously, the possibility of joint co-operation in the event of a war with France was broached and the ambitions of Prussia were laid bare. The meeting at Memel was a personal triumph for Alexander and a powerful stimulant to his vanity. Not only did he

[7] *Ibid.*, VI, 235.

get a triumphant reception and hear the cheers of the crowd while passing through the cities on his way to Prussia, particularly at Riga, but he enjoyed the dominant role he played at Memel. The submissiveness of the King of Prussia in his dealings with Russia was in such marked contrast to the hauteur of Frederick the Great that it showed too well the change in the status of the two courts within a quarter of a century. It also marked for Alexander an important step in the development of his anti-French feelings. As he came back to St. Petersburg he began to listen more attentively to the pro-English circles in Russian society, which were supported by the British envoy, Admiral Waren. With war between France and England once more looming in the spring of 1803, British diplomacy was straining every nerve to win Russia for an ally.

When hostilities between France and England actually started in May, 1803, this event gave a further powerful stimulus to the development of anti-French feeling in Russia. One of the main issues involved in this war was the question of Malta; and, though Russia had ceased to claim the island, its fate nevertheless remained too closely linked with the question of which power would dominate the Eastern Mediterranean not to remain of vital concern to Russia. Nor were affairs concerning Germany satisfactory; in violation of the spirit of the Franco-Russian mediation and the "Recess" of the previous year, Napoleon's policy was to exclude Russia by acting on his own initiative without consulting her. His arbitrary occupation of Hanover was a glaring example which irked the Russian Government. In Russian military circles war fever was rising, based largely on an unwarranted contempt of the French as a result of Suvorov's victories over them in 1799. Joubert, it was argued, was just as good as Bonaparte, and he had been easily defeated by Suvorov. But Suvorov was gone, and the price of this conceit was to be Austerlitz.

In the meanwhile, on June 12, Bonaparte casually observed to the Russian ambassador that he would welcome Russian mediation in his war with England. The French terms for peace were given to Morkov as follows: Malta to be placed under the guarantee of Russia, the principality of Lampedusa to be given to the British, the King of Sardinia to receive an indemnity, and the French to evacuate Holland, Switzerland, and Naples in return for the British evacuation of Malta. Morkov notified his government and wrote to the Russian ambassador in London, Count Vorontsov, cautioning him that Bonaparte appeared to him to be insincere. Alexander accepted the guarantee of Malta and informed the British Government of this step, but Britain refused to abandon Malta, and Hawkesbury wrote to Waren instructing him to offer instead a subsidy for the participation of Russia in the war. On July 19 Alexander submitted to the First Consul his plan of peace on the basis of the latter's terms, but added to them the evacuation by the French of Hanover, the neutrality of the French-sponsored Helvetian, Ligurian, Batavian, and Ionian republics, the granting of a kingdom to the King of Sardinia in compensation for the loss of his territory, and a guarantee of the integrity of the Ottoman Empire. In return for these concessions the British were to evacuate the Dutch colonies. The whole issue was to be settled by a general European conference. Now it was Napoleon's turn to reject this offer. Thus the efforts of Russia came to naught because of the unwillingness of both parties.

The failure of this mediation made the First Consul realize that he had no further use for Russian friendship. He was, furthermore, well aware of the growing hostility to France in Russia, and he had a personal dislike for the Russian ambassador, Morkov, whom he found overbearing and haughty. Hence he followed up this refusal by a demand that Morkov should be recalled on the ground that he had been spying, an issue which under other circumstances he would probably have overlooked. Alexander complied with the demand and recalled Morkov, but not without conspicuously conferring upon him the Grand Cross of the Order of St. Andrew, the highest decoration in Russia. Morkov left Paris on December 18, 1803, and his departure marked the beginning of a definite coolness between the two countries. However, there still existed in Paris a powerful pro-Russian group, a circle of influential members of Paris society whom Morkov had organized and cultivated and who were known as "the friends of Russia."

II

As far as the continent of Europe was concerned the year 1804 opened in perfect calm—the hostilities between England and France were relegated to the colonies and to naval warfare and did not affect the rest of Europe. But the relations between France and Russia were growing steadily worse, and it very soon became apparent that, aside from England, Russia was to become Napoleon's principal and most dangerous foe. Several causes were contributing to this development. The mediation of Russia in the questions pending between France and the princes of the Holy Roman Empire over the mediatization of their territories was still in progress and served to envenom Franco-Russian relations. In this mediation Russia was taking the side of Austria and of the Austrian-protected princes, whose rights had been guaranteed by the "Recess," just as previously Russia had defended the interests of Prussia and the middle German states. On February 18, 1804, the Russian chargé d'affaires in Paris, D'Oubril, who had been representing Russia since the recall of the ambassador, Morkov, presented a note to Talleyrand suggesting the transfer of the mediation from Regensburg to Vienna, so as to bring into the negotiations the Holy Roman Empire. France agreed in principle, on condition that Russia should in turn support France in her demand on Austria to limit armaments. Russia refused to do so; the mediation became deadlocked and had to be dropped.

This latent quarrel was transformed into an open conflict by the kidnaping and assassination of the Duke of Enghien. It will be recalled that Napoleon, having discovered a Royalist plot against his regime, decided to act against the Royalists; and a prince of the Bourbon family, the Duke of Enghien, who was peacefully residing at the Castle of Ettenheim in Baden, was made the innocent victim. On March 15 a force of French cavalry, violating the neutrality of Baden, reached Ettenheim and brought the young duke to Paris, where after a summary trial he was executed in the castle of Vincennes. The impression produced all over Europe by this crime was tremendous, but no one except the Czar and the King of Sweden felt independent enough to express their sentiments openly. Curiously, neither the Elector of Baden, whose territory had been violated, nor his suzerain the Holy Roman Emperor dared to raise their voices in protest. Alexander took up the challenge, declaring that his relative the Prince-Elector of Baden had been affronted.[8] Talleyrand had attempted to placate the Czar by forwarding to the French ambassador in St. Petersburg, General Hédouville, an ex-

[8] Alexander had married in 1793 the Princess Marie Louise of Baden.

planation of the circumstances of the assassination, in which he attempted to throw the blame on British agents. Alexander was not impressed, and in his first moment of impulsive anger wanted to send Hédouville back to France. However, mastering this impulse, he called an extraordinary council of the highest dignitaries of the Empire under his own chairmanship, and with unanimity the council decided that further relations could not exist with a government which could be regarded only as a "den of brigands."[9] The result of the meeting was that Russia as guarantor of Germany under the peace of Teschen sent a note to Paris and to the Diet of Regensburg protesting the violation of the territory of Baden. This note to France further raised the question of violations by France of the territories of Sardinia, Naples, and Hanover, and asked for an immediate reply on these points. Napoleon, taking cognizance of the Russian note, ordered his ambassador in St. Petersburg to leave the capital within forty-eight hours and proceed to Berlin under pretense of ill health.

Bonaparte himself wrote the reply to the Russian note, declaring that in the case of the Duke of Enghien he was acting in self-defense against the machinations of British agents. He ended his reply with a vitriolic allusion to the assassination of Paul I calculated to hurt Alexander bitterly. He further declared that the matter was of no concern to Russia, and he accused Russia not only of giving asylum to French Royalist *émigrés* but of actually taking them into her service. The most prominent of these was Pozzo di Borgo, who had entered the Russian service the year before, and was destined to hold the highest positions in the Empire. Similarly there was the Count d'Antraigues, who was appointed Russian minister in Dresden; and Monsieur de Vernegues, who represented Russia in Rome. These *émigrés,* Bonaparte declared, by intriguing against him made Russia an accomplice in the royalist plots. He made no mention of the other issues Russia had raised, except to declare that he considered the Franco-Russian mediation in Germany to be at an end and was informing the Diet of Regensburg accordingly.

When the note was sent to St. Petersburg, D'Oubril asked for his passports. Napoleon persuaded him, however, to remain in Paris

[9] Edouard Driault, *Napoléon et l'Europe. Austerlitz, la fin du Saint-empire (1804-1806),* (Paris, 1912), p. 552; Sorel, *op. cit.,* VI, 359.

until he received instructions from his government. French diplomacy now became very busy in an attempt to have the Russian note rejected by the Diet at Regensburg. Most of the German states, including Austria, were afraid to show their sympathy with Russia, and acquiesced in the statement made by Talleyrand that the internal affairs of Germany did not concern Russia. The King of Sweden, however, as a member of the Diet for Pomerania; and the Elector of Hanover openly voiced their approval of the note, and the final result was that the note was neither accepted nor rejected by the Diet, a fact which showed that the Russian and the French influences at Regensburg were of about the same strength and neutralized each other.

Just as this affair was in progress a new question arose to increase the tension between Russia and France. By the *Senatus Consultum* of May 18, 1804, Napoleon proclaimed himself Emperor. Austria and Prussia rather humbly and obsequiously recognized the title, though Austria's action was in return for the recognition by France of Francis II as hereditary Emperor of Austria. Most of the German princes of the Empire hastened to follow suit. Only Russia and Sweden (England being at war with France) refused to recognize Napoleon's new title. Russia did more. She blocked the recognition of the title by Turkey as well, and this was a serious blow to France's prestige in the Near East.

The energetic efforts of the new French ambassador in Constantinople, General Brune, to obtain the recognition of the title from the Sultan were no more successful than the effort to bribe the Turkish ambassador in Paris with a gift of forty thousand francs. The Sublime Porte remained adamant in its refusal. Finally, hard pressed by Brune, the Reis Effendi produced a note transmitted by the Russian ambassador in Constantinople, Italinsky, in which Russia insisted that Turkey should recognize the French Empire only when Russia did so; Turkey could count on the powerful protection of Russia and England, but should Turkey recognize the French Empire, Russia would regard her as becoming a mere French province.[10] The Ambassador had further informed the Porte of Russia's intention to fight France. Brune understood that the case was lost and asked for his passports. Talleyrand was furious. "Is the Sublime

[10] Driault, *op. cit.*, p. 89.

Porte a vassal of Russia . . . ? Is the Russian Emperor in the opinion of the Sublime Porte a sovereign superior in power and in dignity to the Emperor of the French?" he asked.[11] But the pertinent fact was that, both in Germany and in Turkey, France was meeting obstacles placed in her way by Russia. Obviously the situation was leading up to a crisis. Both ambassadors, Morkov in Paris and Hédouville in St. Petersburg, had departed, leaving their embassies in care of their chargés d'affaires, D'Oubril and de Rayneval, respectively. D'Oubril, it will be remembered, had asked for his passports as well, but was persuaded to await instructions from his home government. These finally came in September, and the Russian diplomat informed the French Government that since all further negotiations were deemed useless by Russia, he was leaving Paris for Mainz. Thus the break between the two countries was complete, and Russia had definitely committed herself to a policy leading to war.

To get the whole picture in this evolution of Russian policy, we have to bear in mind an important change which had occurred in the direction of this policy. Early in 1804 the old and experienced Chancellor of State, Count A. Vorontsov, had resigned and the Assistant Minister of Foreign Affairs, Prince Adam Czartoryski, had taken over his job.[12] Czartoryski was young and impetuous; but, more important, belonging to the highest Polish nobility, he was an ardent Polish patriot. He was also a personal friend of Alexander, and had been one of the four members of the Secret Council which Alexander had instituted for the purpose of studying the possibilities of reform in Russia. As such he had collaborated daily with the Czar, and he had honestly told his sovereign that he would loyally serve him so long as the interests of his nation, Poland, were not menaced. But the fact remained that Poland dominated the thoughts of the man who had been called to direct Russia's foreign policy, and Czartoryski's aim was to form a European coalition against Napoleon in the hope that the ensuing war would bring back a united Poland, independent and—if necessary he was ready to accept the idea—under the crown of Russia. Thus Czartoryski favored war with France. These views made him many enemies at the Russian court,

[11] *Ibid.*, p. 90.

[12] Count Kochubey had been transferred to the ministry of the interior.

the members of which objected to the injection of Polish interests into Russia's foreign policy. Among these was another influential member of the inner circle, Prince Dolgoruky, who once sharply called Czartoryski to account by saying, "You reason like a Polish prince and I talk like a Russian prince."[13]

It must be pointed out that so far the actual points of contact between Russia and France were to be found directly only in the Mediterranean and Turkey, and indirectly in Germany. But by the Russian occupation of Corfu and the French penetration into Naples the two empires had become virtually contiguous in the lower Adriatic. Hence each accused the other of violating the secret convention of October 10, 1801, which guaranteed both the independence of the Republic of the Seven Islands and the integrity of the territories of the Kingdom of the Two Sicilies. With regard to Turkey, Czartoryski presented to the Czar an important memorandum outlining Russia's interests in that country. This document became the basic charter of Russia's Near Eastern policies, and its ideas, re-endorsed in 1829, formed the guiding principles of Russo-Turkish relations throughout the nineteenth century.

According to Czartoryski, Russia's interest lay in preserving Turkey as it was at the time, that is to say, weak and peaceful, causing no obstruction to the development of Russia's trade in the Black Sea. The picture would change completely if Turkey came under the domination of France, or if some leading power should gain control of Greece, the Archipelago, or the Straits. Therefore, should a threat to the integrity of Turkey develop, it was in Russia's interest to stand by Turkey. If, however, the fall of the Ottoman Empire could not be averted, then Russia should not allow any other power to "establish herself on the ruins" and should get possession of such points as would assure Russian trade a free outlet from the Black Sea into the Mediterranean. Thus Russia had drawn her lines of action. "Ambitious to recreate the Eastern Empire, she was frightened by the near-emergence of the Western Empire."[14]

With the final severance of the relations between France and Russia, the next task of Russia's diplomacy was to obtain allies for

[13] Nikolai Karlovich Schilder, *Imperator Aleksandr Pervyi* . . . (St. Petersburg, 1897-1898), II, 124.

[14] Driault, *op. cit.*, p. 94.

the coming struggle. Sweden and Naples were easily secured, but these were minor powers. The success of the coming war depended upon the support of England, Austria, and Prussia. Russian diplomacy was to be active in all these three countries, but since England was already at war with France, the main attention of Russia now turned to England. Indeed, at this point Alexander took the important initiative of starting negotiations with England for the purpose of forming a coalition against Napoleon. Though Russia had in London an old and experienced ambassador, Count Semeon Vorontsov, it was a young man and a novice in diplomacy, Nicolas Novossiltsev, who was selected for the purpose. Only thirty-four years old, Novossiltsev had played an important role in the reign of Alexander as a personal friend of the Czar and, together with Czartoryski, had been a member of the Secret Committee. Moreover, having been educated in England, he was deemed the right man to deal with the British; and though this led to inevitable friction with Vorontsov, Novossiltsev succeeded in carrying his mission to a successful conclusion. The return of Pitt to power in May, 1804, made the Russian Government believe that the atmosphere in England had become more propitious for negotiating than previously. It must be emphasized, however, that contrary to the generally accepted theory it was not Pitt but Alexander who initiated the negotiations for the formation of the Third Coalition against France. Pitt's role was passive, merely that of listening to Alexander's suggestions. Novossiltsev's mission to London thus assumed an importance in history which has not been sufficiently recognized. So important was this mission considered that Alexander, in collaboration with Czartoryski, and perhaps in response to ideas put forward by a certain Abbé Piatoli, wrote out personally the lengthy instructions to the young diplomat for his visit to London.

III

The "Instructions to Novossiltsev" is an extremely important document, for it reveals the political philosophy of Alexander, which through the run of years and notwithstanding the evolution of the Czar's character, remained constant. It is to be compared, as Sorel points out,[15] with Kutuzov's appeal to the Germans in 1813 and

[15] Sorel, *op. cit.*, VI, 39.

with Alexander's appeal to the French in 1814. These instructions are to be found at the base of the concept of the Holy Alliance, and they finally appear, expanded and developed, at the Congress of Aix-la-Chapelle.

The instructions open with a recognition of the power of public opinion and propaganda: "The most effectual weapon which France now wields . . . is [her] ability to persuade public opinion that [her] cause is that of the liberty and prosperity of all nations."[16] Next comes a proposal for Great Britain to join Russia in the establishment of a new European order, which amounted to the recognition of the principle of self-determination of nations. Thus Sardinia, Holland, and Switzerland were to be restored to independence, but on condition of the granting of "a wise and free constitution" to the Sardinian nation. "The character of the national desires must be considered before deciding upon the form of the government to be established."[17] In the same vein the Allies were to fight, not the French people, but "a government as tyrannical towards France as towards the rest of Europe." As for a durable and final peace, it would be possible only if Europe were organized into a confederacy or a League of Nations by a pact to which the nations would voluntarily adhere and which would become "the basis of the reciprocal relations between the states of Europe." This league would have to establish a law of nations "assuring the privileges of neutrality and consecrating as an obligation never to commence war without having exhausted all the means of mediation by a third party." But to avoid causes of future conflicts, "it would be necessary to fix the frontiers which properly belong to each separate state"; such frontiers ought to follow natural boundaries, leave open to each nation proper means of access for "the interchange of products of their soil and industry," and comprise within their limits a population homogeneous "in agreement among themselves and with the government that rules them." As for the small states, in the name of the balance of power they should either unite with the larger states or group themselves into small federative unions, for "the disturbances which have shaken Europe . . . have only taken place because so

[16] William Penn Cresson, *The Holy Alliance: The European Background of the Monroe Doctrine* (New York, 1922), p. 12.

[17] *Ibid.*, p. 13.

little attention has been paid to any system of equilibrium."[18] In writing these remarkable instructions Alexander not only revealed a great political mind but became the precursor of Wilson, Briand, and Kellogg.

How did Pitt receive these proposals? In his reply to Novossiltsev he paid lip service to Alexander's ideas by suggesting that a treaty be concluded at the restoration of peace between the great powers, guaranteeing the *status quo* "as now established, and engaging the powers to support each other against efforts to disturb and infringe upon their rights." This very practical reinsurance by the great powers of the maintenance of a *status quo* favorable to them was a far cry from the idealism of the Czar. Too, England insisted upon the main point, which was the forming of a powerful and effective coalition against France. Novossiltsev was to find the going difficult; he noticed Pitt's suspicion and jealousy of Russia's policy in Turkey. Protracted negotiations were to follow before an agreement could be reached.

Novossiltsev had arrived in London on November 16, 1804. Having quieted the British Government with regard to Turkey by declaring to Lord Harrowby that Russia desired above all the maintenance of the *status quo* in Turkey, Novossiltsev outlined to Pitt the following immediate aims of the Anglo-Russian alliance: (1) to reduce France to her ancient frontiers, (2) to place natural obstacles in the way of Bonaparte's ambitions, (3) to consolidate the order of things thus created.[19] Pitt consented and offered a subsidy of five million pounds to be paid by England to her allies. Novossiltsev further submitted a plan of convention which Pitt approved and sent on to Lord Gower, the British ambassador in St. Petersburg. But there remained questions of detail, such as the necessity of bringing Prussia into the alliance, the amount of the subsidy to be paid to Russia (Russia demanded £1,600,000 for an army of 115,000 and her fleet), and others. Moreover, Alexander became hesitant, thinking that Novossiltsev was going too far and committing himself too much; hence he was recalled in February, 1805, and the negotiations were transferred to St. Petersburg; here Prince Czartoryski and the British ambassador, Lord Gower, taking their

[18] *Ibid.*, pp. 14-15; Martens, *op. cit.*, XI, 85-88.

[19] Martens, *op. cit.*, XI, 98.

stand on the ground of Novossiltsev's plan submitted to Pitt, negotiated and concluded, on April 11, 1805, a treaty of alliance known as the Convention of St. Petersburg. The sudden speed with which all differences were ironed out and an agreement reached at St. Petersburg indicated the urgency of the situation. This was due to the encroachments of Napoleon on Italy, and differences and jealousies were forgotten in the face of the common danger.

This convention was to become the basic treaty of the Third Coalition. On its lines were modeled the conventions with subsequent members of the coalition—hence its importance. In the preamble it was stated that the King of England and the Emperor of Russia were desirous of giving back to Europe the peace, independence, and happiness which had been disturbed by the ambitions of France, and that they had decided to use for this purpose all the means at their disposal. Accordingly they would pursue the aim of forming a general European union, and invite other powers to become parties to the convention, with the object of bringing into the field against France five hundred thousand men, exclusive of the British forces. Article I stipulated that they would endeavor to achieve such a union by obtaining the evacuation of Hanover and of North Germany by the French, the recognition of the independence of Holland and Switzerland, the reinstatement of the King of Sardinia in Piedmont, the security of the Kingdom of Naples, and the establishment of such an order in Europe as would guarantee the safety and independence of the various states. In Article II Britain promised to furnish the necessary subsidies for the armies in the field. The parties to this convention pledged themselves not to sign a separate peace with France, and not to recall any of their forces before the conclusion of a general peace. Other separate clauses stipulated that Holland was to receive the Austrian Netherlands, and Switzerland was to be given Geneva and Savoy. Austria was to be promised additional territories to be determined later, and Prussia was to be granted that part of the Rhineland ceded to France in 1796. Russia was to mediate the differences between Spain and England, with the aim of obtaining Spain's entrance into the coalition, and was also to put pressure on Portugal for the same purpose. The war was to start when there had been put into the field 400,000 men out of the 500,000 scheduled; of this number Austria was to provide

250,000, Russia 115,000, which would be increased to 190,000 if necessary, and the remainder would be sent from Naples, Sardinia, Hanover, etc. England was to subsidize these forces at the rate of £1,250,000 for every 100,000 men in the field; the Russians were to move up 60,000 men immediately to the border of Austria, and 80,000 to the Prussian frontier. Under the separate Article X, Great Britain promised to surrender Malta should Napoleon make this issue a *sine qua non* of peace. This clause was later amended. The liberal principles expressed in the Novossiltsev memorandum made their way very cautiously into the secret articles of the treaty, in which the two powers pledged themselves to discuss the establishment after the war of a federative system of nations which would assure the independence of the small states. Similarly it was agreed that Holland and Switzerland would be permitted to establish forms of government which would correspond to the desires of the people, and that the King of Sardinia, in his newly acquired territories, would be invited to grant a regime which would meet with the approval of his subjects.

In a more general way a somewhat cryptic article stipulated that the contracting parties were not to influence the public opinion of France or of any other country occupied by the allied armies in favor of any particular form of government; they were not to annex any territories except in the name of the countries to which they legally belonged; and they were to call a general congress in Europe at the end of the war for the purpose of establishing a new European order. The treaty was to be ratified within ten weeks.[20]

However, rather oddly, the main difficulties were encountered not before but after the treaty had been signed, and the ratification had to be postponed. There were two major issues in which the British and Russian governments did not see eye to eye and which not only impaired negotiations, but were to be the stumbling blocks in the establishment of real confidence and friendship between the two countries: these were the question of Malta and the question of the rights of neutrals on the high seas. Though Alexander had relinquished the claims of his father on Malta, it still remained im-

[20] John Holland Rose (ed.), *Select Despatches from the British Foreign Office Archives, relating to the Formation of the Third Coalition against France, 1804-1805* (London, 1904), Appendix.

portant for Russia to see that the island did not fall into too powerful hands. England, on her side, anxious not to allow Malta to become French, had proposed in 1801 that Russia should garrison the island with her troops, while the British navy should occupy the Maltese harbors. Alexander, comparing this offer with the one made by the British to Catherine II to garrison the island of Minorca with Russian troops, rejected it on the ground that Malta was too far away from Russia. Napoleon for his part had categorically refused to acknowledge the right of the British to retain Malta. Hence Alexander suggested as the best solution that the island should be declared neutral and be occupied by Neapolitan troops pending its return to its rightful owner, the Order of the Knights of St. John. But the British Government continued to insist that the Russians should occupy the island militarily, and raised this issue six times in succession. Alexander finally went one step further and declared that he was ready to take the island under his protection and contribute to the restoration of the Order of St. John and the election of its new Grand Master. He refused categorically, however, to occupy it with Russian troops.[21]

With the signing of the Peace of Amiens between England and France, however, the British attitude underwent a sudden and complete change—no longer was Russia requested to hold Malta and, in Article X of the treaty, Russia was mentioned simply as one of the six powers guaranteeing the restitution of the island to the Order of St. John. But, as Vorontsov rightly observed, a guarantee of six powers is no guarantee at all; and, furthermore, Russia was hurt at this change of attitude after the previous British insistence upon her garrisoning Malta. She therefore refused to accede to this article. When the Treaty of Amiens failed to maintain peace and a war between Britain and France was again looming, the British Government once more raised the issue of the Russian protectorate over Malta, coupling it with an offer of alliance against France. Alexander refused the offer of an alliance, but accepted the Maltese protectorate with the proviso that a special and separate act to replace Article X of the treaty should be drawn. Later, with hostilities about to start between France and England, Alexander agreed to occupy Malta

[21] Kotchubey to Count Vorontzov, November 13 and December 22, 1801 (Martens, *op. cit.*, XI, 65).

with Russian troops for a period of ten years, or until such time as the British and French should settle the question; as he put it, "He was taking Malta on deposit." But during the war the British in turn changed their stand, and Hawkesbury declared to Vorontsov that the happiness of Italy and the independence of the Mediterranean and the Levant depended upon Malta's remaining in the hands of Britain. Firmly but politely Hawkesbury now rejected the Russian military occupation of the island. Though Alexander still maintained that the best solution was to give Malta back to the Maltese Knights, he apparently did not then object to this British attitude.

Thus matters stood at the time of the negotiations for the treaty of alliance, and in sending Novossiltsev to London Alexander instructed him merely to discover the final intention of the British Government toward Malta. However, during the negotiations and particularly during their final stage in St. Petersburg, the issue suddenly became acute. The Russians had proposed that the following wording be inserted in the draft of the treaty:

> Both contracting parties agree that should the effort to keep Malta in the hands of England fail, and this result not be achieved, they will desist from it to avoid breaking up the negotiations. In such a case the evacuation of Malta [by the British] will be agreed upon, and this island will receive a Russian garrison of which the upkeep will be settled by an arrangement with his Sicilian Majesty and with the order of St. John.[22]

Lord Gower took strong exception to this wording and proposed as an alternative that the upkeep of the Russian garrison should be settled "by an ulterior arrangement convenient to the natives." This vague wording eliminated both Naples and the Maltese Knights, and left England to decide what was convenient for the natives. Russia was thus invited to pull the chestnuts out of the fire for British Mediterranean interests. Alexander, eager to obtain his alliance with England, took the position that this was a personal move of Lord Gower, due to his obstinate character, and that it would not be supported in London. Hence he ordered his plenipotentiaries to sign the treaty with the English wording in it, but wrote to his ambassador in London: "I would myself have ceased any further

[22] *Ibid.*, XI, 106.

discussions if I believed that the British Government endorsed the feelings of their ambassador." He went on to say that he was convinced that his Britannic Majesty would not balance the possession of Malta, which had already once been ceded by England, against the peace and security of Europe. Russia did not want to keep Malta and favored its return to the Order, but the ambassador must insist that in the ratification of the treaty this article should be inserted without any restrictions; should the British Government refuse to do so, Russia could not ratify the treaty.[23] Thus a crisis had been reached. Vorontsov knew full well that Gower was acting upon instructions of his government and not indulging his personal whim. Nevertheless, the ambassador carried out his mission, informing Pitt of the Czar's letter. Pitt immediately answered that the decision in the matter was not his or the King's, for neither the British parliament nor the people would ever accept the abandonment of Malta; therefore to his sorrow he would be forced to renounce the agreement with Russia, for the Czar's decision appeared to be irrevocable. He put forth the argument that France was now the most formidable military power in Europe and that the Mediterranean was becoming a French lake; therefore France was in a position to menace Turkey and India, which would result in the ruin of England. Consequently, the security of Italy, Turkey, and the Levant would depend upon the possession of Malta by England. In vain did the Russian ambassador argue that England by the Treaty of Amiens had accepted the cession of Malta in return for the island of Lampedusa; Pitt declared this to be "a bad joke." When Vorontsov pointed out that this meant the end of the coalition and of the attempts to bring Austria and Prussia into the war, Pitt merely said that he was sorry but the British decision with regard to Malta was irrevocable: "We will continue the war alone." On June 5 Pitt officially notified the ambassador of the refusal of the British Government to entertain the Russian proposal, and added that in view of the fact that the Emperor had declared that he would ratify the treaty only if modified, he considered the treaty to be henceforth void.

Just as a complete deadlock had been reached on this issue, the question of the maritime code came up further to increase the exist-

[23] *Ibid.*, XI, 107.

ing tension. Russia had long objected that her merchant vessels had been the object of capture and search by the British, who were ruthlessly conducting the war against Napoleon on the seas. A particularly serious case having arisen in April, 1805, Czartoryski instructed Vorontsov to lodge a formal protest. "You will concede, my dear Count," he wrote, "that it is very disagreeable that our merchant marine should continually be subjected to more annoyances by . . . a friendly and allied power than by the enemy itself."[24] Vorontsov was therefore to suggest the calling of a conference to discuss once more the question of international law on the high seas. This proposal was very badly received by the British ministers, who declared themselves shocked by such an unexpected and unfriendly move. England, they declared, would never give up the rights she had exercised since the reign of Queen Elizabeth, the abandonment of which would lead to her ruin.

When Vorontsov reported the negative replies to both Russian demands, Alexander gave vent to a veritable fit of fury. Czartoryski, writing to Vorontsov, said that he was afraid the Czar's anger would make him do something rash, and declared he had never seen him in such a state. Thus the relations between the two countries following the signing of the treaty had reached the pole opposite to friendliness, and the treaty remained unratified and void. But when the prospect of a continental war with France loomed in the fall of 1805, the issues of Malta and of the rights of neutrals lost their significance. Though remaining unsettled, they were shelved, and the treaty was ratified hurriedly in order to obtain the adherence of Austria and Prussia to the coalition. Still, the difficulties which had beset it were a clear indication of the instability of friendly relations between Russia and England, which were not to survive the hostilities.

IV

If the negotiations with England were laborious, the problem of inducing Austria—the second most important partner in the coalition—to join proved much more difficult, and did not augur well for the solidity of the coming alliance. Alexander approached Austria as early as 1803, when the Russian chargé d'affaires in Vienna, Anstett, was instructed on October 6 by the Chancellor, Count Vo-

[24] *Ibid.*, XI, 113.

rontsov, to open negotiations for the purpose of joint action against Napoleon. The Austrian Vice-Chancellor, Count Cobentzl, responded with apparent enthusiasm, declaring to Anstett, "I am convinced that the union of the two Imperial Courts, and this union alone, can save Europe and save us in particular."[25] But upon second thought, out of fear of Napoleon, the Austrian Government adopted a policy of procrastination. Alexander wanted an immediate alliance with Austria and offered concrete terms by which Russia would place an army of 90,000 men at the disposal of Austria, with a reserve army of 80,000 to be used according to need. However, Cobentzl became more and more cautious, stating that Austria, if threatened by France, could be destroyed before Russian aid could be really effective. Count Razumovsky, the Russian ambassador in Vienna, complained to his chancellor that both the Austrian Court and Government were "weak, indolent, and pusillanimous." Early in 1804 Austria offered to renew the alliance of 1792, the terms of which Alexander found too general and vague to suit the circumstances. On April 25, 1804, Alexander sent an autograph letter to Emperor Francis offering a coalition in which Russia would furnish a separate army of 100,000 men, and in addition an army of 50,000 men which would be made a part of the Austrian Army. The Czar asked for an immediate reply, but Cobentzl delayed once more, declaring that the terms of the alliance needed more careful study and that certain points were not sufficiently clear. Meanwhile rumors that Austria was negotiating with France reached St. Petersburg, and in an unguarded moment Emperor Francis said to Razumovsky, "Besides, the French have done nothing to me and I am pleased with them." Austria now demanded that the Russian Army should be raised to 150,000 men and that Russia should guarantee any Austrian acquisitions made in Italy in the event of a successful campaign. Alexander refused the increase of the army, but accepted the other clause. Still Austria delayed. Losing patience, Alexander in September ordered Razumovsky to demand an immediate and final reply. The upshot of this move was the signing on November 6 of a convention by which both powers, Russia and Austria, pledged each other aid should Germany or any adjacent territories, including Naples, be attacked by Napoleon. Under Article VIII of this convention the

[25] *Ibid.*, IV, 399.

contracting powers agreed to put jointly in the field 350,000 men, of which Austria's share was 235,000. Russia guaranteed Austria's acquisitions in Italy, and both powers agreed not to sign a separate peace. A special secret article dealt with Prussia. Should Prussia attack Austria, Russia was to bring into action an army of 80,000 men mobilized for that purpose on the Prussian border. A further convention dealt with the problems of the subsidies granted by England.

The Austro-Russian Convention of November 6, although specific in its details, remained purely defensive, and was entirely conditional on the attitude adopted by Napoleon—its purpose being merely to guard against any further encroachments by France, particularly in Naples. Having gone this far, Austria lapsed once more into her policy of cautious reserve, although she increased the number of her troops stationed in Venetia under the pretext of establishing a sanitary cordon against an epidemic of yellow fever raging in Leghorn.

The truth of the matter was that she feared Russia as much as France, and she hated and was jealous of Prussia. Under these circumstances the entreaties of Razumovsky to rouse her to be more aggressive fell on deaf ears, and she constantly pointed out her unreadiness for war. However, while Russian policy was defensive, Napoleon's policy was more and more aggressive, particularly in Italy, and Austria was being compelled by the very force of circumstances to take sides. In July General Winzingerode in the name of the Russian Army arrived at Vienna to discuss with Prince Schwartzenberg and General Mack joint action by the two armies in the event of war; these conferences were terminated on July 16 by a complete agreement reached between the two general staffs. When Napoleon occupied Genoa the last hesitations of Austria vanished, and she notified Russia of her willingness to join the British-Russian alliance. A series of conferences was held once more in St. Petersburg, between Czartoryski, Lord Gower, and Count Stadion, and resulted in the issuance of five declarations signed on August 9, 1805. By these declarations exchanged between the three parties concerned, Austria officially adhered to the Anglo-Russian treaty of April 11, 1805, and both England and Russia acknowledged Austria's move. Furthermore, the military dispositions worked out in the Vienna conferences between Winzingerode and the Austrian generals were put into effect. Thus Austria finally had become an active member of the coalition. But still the coalition could not be considered complete: its success and in fact its very existence depended upon the attitude which Prussia would assume.

By her geographical position Prussia had become, contrary to her will, a key strategic position in the coming war. Indeed, if she sided with the allies she would endanger Napoleon's left flank from Holland to Switzerland, and furthermore, in the event of his advancing on Austria through the valley of the upper Danube, she would be in a position to cut his communications. She would also facilitate the movement of the Russian armies marching to join the Austrian forces through Silesia, and lastly she would link up Austria with Sweden. Conversely, if she joined France she would thereby protect Napoleon's flank and hinder considerably the co-ordination of the allied armies. For this reason Prussia was subjected to strong pressure from both sides, and Alopeus and Metternich, Russian and Austrian ministers in Berlin, did everything they could to induce Prussia to join the coalition. But terrified and uncertain, King Friedrich Wilhelm tried to stave off the storm by remaining strictly neutral. In vain the Czar sent a very friendly letter to the King through his personal aide-de-camp, Prince Dolgoruky, and in vain the Russian minister farsightedly pointed out the dangers to Prussia and Europe of Napoleon's ambitions, which could result in the expulsion of the Bourbons from Naples and Spain, the establishment in neighboring Holland and Switzerland of rulers appointed by Napoleon, and the creation of a federated Europe under French domination—the King was adamant in his decision to remain neutral.

In St. Petersburg, however, Czartoryski was playing an intricate game for his own secret ends: as already stated, he dreamed of recreating Poland under the crown of the Czar. As the larger part of Poland, including its capital, Warsaw, had gone to Prussia, he secretly hoped to maneuver Russia into a war with Prussia to obtain this territory. He therefore heartily disapproved of the Czar's policy of warm friendship with Prussia inaugurated at Memel, and, when persuasion failed to move the King, he embarked on a more aggressive policy of terrorizing Prussia. She was notified that if she did not join the coalition the Russian troops would pass across

Prussian Silesia without her consent. This move so irritated Friedrich Wilhelm that he ordered the immediate mobilization of Prussian forces in Silesia and Pomerania and announced his decision to fight any violators of his neutrality. Napoleon immediately saw his chance to win over Prussia and sent General Duroc to Berlin on a secret mission.

Arriving there on September 1, Duroc was to offer a military alliance with France on the following terms: Napoleon would guarantee the integrity of Holland and Switzerland and would pledge himself not to retain in his possession any conquests he might make in Germany. In return for Prussia's co-operation with France, Prussia would be given full possession of Hanover, which Prussia coveted greatly. The offer was alluring, the more so because Napoleon astutely removed the French forces of occupation from Hanover, allowing the Prussians to occupy it. Thereby he was not only showing good will to Prussia but covering the line of the Elbe River, obtaining the freedom to act unmolested along the line of the Danube. Though afraid to commit himself, the King nevertheless ordered Hardenberg to carry on negotiations with Duroc on the basis of Napoleon's offer. His perplexity was further increased by the rapidity with which Napoleon was gaining allies in southern Germany. On August 24 France signed a treaty of alliance with the Elector of Bavaria, in which in return for Bavarian military aid Napoleon guaranteed the integrity of Bavaria and promised Bavaria in the event of victory to round out her possessions. At the same time he pledged himself once more not to take any territory for France beyond the Rhine. On September 5 a treaty very much along the same lines was signed with Baden, followed by a treaty with Württemberg. But on October 5, while negotiations were still proceeding between Duroc and Hardenberg, Napoleon decided to begin hostilities against the coalition by striking at Austria along the Danube. Bernadotte, who was occupying Würzburg, was ordered to march into the Margravate of Anspach lying athwart his line of advance. Since Anspach belonged to Prussia, the news of this invasion produced an outcry of indignation in Berlin; the reaction was the same against France as it had been against Russia when she threatened to invade Silesia. It was declared that this violation by the French of Prussian neutrality was an "insult to the King, to the dignity of his crown and the independence of his monarchy."[26]

Alexander now made the same use of this seesawing of Prussian moods as Napoleon had made a month earlier. From Pulawi, the palatial estate of the Czartoryskis in Poland where the Czar had been visiting on his way to the front, he had written to King Friedrich Wilhelm offering to come to Berlin to talk matters over. The cautious King had replied that he was afraid that this visit might compromise him in the eyes of Napoleon. Now, however, under stress of the indignation felt over the Anspach affair, he threw caution to the winds and said that he would be delighted to see the Czar. Alexander immediately proceeded to Berlin, where, as before, he found the Queen working in his favor. "You must strike while the iron is hot," said Vorontsov, and this the Czar did, with unexpected success. Traveling incognito under the name of the Comte du Nord, Alexander remained in Prussia for nearly two weeks, between October 25 and November 5. Residing in the castle at Potsdam, he had the opportunity of intimate contact with the King, in which his stronger personality overcame the latter's irresolution. Hence, on November 3, Prussia signed the Treaty of Potsdam which made her a member of the coalition. By this treaty Prussia was to act as mediator between France and the allied powers and to offer peace to France on the following terms: the King of Sardinia was to be compensated either by territorial acquisition of Genoa, Piacenza, Parma, and other small states, or by financial recompense. France was to evacuate Naples and Holland and guarantee their independence, as well as that of the Holy Roman Empire and Switzerland. The independence and integrity of the Ottoman Empire was guaranteed; Austria was assured the lines of the Mincio and Po as frontiers in Italy, and in turn recognized Napoleon as King of Lombardy. Russia in turn promised to recognize Napoleon as both Emperor of the French and King of Lombardy, and to evacuate the island of Corfu. These terms were to be carried by a Prussian negotiator to the French Headquarters, and were valid up to December 15. Should Napoleon accept the terms, an immediate armistice followed by a European peace congress was to take place; whereas should he reject them, Prussia pledged herself to enter the war on the side

[26] Driault, *op. cit.*, p. 247.

of the allies with eighty thousand men. A secret clause assured Prussia of Russia's aid in securing England's consent to the occupation of Hanover.

The following night, in the romantic mood in fashion at the time, the Czar, the King, and the Queen met in the underground crypt where lay buried the bodies of the Great Elector and Frederick the Great, and there over the tomb of Frederick the Great swore to each other eternal friendship and loyalty.

Thus the magnetic personality of the Czar and his quick energetic action had scored a signal diplomatic victory. But this victory proved more apparent than real. Frightened by the rapid French successes in the war, particularly after Napoleon's victory at Ulm, Prussia once more lapsed into a cautious "wait and see" policy, carrying on her military and diplomatic preparations with extreme slowness. After the capitulation of Mack, as the Russians were falling back in danger of encirclement, Alexander sent a desperate appeal for haste to his friend Friedrich Wilhelm:

> I am abandoning all formality [he wrote on November 19], as you allowed me, Sire, to address you as a friend. Never was I in more need of one. Our position is most critical, we are absolutely alone against the French. . . . As for the Austrian Army, it does not exist. Our troops are fighting with amazing courage. Mortier has been completely beaten at Krems and it is rumored that he has perished there. But all this is of no avail, for the superiority of the French is too great. . . . If your armies advanced, the position would change entirely, as mine then could resume their offensive.[27]

To this the King replied merely with a promise to concentrate troops in Franconia. In reply to a second urgent appeal sent directly through Dolgoruky, Friedrich Wilhelm answered that he was getting ready as fast as possible, but was awaiting the results of the negotiations with Napoleon under the terms of the Treaty of Potsdam. But Count Haugwitz, who had been appointed to carry the peace proposals to Napoleon, procrastinated so long that he arrived at the French Headquarters and communicated with Napoleon only on November 29, three days before the battle of Austerlitz put

[27] *Ibid.*, p. 257.

an end to the campaign. The Count subsequently became the head of the pro-French party in Prussia.

Thus Prussia's aid in the campaign had been nil; and even in the north, where the British, Russians, and Swedes were operating against the French in Holland, her conduct was ambiguous—she occupied Hanover with a powerful force, but did not molest the little French garrison holding the city of Hameln. This conduct permitted each side to claim that Prussia favored it.

CHAPTER IV

The Campaign of Austerlitz

I

TURNING to the study of the two months' war which was terminated by the battle of Austerlitz, we find that the campaign brought little credit to the Russian armies except for the masterly retreat of General Kutuzov into Moravia. The general plan of campaign of the allies provided for a broad advance toward France on a front stretching from the Baltic to Italy. Pending the arrival of the Russian armies, the Austrians were to wage a defensive war in Germany. An Austrian army 58,000 strong under General Mack was to advance up the Danube and take up a defensive position on the Iller River, with headquarters at Ulm, where Mack would be in a position to block the French offensive through the Black Forest. A second Austrian army 22,000 strong under Archduke John covered the passes of the Tyrol. The main Austrian army of 95,000 men under Archduke Charles was meanwhile to advance in Northern Italy and join an allied British-Russian-Neapolitan army which was to work its way up from Naples. The main Russian army under Kutuzov was to come from Poland to support Mack. But in the event that Prussia remained hostile, a part of the Russian forces were to be diverted against the Prussians. Lastly, on the Baltic, a Swedish-Russian army assembled at Stralsund was either to threaten Prussia from the north, or to co-operate with a British force coming through Holland to eject the French from Hanover.

Accordingly, the disposition of the Russian armies along the western border of Russia was as follows: In the Ukraine, with headquarters at Radzivillov, 50,000 men under General Kutuzov; this army was to march through Galicia and Bavaria and effect a junction with General Mack. Farther to the north, between Grodno and Brest-Litovsk, 90,000 men under General Michelson; two corps of this army under Generals Buxhoevden and Essen, including the Imperial Guard, were to cross Silesia and march into Moravia to form the reserve of the Austrian army. Should Prussia not permit the passage through Silesia, these two corps were to join the third and augmented corps, 40,000 strong, under General Baron Bennigsen, which was to demonstrate against Prussia. On the extreme right, coming by sea from Kronstadt to Stralsund, the corps of General Count Tolstoy was to join with the Swedish forces either to threaten Prussia or to advance from Pomerania on Hanover. Facing the Dniester along the Moldavian border was the reserve corps of General Tormasov, with 15,000 men, and finally in Naples the division of General Lascy, with 13,000 men.[1]

Napoleon's obvious move was to profit by the fact that the allies were scattered and, by means of speed, to crush them separately. Hence, leaving Masséna with 50,000 men to cope with Archduke Charles, Napoleon himself marched against Mack. The only chance of salvation for the allies depended upon the ability of Mack to resist and the speed with which the Russians could come to his aid. Neither of the two requisites was fulfilled. On October 20 Mack capitulated to Napoleon, after blindly allowing himself to be surrounded by the French armies—thus the allies, practically without battle, lost 30,000 men and 60 cannon. Mack had sent 22,000 men under General Kienmayer to establish contact with Kutuzov's army, which was approaching the river Inn, and this force was able to escape the French. Kutuzov reached Braunau on the twenty-third, his forces having dwindled during the march to 32,000 men. The 22,000 Austrians now under the command of Meerveldt, who had replaced Kienmayer, brought the allied forces holding the line to 54,000. Back of Kutuzov the nearest Russian corps (Buxhoevden) was approaching Olmütz, whereas Bennigsen was still in Russian Poland. The plan of the allies was to gain time to let Buxhoevden and Bennigsen come to the support of Kutuzov, and to let the Austrian Archdukes John and Charles, who were falling back toward the Danube, complete their retreat and unite their forces. There was also hope that the Prussians would finally come in. In the

[1] For disposition of Russian Army, see Schilder, *Imperator Aleksandr Pervyi*, II, 124; for plan of campaign, see Commandant Hubert Camon, *La Guerre napoléonienne. Précis des campagnes* (Paris, 1903), I, 117; and Colonel Emile-Hippolyte Bourdeau, *Campagnes modernes* (Paris, 1916), II, 29.

meanwhile Kutuzov and Meerveldt found themselves in a very dangerous and exposed position on the Inn, as Napoleon's obvious move was to strike at Kutuzov and destroy him before he was reinforced; hence Kutuzov began falling back along the Danube, covering himself by the various tributaries of this great river, while Archduke John was marching down the valley of the Drave in an effort to effect his junction with Archduke Charles, who was then retreating toward Laybach in Slovenia. But neither of these armies could be of any immediate assistance to Kutuzov, as their line of march diverged from the line of Russian retreat; furthermore, as they were out of reach of the Napoleonic armies, Napoleon had a chance to concentrate his forces against Kutuzov. Thus began the second phase of the war.

Kutuzov was an able and experienced general with a distinguished record in both war and diplomacy. Suvorov had spoken of him as his "right hand," and had a very high opinion of his personal bravery and his ability. However, he was now sixty years of age and had been twice severely wounded. Consequently he did not have the driving power and energy required to face such a formidable opponent as Napoleon, but to some extent he made up for this by his ability in maneuvering and in sizing up a situation. It is interesting to notice that in each of his two encounters with Napoleon, in 1805 and 1812, he used the same strategy and outmaneuvered his enemy.

Napoleon started his advance against Kutuzov on October 25, with the intention of repeating the encircling maneuver which had trapped Mack's army. On that day the French army crossed the Isar in three columns on a wide front between the Danube and Munich and, moving along the right bank of the Danube, approached the line of the Inn, which Kutuzov abandoned. Not knowing just where Buxhoevden was, Napoleon thought it prudent to cover his march on the left bank as well; hence, at Passau where the Inn falls into the Danube, he ordered Mortier's corps to cross the Danube and follow the left bank of the river. Kutuzov, in the meanwhile, had fallen back to the line of the river Enns and was approaching Vienna. Here his road divided from that of the Austrian corps of Meerveldt, who, in an effort to join Archduke John, turned south and proceeded to go up the valley of the Enns. Napoleon, quick to see his chance, sent Davout after him; and the latter, on November 8, routed

Meerveldt at Maria-Zell. At the same time Napoleon ordered Marmont to go to Leoben to block the route of Archduke Charles. By these maneuvers he separated the Russians from the Austrians for the rest of the campaign, and isolated Kutuzov.

The two contending armies first established contact on November 5; Murat, followed by Lannes, advancing in the van, stumbled against the Russian rear-guard division of Bagration holding the fortified line of the river Ips. A very hot engagement ensued, lasting late into the night. Bagration was forced to abandon his position and lost 1,800 prisoners, but he had delayed the French advance sufficiently to give Kutuzov time to carry out a very delicate maneuver. Faced with a French army twice the size of his own, Kutuzov could not stop until he had joined his forces with Buxhoevden's. To reach him he had to cross to the left bank of the Danube. This he managed to do unmolested, on the nights of the eighth and ninth, over a wooden bridge at Mautern. Here Murat, following upon Kutuzov's heels, made a bad mistake. Instead of crossing the river after the Russians, he saw a chance to seize Vienna and, without referring the matter to Napoleon, marched on the capital. He thus placed the French corps of Mortier—which as we have seen was coming down the Danube on the left bank—in a very precarious position. Kutuzov saw his chance, stopped his retreat, and on November 11 in a rapid and daring counteroffensive fell upon Gazan's division of Mortier's corps just as it was entering a narrow defile, through which the river flows near Durrenstein. The French sustained a bloody reverse. After an extremely fierce hand-to-hand struggle in the narrows, Gazan's division was saved from complete annihilation only by the arrival of Mortier's two other divisions, which were attacked in turn. Mortier finally succeeded in breaking through the Russian lines, but at a cost of 1,700 prisoners and all his artillery. Napoleon called this battle "the day of the massacre," and sent a violent rebuke to Murat for having disobeyed his orders.

However, Kutuzov could not profit by this victory, for Murat was in a position to threaten the Russian rear by crossing the Danube at Vienna. This was precisely the plan which Napoleon decided upon; he intended to make the best of Murat's blunder. Accordingly, he ordered the corps of Murat, Lannes, and Soult to seize the crossings of the Danube at Vienna, and to cross over to the left bank of the river. At the same time Bernadotte was to cross upstream at Mautern and join Mortier. This was the maneuver of Ulm all over again. "By this maneuver this Russian army might be captured. I will join you myself tomorrow," he wrote to Murat.[2] Indeed, he had placed Kutuzov in a very difficult position. Kutuzov was at Krems on the Danube halfway between Linz and Vienna; immediately back of him, i.e., upstream, were two French corps (Bernadotte and Mortier), or between 50,000 and 60,000 men, and ahead of him along his line of retreat, i.e., downstream, three corps (Murat, Lannes, and Soult), or 75,000 men. Although Kutuzov's army had been strengthened by Rosen's division, he had not more than 40,000 men with which to face 125,000 men, and in addition his line of retreat had been cut.

On the thirteenth, Murat, pretending that an armistice had been signed, tricked the Austrian general, Prince Auerspeg, who was holding the Vienna bridges, into surrendering them, and started crossing the river. But Bernadotte, who was to cross simultaneously at Mautern, was slow and lost a day. Mortier, after his defeat at Durrenstein, was in no position to attack Kutuzov alone; hence Kutuzov could make good use of this lack of synchronization of the French, and outmaneuvered them on the night of the thirteenth by abandoning the line of retreat along the Danube. He turned sharply at right angles to the river and proceeded north toward Znaym, on the road leading to Olmütz, where Buxhoevden was stationed. But the direct highway from Vienna to Znaym met the Krems-Znaym road at a point north of Hollabrün; accordingly, to protect himself against danger from Vienna, Kutuzov sent the division of Bagration supported by eight squadrons of cavalry (Nostitz), and he himself with the bulk of the army marched to Znaym, thus outmaneuvering Napoleon. Murat and Lannes, followed by Soult, proceeded by forced marches to attempt to cut Kutuzov's retreat at Hollabrün, where they came into contact with Bagration's division. Kutuzov now played the same trick on Murat that the latter had played on Prince Auerspeg. He sent his aide-de-camp Baron Winzingerode to Murat's headquarters on the morning of the fifteenth to discuss the terms of an armistice. Murat suspended hostilities and passed the offer on to Napoleon. By the time Napoleon had sent back an irate order

[2] Camon, *op. cit.*, I, 136.

to Murat to resume hostilities immediately, twenty-four hours had passed and Kutuzov had slipped past Znaym safely out of reach. Enraged, Murat at 4:00 P.M. on the sixteenth fell upon Bagration with all his forces; the 6,000 men of Bagration's division were pitted against Murat's cavalry, two divisions of Lannes's corps, and two divisions of Soult's corps, thus fighting against a massed attack of some 30,000 men. Bagration resisted desperately, the battle lasting until 11:00 P.M. Threatened with complete encirclement, he broke through to Guntershofen, losing a third of his forces (1,800 prisoners and twelve cannon), but his heroic resistance had allowed Kutuzov to get away safely. Kutuzov carried out his junction with Buxhoevden near Wachau, and established his headquarters at Olmütz, where he was further strengthened by the Russian Guard Corps and by a newly raised Austrian force of 13,000 under the command of Prince Lichtenstein. As for the French, Murat entered Znaym on the seventeenth of November and pushed on to Brünn on the nineteenth. Napoleon followed Murat and established his headquarters at Brünn, and the Emperors Alexander I and Francis II rejoined Kutuzov at Olmütz.

Summing up, it may be said that Kutuzov by his skilful maneuvering extricated himself from a very difficult and perilous position, and, except for the division of Bagration, deliberately sacrificed to save the army, brought his men through safely.

After a few days' rest the Russian army started a counteroffensive supported by a force of 13,000 Austrians, but without waiting for the Russian corps of Essen, 12,000 strong, to come up. On the twenty-seventh of November Kutuzov advanced from Olmütz toward Brünn in three columns and a reserve corps—the right column under Prince Lichtenstein, the center under the Austrian General Kollowrat, the left wing under Buxhoevden, and the reserve under Grand Duke Constantine, the whole totaling 86,000 men. Thus began the operation which resulted in the disastrous battle of Austerlitz. Although Kutuzov was in command, his power had become merely nominal, the actual direction of operations being in the hands of Czar Alexander himself, who was counseled by the Austrian General Weirother. Kutuzov disapproved of the whole operation; his plan was to evade a battle until the Prussian army, slowly mobilizing, came into action, or until Archduke Charles was able to join the allied forces. He argued that by offering battle to Napoleon the allies were playing into his hands, for there was nothing that Napoleon wanted more than to engage the allied armies in a battle. The wisdom of Kutuzov's views was borne out by subsequent events, but at the time they succeeded only in arousing Alexander's antagonism. The twenty-eight-year-old Czar was eager to cover himself with military glory, and came entirely under the influence of Weirother, who was a cabinet strategist. The Czar's antagonism toward Kutuzov reached the point where, when the latter asked to see the plan of march for the armies, he rebuffed the old general with a sharp, "This does not concern you." Thus the disaster of Austerlitz must be placed squarely on the Czar's shoulders. Furthermore, it was essentially a defeat of the Russian Army, for the Austrian contingent, as we have seen, did not exceed fifteen thousand men. On the very day the Austro-Russian army started its counteroffensive, Emperor Francis offered Napoleon an armistice. Napoleon, mistrusting this offer, pretended to accept it and asked for an interview with Czar Alexander. Nevertheless, expecting battle soon, he started concentrating all his forces which were scattered between Vienna and Brünn. Marshal Soult, who was occupying the heights of Austerlitz, was ordered to retreat, so that the enemy should gain the impression that he was eager to avoid battle. Soult carried out his retreat during the night and, falling back several miles, began hurriedly to erect a fortified line, thus giving a further impression of fear. In this way Napoleon set a trap into which the allies fell.

Meanwhile the allied advance was progressing on a broad front. On the twenty-eighth Bagration drove Lannes's cavalry out of Wischau. Murat in turn abandoned Rausnitz. Believing the French were retreating, the allies started a converging movement against the French right flank, with the intention of cutting it off from the Danube and Vienna. The allies continued their advance beyond Wischau, crossed the river Littawa on December 1 and, on the left bank of that river, spread out their lines, executing a flanking movement from Wischau to Austerlitz. In so doing they were dangerously exposing themselves to French counterattack, but the fact that the French did not move strengthened further their belief that Napoleon was avoiding a battle. In the meanwhile General Savary was sent to the Russian Headquarters by Napoleon. Savary was courteously received, remained there three days, and, according to Napoleon's own words, found, as a result of interviewing various members of the Czar's entourage, that "presumption, impudence, and inconsideration were reigning in the decisions of the Military Cabinet as they had reigned in the decisions of the Political Cabinet. An army thus conducted could not but commit errors. The Emperor's plan was, from this time on, to wait for mistakes, and to select the moment to profit by them."[3]

In reply to the communication of Napoleon suggesting an interview with Alexander, the Czar sent his aide-de-camp Prince Dolgoruky to the French camp, and Dolgoruky was so impressed by what appeared to him to be preparations for a French retreat that he passed the night before the battle watching anxiously to see whether the enemy would escape. Weirother's extremely complicated plan of attack was conveyed to the Russian command at a council of war in which Kutuzov pointedly went to sleep. The order for the disposition of troops was issued so late at night that it could not be carried out in time, and some columns were still marching when the battle started next morning. Kutuzov complained bitterly that he was being given the responsibility of executing a plan of which he disapproved and in the making of which he had had no voice. He was again reprimanded by the Czar on the very morning of the battle for being purposely slow in evacuating the heights of Pratzen, which Kutuzov deemed necessary to retain in his hands. It was in such an atmosphere, of friction and confusion, that one of the greatest battles of modern times was fought.

To understand what happened it is necessary to have a clear picture of the topography of the battlefield. On two sides of the battlefield were two highways, one on the north running east-west from Olmütz to Brünn, and one at right angles to it running north-south from Brünn to Vienna. Branching south from the Olmütz-Brünn road another road led to the village of Austerlitz, located in the east-center of the battle field. Thus these three roads framed the field on the east, the north, and the west. At Austerlitz the two Emperors, Alexander and Francis, established their headquarters; and Napoleon established his at Brünn. Due west of Austerlitz were the heights of Pratzen, running north-south, and farther north

[3] Bulletin of the Grand Army, December 3, 1805.

and slightly more to the west, immediately across the Brünn-Olmütz highway, stood an isolated butte, the Santon. West of the Pratzen heights and flowing parallel to them was a stream, the Goldbach. Slightly southwest of the heights of Pratzen was the fairly large lake of Satschau, and passing through it, the stream of Littawa, running east of the Pratzen plateau, joined its waters with the Goldbach's.

Having crossed the Littawa, the allied army took a position north-south facing the heights of Pratzen. On the extreme right flank Bagration was astride the Brünn-Olmütz road. In the center was Kollowrat's division; the Austrians were due west of Austerlitz; farther to the south on the heights of Pratzen was Buxhoevden with the divisions of Pribyshevsky, Langeron, and Dokhtourov; and finally between the Pratzen heights and the Satschau lake on the extreme left flank, Kienmayer. The Russian Guard was in reserve covering Austerlitz. The objective set by the allies was to force their way across the Goldbach and cut the Brünn-Vienna highway, always on the assumption that Napoleon was anxious to retreat. For this purpose Weirother had worked out the following plan. There was to be one minor and one major attack. As the Santon to the north was a strong position from which the French could counterattack, the minor attack had the purpose of immobilizing the French forces there. Accordingly Bagration was to advance along the Brünn road, sustained by Lichtenstein, who was to keep in touch with Kollowrat. If a gap formed there, it was to be filled by the Guards. The main attack was to be directed southwest and was to converge on the Goldbach beyond the Pratzen. It was to be carried out in stages, the division on the extreme left (Kienmayer) starting the attack and followed one by one by the divisions spread out northwards. Thus Kollowrat's right flank (Miloradovich) would be the last to come into action and would form a pivot. The other divisions which had advanced earlier would converge around this pivot after crossing the Goldbach, and eventually form a line facing due north. Then they would push the French northwards into the arms of Bagration and Lichtenstein, who were operating along the Brünn road. All this required very complicated timing and presupposed that the enemy would remain inactive. Furthermore, as the attacks developed, the southern attack would diverge farther and farther from the northern attack, thus thinning out the center and opening a gap. Finally, the complexity of the maneuver was such that whereas Miloradovich's division was to march southwards, Lichtenstein, who was on his left flank, was to countermarch northwards: i.e., these two columns were to proceed in opposite directions like two railway trains passing each other.

All this played directly into the hands of Napoleon and permitted him to apply his favorite maneuver. This consisted in assembling his reserves at a point opposite the enemy line and then sending a column around the enemy's flank. Faced with this threat to his flank, the enemy would be likely to weaken the section of his line opposite which Napoleon's reserves were assembled. Profiting by this temporary weakening, Napoleon would deliver a smashing blow against this spot and break through the line. But in this case Napoleon had no need for such intricate maneuvering, for the Austro-Russians did the work for him by thinning out their line at the point where the north and south attacks were hinged. To draw the enemy out, Napoleon had purposely abandoned the Pratzen and assembled his army in a close mass west of the Goldbach and immediately south of the Olmütz road. The Santon, however, he had heavily fortified and garrisoned, while Davout alone was left to hold the lower course of the Goldbach where the main allied attack was coming.

We must now see how the allied plan worked out. Early in the morning of December 2, Bagration started the northern attack with the object of capturing the Santon, and encircled the hill from the north. Lichtenstein moved behind him, considerably delayed by the distance he had to cover. The Russian Guards moved up to his left and occupied Blazovitz. Lichtenstein's cavalry pushed Kellerman's cavalry back on the infantry of Lannes, astride the Olmütz road. Thus the northern attack developed successfully.

Buxhoevden started the southern attack at 7:00 A.M.; and Dokhturov, supporting Kienmayer, captured the village of Tellnitz on the Goldbach, which the Austrians of Kienmayer had been unable to take in a previous attack during the night. Farther to the north Langeron and Pribyshevsky, after a delay, crossed the Goldbach and occupied the Castle of Sokolnitz. Thus the first part of their objective was accomplished. Davout put up a fierce resistance, and both Tellnitz and Sokolnitz changed hands several times. Further to the north Miloradovich in the first line and Kollowrat in the second had to wait until 8:30 for Pribyshevsky's division, which was obstructing the road, to get out of their way. They then advanced toward Kobelnitz, but as they did so they opened the fatal gap between the northern and southern attack. Napoleon ordered the combined corps of Soult, Murat, Bernadotte, Oudinot, and the Guards to recapture the Pratzen, and in an overwhelming mass attack to break through this weak point on the Russian front. Realizing the peril, Kutuzov did what he could to fill the gap. He recalled Lichtenstein and the Russian Guards from the northern attack, leaving Bagration to his fate. He further detached the brigade of Kamensky, which formed the end of Langeron's column, veered it around, and sent it to the support of Miloradovich, who was desperately clinging to his ground. But the French attack was so crushing that at noon Miloradovich fell back, and Kamensky was pushed southward. Soult captured the Pratzen, just as the Russian Guards came up to meet the combined impact of Bernadotte, Oudinot, and the French Guards. A charge of the French Guards Cavalry was beaten back, followed by a countercharge of Russian cavalry. A second massed French attack pushed the Russian Guards back, halfway between the Pratzen and Austerlitz, and this resulted in the allied army's being cut in two. Now while Bernadotte followed the retreating Russian columns, Oudinot and Soult wheeled to the right and began advancing south on a broad front between the Goldbach and the Littawa, falling upon the flank and the rear of the columns of the Russian southern attack, which were scattered and unable to sustain each other. Pribyshevsky and Langeron were made prisoners at Sokolnitz. Buxhoevden with his cavalry escaped past Satschau. Dokhturov remained alone. Heroically, he rallied the remnants of three Russian divisions and made a last stand near Tollnitz with his back to Lake Satschau. But he was attacked frontally by the divisions of St. Hilaire and Vandamme, and on his right flank by Friant's division (Oudinot's corps). He tried to break through along a causeway connecting Lake Satschau with the pond of Moenitz; but his infantry was forced off the causeway onto the ice of Lake Moenitz, which, riddled by the French artillery, gave way; and his men drowned by thousands. Dokhturov, however, succeeded in rallying those who were left and managed to bring the remainder of the army out, covered by Kienmayer's cavalry. In the meanwhile

Bagration, left alone in the north, was attacked by both Lannes's and Suchet's corps, as well as Murat's cavalry. He threw his own cavalry into one charge after another to save his infantry, which fell back to a second line at Pozoritz. There he resisted until afternoon. Virtually surrounded, he managed to break away at 4:00 P.M., losing 1,200 prisoners, and in the evening he passed through Austerlitz and rejoined the rest of the army. The day had cost the allies 26,000 men, 45 colors, and 180 cannon; the French lost between 8,000 and 9,000 men. On the next day the allies fell back to Goding southeast of Austerlitz and crossed the Morava. The French pursued weakly. Two days later an armistice was signed, and Kutuzov marched the remnants of his army back to Russia, through Galicia into the Ukraine, where the troops went into winter quarters.

Appraising the role played by Kutuzov in this campaign, a distinguished French military authority wrote:

> One must render justice to Kutuzov, who did all that was possible to remedy the bad decisions made by the Czar; and also to the intrepidity of the Austro-Russian troops and to the tenacity of Doktorof [Dokhturov], who fought until the last moment. Following the fine retreat executed in the face of the Grand Army . . . Kutuzov had suggested a retreat behind the Morava, or at least a time of immobility to await the arrival of the corps of Essen—he alone had seen aright, he alone, in the absence of Archduke Charles, was of the stature to fight an adversary like Napoleon.[4]

II

Although the campaign of Austerlitz, by the extreme swiftness of its development, rendered useless the action of the allied armies on the flanks in both Italy and Northern Germany, Russia's moves on these fronts present a colorful chapter of history which should not be overlooked. The interest Russia was showing at this time in the fate of the Kingdom of Naples was the logical consequence of the powerful hold Russia had secured in the Adriatic through the occupation of Corfu. Naples formed a bulwark against Napoleon's encroachments in Italy, which were threatening the allied position in the Mediterranean. Had Napoleon succeeded in extending his sway over Naples and thereby gained control of the seacoast of Southern

[4] Bourdeau, *op. cit.*, II, 75.

Italy, the British hold over Malta as well as the Russian position in Corfu would have been endangered, for with either Naples or Sicily in his possession, Napoleon would have been in a position to extend his control over the whole Eastern Mediterranean.

Whereas in Turkey British and Russian joint action was marred by mutual suspicion and jealousy, here the similarity of interests made for unity of action. In the great frontal attack on France which was being planned by the Third Coalition, Naples had assumed an important position as a point of departure; indeed, it was to be the extreme left flank of the allied front. An Anglo-Russian force landing in Naples and joining forces with the Neapolitan Army could work its way northward and attempt a junction with the Austrian army coming from the Mincio; such an operation not only would liberate Italy from the French, but would offer the possibility of renewing Suvorov's campaign of 1799, and lead to the invasion of southern France. Lastly, the Court of Naples, through the energetic stand taken by Queen Marie Caroline, showed itself one of the most adamant of Napoleon's foes, and as such was worth the support of the great powers able to be of aid, that is to say, Great Britain and Russia. Russia had a force of some ten thousand men on Corfu, and was awaiting the arrival of a squadron and a further division of reinforcements which were making their way from the Baltic to the Mediterranean through Gibraltar. With these additional forces she would be in a position to act effectively in Italy. It was Napoleon's own moves in Italy, however, which forced the Neapolitan issue upon Russia and made her hasten her action. On March 17, 1805, Napoleon proclaimed himself King of Italy. In June he incorporated into this new state the republics of Lucca and Genoa, or Liguria, as it was then named. These annexations in time of full peace and in flagrant violation of international law stirred Europe and foreshadowed further arbitrary actions by the French in Italy. Naples seemed directly menaced, Austria was profoundly irritated, Russia was worried. Alexander I said, on hearing the news of the annexation of Genoa, "The man is insatiable—his ambitions know no limits; he is a menace to the world; he wants war; he will have it, and the sooner the better."[5] Russia was thoroughly cognizant of the dangers in the Italian situation, but she also saw in it an important advantage:

[5] Driault, *op. cit.*, p. 213.

it was the one issue which brought her into perfect harmony with England and Austria, and would be a determining factor in helping to overcome the mutual jealousies elsewhere.

It was naturally in Naples that the most acute alarm was felt. Queen Marie Caroline, already violently anti-French, after the proclamation of the Kingdom of Italy saw war as inevitable and turned to both England and Russia for aid. The British, in virtual control of Sicily as well as Malta, and the Russians in Corfu, were in constant communication with her, encouraging her in her bellicose preparations. A secret military mission of Russian staff officers under General Lascy arrived in September and proceeded to examine the Neapolitan defenses as well as the topography of the country. The French, who were still in partial occupation of Neapolitan territory, were indignant at the presence of the Russian mission. Alquier, the French minister, threatened to bring in a force of twenty thousand men to occupy the city of Naples, but confident of the support of her powerful allies, the Queen was unimpressed. On September 10 she signed a treaty of alliance with the Russian minister, Tatishtchev, by which, should the French increase their forces of occupation in Naples, she pledged herself to admit British and Russian troops on Neapolitan territory. In such an eventuality, furthermore, the Neapolitan Army as well as the defenses and the fortresses was to be placed under the command of the Russian Commander in Chief. Exasperated, Napoleon ordered Marshal Gouvion de St. Cyr to advance into Naples and dethrone the Bourbons; but, at the last moment, fearing that his forces there might be cut off, he withdrew his order. Instead Napoleon forced the Queen to sign a convention, dated September 21, pledging Naples to remain neutral in the event of war, the Neapolitan Government promising not to admit any foreign troops on her soil. The Queen informed the Russian Government that this convention was not valid since it had been extorted by force, and that she was anxiously awaiting the arrival of the Anglo-Russian expeditionary force.

On November 19 the Anglo-Russian force arrived with 50 vessels: 13,500 Russians and 5,600 British landed and joined the Neapolitan Army, 40,000 strong. The British under General Craigh occupied Naples, but characteristically refused the joint command and remained a separate force. The Russo-Neapolitan Army was placed under the command of the Russian General Lascy. In December Lascy started his advance northward with about 30,000 men, the rest remaining in reserve. The British marched as a separate column along the seaboard on the left flank, the Russians in the center, and on the right flank 10,000 Neapolitans supported by 2,000 Russians, under a French *émigré*, Damas. The army was to effect a junction with the Austrian army of Archduke Charles between Mantua and Piacenza. But in the meanwhile, before Lascy had left the territory of Naples, Archduke Charles had hurriedly evacuated Italy and gone north. These tidings, followed by the news of Austerlitz, reached Lascy as he was approaching Rome, and rendered his advance meaningless. He therefore started a retreat back to Naples and, stopping near the city, covered it from the north. In the meanwhile the Treaty of Pressburg was signed. By this Austria terminated the war, and the Russian armies in Moravia withdrew from Austria and started back to Russia. The following day, December 27, Napoleon issued the proclamation of Schönbrunn, declaring that the Bourbon dynasty had ceased to reign; and on January 6 Massena set out to invade Naples, accompanied by Joseph Bonaparte, waiting to be proclaimed King of Naples. Left to themselves without support, Lascy and Craigh decided to evacuate the city. On January 11 the allies started embarking in their vessels; and the British, followed by King Ferdinand of Naples, retreated to Sicily, which was to become their base. The Russian division was sent back to Corfu and was subsequently used in operations on the Dalmatian coast. Naples fell to Joseph without resistance on February 15, but in the south, particularly in Calabria, the French for a long while were to face the resistance of fierce guerilla bands under such chiefs as the famous Fra Diavolo. The British operating from Sicily made a few thrusts at the mainland, but without much success. In these operations the Russians took no more part.

III

A curious parallel may be noted between the situation in Naples—which, as we have seen, formed the extreme left flank of the coalition—and that in Pomerania and along the Baltic, which was to be the extreme right flank. In the north, as in Naples, the Russians were to form part of a combined army and co-operate with the British, who were to land in Holland for the purpose of driving the French out of the Kingdom of Hanover. Moreover, in Naples the Russians joined the Neapolitan Army, and in Pomerania they were to form part of an allied Swedish-Russian force. Again, like Queen Marie Caroline of Naples, King Gustavus Adolphus IV showed himself extremely aggressive toward Napoleon, his hatred against the French Emperor being due partly to a personal insult inflicted upon him, and partly to the extremely autocratic views which he held. He was the first European monarch to ally himself openly with England against Napoleon; and on December 3, 1804, he signed a convention with the British, by which in return for a subsidy of eighty thousand pounds he placed the island of Rügen and the important harbor and fortress of Stralsund at the disposal of England.[6]

Negotiations had been proceeding since the beginning of 1805 for a joint Russo-Swedish expedition, to be subsidized by England, for the defense of Swedish Pomerania. King Gustavus's demand for absolute command of this force caused a great deal of wrangling. Finally an agreement was signed in February, 1805, by which Russia was to provide 40,000 to 45,000 men, Sweden 20,000 to 25,000; and the British were to pay for the upkeep of these forces. The treaty was to take immediate effect in the event that the French, occupying Hanover, should advance either toward Oldenburg, Mecklenburg, or Holstein. But further wrangling delayed the signing of a treaty of alliance between Russia and Sweden until September, and it was only in October that the combined forces began to move. A corps of 20,000 men (15,836 infantry, 1,705 cavalry, 1,749 artillery with 5,400 horses)[7] under General Count Tolstoy was transported by sea from Kronstadt to Stralsund, where it landed on October 5 and joined a Swedish force of some 10,000 to 15,000 men. At the same time a British force of 6,000 men of the King's German Legion under General Don were ordered on October 10 to embark for Germany. They were to disembark at Glückstadt on the Elbe; occupy and hold Stade, Cuxhaven, and Bremerlehe; and then await the arrival of further forces numbering 11,000 men; after this they would advance in conjunction with the Russo-Swedish army. The

[6] John Holland Rose, *Life of William Pitt* (New York, 1924), p. 516.

[7] Sir John William Fortescue, *A History of the British Army* (London and New York, 1899-1930), V, 284 n.

British for this purpose were to concentrate on the Weser and march toward Nienburg, while the Russians and the Swedes marched into Hanover via Luneburg and Zell. For a while the idea of occupying Holland as well was entertained. While the British were awaiting the arrival of additional forces from England, the Prussians suddenly moved—profiting by the evacuation of Hanover by the French—entered that state, and secured the chief passage to Holland by occupying Blenheim. The Swedish-Russian force in the meanwhile had started its advance. A delicate situation had arisen, and the commanders of the three armies—the British General Don, the Russian Tolstoy, and the Prussian Duke of Brunswick, met at the General Headquarters of the Prussian Army. Here it was decided to draw a line of demarcation between the respective armies of occupation. The British accordingly were to hold the lower Weser up to Werden, Tolstoy's right was to hold the Weser toward Minden, and his left to blockade Hameln. But the King of Prussia kept on wrangling, and both the British and the Russian contingents were immobilized for lack of transportation. Accordingly, though London was urging immediate action, and an additional British division was sent under Lord Cathcart to be used for a march on Holland (the main objective of the British), it was decided in a consultation between Don and Tolstoy not to move until the Swedes who had remained behind should come up.

Meanwhile, on November 28 in an interview with Napoleon, the Prussian Minister, Haugwitz, obtained Napoleon's acceptance of a Prussian scheme of mediation on condition that neither the British nor the Swedish-Russian forces should invade Holland. The King of Sweden, after allowing a part of the Swedish forces to reach the Elbe, declared that he would advance no farther in view of the threatening and uncertain attitude of Prussia. Then came the news of the disaster of Austerlitz, and the signing on December 15 of a treaty between Prussia and France, in which Prussia pledged herself not to take Hanover. The situation was now so confused and the attitude of Prussia so equivocal that Lord Cathcart, even though he had received further reinforcements, decided not to move, and came to terms with the Prussian General Kalkreuth. By these terms the British were to hold Bremen and Werden, the Russians Hoya and Nienburg, while the Swedes remained in reserve on the Elbe and the Prussians covered the British left along the Ems. The French, however, increased their army in Belgium west of the Yssel; and Augereau was now threatening Hanover from Frankfurt-on-the-Main. In view of this, in January, while negotiations were still proceeding between Prussia and France, a Prussian army of fifty thousand men marched into Hanover and occupied it by force. With a strong French army holding Holland under Napoleon's brother Louis, and the Prussians holding Hanover, the position of the allied forces on the Weser became untenable; and in February the British received final orders to re-embark for England. As for the Russians, after being placed temporarily under the command of the King of Prussia, they were ordered to proceed home overland. Thus came to an end this inglorious and unfruitful campaign.

Chapter V

Austerlitz to the Peace of Tilsit

I

Alexander, crushed by the defeat of Austerlitz, passed a feverish night on the battlefield, physically and morally ill, requiring medical attention; and Emperor Francis asked Napoleon for an immediate armistice. Accordingly the French and Austrian Emperors met on December 4, and Napoleon agreed to the cessation of hostilities on condition that the Russian Army should forthwith return to Russia. He felt that Austria was at his mercy, and he was eager either to get Russia out of the way or to win her over to his side. This he intended to do by indirect action—offering more favorable conditions to Emperor Francis if the latter would put pressure for peace on his ally, and in direct negotiations with Alexander stressing his friendliness toward Russia, as contrasted to the hard terms to be imposed upon Austria.

Thus the following day (December 5) General Stuttenheim, in the name of Emperor Francis, and General Savary, representing Napoleon, presented themselves at the Czar's headquarters with parallel missions. Stuttenheim, received first by Alexander, notified him of Napoleon's offer to Emperor Francis. Alexander immediately and definitely refused any negotiations for peace, but was prepared to accept an armistice. "I brought my army to the aid of Austria," he said. "I will withdraw it if Austria does not require my aid any longer."[1] When Savary was introduced into the presence of the Czar, the latter had regained his composure and revealed himself once more the supreme diplomat he was. "Tell your master," he said to Savary, "that he has done wonders." "Sire, it is the art of war. This is the fortieth battle of the Emperor." "That is true," said Alexander; "he is a great captain. As for myself, this

[1] Sorel, *op. cit.*, VII, 5.

is the first time I have been under fire."[2] Savary then stated that Napoleon had given orders not to hamper the retreat of the Russian Army and that the word of honor of the Czar would suffice as a guarantee. "I give it," said the Czar simply. As a further token of good will Napoleon ordered the return to Russian headquarters of all the prisoners of the Russian Guards taken in battle, a measure which elicited from old General Vandamme the grumbling remark: "Let those fellows go, and in six years they will be in Paris."

The armistice was signed the following day, and the Russian Army began its withdrawal. Napoleon, after Austerlitz, had a feeling of justifiable pride: "In Italy he [Napoleon] had faced only the Austrians. This time he had crushed the redoubtable Russian infantry, the infantry of Suvorov, rival and victor of the French."[3] But there were still dangers ahead for Napoleon. Prussia, so slow to move, had finally completed her military preparations and was about to come into the war. Alexander having accepted only an armistice, the war was technically still on; and it was imperative to prevent the formation of a new coalition by England, Prussia, and Russia, with Prussia taking the place of Austria. Therefore Napoleon lost no time in approaching Prussia; and while the negotiations for peace with Austria were proceeding, first in Vienna and then in Pressburg, the Prussian ambassador in Vienna, Count Haugwitz, received a hint from Napoleon that an alliance with France would give Prussia some valuable territorial compensations. Haugwitz responded with alacrity, and a treaty was signed by him on his own authority, on December 15 at Schönbrunn, which stipulated that Prussia and France were to be bound by an offensive and defensive alliance, with Prussia to receive Hanover in return for the cession to Bavaria of Anspach and the Principality of Neufchâtel, and Cleve to be given to a prince to be designated by Napoleon. Thus Napoleon had achieved his aim.

But Alexander was equally impressed by the importance of Prussia; and on the very day that the Treaty of Schönbrunn had been signed, Prince Czartoryski wrote to the Russian minister in Berlin, Alopeus, about the conditions which Napoleon was imposing upon Austria.

[2] *Ibid.*
[3] *Ibid.*, VII, 2.

> If such terms are accepted, Austria will be eliminated from the number of independent states of Europe. In such a critical moment the only hope resides in the energy of the King of Prussia, in his loyalty and fidelity. Should he pronounce himself in accordance with the stipulations of the Treaty of Potsdam, things will soon take a different turn.[4]

In this spirit Alexander ordered the army of Bennigsen and the corps of Count Tolstoy to be placed at the immediate disposal of King Friedrich Wilhelm; also the army of Kutuzov was eventually to form a junction with the Prussian armies. He further sent his aide-de-camp Prince Dolgoruky to Berlin to establish contact with the King. But Dolgoruky found the utmost dejection in the Prussian capital. The news of Austerlitz had produced such fear and consternation that all warlike measures were immediately canceled, in flagrant violation of the Treaty of Potsdam. The timorous King did not want to become involved on either side, either against France or against Russia and England. Dolgoruky did his utmost to persuade him to align his country with Russia against France, stressing the honor and the treaty obligations of Prussia, as well as the fact that should Prussia yield to France, Russia would be exposed to an invasion of Napoleon which would be fatal to both of them. The King merely conveyed his assurances that he would never separate his fate from that of Emperor Alexander.

On December 26 Austria signed the Treaty of Pressburg, losing thereby all her acquisitions in Italy and Dalmatia, as well as the Tyrol, Vorarlberg, Brixen, Trente, Passau, Lindau, and five cities on the Danube. She lost some three million inhabitants, and what was even more important, she lost the passes into Germany. Thus cut off and weakened, Austria would not be in a position to wage war or be of much use to the anti-French powers.

Haugwitz arrived in Berlin on the same day, bringing his treaty with him for ratification. In the court and political circles a wild outcry of indignation greeted him. In particular the Queen, Prince Louis Ferdinand, Hardenberg, Stein, and the military circles led by Blücher were set against an alliance with France. The King, however, after a council with his ministers in which the utmost irresolution prevailed, agreed to the treaty, provided that some important amendments were made. At the same time the King made a feeble

[4] Martens, *op. cit.*, VI, 368.

attempt to reconcile the contradictory trends of his policies by writing to Napoleon in January, suggesting a reconciliation between France and Russia. But when Haugwitz reached Paris with the amended treaty, he found that Napoleon was not only in no mood to tone down his demands, but on the contrary had raised them. Faced with an ultimatum from Napoleon, Haugwitz signed the new version of the treaty, which imposed upon Prussia much stiffer obligations, including the closing of ports to British vessels, the recognition of the Treaty of Pressburg, and above all the obligation to join forces with France in any future war. Furthermore, Hardenberg was to be replaced by the pro-French Haugwitz in the conduct of Prussian foreign affairs. The King ratified the new treaty on February 26, and thus technically found himself at war with Russia, since the hostilities between France and Russia had not ceased.

Yet as early as January the King had written to Alexander, stating expressly that his relations with France would in no way hinder his close relations with Russia. In February the King sent the elderly Duke of Brunswick, of 1792 fame, to St. Petersburg to announce the signing of the treaty, and to explain why Prussia had been forced to sign it. On the very day of the ratification of the treaty Friedrich Wilhelm wrote to Alexander, "I recognize only two judges, my conscience and yourself. The former tells me that I have to rely on you, and this conviction is sufficient for me."[5]

The Duke of Brunswick was cordially received by Alexander, who sent him to confer with Czartoryski. The latter bluntly stated with regard to the acquisition by Prussia of Hanover that "any increase in the power of Prussia suits us"; and Goltz, the Prussian envoy in St. Petersburg, reported that Russia was disposed "to uphold Prussia and by all means."[6] But as a preliminary measure Alexander demanded guarantees against any further yielding to Napoleon. He therefore handed to the Duke a memorandum for the King, in which he promised to place his whole might on the side of Prussia, provided the latter gave a solemn promise not to consider her treaty with France binding in the event France should attack Russia. Russia for her part would come to the aid of Prussia, should the latter find herself at war with France. These engage-

[5] Sorel, *op. cit.*, VII, 34.
[6] *Ibid.*, VII, 41.

ments were to remain absolutely secret, and Russia was prepared to cover them by herself initiating negotiations with France for the re-establishment of a general peace in Europe. These pledges were reiterated in a personal letter from the Czar to the King, brought back from St. Petersburg by Brunswick, in which Alexander promised "to fly to the aid of Prussia at her first appeal." Friedrich Wilhelm replied that he had never had any faith in his French alliance, which he considered virtually annulled, and that, though he could not break off with Napoleon, he was determined to side with Russia and to prepare to resist France jointly with Russia. As for the declaration not to fight Russia: "With what joy I am giving it to you, Sire, and what a need for my heart to repeat incessantly that my first duty is toward you."[7] As Haugwitz put it later to Gentz, "If there ever existed a power which he had intended to trick, it was France."

A situation without parallel now developed in Berlin. Hardenberg, who because of the hostility of Napoleon was officially in retirement and could see the King and the Queen only secretly, was placed in charge of the secret department which dealt with Russia, whereas Haugwitz, the official Minister of Foreign Affairs, became merely a smoke screen. The real affairs were conducted behind his back by Hardenberg. Russia met this abnormal situation by appointing Baron Stackelberg as the official envoy to deal with Haugwitz, and Alopeus, the more experienced former minister, to deal with Hardenberg. Stackelberg did not share the enthusiasm of Alopeus concerning Prussia, and with remarkable foresight wrote to his government: "Things have come to a point where an alliance with Prussia would be for us more onerous than useful. . . . Prussia will demand our assistance when it will perhaps be too late to give her efficacious aid."[8] Nevertheless Alopeus was instructed to proceed with his negotiations with Hardenberg, and on April 16 Czartoryski wrote to him giving Russia's conditions: the treaty of alliance between France and Prussia was not to affect the engagements accepted by Prussia toward Russia; Prussia was to pledge herself not to fight Russia in the event of a war between France and Russia over Turkey or Italy; Prussia was to guarantee the integrity of the Ottoman Empire, as well as the possessions of the Kings of Denmark

[7] *Ibid.*, VII, 42.
[8] Martens, *op. cit.*, VI, 374.

and Sweden in Germany; she was to reorganize her armed forces and do her best to obtain the evacuation of the French armies from German soil. In return Russia promised to defend the integrity and independence of Prussia with all her armed might, and undertook to maintain complete disinterestedness in her dealings with European powers. This agreement was to remain strictly secret, and Russian diplomacy was to persuade France of the loyalty of Prussia to her French alliance.

To maintain this secrecy an interesting piece of diplomatic subterfuge was resorted to. In co-operation with Hardenberg, Alopeus wrote the text of a bogus treaty, which was copied by the hand of Mme Alopeus and presented to the "official" cabinet of Haugwitz, well knowing that through this channel it would reach Paris. Meanwhile the secret treaty along the lines above indicated was signed by the King on July 1, and Prussia found herself in the peculiar position of being at once the ally of France and of Russia, though these countries were at war with each other.

But although the treaty had been signed, Russian diplomacy was uncertain about the value of this alliance so long as Haugwitz and the pro-French clique remained in power in Berlin. In vain did Queen Louise intrigue against them and even seek through secret messengers the co-operation of Alexander to oust them; it was not until November that Haugwitz fell. In August, a month after the signing of the treaty, Russia's distrust appeared clearly in a confidential inquiry from St. Petersburg to Stackelberg, to determine what attitude Prussia would take in the event of a war between France and Russia, and what the condition of the Prussian Army was. The answer came more quickly than expected, in the disaster of Jena. It was, however, only two weeks after the Prussian Army had been destroyed by Napoleon in this battle that the first military convention between Russia and Prussia was signed on October 28 at Grodno, regulating purely technical problems of the passage of the Russian Army over Prussian territory. After Jena, on November 8, Friedrich Wilhelm wrote in despair that his only hope lay in help from Russia. Alexander replied encouragingly, urging the King not to lose courage, and promising to fight until the French were driven back across the Rhine. The King sent effusive thanks for this "generous procedure" and asked permission to seek asylum in Russia should circumstances make it necessary. After the fall of Berlin plans were made to have Queen Louise and the children removed to Riga, though these did not materialize.

In the meanwhile, just at the time of the negotiations for the secret treaty with Russia, an important change took place in the conduct of Russian foreign affairs. Prince Czartoryski came to a parting of the ways with Emperor Alexander and was replaced by an obscure personage, Baron Budberg, who in turn a year later was replaced by a man once more of strong caliber, Count Rumiantsev. Czartoryski, in a letter remarkable for its bold and outspoken criticism of the Czar's conduct of affairs, explained why he could not serve him longer. He reveals his Polish dislike of Prussia when he writes:

> I consider the meeting [at Memel] one of the most unfortunate events which has occurred for Russia. The close friendship, which after a few days of acquaintance Your Majesty contracted with the King, resulted in your seeing in Prussia not a state but a person who was dear to you. . . . Your Majesty felt it to be contrary to your personal sentiments for the King, to endorse any plan hostile to Prussia. . . .

He goes on to say that Russia ought to have fought Prussia instead of being allied to her. Obviously such views were in contradiction to the present trend of Russian diplomacy. More pertinent were his observations on the character of the Czar:

> Your Majesty is acquainted with the words of Suvorov that a moment decides a battle, an hour the issue of a campaign, and a single day the fate of empires. . . . In Europe there is only Bonaparte who knows the value of time. . . . He knows how to undertake now what would be impossible in eight days. . . . I have discovered, too late perhaps and with great pain, that Your Majesty has no profound and decided convictions on questions debated by your cabinet. After discussing the matter thoroughly, after deciding the principles, Your Majesty after a while would change your views, have regrets painful to yourself and still more so to your cabinet. Whereas by your own decision, Sire, events have taken a certain direction . . . we were never sure of the point from which we started, obliged as we were to reverse our decisions as if nothing had been decided and agreed upon. . . .

He further accused Alexander of causing the disaster of Austerlitz by interfering with the dispositions of General Kutuzov.[9] Though Alexander's feelings were hurt, he retained his friendliness for Czartoryski, and the latter was still to play an important role in Russian affairs.

As a constructive measure, Czartoryski advocated in his letter the seeking of a reconciliation and the establishment of friendly relations with Napoleon, thereby foreshadowing the meeting of Tilsit a year later. But at this juncture Alexander was not yet prepared for so revolutionary a change in his policy, and since he was bent on maintaining at least in theory the war against France and since Prussia was so uncertain a factor, the relations with England were acquiring an increasing importance in his eyes. The death of Pitt in January, 1806, affected Alexander very greatly and was considered in St. Petersburg an event as unfortunate as the Battle of Austerlitz, for Pitt was credited with being a staunch supporter of the Russian alliance. Count Vorontsov, the long-time Russian ambassador to London, had been a lifelong friend of the British statesman. He did not get along so well with Pitt's successor, Fox, even though Fox maintained the former's pro-Russian policy. Mutual antipathy developed between the two men, and Vorontsov suspected Fox of double dealing—he had proofs of a secret correspondence carried on by the latter with Talleyrand—and feared separate British peace negotiations with Napoleon. These fears were not justified, considering that Fox wrote to Talleyrand, "England is united with Russia by ties so close that she wishes to negotiate only in concert with the Emperor Alexander."[10] But realizing that the secretiveness of Fox was largely due to the latter's personal dislike of himself, Vorontsov tendered his resignation. Count Stroganov was sent to replace him temporarily, pending the appointment of a new ambassador, who was to be Alopeus, transferred from Berlin. At the farewell audience which Vorontsov had with King George III the later made the following remarkable statement:

> You know yourself, as I have frequently said during the twenty-one years that we have known each other, that a good Englishman must be a good Russian and a good Russian, a good Englishman. . . . one would have

[9] Le Prince Adam Jerzy Czartoryski, *Alexandre Ier et le prince Czartoryski, correspondance particulière et conversations* (Paris, 1865), pp. 19-56.

[10] Sorel, *op. cit.*, VII, 47.

to renounce all common sense . . . to imagine that there could exist an alliance more natural and more solid in the world than the alliance between Great Britain and Russia, which countries are not neighbors, neither of them having the same kind of power . . . the one being the most formidable military power on the Continent, the other insular with the largest navy that any country has ever had.[11]

Indeed, the interests of England and Russia were so closely interwoven on the Continent, and particularly in the Mediterranean and the Near East, that they both attracted and repelled each other.

"Austerlitz," writes Sorel, "had hit Alexander in his illusions, the Russian name in its prestige, the Empire in its interests. It was for supremacy in Poland and in the Ottoman Empire that Russia had fought in Moravia. It was her advanced posts that Russia was defending on the Danube and at Naples, and now France was mistress of Naples and presenting a formidable claim to the succession of the Sultan."[12] Czartoryski had been well aware of this danger, and in a memorandum to Alexander he outlined the situation thus: Bonaparte is menacing Poland through Prussia, and Turkey through Dalmatia, and is on the way to dominate the Mediterranean. These moves directly endanger Russia, and to counteract them Russia ought to assemble a fleet in the Mediterranean, an army at Corfu, and one hundred thousand men in Moldavia; she should also seek an agreement with Britain for joint military action—the British to land in Egypt and the Russians to occupy the Danubian Principalities. Should this lead to a partition of Turkey, Russia should form a Slav state along the Adriatic, and a Greek state to include Greece and the Ionian Islands. As the supreme and ultimate goal of Russia's diplomacy Czartoryski envisaged a federation of Slav states under the sponsorship of Russia. These ideas were conveyed to Stroganov in London by a letter of May 23, 1807, to form a basis of discussion for joint action with the British Government. But Fox did not share the imaginative flights of Russian diplomacy—he merely observed dryly that he foresaw "with sadness" the destruction of the Ottoman Empire, and that in such an event Great Britain would take the island of Crete and the port of Alexandria in Egypt. He pointedly did not mention the creation of the new

[11] Martens, *op. cit.*, XI, 123.
[12] Sorel, *op. cit.*, XI, VII, 36.

states proposed by Russia. On the other hand, Russia, as we have seen, wholeheartedly endorsed the acquisition of Hanover by Prussia. The British Government refused sharply to accept this transaction. Thus points of friction and divergence were appearing between the allies. Further, Russia complained once more to England about the freebooting attacks of the British on Russian vessels. The British Government promised to put an end to the molesting of vessels flying the Russian flag. On the British side, however, much ill feeling was caused by D'Oubril's mission to Paris to negotiate a separate peace for Russia.

It will be recalled that Alexander promised the Duke of Brunswick in St. Petersburg that he would initiate talks of peace with France, to cover up his alliance with Prussia. Subsequently Napoleon opened negotiations with England through the intermediation of Lord Yarmouth, and the British Government loyally informed Russia of this step. Accordingly one of Russia's most astute diplomats, D'Oubril, was sent to Paris on the pretext of negotiating for the repatriation of Russian prisoners of war. D'Oubril's secret instructions provided (1) for a close watch on Lord Yarmouth to prevent England from concluding an agreement with France prejudicial to Russia, and (2) for making a separate arrangement with France "should such an arrangement present infinitely marked advantages for Russia." In return Russia notified the British Government of this step. Arriving in Paris on July 6, D'Oubril saw Talleyrand the same day. The French minister was not fooled by the official pretext concerning the prisoners, and asked point-blank, "Is it with a British minister that I am dealing in negotiating with you?"[13] D'Oubril replied that his mission was to maintain the existing good relations between Russia and England, but that if Talleyrand raised confidential matters concerning Russia alone, he would not convey them to London. Thus encouraged, Talleyrand went ahead and proposed a truce of eight or ten years. D'Oubril replied that he was not averse to such a truce, but that it was not feasible since the French Empire's borders were contiguous to Turkey. Although D'Oubril said that he had no powers, Talleyrand and his aide Clark put all pressure possible upon him to obtain a peace treaty. D'Oubril was in a quandary. He feared that the col-

[13] *Ibid.*, VII, 73.

lapse of negotiations would lead to the immediate resumption of hostilities. Napoleon further offered as bait a promise that if Russia ceded Cattaro to France, he would evacuate the Germanies. After much hesitation and after obtaining the views of Fox, D'Oubril took upon himself to accept the bargain, and on July 20 signed a treaty of peace along the following lines: Russia would recognize Napoleon as Emperor and King of Italy, cede Cattaro to France, and acknowledge the possession of Dalmatia by France. France in return would respect the independence of the republic of Ragusa and of the Seven Islands. She further pledged herself to evacuate Germany within three months of the signing of the treaty and after cession of Cattaro by Russia. Both parties were to arrange a peace between Prussia and Sweden, Russia was to acknowledge Joseph as King of Naples, and King Ferdinand was to be given in compensation the Balearic Islands to be obtained by joint action from Spain. The integrity of the Ottoman Empire was to be guaranteed, and Russia offered her mediation to re-establish peace on the seas. The treaty was to be ratified within twenty-five days.

This treaty produced an outcry of indignation in London, and the relations with Russia became so strained that Stroganov refused all invitations, remaining secluded in the Embassy.

But scarcely had D'Oubril left Paris to return to St. Petersburg when Napoleon announced the establishment of the Confederation of the Rhine, and imposed upon Austria the subsequent dissolution of the Holy Roman Empire. These measures, which made Napoleon's domination over Germany an accomplished fact, were a direct menace to Prussia and an indirect one—through Saxony and Poland—to Russia. When D'Oubril reached St. Petersburg he was met with a storm of protest against his "infamy" and against the duplicity of Napoleon, who at the very time he pledged himself to evacuate Germany was establishing himself there more or less permanently through the new confederation of which he was the Protector. The Czar called a session of the Council of State, which accused D'Oubril of having abused his powers. D'Oubril was ordered to leave the city and reside on his country estate, and the new Minister of Foreign Affairs, Budberg, notified Talleyrand (August 14) of the refusal of Russia to ratify the treaty, declaring that peace could be arranged only if France renounced her claims to Albania and Dalmatia, guaranteed Sicily to King Ferdinand of Naples, and obtained an indemnity for the King of Sardinia. The news of Russia's refusal to accept peace was received with rejoicing in England, and the King in a proclamation to his people announced on October 21, 1806, that the honesty of Russia had "imposed on him an increased obligation not to separate his interests from those of so faithful an ally."[14] In Prussia, Russia's action strengthened the hand of the very active war party, already incensed by Napoleon's policy of encircling Prussia, and on September 6 Friedrich Wilhelm wrote to Alexander, "I have no more choice but war. . . . It is I who, as it appears, will have to take the initiative of decisive action. My troops are marching on all sides to speed the moment."[15] War was merely a few weeks off.

Before studying the events in this great new campaign in which, by the rapid defeat of Prussia, Russia was once more to come face to face with Napoleon, it is necessary to turn our attention to a relatively remote part of Europe—the Dalmation coast and the Ionian Islands, which by the nature of their geographical position had assumed a focal importance in the present situation. Here alone, fighting continued unremittingly after the battle of Austerlitz, between the French and Russian forces centering around Cattaro, and the importance of that city was not lost on Czartoryski. "If we keep Cattaro," he wrote, "Turkey will become dependent on us. . . . All the plans of Bonaparte for the Levant will disappear forever. The conquest of Italy would become precarious. . . . Bonaparte is well aware of the importance of Cattaro."[16] Thus the Dalmatian coast with the great Bay of Cattaro and the islands off the coast became the key to the supremacy of the Eastern Mediterranean, both for the French and for the Russians, and the story of the Russian conquest of the Adriatic, little known and little told, marks a colorful if transitory chapter in Russian naval imperialism.

II

We have seen how Russia in 1798 obtained control of the Ionian Islands and thus got a strong foothold on this valuable base, which she succeeded in maintaining even after the collapse of her Nea-

[14] Martens, *op. cit.*, XI, 129.
[15] Sorel, *op. cit.*, VII, 97.
[16] *Ibid.*, VII, 39.

politan venture in the campaign of Austerlitz. Corfu and the Ionian Islands had served as a base for operations against the French in Italy; they were to serve the same purpose against the French forces operating on the Dalmatian coast.

Indeed, after the occupation of the Ionian Islands the Russians extended the field of their operations to the eastern coast of the Adriatic, that strip of territory between the Dalmatian Alps and the sea, extending from the county of Zara to Montenegro. This territory, as well as the numerous coastal islands, comprised the former Venetian province of Dalmatia, the independent republic of Ragusa, and, bordering Montenegro, the region of the Bocca di Cattaro. By the Treaty of Campo Formio (October, 1797) Dalmatia and the Bocca di Cattaro came under Austrian domination, but after her defeat at Austerlitz Austria was compelled to re-cede these territories to France under the Treaty of Pressburg, and they were attached to Napoleon's Kingdom of Italy. As for the rich and flourishing aristocratic Republic of Ragusa, it had succeeded in maintaining a somewhat precarious existence. Napoleon had attached special importance to the possession of this coast because he regarded it as the keystone of his whole Eastern policy and as a gateway giving access to far more important regions. From there he could hope to establish a direct contact with the Serbs, in rebellion against Turkish authority, either through the northern passes or through Bosnia. Cattaro gave access to Albania and Montenegro, and permitted an attack from the rear on the Ionian Islands, which in turn led to direct contact with Greece. Through the possession of the Dalmatian coast the French Empire bordered on Turkey, and Turkey could either be dismembered or be used against Russia, England, or Austria. Through Turkey, Napoleon could menace British trade in the Levant, Russian predominance in the Black Sea, or, using the Danube, could either march around Austria or invade Russia from the south, while another army could march through Germany and Poland. For precisely these reasons the Russians were anxious not to allow the French to dominate this territory, and they found a natural ally in their coreligionists and Slav brethren, the Montenegrins, who were covetous of extending their sway to the north.

Russian relations with Montenegro dated from the reign of Peter the Great. Faced with an unexpected Turkish attack in the midst of his war with Sweden, Peter in 1710 had sent an emissary, Milo Radonich, to raise the sturdy mountaineers of the Black Mountain against their traditional foe, the Turks. The Elective Prince-Bishop of Montenegro (the *Vladika*), Danilo Petrovich, responded to the call; and Peter in return granted a subsidy of ten thousand rubles and one hundred and sixty gold pieces when Danilo visited Russia in 1715. His successor, *Vladika* Vassili, also again went to Russia and received from Empress Elizabeth a regular annual subsidy of three thousand rubles. Furthermore, the Empress gave a thousand ducats for schools in Montenegro and admitted fifteen young Montenegrins into Russian military schools. Vassili died in 1765 and was buried in the monastery of St. Alexander Nevsky in St. Petersburg. Upon his death an impostor, Stephen Mali, who claimed to be Czar Peter III, husband of Catherine the Great, succeeded in mounting the throne of the *Vladikas*. He proved to be an energetic and able ruler, fighting both Turkey and Venice. Catherine sent Prince Dolgoruky to bring munitions as a gift to the Montenegrins, but also to expose the impostor. Dolgoruky denounced Stephen in a public assembly in Cettinje and the latter, admitting fraud, was arrested. But as he had proved to be a good administrator and furthermore a sworn foe of the Turks, Dolgoruky not only had him released, but made him regent. Following the death of Stephen at the hands of a Greek spy sent by the Pasha of Scutari, Montenegro was ruled by its greatest *Vladika*, Peter I, who was to be the ally of the Russians in the present strugle.

With the republic of Ragusa, the relations of Russia in these years immediately preceding the Russian attack were stormy. The little republic, terrified at being drawn into a crisis which would undermine its prosperity and eventually its very existence, had attempted to remain at peace with all parties concerned—the French, the Russians, and the Austrians alike. A number of liberal-minded senators of Ragusa showed, however, their distinct predilection for France, out of fear of Austria; and the news of Austerlitz was the signal for rejoicing in certain quarters, which provoked an official protest by the Russian consul-general, Fonton. The Russian Government had an earlier grudge against the republic for the aid it had given to France by supplying her squadrons operating against the Russians; hence instructions had been given to the Russian consul to intimidate the Senate, which he did. A quarrel over the accommodations assigned to the Russian consulate, over the Orthodox Church in the city—every occasion was used as a pretext for violent remonstrances. Terrified, the Senate presented apology after apology to the chancellor, Count Vorontsov, in St. Petersburg, through the agency of the papal nuncio in Russia.

During the war of 1805 the Russian forces occupying the Ionian Islands were considerably strengthened. Indeed, already in 1804 the Russian forces in the Adriatic had been brought up to one infantry division, with four additional vessels joining the Adriatic squadron the following year. In 1806 Admiral Seniavin arrived from the Baltic, and with his squadron the Russian naval forces reached their maximum strength of ten vessels of the line, three frigates, six corvettes, and seven brigs; the land forces were composed of thirteen thousand men plus the so-called Albanian Legion in Russian pay. A further twelve thousand Montenegrins joined the Russians at Cattaro. When the Austrians under the Treaty of Pressburg ceded Dalmatia to France and the French General Molitor proceeded to occupy the territory, the population of the Bocca di Cattaro, mostly Orthodox and Slav, showed signs of utmost unrest, and sent an invitation to Admiral Seniavin to come and protect them against the French. Simultaneously the *Vladika* of Montenegro held a great assembly at Risano on February 26, where, with the aid of the Russians, he pledged himself to fight the French. Two days later an advance squadron of the Russian fleet sailed into the bay of Porto Roso, capturing a French vessel. On March 5 the main squadron appeared, and at the same time Montenegrin forces crossed the border and occupied the various cities in the region which was not garrisoned by Austrians. Summoning the Austrian Commissioner Ghislieri, Admiral Seniavin gave him a virtual ultimatum to evacuate immediately the fortress of Castelnuovo, which commanded the entrance to the Bay of Cattaro.

Ghislieri complied, and the Austrian garrison, 2,500 strong, was transported by the Russians to Trieste. The way was now open for the occupation of Cattaro itself, and indeed the next day after the capitulation of Castelnuovo, the *Vladika* of Montenegro celebrated a solemn mass, following which he addressed the Bocchese and said: "The very powerful ruler of the Russians has admitted you amongst his children. God be praised." And while the people were giving their oath to Russia, the Russian flag was hoisted over the forts with a salute of 101 guns, after which the *Vladika* returned to Montenegro, leaving the Russians in sole possession of the region. Seniavin made Cattaro his base, occupied the forts with strong detachments of infantry, and immediately proceeded to expand his conquest so as to forestall the advance of the French. Indeed, on March 30 a Russian vessel appeared before the island of Lissa and captured it. The Russians appeared next before Curzola, where the small French garrison surrendered. But at the island of Lesina the French made a determined stand, forcing the Russians to retire. Curzola commanded the entrance into Ragusa; hence the Senate of the republic was compelled to renew negotiations with Seniavin. But fearing the French more than the Russians, the Ragusans, at the news that a powerful French force under General Lauriston was marching into Dalmatia, showed the utmost servility to the conquerors, and promised all possible aid in providing transportation for the French. Thereupon Seniavin informed the Senate that should any aid be given to the French, he would occupy Ragusa-Vecchia. Terrified, the Senate sent a special courier to Emperor Alexander I,—its "well-beloved protector." Seniavin, on March 4, dictated his conditions to the Senate in an ultimatum bearing a forty-eight-hour time limit: viz., absolute neutrality of Ragusa, all supplies prepared for the French to be transported south of Ragusa, and Ragusa to give all information available on movements of French armies. The Senate meekly complied, trying to gain time. Under these circumstances Seniavin was averse to occupying Ragusa, an independent state which had regular diplomatic relations with Russia. The result was that Seniavin lost valuable time cruising off the coast of Ragusa, and finally on May 18 he headed for Trieste in the hope of capturing some French vessels, leaving only a few vessels near Ragusa for observation purposes. In the meanwhile the French offensive under General Lauriston got under way, and on May 26 Lauriston reached Ragusa, by forced marches. More determined, the French general summoned the city to surrender, and once more the Senate complied. Thus the French entered the city and ordered the Russian consul-general to leave within forty-eight hours. But, as might have been expected, the Russians, outwitted, counterattacked. Lauriston's plan had been to proceed further and to reconquer Cattaro. Instead, he faced a siege of twenty days by a combined force of some three thousand Russians and several thousand Montenegrin auxiliaries. The French, variously estimated at two thousand,[17] four thousand,[18] or seven thousand,[19] were now put on the defensive.

The siege progressed rapidly. The Russians and Montenegrins bombarded Ragusa, burned some of its suburbs, and in a series of bloody engagements brought Lauriston to the point of capitulation. When negotiations had already started, the tables were turned suddenly by the appearance of French reinforcements. General Molitor, by an audacious march over the mountains, made his way into the rear of the Russian lines and forced them to withdraw. The Russians and their allies fell back to hold Ragusa-Vecchia, and, as peace negotiations had in the meanwhile started, a lull in the war ensued. Ragusa had remained in French hands. But since Seniavin had virtually complete control of the Adriatic, the city was isolated by sea, and only occasional French supply ships succeeded in reaching it by running the Russian blockade. The hostilities flared up anew in September, 1806, after peace negotiations had failed. Indeed, on August 3 the treaty of peace negotiated by D'Oubril had been signed in Paris, whereby Russia was pledged to evacuate Cattaro; but Seniavin, upon receipt of this news, merely played for time, and in September he was informed that, the Czar having refused to ratify the treaty, hostilities were to be resumed. Fearing a new siege of Ragusa, Marmont now took the offensive, since his intelligence service informed him of the arrival of a new Russian regiment from Corfu. The result of this offensive was the bloody but indecisive engagement at Castelnuovo which cost the Russian forces some 350 dead and 600 wounded; after this Marmont locked himself up once more in Ragusa. Seniavin on his side attacked and reoccupied Curzola, before winter put an end to the fighting. But Seniavin's position was suddenly made dangerous by Turkey's declaring war on Russia at the instigation of Napoleon (December 30, 1806) and by negotiations which were proceeding between the French

[17] Lauriston's report; see Chanoine Paul Pisani, *La Dalmatie de 1797 à 1815, épisode des conquêtes napoléoniennes* (Paris, 1893), p. 173 n.

[18] Marmont's figure (Pisani, *op. cit.*, p. 173 n.).

[19] Milakovich, a Montenegrin historian (Pisani, *op. cit.*, p. 173 n.).

command and the Turks for joint action against the Russians. Moreover, French officers were sent to fortify the Dardanelles, and the Turkish Pashas of Bosnia and Jannina—immediate neighbors of Dalmatia—were establishing friendly relations with Marmont. Seniavin therefore was ordered to proceed into the Greek Archipelago to attack the Turks as soon as his forces had been strengthened by the arrival of a new squadron from the Baltic.

Accordingly, Seniavin sailed into the Greek Archipelago with a squadron of eight vessels carrying three battalions of infantry. His appearance in Greek waters stirred the population of Morea to revolt. Seniavin declared the Greek islands under Russian protectorate and landed a Russian garrison on the island of Tenedos. The Turkish Fleet put out to sea but was chased back to the entrance of the Dardanelles. On June 10 a Turkish fleet composed of ten ships of the line, nine frigates, and one brig made a second appearance, cornering Seniavin in becalmed waters near the island of Samothrace, after which the Turks landed forces on the island of Tenedos. But nine days later Seniavin inflicted a crushing defeat on the Turkish Fleet at Mount Athos, capturing the Admiral's flagship and sinking a number of other vessels. This victory having relieved the besieged Russian garrison at Tenedos, Seniavin now joined forces with the British Admiral Duckworth for a thrust at the Dardanelles, but the end of the hostilities with Turkey caused him to return to the Adriatic.

Here he once more proceeded to the conquest of the islands north of Ragusa. He captured Brazza and Solta but failed before Lesina, where an attempted landing was foiled by French artillery. At the same time Russian agents organized an insurrection of the Slav population on the mainland, and Russian forces were landed in the neighborhood of Makarska in support of the insurgents. Thus half of the Dalmatian territory northwest of Ragusa was lost to the French, and their isolated detachments scattered through territories held by rebels were in a critical position when on July 29 came the news of the signing of the Treaty of Tilsit, which will be discussed subsequently. The Russians, under this treaty, found themselves the unexpected allies of the French, and proceeded to transfer to them the territory they held in Dalmatia, as well as the Ionian Islands. Prince Bariatinsky embarked a force of 4,740 men on six transports and, escorted by six vessels of the line and three brigs, headed for Trieste, where the infantry and artillery disembarked to make their way home overland through Austria, while the vessels were turned over to the French. But the lengthy and continuous service they had seen in the Adriatic without repairs had made them unseaworthy, and the French had to scrap them. The remaining squadron under Seniavin set sail for the Baltic through Gibraltar, the Dardanelles being closed by the Turks. But Seniavin's troubles were just starting.

The international situation of Russia had changed so rapidly that, by the time Seniavin reached the coast of Portugal, Russia was at war with her former ally, England. This put Seniavin's squadron in a critical position. Badly battered by a gale, he put in to Lisbon for repairs and there learned the unwelcome news. Just as his ships were lying disabled in dock, a British squadron sailed into Lisbon to convoy the Portuguese royal family on their journey to Brazil, and Seniavin found himself trapped. One Russian frigate which had remained in the Mediterranean was pursued by the British and escaped only by putting into Palermo and there, with permission of the Court of Naples, raising the Neapolitan flag. Another ship was captured by the British in Portsmouth, where the declaration of war found it. In August, 1808, Seniavin, still blocked in Portugal, finally negotiated a capitulation for his squadron, on condition that the ship should be returned to the Russian Government upon conclusion of peace, that his crews should be permitted to return to Russia at the expense of the British, and that military honors should be accorded them when they abandoned their ships. Accordingly the crews reached Russia in September, 1809, and finally in 1813 the British Government returned two vessels to the Russian Government. Thus ended the second and last venture of Russia to dominate the Eastern Mediterranean.

The failure of this venture was due not to the events which took place in the Adriatic but to the fact that, though this sea was important to Russia, it nevertheless remained of subordinate value on the chessboard of Russia's struggle against French imperialism. Thus, paradoxically, it is in the war which flared up between Prussia and France, and in which Russia became involved only after the collapse of Prussia, that the reason must be sought for the abandonment of Russia's hold both on Corfu and on the Dalmatian coast. Of what import for Russia were these now remote outposts when, in that fateful month of October, 1806, the Prussian army was destroyed at Jena, Berlin captured by the French, and the Prussian royal family forced to seek the safety of Königsberg, so close to the Russian border? Furthermore, with Napoleon following up his triumph in Prussia by an invasion of Poland, Russia became actively involved, single-handed, in the struggle; and her ultimate defeat resulted in the unavoidable about-face of the alliance of Tilsit—an alliance which produced as a corollary the war with England. Thus it was on the battlefields of East Prussia and Poland that the fate of Corfu and Cattaro was sealed. Before turning to the study of these major events on the Continent it is necessary to realize the close linkage existing among the various segments of the broad pattern of Russia's action, scattered over the map of Europe from the Baltic to the tip of Italy and the coast of Greece. Indeed, in Napoleon's mind they were all integrated in one vast scheme, and it is impossible to disentangle the web of subsequent events without having a view of the whole.

III

As the Grand Army was marching into Poland, after crushing Prussia, Napoleon envisaged a grandiose plan of attack on Russia with a double spearhead composed of Poland and Turkey. Hence he turned to defeated Prussia and Austria to join him in the great alliance. To Friedrich Wilhelm III he held out as bait the return of those of his possessions occupied by the French armies, on the sole condition that the King should become a party to the guarantee of the integrity of Turkey against Russia. But, smarting under the memory of Jena, Friedrich Wilhelm refused and remained faithful to Russia. In Vienna, where both the renascence of Poland and the fate of Turkey were major concerns, Talleyrand proposed joint action in the Near East (December 9, 1806) and tried to offset the French policy of re-creating Poland by stressing the menace of Russia in the Danubian principalities and in the Adriatic. Furthermore, in return for the cession of Galicia to Poland, Austria was offered Prussian Silesia. But Austria, unprepared for a struggle, was not desirous of abandoning a prudent neutrality, and General Andreossy's mission to Vienna resulted only in vague and noncommittal assurances of friendship.

Thus Napoleon had failed to line up the two Central European powers which would have strengthened the middle portion of the unbroken front designed to threaten Russia from sea to sea. But through Saxony and the States of the Confederation of the Rhine he still had control of the wide corridor which connected France and Poland through Central Europe, and through Italy and Dalmatia he had direct access to Turkey; hence he resolved to make the best of these advantages. Prussian Poland was in rebellion at the approach of the French, and Napoleon promised the Poles independence on condition that they arm and fight for him. Equally successful was his diplomatic action in Turkey. In November, 1806, General Sebastiani was appointed French ambassador to Constantinople with the task of bringing Turkey to declare war on Russia, which resulted in the naval operations against Seniavin already discussed. Encouraged by the support given him by Napoleon, Sultan Selim closed the Straits and deposed the reigning Hospodars of Moldavia and Wallachia, thereby flaunting Russian treaty rights. Supported by England, the Russian Ambassador Italinsky threatened the immediate rupture of diplomatic relations, while Russian forces were ordered to occupy the Principalities. Terrified, the Turkish Divan revoked the firman deposing the Hospodars, but the advance of Napoleon into Poland gave the Sultan and his government new courage, and war was declared, while an embassy was sent to conclude a formal military alliance with France.

Napoleon's plan now was for a direct attack through Poland with the support of such Polish forces as he would be able to muster, while the Turks would march up the Danube and the Dniester, backed by thirty-five thousand French who would follow up from Dalmatia. Furthermore, Polish and French agents were to raise a rebellion in the Russian provinces of Volhynia and Podolia. The guerilla bands formed there would serve as liaison between the two invading forces, from the north and the south; and lastly the Turkish fleet was to attack the Russian coast of the Black Sea. For purposes of co-ordination headquarters were established at Viddin, whence the French could keep in touch not only with Constantinople but with the semi-independent Turkish pashas in Bulgaria, Serbia, and Albania. As usual, Napoleon overreached himself, and the subsequent reality fell far short of these grandiose schemes.

The Russians countered with an attempt to win Austria to their side. Pozzo di Borgo was sent on a special secret mission to Vienna to strengthen the position of the Russian ambassador, Count Razumovsky, who was working feverishly to persuade Austria to come into the war on Russia's side. Pozzo arrived on December 13, a few days after Andreossy, bringing with him personal letters from the Czar to Emperor Francis and Archduke Charles. But the Emperor frankly told the Russian envoy, "I will fight as late as possible," and the sole result of the mission was to ascertain that Austrian sympathies were with Russia and not with France, but that the Court of Vienna would not for the present be drawn into any active participation in the struggle.[20] The reason for this was not only Austria's lack of preparedness, but a factor which became apparent in Pozzo's interviews with Count Stadion, when the latter raised with considerable bitterness the question of the Russian occupation of the Danubian Principalities. Thus the Balkans, then as later, were to become the stumbling block in all attempts to build a solid friendship between Austria and Russia. The failure of Pozzo di Borgo's mission threw Russia back on her two former allies, England and Prussia. Alexander was beginning to distrust England, and Prussia, prostrate, was more of a liability than an asset.

Meanwhile the Russian armies, holding a line roughly behind Warsaw, had in December established contact with the French; and the whole intricate game of alliances depended upon the outcome of the hostilities. As Pozzo reported to the Czar, the military results would be the "thermometer of the courage" of the Austrians, who would join in if the Russians could show that Napoleon could be defeated.

IV

After the crushing defeat sustained by the Prussian army at Jena on October 14, 1806, Prince Hohenlohe with the remnants of the Prussian Army, leaving a garrison at Madgeburg, fell back to Stettin to cover himself by the line of the Oder, and there to reorganize his forces and await the coming of the Russians. But the French, overtaking the Prussians, captured Stettin and Madgeburg and forced Hohenlohe to capitulate at Prenzlow. The whole Prus-

[20] Albert Vandal, *Napoléon et Alexandre Ier. L'alliance russe sous le premier empire* (Paris, 1891-1896), I, 19.

sian Army was thereby destroyed except a force of fifteen thousand men under General Lestocq, left to defend the bridgehead at Thorn, and another five thousand men garrisoned at Warsaw. Except for these detachments Russia had to face Napoleon alone. On November 1 the Russian Army crossed the Niemen at Grodno and occupied Warsaw and Plock, but with the approach of Napoleon it fell back behind the Narev. The original plan of the Russians was to march through Poland into Silesia to effect a junction with the Prussians, but the rapid collapse of Prussia reversed the picture and resulted in a French invasion of Poland. Napoleon was anxious to advance on Warsaw as fast as possible to defeat the Russians and obtain a peace, and thus cancel all possibility of Prussia's reconstituting her power. Should this plan fail, he was determined to force the Russians out of Poland so that Russia would lose contact with Prussia. Finally, he was hoping to obtain from the Poles, who were to take up arms upon his arrival, an auxiliary force of at least 40,000. He ordered the corps of Davout, Lannes, and Augereau, as well as his cavalry, to march on Warsaw under the general command of Murat. The corps of Ney and Bernadotte advanced toward Thorn, and Soult linked up with Murat by advancing from Thorn to Warsaw. Thus the French Army was stretched along the Vistula from Thorn to Warsaw, and had some 150,000 men in the front line. Another 150,000 were in reserve, scattered over Germany east of the Rhine, and in France and generally west of the Rhine there were some 350,000 more. The grand total of all forces available represented 580,000 French and 70,000 Germans of the Confederation of the Rhine. Opposing these forces on the Russian side were the First Army under Bennigsen, 60,000 men, and the Second Army under Buxhoevden, 50,000 men, which was coming up from Lithuania, plus 20,000 Prussians.[21] In addition two divisions under General Essen, detached from the army operating in Moldavia, made their way up the Dniester and reached Poland in January, 1807. The supreme command of the Russian Army was given to the seventy-five-year-old Field Marshal Kamensky, a former lieutenant of Suvorov, "of whom he had the hardness without having his other characteristics."[22] Kutuzov, nursing a wound he received

[21] Eight Russian divisions of the first line as against fifteen French divisions.
[22] Bourdeau, *op. cit.,* II, 166.

at Austerlitz, and in disgrace since that battle, had a rear command as Governor of Kiev.

On November 28, Murat entered Warsaw without resistance; at the same time Bennigsen retreated due north along the Narev and established his headquarters at Pultusk. Four days earlier, on the twenty-fourth, Napoleon himself left Berlin and proceeded to Warsaw, which he made the center of his operations. A lull of nearly a month followed, while the French were bringing up their forces and building bridges and Bennigsen was awaiting the coming of Buxhoevden, who was following the course of the Narev and the Bug. Having retreated north, Bennigsen was in a position to keep in touch with the Prussians and to cover Königsberg. "One can expect," wrote Napoleon on December 13, "that the plan of the enemy is to form a line with his left wing based on Pultusk and the Bug, the Narev and the little stream of Orzyca, extending so as to touch hands with the Prussians who are strung out along the little stream of Passarge, with their right wing extending to the sea."[23] Accordingly Napoleon decided to take the offensive and to attack Bennigsen on either December 21 or 22.

His plan was simple. The corps camped around Thorn were to advance due east toward Biezun on the Ukra, approximately halfway between Thorn and Pultusk, so as to draw Bennigsen in that direction. In the meanwhile Napoleon, with the eighty thousand men concentrated under Murat, was to march north, attacking Pultusk from the south and cutting Bennigsen off from the crossing on the Narev. Thus Bennigsen was to find himself trapped between these two attacks and separated from the Prussians. However, in the meanwhile, Buxhoevden's Second Army having effected its junction with Bennigsen's, Field Marshal Kamensky in turn ordered an offensive to start on the twenty-second. Bennigsen advanced two divisions toward the Ukra, meeting the French corps from Thorn coming in the opposite direction. Thus both armies were set in motion at the same time, and the next day they came into contact. Davout attacked Czarnovo, occupied by a Russian division, and the battle raged for nearly twelve hours. The French lost 800 men; and the Russians, who counterattacked twice, 1,300 men. Finally Davout gained the passage of the Ukra, though "the stubbornness of this

[23] Camon, *op. cit.*, II, 195.

first encounter forecast for the future a resistance to which our troops were not accustomed."[24] Bennigsen fell back once more to Pultusk, concentrating his scattered divisions, while the advance guards of Buxhoevden's army (Dokhturov) reached Golymin.

It is at these points that parallel battles were fought on December 26. At Golymin, Dokhturov with sixteen thousand men had to face an attack of the combined forces of Davout, Augereau, and Murat, more than double his effectives. Furthermore, Davout had advanced so rapidly that he had caught the Russian columns still converging toward Golymin. The battle, which started at 3:30 P.M., was fought with the utmost fierceness until ten in the evening. A great cavalry charge launched by Murat nearly finished in disaster when one of his brigades (Lasalle) broke and fled in panic. But Davout's superiority in numbers was such that finally, after one more repulsed attack, Golymin was captured and Dokhturov was forced to retreat, losing a thousand men and ten cannon. The French losses (according to French sources) amounted to six hundred men. In the meanwhile, Napoleon directed Lannes to capture Pultusk, but there he clashed with Bennigsen's main corps. "Since I have fought wars, I have never seen such a fierce battle," said Lannes.[25] Indeed, all his attempts to break into the city failed, and his left wing was nearly crushed by Russian counterattacks. Only the timely arrival of a division of Davout's corps saved him from complete disaster. After fighting the whole day he was forced to abandon his attack and to fall back to his initial positions. During the night, however, Bennigsen ordered the abandonment of Pultusk, and Lannes could claim a technical victory. The losses on both sides were very great and, according to French sources, amounted to 3,000 for the Russians, and for the French, 1,200. The battle of Pultusk produced a wide sensation in Europe and accounted for the hardening of the Austrian attitude toward Napoleon. Joseph de Maistre wrote gleefully that it was the first setback in Napoleon's career since St. Jean d'Acre. Napoleon had deliberately repeated the maneuver of Jena in the hope of destroying the Russian Army in the same way he had destroyed the Prussian Army. But just as he had failed at Ulm when he tried to apply the maneuver to Kutuzov, an attempt

[24] Bourdeau, *op. cit.*, II, 172.
[25] *Ibid.*, II, 177.

which had resulted in the capture of Mack, so here his sanguine hopes, as announced in his correspondence, merely resulted in pushing the Russians farther north up the Narev. "We had changed enemies," observed Chateaubriand; and Bourdeau wrote:

> As for the Russian army, it was not commanded. Marshal Kamensky did himself justice by vanishing. The cold and indomitable courage of the Russian soldier alone offered us a fierce resistance: Frederick the Great has already said of the Russian soldier, that after killing him it is still necessary to push him to make him fall to the ground.[26]

Like the rounds of a prize fight, this war was interspersed with lulls separating one bout of the fighting from another. After Pultusk a lull of a month occurred, during which Bennigsen, having replaced Kamensky in command, moved his headquarters to Ostrolenka. On January 25 Bennigsen, suddenly taking the offensive, fell upon the encampments of the French First Corps (Bernadotte). At this news Napoleon set his army in motion, and the second maneuver of the war, culminating in the Battle of Eylau, took place. The position of the armies before this second resumption of hostilities was as follows. The bulk of Bennigsen's and Buxhoevden's forces had moved north of Ostrolenka and was concentrated around Biala, covered from the west by the Mazurian Lakes, whereas Essen's reserve corps was still at Brest-Litovsk. The Prussian corps of Lestocq was covering Königsberg, where the Prussian royal family had taken refuge. On the French side the bulk of Napoleon's forces was concentrated around Pultusk, with the cavalry at Ostrolenka. The rest was stretched out in a line reaching all the way to the seacoast. Covering the siege of Danzig conducted by Marshal Lefebvre, and farthest to the north, was Bernadotte's corps in the region of Osterrode—Marienwerder, watching the Prussians at Königsberg. Farther to the south Ney in the region of Soldau-Mlava linked up with Soult at Golymin and the main army at Pultusk. Napoleon had once more 140,000 men in the first line and 100,000 men in the second line. He thus maintained his crushing numerical superiority over the Russians.

By concentrating his army around Biala, Bennigsen had the double advantage of covering his main line of communications, which

[26] *Ibid.*, II, 187.

passed through Grodno and Kovno to St. Petersburg, and at the same time remaining in a position to lend a hand to Lestocq's Prussian corps, dangerously isolated at Königsberg. However, any movement westward to aid the Prussians entailed this danger for Bennigsen: that, since Napoleon's main army was due south of him, it could by moving northward cut the Russian line of communications—a maneuver which was in fact attempted by Napoleon. It is therefore difficult to understand why Bennigsen risked such a dangerous move. The explanation is to be found in the pressing appeals for aid from the Prussian royal family. The action, strategically unsound as it was, was motivated by political considerations. Be that as it may, Bennigsen on January 10 started his march on Bishoffstein, crossing the Alle. Ney in the meanwhile, disobeying the orders of the Emperor, had pushed some seventy miles beyond the region assigned to him and thus found himself farther north and east than Bernadotte, in other words, nearer to Königsberg. It was this thrust of Ney's which brought the request of the Prussians for aid and the consequent advance of Bennigsen. On the eighteenth the Russian cavalry first clashed with Ney's cavalry. On the twentieth Ney had to fall back precipitously toward Soldau, and Bernadotte, warned by Ney, did the same just in time to escape a perilous position, for on the twenty-fourth the Russian vanguard (General Markov) destroyed a French regiment of cavalry and part of the infantry of Rivaud's division. Ney had retreated so fast, however, that he left Bernadotte in an exposed position; and the next day Bennigsen, having crossed the Passarge, fell upon Bernadotte at Mohrungen. A bloody engagement ensued which forced Bernadotte to retreat south toward Osterrode. This battle induced Napoleon to raise his winter quarters prematurely. So far he had thought that the Russian offensive was merely of a local nature directed against his too extended left flank, but the full import of the Russian advance now became clear to him, and he ordered a general counteroffensive.

His plan was to march his main forces due north from Pultusk and cut the line of Russian retreat on the Alle by occupying the two crossings of the river at Allenstein and at Güttstadt. Thus the Russians would find themselves facing Bernadotte and Ney in front of them, with Napoleon himself and the bulk of his army in their rear. They would then have three alternatives left: to attempt to make their way out of the trap by returning to Allenstein or Güttstadt, to turn north toward Königsberg and lock themselves up there, or, still pursuing their westward movement, to force their way into Danzig and allow themselves to be blocked in that fortress. Once more the situation was identical with the dispositions made by Napoleon at Jena against the Prussians. However, Bennigsen again got out of the trap. In the hope of putting an end to the war with one blow, Napoleon had assembled all his corps, including the Guards brought up from Warsaw, except for the corps of Lannes (under the temporary command of Savary), which was left on the Narev to hold back Essen's corps. On February 2 Murat's cavalry in the vanguard approached Allenstein and stumbled against important Russian forces. What had happened was that Bennigsen, having got wind of Napoleon's plan through the capture of a French officer carrying instructions to Bernadotte, had been able to reassemble his scattered forces and occupy a position at Joukovo, ten miles northwest of Allenstein. Thus Napoleon, in place of the elaborate turning movement he had planned, now faced the necessity of a frontal attack, which left Bennigsen free to retreat.

Napoleon ordered an attack the next day, but it was 1:00 P.M. before the engagement started, a delay having occurred in bringing the French corps into position. By nightfall no decisive result had been obtained, except for a menace to the Russian left flank by a movement of Soult. During the night Bennigsen retreated toward Deppen, with the obvious intention of coming nearer to Königsberg and joining with the Prussian corps of Lestocq. During the subsequent days the Russian movement northward continued unhampered and the French followed closely behind, which merely resulted in a series of rear-guard engagements. One such engagement at Hoff in February was an actual battle costing each side two thousand casualties and was an entirely useless action. All attempts of Napoleon to speed up his march in order to overtake the enemy failed, and Bennigsen pursued his retreat unmolested. Thus finally he reached Eylau, some thirty miles due south of Königsberg, and the sea. Bennigsen realized here that he must now either fight a battle or lock himself up in Königsberg, for he was within marching distance of the Prussians, and to come closer to the sea and to the city would paralyze his freedom of maneuvering. Thus he decided to stop and give battle the next day, February 8.

Leaving a strong rear-guard force under Bagration to hold the city of Eylau, Bennigsen went beyond it to select an appropriate position. During the night of the eighth Soult and Augereau, supported by Murat, attacked Bagration; and the struggle developed into a hand-to-hand fight from street to street and house to house. During this engagement General Barclay de Tolly, hero of the campaign of 1812, was severely wounded. Soult finally succeeded in gaining possession of the city late at night, and by the next morning the positions of the two armies were clearly drawn. Bennigsen with seventy thousand men and four hundred cannon had disposed his forces in two parallel lines, about a mile east of the city, his lines running northwest to southeast. The French positions, somewhat more zigzagging because of the nature of the ground, spread out parallel to the Russian line and covered the city along its immediate outskirts. Just south of the city a cemetery and church offered a good point of observation from which Napoleon could direct the battle. Bennigsen worked out a plan for attempting to break the French line in two by striking at the city proper. For this purpose he was going to use his massed artillery. Napoleon had at his disposition about sixty-five thousand men and two hundred cannon. His plan was the classical one he had used many times before. Soult was to hold the enemy immobilized along the front, while Davout, with three divisions, was to march around the enemy's left flank. Napoleon thought that the Russians, frightened by the threat of Davout's attack, would weaken the section of the front nearest to Davout by taking troops from the trenches to stem Davout's attack. Augereau, supported by the Guards and Murat, was then to attack frontally at the weakened spot and break through the Russian front. Ney was to support Soult in immobilizing the rest of the enemy line.

Thus the main action was to develop southeast of the city of Eylau, and Napoleon from his point of observation was in a position to control it directly. The Russian front was about four miles in length and the French was two miles longer, owing to the thinning out of the sector held by Soult. The battle opened at 7:00 A.M. with a violent artillery duel which lasted two hours; then one

Russian division (Tuchkov) attacked a division of Soult's corps (Leval) immediately north of Eylau. This attack remained isolated and was not supported, both sides soon concentrating on the sector south of the city where Davout had started his flanking movement.

At 10:00 A.M. Davout's columns reached the village of Serpallen, and his vanguard division (Friant), supported by cavalry, pushed on to Klein Sausgarten. The first village was on the extreme left flank of the Russian line and the second a mile and a half farther east. From Sausgarten, by turning sharply to the left, the French would have been in a position to get behind the Russian line. General Baggovut, commanding the Russian left-wing division, saw the danger and attacked this column, but was forced to fall back to cover Sausgarten, making the Russian line curve backwards. General Ostermann, next in line, came to his support and attacked the French from the flank with eight thousand men. But Davout's other two divisions came up, forming an overwhelmingly stronger force, which could have crushed the two Russian divisions. Seeing this peril, Bennigsen threw in his main reserves to the support of his hard-pressed flank. From his point of observation Napoleon decided that the moment had now come for the frontal mass attack. Accordingly Augereau, with three divisions supported by cavalry, hurled himself against the one Russian division (Sacken) which was holding the line immediately to Ostermann's right. But a heavy snowfall made visibility poor, and the French columns, deviating too much to the left, came under the direct fire of Russian batteries. As the columns stopped, a charge of Russian cavalry completed their demoralization; and, breaking, the French fell back in disorder. Augereau himself was wounded and his corps lost 50 per cent of its effectives. Now the Russians counterattacked in their turn, and, as the weather cleared, Napoleon suddenly saw masses of Russian infantry advancing toward the very cemetery where he was with his staff. A column of Russian grenadiers actually reached the entrance of the cemetery, but was met here by a battalion of the Guards and the Emperor's personal escort. This was one of the most critical moments in Napoleon's career, and he was very nearly taken prisoner. The situation was saved by Murat's cavalry, whose mass charge of eighty squadrons remains one of the greatest cavalry charges in history. The first wave of twenty-nine squadrons (of cuirassiers), clashing with the Russian cavalry, was beaten off and fell back in disorder; but the second wave reached the Russian infantry, after which the battle degenerated into a melee of men fighting hand to hand, with batteries from both sides firing indiscriminately into the mass, unable to distinguish friend from foe. Finally out of sheer exhaustion the fighting dwindled to an exchange of rifle fire and gradually died away.

In the meanwhile a heated struggle was going on around Sausgarten, which was taken by Davout's advance guard, then retaken by the Russians of Kamensky's division sent to back up Ostermann, and once more retaken by the French. The battle here swayed back and forth. It was not until late in the afternoon that Davout finally began making headway and reached Anklappen in the rear of the Russian line. But with the failure of the main attack this advance was of little avail. At that moment Lestocq's Prussian corps (7,000 men) came up, Kamensky's division once more regained the lost ground; and the battle here came to an end on the line of Sausgarten, where it had started. Thus when the fighting had ceased both armies were holding their lines. The losses had been extremely severe, about 20,000 men on each side with 7,000 to 8,000 killed. The Russians lost 16 colors, 26 cannon, and 2,000 prisoners. The French lost 5 colors, over 1,000 prisoners, 6 generals killed, 1 marshal and 14 generals wounded—a loss of high officers very difficult to replace at this distance from France. Thus the Battle of Eylau, one of the bloodiest in history, finished in a draw, both with regard to the position of the armies and their respective losses.

But Napoleon had kept one great advantage over his enemies. Whereas the Russians had used up all their forces, Essen being out of reach on the Narev, Napoleon still had two corps which had not participated in the action. Indeed, at 7:00 P.M., after the fighting had ceased, Ney came up and began threatening the Russian right flank with Bernadotte following him. Moreover, Davout remained at Sausgarten, menacingly poised on the Russian left flank. It was these considerations which induced Bennigsen to abandon the line during the night, thus permitting Napoleon to claim a technical victory. But the French were too exhausted to attempt to pursue the enemy. Not only was the loss of generals felt, but the army was demoralized, and for the first time in his career Napoleon after the battle heard not cheers but sullen recriminations. Desertions began. Therefore, while the Russians fell back behind the line of the Alle, with headquarters at Bartenstein, Napoleon fell back beyond the line of the Passarge with headquarters at Osterrode.

A lull of nearly three months occurred in which both sides, separated by two rivers, were busy reorganizing their depleted forces. The only engagement occurring during this period was an inconclusive battle between Essen and Savary at Ostrolenka, which was captured by the Russians, then retaken by the French, leaving things very much as they were before (February 16). In May Danzig fell, after a long siege, giving Napoleon an excellent base for operations on the lower Vistula. The fall of this fortress had a serious effect on the position of the Russian armies. Danzig was defended by a garrison of 18,000 men under the Prussian Marshal Kalkreuth. Of this force 4,000 were Russians. The fortress had been besieged by Marshal Lefebvre's corps since January, and gradually the French forces had been increased to 24,000 men. Attempts of the garrison to break through the besieging line on the twenty-sixth of March and again on April 27 had failed, and the French gradually completed the investment of the fortress. On May 12 a Russian division of 8,000 men under General Kamensky was sent by sea from Pillau to Weichselmunde in an effort to liberate the city. Landing at the fort of Weichselmunde, located at the very mouth of the Vistula, this detachment proceeded to attack the French positions at Nehrung. British men-of-war meanwhile were to make their way upstream to the city of Danzig itself. However, Napoleon was able to bring up formidable reinforcements—the corps of Lannes supported by the grenadiers of Oudinot, followed by Mortier's corps, which had been operating in Pomerania against the Swedes but was now freed by the armistice with Sweden. In the presence of such forces Kamensky lost 2,000 men in a futile attack on the French positions, and re-embarked at Weichselmunde. Two weeks later, on May 26, Kalkreuth capitulated.

The fall of Danzig placed Königsberg in a very precarious position, as Napoleon had now merely to advance along the seacoast to reach the city. Since Bennigsen was decidedly inferior in numbers to the French, strategically, under these circumstances; his best decision would have been to await the reserve army 30,000 strong which was coming up under the command of Prince Lobanov-Rostovsky. Also, by drawing the French away from the Vistula toward the Nieman, and at the same time weakening them by such thrusts as Pultusk and Eylau, he would eventually have seen the French frittering away their forces. But political considerations centering in Königsberg outweighed strategic caution, and with the coming of spring Bennigsen decided once more upon a dangerous offensive. Napoleon had raised his effectives considerably and had now 150,000 men in the first line and 135,000 men in the second line. Moreover, his first-line army had been strengthened by the inclusion of Mortier's corps, and the second-line army was immediately at hand in Poland, Silesia, and along the Baltic coast. Bennigsen had only 100,000 men, including the Prussians. By the very size of the respective armies, Bennigsen's offensive was an adventure, and his sole chance of success lay in crushing Ney, located somewhat in advance of the French line, and then in attempting to crush whatever other corps presented itself before it was sustained by the rest of the army. Speed therefore was essential.

Accordingly, on June 5 Bennigsen started his offensive by falling upon Ney, who had spread his corps between the upper courses of the Passarge and the Alle. But the attack, conducted with insufficient vigor, permitted Ney to escape, though with heavy losses, by falling back to Deppen on the Passarge. The next day Deppen was taken and retaken six times, but Ney eventually succeeded in crossing the river; and, with the bridges destroyed and the two armies separated by the Passarge, there occurred a delay which permitted Napoleon to organize his counteroffensive. Realizing the seriousness of the situation, Napoleon brought up the corps of Soult, Davout, Victor, and Murat, who lined themselves up on both flanks of Ney. Bennigsen, now realizing that his surprise offensive had failed, decided to fall back to the line of the Alle, where at Heilsberg he had prepared a retrenched camp, precisely for such an emergency. Napoleon came up the following day with 135,000 men. However, in view of the narrow defile of Launau, leading toward Heilsberg, he divided his army into two portions, one section 55,000 strong under Murat, Soult, and Lannes marching ahead with the task of keeping the enemy busy, until he himself with the remaining 70,00 could come up. Thus when the battle opened it was with the advance corps that the Russians had to contend. Murat, misunderstanding his orders, which were to keep the enemy immobilized, threw Soult against the Russian positions at 2:00 P.M. while Lannes was still engaged in the defile. The attack was beaten off, and by 8:00 P.M. Soult's corps had fallen back in great disorder, having lost over 6,000 men. Lannes, who by this time had reached the battlefield, came to the aid of Soult, but his attack was beaten off in turn. Napoleon, arriving at this point, ordered the battle to cease; the French had suffered a bloody reverse which cost them over 10,000 men, owing to the fact that they attacked a very strong position in successive waves. If Bennigsen had followed up his victory by a vigorous counterattack, the French reverse might have turned into a disaster, but Bennigsen was physically ill that day; besides, he knew that he would have to meet the second half of the French army, which was very nearly the size of his own army. These considerations may explain his lack of initiative and his decision not to come out of the fortified camp. They do not, however, explain his decision to abandon Heilsberg the following night without giving battle and to continue his retreat toward Königsberg, following the right bank of the Alle. The Prussians of Lestocq now fell back to cover the city itself, and Bennigsen sent Kamensky's division to strengthen Lestocq's corps. Bennigsen himself moved down the Alle, always following the right bank, via Bartenstein and Shippenbeil. But by so doing he left the French on the left bank in possession of the direct route to Königsberg. Under instructions from the Czar to protect Königsberg, for the sake of the Prussian royal family, Bennigsen therefore had to recross the Alle at some point farther down stream and turn his march northwestward, leaving the course of the Alle. Bennigsen selected Friedland as the place for his crossing and there had three bridges set up. His advance guard reached this point on the thirteenth.

Napoleon once more divided his army into two sections. Murat with sixty thousand men was sent toward Königsberg to keep Lestocq and Kamensky separated from Bennigsen, and also to watch the course of the Pregel, should the Russians follow the Alle down to its confluence with the Pregel. Napoleon, with the main body, remained at Eylau awaiting information about the moves of the enemy. Upon receiving intelligence from Lannes that the Russians were holding Friedland, he sent the corps of Oudinot and Grouchy's cavalry to the aid of Lannes, whose attempt to take the city had failed. Thus Lannes, with Oudinot's divisions and Grouchy's cavalry, was left to face the Russian army through the day of June 14. When Napoleon realized that he was dealing with an attempt of Bennigsen to cross the Alle, however, he brought the rest of his forces up and reached Friedland by that afternoon. By this time Bennigsen had thrown most of his forces across the river and had been sustaining a sharp vanguard engagement with Lannes's corps. It was 5:00 P.M. by the time the last units of the Grand Army came up. Because of the late hour Napoleon was advised by his marshals to postpone the battle until the next day. "One does not twice catch an adversary committing such an error," was the reply, and he ordered an immediate attack. Indeed Bennigsen's position was more than precarious—his army's back was to a river, with some of its units still on the other side. Accordingly, he hesitated between accepting the battle and recrossing the river. In this case he would have been better inspired to follow the latter course. With the exception of the preliminary engagements against Lannes, the Battle of Friedland began at the late hour of 5:00 P.M., with a cannon shot followed by three rifle salvos, which was the signal given the French troops for a general attack. It was one of the shortest battles in history, for it lasted only three hours and resulted in a complete defeat of the Russians.

The Alle at Friedland makes a sharp bend, and the city itself is nestled in the curve of the bend on the left bank of the river. South of it the forest of Sortlack, and north of it the forest of Damereau, formed the limits of the battlefield. The road from Friedland to Königsberg, leading northwest, cuts the battlefield in two, passing, a few miles out of Friedland, through the village of Heinrichsdorff and along a forest of the same name. According to his custom, Bennigsen disposed his forces in an arch from Damereau around Friedland toward Sortlack: the main body under Gorchakov, astride the Königsberg road, with Ouvarov's cavalry on the extreme right flank toward Damereau, and the left flank under Bagration from Friedland to the forest of Sortlack. His reserves were unfortunately concentrated on the other side of the river. During the preliminary stage the struggle centered around Heinrichsdorff, which, after changing hands several times, remained in possession of the French by the time Napoleon had come up. The general attack which the French opened at 5:00 P.M. was directed concentrically toward Friedland—the corps of Ney, Victor, Lannes, and the Guards against Bagration, weaker in numbers; and the corps of Mortier and Grouchy against Gorchakov. The plan of Napoleon was to crush Bagration with forces four times superior in numbers, whereas Mortier and Grouchy were to hold Gorchakov immobile and if possible to draw him toward Heinrichsdorff, so as to detach him from Bagration. The semicircular Russian line made it impossible for Gorchakov to support Bagration without exposing his own line of retreat. As the main French attack developed, Bennigsen threw in the Russian Guards to the support of Bagration. The latter counterattacked Ney, whose corps broke and retreated in disorder, but Victor's corps and the divisions of Dupont and Latour-Maubourg came to the rescue of Ney and overwhelmed the Russians. The latter fell back to Friedland but could not hold it. The city was captured by the French by 7:00 P.M., and the French artillery succeeded, by destroying the bridges which connected the city with the right bank of the river, in cutting off the Russian retreat. Bagration's corps was trapped, and only a portion of it succeeded in getting across the river.

As for Gorchakov, he was attacking the French at Heinrichsdorff when the news of the fall of Friedland reached him. Napoleon was now free to throw his whole army against Gorchakov, who found himself pressed frontally by Lannes, Mortier, Grouchy, and the Guards, whereas Victor and Ney encircled him on the flank and in the rear. In despair the Russian infantry then formed squares and put up a stiff resistance, permitting a part of the artillery to get away. But once more Napoleon was able to concentrate such overwhelming forces that the infantry eventually broke and made a desperate attempt to cross the Alle. Some succeeded in getting across; others drowned in the river or were taken prisoner. The cavalry on the extreme left flank made its way up the left bank of the Alle and reached Allenburg. The firing ceased at 10:00 P.M., and the day had cost the Russians 10,000 killed, 15,000 wounded, and 80 cannon, whereas the French lost around 10,000 men. This battle put an end to the campaign.

Rallying the remainder of his forces, Bennigsen marched along the right bank of the Alle to its confluence with the Pregel and from there gained Tilsit, where negotiations for an armistice were opened. It must be said that Bennigsen showed very poor generalship in this battle. He lacked energy in attacking Lannes while the latter was weak, and he accepted battle in a position with his back to the river and with forests obscuring the vision of his troops and permitting easy concentration of the enemy. Moreover, he strung out his forces in such a way as to allow Napoleon to concentrate the bulk of his forces first against Bagration, who was isolated, and later against Gorchakov. But summing up the campaign as a whole, we may say that Bennigsen showed skill in his retreats and his thrusts at the enemy, which were so costly for the French. In the words of Bourdeau:

> Napoleon took a few weeks to defeat the King of Prussia and to conquer his kingdom. He required eight months to beat the Russians without even encroaching upon their immense territory, and this he achieved only at the cost of incredible hardships and privations for the Grand Army. The campaign of Poland was for Napoleon a warning and a lesson: with highly trained, well-commanded troops, fired by the enthusiasm of unprecedented victories, with an army often superior in numbers to the enemy army, the Emperor had to make the greatest efforts to overcome his enemy.[27]

As one of the reasons for this, the French writer gives the severity of the winter climate. It is true that the Russians were better prepared to withstand the rigors of the northern winters, but nevertheless this factor brought hardships on both armies equally. A second reason was "the unforeseen resistance of the Russian soldier who lets himself be killed without retreating. . . . Already Masséna's troops had met the heroism of Suvorov's soldiers in the mountains of Switzerland during the winter of 1799, but the lesson was forgotten and Napoleon had committed a grave error in disdaining such adversaries."[28]

Casting a retrospective glance on both campaigns, that of Auster-

[27] *Ibid.*, II, 240.
[28] *Ibid.*, II, 241.

litz and that of Poland, we may make several deductions. First, with the exception of the Battle of Austerlitz, every time Napoleon had a clear-cut victory he always was greatly superior in numbers to the Russians; whenever the numbers were about equal on both sides, as at Eylau, there was a draw; and when the French were inferior in numbers, as at Mohrungen, at Pultusk, and at Heilsburg, there was a Russian victory. However, the Russian command lacked the energy to follow up such victories, and used the obstinately contested strategic retreat in both campaigns; this strategy was made necessary precisely by the inferiority of numbers, as the two abortive advances of Bennigsen and the first march of Kutuzov toward Ulm proved. This inferiority in numbers was due to the fact that all the plans of joint action with the allies were vitiated by the defeat of the allies before the Russians came up—the defeat of the Austrians at Ulm and of the Prussians during the campaign of Jena. Thus Kutuzov had to face Napoleon alone, with merely an auxiliary force of fifteen thousand Austrians at Austerlitz; and similarly Bennigsen could count only on Lestocq's corps of twenty thousand men (but in actual fact much reduced in numbers because of the dispersal of the Prussians). Thus the actual contribution of the allies to the struggle was very small, and in the case of Bennigsen the ally who should have helped actually became a liability, for the need to go to the aid of the Prussian royal family forced upon him the strategically unsound maneuver of covering Königsberg, which led to his final defeat.

All these military considerations have to be taken into account to understand the remarkable parallel evolution of Napoleon's and Alexander's thought, which made possible their coming together at Tilsit, to open a new chapter in their relations.

We have now to examine the story of the diplomatic activities on both sides, after the Battle of Eylau had formed the initial point of this psychological evolution.

Chapter VI

The Peace of Tilsit to the War of 1812

I

The importance of the battle of Eylau must not be judged by the military factor alone, for it was responsible for a momentous change in the psychology of both Napoleon and Alexander which foreshadowed the alliance of Tilsit. Indeed, the setback to Napoleon's prestige produced by this battle was sufficient to force him to abandon all hopes of bringing Austria into the conflict on his side. Thus he turned to Prussia, six days after the battle, offering to return the occupied territory to King Friedrich Wilhelm, provided the latter abandoned his alliance with Russia and changed over to the side of France; but his proposal met with no success. Thus all hopes of obtaining allies in an increasingly difficult campaign were nullified by the semireverse of Eylau. Under these circumstances his attitude toward Russia changed. As Vandal writes:

> The Russian Army killed off several thousand of his soldiers and some of his best officers . . . does he aspire to vengeance and the redoubling of military ardor against the nation which caused these misfortunes? No, he admires it. He now appreciates Russia at her true value, and thinks that if he could rally this power [Russia] to his side, she would be able to help him better than any other to control Europe and to raise it against England.[1]

And as early as March 14 Napoleon wrote to Talleyrand: "I am of the opinion that an alliance with Russia would be very advantageous, if the idea were not fantastic."[2] He ordered negotiations to be started with Bennigsen, who, however, cut them short by replying that his task was to fight and not to negotiate. At the same time Napoleon turned once more to Austria in a last endeavor to win her over. But Alexander had already approached Austria,

[1] Vandal, *op. cit.*, I, 33.

[2] *Ibid.*, I, 36.

and his emissary Pozzo di Borgo had a talk with Count Stadion on May 13 in which he told the Austrian statesman plainly that if Austria persisted in remaining neutral, Russia would see no reason to fight alone in a common cause, and therefore would consider negotiating peace if the terms offered by Bonaparte should be sufficiently favorable to Russia.

Thus approached by both sides, Austria had a difficult decision to make, and replied by offering her mediation to both parties. Alexander, however, was loath to give in without one more try to bolster up a really effective coalition against Napoleon. On April 26, after an interview with the King and Queen of Prussia at Bartenstein, he signed a new convention between Russia and Prussia in which both countries pledged not to sign peace independently of each other. Russia furthermore renounced all territorial acquisitions and promised Prussia the restitution of her lost provinces. She also acknowledged the principle of the integrity of the Ottoman Empire and set as ultimate goal in the war the dissolution of the Confederation of the Rhine. A new form of Germanic confederation was to be constituted under the domination of Prussia and Austria. The status of Italy would also be altered under the guidance of Britain and Austria, and the latter was to recover territories up to the line of the river Mincio. These terms were to be submitted to Sweden, Great Britain, and Austria, with the purpose of obtaining from these countries an effective support in men and money. The results, however, were not encouraging. Austria hesitated, and Emperor Francis sent General Stullerheim to the Russian General Headquarters for further negotiations. England and Sweden remained cold to the Russian suggestions. Furthermore, signs of suspicion of Russia's policy showed by England irritated Alexander profoundly. The narrow egotism of these countries, which wanted Russia to do a work that concerned the whole of Europe, produced the inevitable impression upon the idealistic Czar that he ought to concern himself with Russia's interests alone and not worry about the rest of Europe. Thus an evolution parallel to the one taking place in Napoleon's mind began developing in Alexander's as well.

In the meantime the battle of Friedland was fought, and led both rulers to start negotiations for peace and to seek each other's friendship. Indeed, prior to this Napoleon had felt that in view of the mediocre results of the preceding campaign he could not embark upon a course to end the war without a serious loss of prestige until he had gained at least one signal victory. At the same time this battle left Alexander with no alternative but to start negotiations for a truce, for he needed time to reorganize his forces. Thus the climax had been reached, and the way was now open to both sides for negotiations which were going to be extremely important in their ultimate results.

II

The day after the battle of Friedland, on June 15, 1807, Bennigsen wrote a letter to Czar Alexander, accompanied by another one to Grand Duke Constantine, asking that steps be taken to stop any further hostilities. Accordingly General Prince Lobanov-Rostovsky, who had been in command of the Russian reserve army, was ordered to proceed to Tilsit; and at the sight of his white flag firing stopped on both sides. On June 19 Lobanov had an interview with Marshal Berthier, the Prince of Neufchâtel, and the next day with Napoleon's Grand Marshal, Duroc. Alexander having agreed to sign a separate armistice and to start negotiations for peace without the concurrence of Prussia, Napoleon on June 22 invited Lobanov to dinner and made his historic remark that the Vistula ought to be the frontier of Russia and the dividing line of their respective spheres of influence—thus lightly hinting at the division of the old world between the two empires. Two days later Lobanov returned with written instructions in which the Czar unexpectedly declared that only an alliance between France and Russia would guarantee the happiness and peace of the world, and that a new political system had to be established. He added that he believed that he could easily come to an understanding with Napoleon, "provided we negotiate without intermediaries."[3] Napoleon immediately suggested a personal meeting with the Czar for the following day, June 25, at 1:00 P.M. For this occasion a raft was hastily constructed by French engineers in the exact middle of the river Nieman, the dividing line between the two armies. Thus the delicate question of who would be visiting whom was settled by having the meeting take place on neutral territory. At precisely the same moment boats carrying both Emperors

[3] *Ibid.*, I, 53.

left the opposite banks, while the troops lined up on each side cheered and the Russian and French artillery fired the imperial salute. Napoleon ordered his men to row faster and thus was able to arrive a few minutes earlier and play host to the Russian Emperor. Alexander charmed Napoleon by his graceful and friendly simplicity, and it is said that his first words were "Sire, I hate the British as much as you do." "In that case," replied Napoleon, "peace is made."[4]

The fate of Prussia, however, remained an issue of prime importance to Russia, the more so that Alexander had violated the convention of Bartenstein by opening negotiations with Napoleon. Hence, knowing that Napoleon demanded the complete evacuation of Silesia and Pomerania and the surrender of the remaining Prussian garrisons, Alexander requested Napoleon to spare Prussia any unnecessary humiliation and to sign an armistice with her at the same time. Napoleon suggested that both Alexander and Friedrich Wilhelm should be his guests at Tilsit, and Alexander accepted the invitation. Writing to Josephine on the same evening, Napoleon said, "I have just seen the Emperor Alexander and have been very pleased with him. He is a handsome, good young Emperor, and is more intelligent than is commonly believed."[5]

The second meeting on the raft occurred on June 26, this time in the presence of the King of Prussia. This interview was cold and strained because of the reserved and constrained attitude of Friedrich Wilhelm. During the interview Napoleon invited Alexander to dinner the same evening, in the presence of the King, who was not invited. After a solemn entry into Tilsit, the Czar took up quarters in that city, and work started on the treaty to be concluded between France and Russia. Talleyrand was appointed negotiator for France, and the Princes Kurakin and Lobanov-Rostovsky for Russia, but in reality it was in the constant personal interviews between the sovereigns that the general principles of their policies were worked out. The first stumbling block was easily overcome when Alexander declared himself prepared to recognize all the conquests of France. There remained three outstanding problems to be settled: the question of Prussia, the relations with England, and

[4] *Ibid.*, I, 58.
[5] *Ibid.*, I, 60.

the question of the Near East. Napoleon's policy of building up a chain of states under his control, forming a belt across Germany to connect with a Poland re-created from the territories taken from Prussia, would mean the strangling of Prussia and a possible future menace to Russia. Here were to be found seeds of future conflict. Furthermore, Napoleon wished to take Silesia away from Prussia, giving in return some territory between the Elbe and the Rhine. A serious discussion ensued, the Russians fighting every step of the way to retain as much territory for Prussia as possible, but Napoleon remaining adamant, stipulating as a general principle that Prussia should under no circumstances be left wider than fifty leagues along a line running from Königsberg to Berlin. Alexander kept the Prussian Court informed of the progress of his negotiations, and at the crucial moment the beautiful Queen Louise, counting on the power of her charm, called upon Napoleon in person in an effort to retain for her country at least the important strategic city of Madgeburg. But her mission failed, Napoleon refusing to discuss politics with her; and on July 9 he imposed a brutal treaty on Prussia whereby that kingdom lost one third of its territory, including all territories west of the Elbe and all of its Polish possessions. On the twelfth a second convention was signed, stipulating that the French were to evacuate the occupied territory in Prussia by stages, but only after Prussia had paid the contribution which was to be levied upon her. Thus Napoleon not only retained his strangle hold over that country, but found an excuse for postponing the evacuation of the country by imposing such an exorbitant indemnity that Prussia would be in no position to pay it. True, Napoleon consented to list in his treaty with Russia the names of the Prussian territories he was pledging himself to evacuate, "out of special deference to His Majesty the Emperor of All the Russias,"[6] but his policy of delaying this evacuation until the fulfilment of the convention of July 12 virtually annulled this clause.

The two other issues, the British and Turkish, were interrelated. Alexander promised to act as mediator between England and France and, should this mediation fail, to come to the aid of France by fighting England, and Napoleon promised the same with regard to Turkey. This brought to the forefront a matter which was upper-

[6] Article IV, Treaty of Tilsit.

most in the minds of both Emperors, but which both were loath at first to mention—the question of the partition of Turkey. Curiously, it was the Prussian Minister Hardenberg who raised the issue in the hope of saving Prussia. He presented a memorandum in which he suggested that Russia should be given Bulgaria, Rumelia, and the Straits; Austria should be given Dalmatia, Bosnia, and Serbia; and France was to receive Greece and the Archipelago, in return for which Russia, Austria, and Prussia would renounce their hold on their respective parts of Poland. Poland thus re-created should be given to the King of Saxony, who in turn would abandon Saxony to Prussia. This fantastic project, coming together with the news of a revolution in Constantinople, raised the issue, but it was discussed merely in a general way. On one point, however, Napoleon was clear: Constantinople was not to become Russian.

The treaties were signed on July 7, ratified on the ninth; and Alexander left Tilsit the same day. A military review held jointly by the two Emperors the day before marked the official closing of the festivities. As Napoleon was inspecting a battalion of the Preobrajensky Guards, he took from his coat the cross of the Legion of Honor and decorated a soldier by the name of Lazarev, who had been pointed out to him as being the bravest in the battalion.

To sum up the effects of this meeting, which resulted in a complete change in the course of Russia's foreign policy, it is necessary to analyze the treaties concluded at Tilsit. First came the treaty of peace between France and Russia signed by Talleyrand and the Princes Kurakin and Lobanov-Rostovsky. The first three articles deal with the cessation of hostilities. Article IV stipulates in great detail the territories to be retroceded to Prussia after the evacuation by French troops. Its preamble is interesting:

> His Majesty the Emperor Napoleon, in deference to His Majesty the Emperor of All the Russias and desirous of giving proof of his sincere desire to unite the two nations in a bond of confidence and unalterable friendship, agrees to restore to His Majesty the King of Prussia the conquered countries, cities, and territories named hereafter.[7]

By Article V the provinces owned by Prussia, but which were Polish up to January, 1772, became the Grand Duchy of Warsaw under the

[7] Vandal, *op. cit.*, I, Appendix.

sovereignty of the King of Saxony, whereas Danzig and adjoining territories became independent (Article VI). The Dukes of Saxe-Coburg, Oldenburg, and Mecklenburg-Schwerin regained possession of their states. Russia recognized Joseph as King of Naples and Louis as King of Holland (Article XIV). Russia also recognized the Confederation of the Rhine, and promised to recognize any further adhesions to this Confederation (Article XV), as well as the creation of the Kingdom of Westphalia, to be composed of territories on the left bank of the Elbe ceded by Prussia (Article XIX).

In Article XXI Russia promised to cease hostilities with Turkey and to withdraw her troops from Moldavia and Wallachia. Both France and Russia guaranteed their respective possessions according to the *status quo* at the time of the signing of the treaty and pledged themselves to resume commercial relations and to accredit ambassadors on equal terms to each other's government (Articles XXV, XXVI, XXVII).

More important to France were the secret articles in a separate convention by which Russia abandoned to France the region of Cattaro and the Seven Islands, with Corfu, on the pledge that the French should not persecute the local inhabitants for their participation in the struggle against France, this referring particularly to the Montenegrins. Finally came the treaty of alliance between France and Russia. By Article I each contracting party pledged to come to the aid of the other in any war with any European power which might involve either of the contracting parties. Articles II and III stipulated the military measures to be taken in concert, and both parties promised not to sign a separate peace. Should England refuse to make peace with France by November 1, 1807, Russia was to join France in her war against England (Article IV). In such an event the two allied powers would jointly invite Denmark, Sweden, and Portugal to close their ports to British ships and to break off diplomatic relations with England and declare war; any nation failing to do so would be treated as an enemy (Article V). Similarly, the two allies would put joint pressure on Austria to bring her into the war against England (Article VI). Should England consent to the conditions of peace, Hanover would be ceded to her in compensation for the return of French, Dutch, and Spanish colonies (Article VII). Lastly, if Turkey refused to accept the conditions of peace with

Russia, "the two high contracting parties will come to a mutual understanding for the purpose of liberating all the provinces of the Ottoman Empire in Europe, the City of Constantinople and the Province of Rumelia excepted, from the yoke and the vexations of the Turks."[8] This treaty was to remain secret.

III

The immediate result of the meeting at Tilsit was the resumption of diplomatic relations between Russia and France. But until all the formalities for the exchange of regularly accredited ambassadors had been completed, Napoleon appointed an unofficial envoy to the Russian court—General Savary. The latter's task was to maintain Alexander in the friendly disposition which had originated at Tilsit, and to find out more about Russia, so as to permit Napoleon to assess the real value of his new alliance. He was also, if possible, to win over to France any important persons whose attitude toward the new alliance was considered doubtful or openly hostile, and to offset other influences, particularly British. The measure of hostility of society and the populace in Russia to the French was soon made evident to Savary upon his arrival in the Russian capital. He could not find living quarters to house his mission, as no one wanted to receive Frenchmen. As for the various social cliques, he found them equally forbidding and openly expressing their hostility to France. At court the Dowager Empress Maria Feodorovna, the wife of Emperor Paul I, who dominated the social life of the capital, received the French envoy so coldly that the interview did not last more than a minute. This dislike for the French was intensified by a personal factor, for Savary had played a conspicuous part in the assassination of the Duke of Enghien. Only Alexander was extremely cordial, and it soon became apparent that the alliance arose entirely from a personal policy and was supported by a mere handful of statesmen, of whom the most important were Count Rumiantsev, Minister of Commerce and later Minister of Foreign Affairs, Baron Budberg, present Minister of Foreign Affairs, and General Prince Lobanov-Rostovsky. By dint of indefatigable persistence and the support of his imperial patron, Savary ultimately succeeded in having himself received in a few houses, but the general tone of Russian so-

[8] *Ibid.*

ciety remained hostile. This hostility was further fanned by a large colony of French royalist *émigrés,* many of whom belonged to the highest French nobility, and hence were heartily welcomed in the aristocratic houses of the Russian capital. Conspicuous amongst these *émigrés* for the important role he played was Count Joseph de Maistre, who was to become famous as a writer and philosopher. In his semiofficial capacity of envoy for the Sardinian King in exile he had access to circles which were closed to the average *émigré.* Equally, if not more, active against France was the British Colonel Sir Robert Wilson, who was lionized in fashionable circles. He had been attached to the Russian General Headquarters during the campaign of 1807, and now was using all the contacts he had acquired in Russia in an implacable struggle against the influence of Napoleon's envoy.

Under the Treaty of Tilsit Russia was obliged to offer her mediation in the war between France and England. Accordingly, the Czar had his ambassador in London approach the British Government. The British reply issued on August 29 was not encouraging. It asked to know the conditions upon which France was prepared to negotiate, and also demanded that the secret clauses of the Treaty of Tilsit should be revealed to the British Government. This put an end to all further steps with regard to the mediation. The alternative could only be war, and presently Britain took the step which made this war inevitable. The British Government had been greatly perturbed at what had leaked out about the negotiations at Tilsit, and though not able to discover the exact extent of Russia's commitments, had rightly guessed Napoleon's plans. In Tilsit the British saw the beginning of an attempt on the part of Napoleon to build up a great naval coalition against England, in which not only Russia but Sweden and Denmark were to co-operate. They drew a comparison with the attempt of Czar Paul I to build up in 1801 a league of neutral powers, which by its essence was directed against England. Then as now, by its geographical position and also by its well-equipped fleet, it was Denmark which could do the most harm. Britain resolved to strike first and strike at Denmark. Hence the attack on Copenhagen on September 1 by the combined naval and military forces of Admiral Gambier and General Cathcart, which reduced the city to ashes after a five-day bombardment. This sudden attack in time of peace against a small, weak, neutral state produced tremendous indignation all over Europe, but nowhere was anger greater than in St. Petersburg. Pressed by Napoleon, who urged Russia to attack, Russia sent a note of protest to the British Government. The British were convinced that Russia was not eager to fight and hoped to placate her by some concessions, such as by declaring both Denmark and Sweden neutral and placing them under the guarantee of the Czar. The offensive power of Denmark having been destroyed, this would have been merely a gesture without any real significance.

In the meanwhile, as a precautionary measure, the British Fleet proceeded to the Baltic as a potential menace to the Russian coast, left unprotected, since the Russian Baltic Fleet under Admiral Seniavin was cruising in the Mediterranean. However, an early winter which covered the Baltic with ice in October obviated this threat.

In the meanwhile, in September, Count Nicholas Rumiantsev exchanged the portfolio of Minister of Commerce for that of Minister of Foreign Affairs, and his appointment marked a stiffening in the Russian attitude. Son of the renowned Field Marshal, Rumiantsev, reared in the great tradition of Catherine's policies, advocated the concentration of Russia's efforts in the Balkans and in the Near East. He deplored the spending of national energies on European problems and on what he deemed a futile struggle against Napoleon, which was not Russia's concern, and advocated the fulfilment of Russia's historical ambitions toward Constantinople. The peace of Tilsit, by putting an end to the struggle against France and reopening the Eastern Question for Russia, made of Rumiantsev the man of the day. If the price for the realization of Russian ambitions in Turkey was to be the support of Napoleon in a war with England, Rumiantsev was prepared to pay it. Alarmed by this appointment, the British Government sent Colonel Wilson, who had gone to London, back to St. Petersburg. Upon his return to Russia the confidential emissary of Canning saw the new minister on October 30. Wilson first proposed the settlement of the Danish and Baltic issues along the lines already mentioned, then attempted to buy over Russia by declaring that England would be willing to recognize the special interests of Russia in the Danubian Principalities, provided these did not presage a complete partition of Turkey and provided Austria would consent to the annexation by Russia of Moldavia and Wallachia. These provisos, and especially the stress on the consent of Austria, completely nullified the value of the British offers in the eyes of Rumiantsev, and he received them with extreme reserve. Seeing that he was getting nowhere, Wilson attempted, with the connivance of the British ambassador in St. Petersburg, Lord Gower, to stir up public feeling against France by spreading a pamphlet published in London entitled *Thoughts on the Peace of Tilsit*, which contained some insulting remarks about the Czar. Alexander was furious, especially when he discovered that these pamphlets had been traced to the British Embassy. He left unanswered a letter of Wilson addressed to him, and a few days later on November 7 the Russian Government in a violently worded declaration announced the rupture of diplomatic relations with Great Britain and the reaffirmation of Russia's stand concerning the maritime law contested in London. War between the two countries followed shortly afterwards, and thus a month before the date set by the Treaty of Tilsit Russia had fulfilled her engagements with regard to her attitude toward England. The hostilities were negligible from a military point of view, the most salient episode being the capture by the British of Seniavin's squadron in Lisbon, an event which has been described elsewhere. In the Baltic, in the summer of 1808, the British squadron co-operating with the Swedes attacked the Russian coast and in June captured a Russian sloop, and in July the Russian ship of the line *Vsevolod*. Three more sloops were captured the following summer, after bitter and bloody engagements. At the same time the British attacked the city of Kola in the White Sea and ravaged the fishermen's settlements along the Murman coast. By 1811 the fighting had subsided, and the war came to an end with the treaty of July, 1812.

But the result of the war against England was another and much more serious war against Sweden. This was made inevitable, not only by the clauses of the Treaty of Tilsit by which Russia had pledged herself to put pressure upon Sweden to force her into the Continental alignment against England, but by the inescapable logic of geography as well.

IV

Once Russia had shifted from the English to the French side, unless Sweden followed suit, the Baltic question would be reopened most ominously for Russia, and not only St. Petersburg but the whole of Russia's Baltic coast would be in danger. Indeed, for Sweden to remain in alliance with an England hostile to Russia meant the access of the British Navy to the Baltic, as it had always meant it in the past. The Åland Islands would form an excellent naval base from which the British Navy could block the Gulf of Finland, while land forces, British or Swedish, could directly threaten St. Petersburg from the frontier running along the river Kumen at the entrance to the Karelian bottleneck. Thus not only the commitments made to Napoleon at Tilsit but strategic necessity made it imperative for Russia to wean Sweden away from the British alliance; the British attack on Copenhagen not only gave an excellent pretext for such a move but, by resulting in an open breach between Russia and England, made the issue of prime importance. Indeed, immediately after the news of the bombardment of Copenhagen had been received in St. Petersburg, Alexander addressed a personal appeal to King Gustavus, which was further backed by a note presented by the Russian minister in Stockholm, Alopeus. Alopeus was to inform the King that the Czar was indignant at the British attack on Denmark, and would like to know Sweden's reaction to the event.[9] The reply of Gustavus was so vague as to leave room for several interpretations, but appeared to be a veiled invitation to Russia not to abandon the alliance with England. However, at an audience given to Alopeus on October 15 the King was much more explicit and openly supported the British. Thus a situation was created in which the only alternative for Russia was to force Sweden away from England by war, should diplomacy fail to achieve the same end. Both King Gustavus and Count Stedingk, however, apparently decided that the safest course lay in remaining indefinite on the issue and not disclosing their stand. Thus the negotiations dragged on, and Rumiantsev became more and more pressing. In his instructions to Alopeus dated November 28, 1807, he wrote: "You will not conceal from the Ministry and the King that since we are forced to take measures against England it is imperative for us to know precisely whether

[9] Rumiantsev to Alopeus, October 6, 1807.

the King . . . desires to join us in closing the Baltic to the British and in avenging the outrage which she [Great Britain] has committed against Denmark."[10] But the reply given by the King to this *démarche* of the Russian minister was once more worded cautiously and evasively. In Stockholm news had been received of the concentration of Russian troops on the Finnish border; Sweden was exhausted by her unsuccessful effort in Pomerania and had merely some twelve thousand men in Finland, poorly equipped and with inadequate supplies. She knew she had to be cautious. Deeming the reply unsatisfactory, Rumiantsev went one step further and on January 11, 1808, presented to the Swedish Minister a note so threatening as to be a virtual ultimatum. The Emperor, said the note, could not wait any longer, having used all the means in his power to persuade the King of Sweden to return to "the sole system" which would give security to Russia.

> His Imperial Majesty desires a precise and final reply on this issue and desires it without delay. . . . Should the reply of His Majesty the King not conform to the wishes of the Emperor, His Imperial Majesty will be forced to take without delay such measures as Providence has put at his disposal for the purpose of assuring the security of his Empire, and he warns the King to this effect.[11]

No more evasions were possible. The Russian ultimatum of January 11 remained unanswered. On February 22 war was declared by Russia; five days later Baron Stedingk, the Swedish minister in St. Petersburg, was given his passports.

In the first days of March, before the Russian legation had left Stockholm, an aide-de-camp of the King suddenly presented himself to Alopeus with an armed force at night, and declared that he had orders to place the Minister and his whole staff under arrest and to place under seal all the archives of the legation. Alopeus remained confined in his home under police supervision until May, when he finally was permitted to leave the country. As the Swedish minister was still in St. Petersburg at the time, the question of retaliation was raised, but by order of Alexander, Rumiantsev wrote the following letter to Baron Stedingk on March 26:

> The Emperor has been informed that His Majesty the King of Sweden has ordered the arrest of the Russian Minister Alopeus with his whole

[10] *Sbornik,* II, 71.

[11] *Ibid.,* II, 75-77.

staff. His Imperial Majesty has instructed me to inform Your Excellency that, not wishing to take the Turks as a model and remaining faithful to his own principles, he has ordered me to double my care and my consideration toward you.[12]

V

The Russian invasion of Finland started in February, 1808. An army of 24,000 men "well equipped and well disciplined,"[13] under the command of General Buxhoevden, advanced in three columns and by March 1 had occupied Helsingfors. Opposing the Russians was a Swedish-Finnish force of 20,000 men under General Klercker, of whom 7,000 were concentrated at the fortress of Sweaborg near Helsingfors, 700 at Swartholm, and the remainder, some 12,000, scattered in garrisons throughout the country. The newly appointed Commander in Chief of the Swedish Army, General Count Klingspor, had worked out a plan whereby the forces of Sweaborg and Swartholm would offer sufficient resistance to delay the enemy, while the field army could retreat and concentrate in the north near Tamerfors. King Gustavus approved of the plan provided the army offered resistance in retreating, but this Klingspor failed to do. The result was that the Russians swept over the country. A division under Count Kamensky was detached to besiege Sweaborg, another one under General Tuchkov marched on Vasa to cut the Swedish line of communications by sea, and Bagration with a third division followed the retreating Swedes, occupying Tavasthus on March 7. The Swedes, however, retreated to Uleaborg and Swartholm so fast that Hango and Abo surrendered without resistance. With Sweaborg isolated, the seacoast of the Gulf of Bothnia and the Gulf of Finland had come into Russian hands, and a thrust was made to occupy the Åland Islands as well. While this operation was in progress a detachment was put on board transports at Libau, and sailed on April 22 to occupy the large and important island of Gothland. Thus the Russians had wrested control of Finland nearly up to the Arctic Circle, and also the Baltic with its main islands.

An even more crushing blow was to follow with the capitulation of Sweaborg, "the Gibraltar of the North," on May 3. This keystone of the Swedish defense was commanded by a naval officer, Karl

[12] *Ibid.*, II, 83.
[13] A. A. Somberg, *A History of Sweden* (New York, 1931), p. 602.

Cronstedt, brave but irresolute. The garrison was demoralized by Russian propaganda, skilfully conducted by a Swede in Russian service, Sprengtporten. The Russians flooded the Swedish lines with especially edited Swedish newspapers, and some of the officers were accused by the Swedes of having been too susceptible to Russian gold; Cronstedt himself was said to have accepted, after the war, a pension of 4,500 rubles paid to him by the Russian Government. At all events, on April 6 Cronstedt signed a convention whereby if by May 3 no assistance should be forthcoming from Sweden he would surrender the fortress, which he did on the appointed day. Thus 7,000 Swedes surrendered to a Russian besieging force of 6,500 men, and the Russians captured in addition 2,000 guns and 100 small war vessels. But, luckily for Sweden, she was better served by her field army—not by Klingspor, who showed little competence or courage, but by his chief of staff, Colonel Adlerkreutz. Adlerkreutz realized that the Russians in their rapid advance had dangerously scattered their forces. Therefore, acting against Klingspor's orders, he stopped the retreat, rallied the Swedes, and, arming the formidable Finnish guerillas, started a counteroffensive. With 10,000 men he attacked the most exposed Russian division of Tuchkov, a bare 4,000 men, and at Revolaksa inflicted a crushing defeat on Tuchkov's vanguard under Colonel Bulatov. The forests around began swarming with Finnish guerillas, and Tuchkov extricated himself by retreating to Gamle-Karleby, but with the loss of his transports and hospitals, which were captured by the Finns. Encouraged by this success, the Finns took up arms, and an insurrection broke out in the Russian rear. At the same time, around the Åland Islands, the ice broke, trapping the garrison. Faced with an insurrection of the islanders and an attack of Swedish naval forces, Colonel Vouich, commanding the garrison on the island of Kumlinge, surrendered with 700 men. On Gothland, Rear Admiral Bodisco with 1,500 men, facing a Swedish landing party 5,000 strong, evacuated the island and brought his force back to Libau. Thus the position of the Russian forces suddenly became critical. Happily the spring thaw stopped all operations for a month, during which time Buxhoevden received reinforcements amounting to 12,000 men. He reorganized his forces, with General Rayevsky, replacing Tuchkov, holding Gamle-Karleby with 7,000 men; Barclay de Tolly with another 7,000 along

Lake Saima from Wilmanstrand to Neishlot; and Kamensky and Bagration with 16,000 men spread out along the coast of the Baltic from Lovisa to Vasa. At the end of May the British General Moore brought a force of from 10,000 to 14,000 men to Sweden, but was not permitted by the King to land, and so sailed to Spain. The British Fleet, however, remained in the Baltic; and this resulted in one or two petty naval engagements.

In June, having received reinforcements from Sweden, Klingspor suddenly attacked Rayevsky with forces twice as large and forced him to retreat to Tavasthus. Barclay tried to go to the aid of his colleague by moving from Neishlot to Kuopio, but found the roads infested with Finnish guerillas under the energetic Sandels. Notwithstanding constant attacks by the Swedish regulars Barclay duly reached Kuopio, where he left a force 3,000 strong under General Rachmanov, and proceeded to advance toward Gamle-Karleby to join Rayevsky. However, scarcely had he left Kuopio when Sandels with a strong force of Finnish irregulars attacked Rachmanov. Fearing for his communications, Barclay hastily returned to Kuopio and drove Sandels away. In the meanwhile the Russian Fleet, sailing from Sweaborg, successfully thwarted a Swedish attempt to land reinforcements at Abo. Through the summer the situation remained fairly stationary, Barclay and later Tuchkov, who replaced him because of illness, holding Kuopio against Sandels, Rayevsky at Tavasthus with a detachment of 1,000 men at Bjerneborg, and the Russian General Headquarters with a force of 4,000 men at Abo. Kamensky replaced Rayevsky and retreated from Tavasthus to Tammerfors, but Klingspor did not pursue the retreating Russians. He followed cautiously and took up a strong defensive position at Salmi. The position was still deemed so critical that Buxhoevden asked for 50,000 men as reinforcements. This number could not be spared because of the situation elsewhere, but nevertheless Buxhoevden obtained sufficient reinforcements to bring his army up to 45,000 men. Kamensky, having reorganized his forces and assembled 10,500 men with 38 guns, suddenly attacked Klingspor on September 1.

The Swedish General was now caught in the same error which had cost the Russians so dearly in the spring: he had scattered his forces. He had 7,000 men with 30 guns at Salmi, and 2,000 men with eight guns fifty miles away at Lindulaksa under Sandels. Accordingly, while Kamensky attacked Klingspor frontally, he detached Colonel Vlasov to Lindulaksa. Klingspor fell back to Orovais, where the next day, September 2, the decisive engagement of the war was fought. Klingspor was defeated with a loss of 1,000 men, which he could ill afford, while Vlasov, after driving the Swedes out of Lindulaksa, marched to Gamle-Karleby, threatening Klingspor's rear. This induced the Swedish commander to ask for an armistice, which Buxhoevden accepted, conditional upon Klingspor's retiring his troops north to Himango, while Sandels was to move back to Idensalmi. The negotiations conducted on the Russian side by Kamensky and Suchtelen were duly terminated on September 29, and military operations ceased.

But when the news of the armistice reached St. Petersburg, neither the Czar nor the Committee of Ministers approved of it; and Buxhoevden was given strict orders to attack Klingspor at once. Thus the truce had lasted only one month. During this time the inefficient Klingspor was recalled and replaced once more by General Klercker, and the Swedish army was reinforced by 3,000 men sent over from Sweden. But the Swedes were exhausted and suffering from disease and hunger; their morale was broken. Hence when the Russians resumed the offensive, Klercker, realizing the disproportion in numbers—he had only 14,000 against the Russian 45,000—retreated, while Tuchkov attacked Sandels and forced him back. Klercker asked for a second truce, and under the convention signed on November 15 at Olkioki, accepted the most drastic terms: the Swedes were to abandon the whole of Finland up to the river Kemi, and all war materials left behind were to be taken by the Russians. At Uleaborg alone the Russians captured 18 guns and 2,000 rifles. Sandels, however, attempted to attack Tuchkov once more, a few days before the convention was signed, but was beaten off.

Finland was now in Russian hands, but the war was still on and Alexander was not pleased. "The armies defending Finland," he said, "notwithstanding our tremendous preponderance in numbers, are still in the field and have maintained their fighting capacity and therefore the war cannot be considered to be at an end."[14] Bux-

[14] General Modest Ivanovich Bogdanovich, *Istoria Tsarstvovania Imperatora Aleksandra I i Rossia v ego Vremia* (St. Petersburg, 1869-1871), II, 391.

hoevden was removed from command and replaced by General Knorring, who was given specific instructions to carry the war into Sweden. The Czar's bold plan was to write a spectacular final chapter to this otherwise drab campaign. Alexander ordered that three attacks should be made over the ice of the Gulf of Bothnia on the coast of Sweden: (1) from the Abo through the Åland Islands in the direction of Stockholm, (2) from Vasa to Umea, and (3) from Uleaborg across the northern end of the gulf near Torneo. An army of 35,000 men with 62 guns was assembled to carry out the undertaking. But such an expedition required the most careful preparations, and the timorous Knorring, who considered the plan infeasible, kept on postponing the expedition on pretense of not being ready. Thus three months passed; then the condition of the ice made further delay impossible. Alexander, exasperated, sent his Minister of War, General Arakcheev, to Knorring's headquarters at the end of February with orders to proceed immediately.

Accordingly, the main column of 15,000 men with 22 guns under Bagration set out across the ice on March 10 from Abo, and reached the island of Kumlinge in the Åland Archipelago on the thirteenth. The march was difficult owing to the fact that a warm wind had melted the surface of the ice and covered it with a layer of water. Furthermore, the Åland Islands were held by a Swedish garrison 5,000 strong under General Döbeln, with an additional 4,000 irregulars; the inhabitants, fearing reprisals for the insurrection of the preceding May, took up arms and adopted a "scorched earth" policy of burning and destroying all habitations. As the army approached, General Döbeln offered to cede the islands, but General Arakcheev, who was accompanying the expedition, insisted upon the surrender of the garrison as well. This Döbeln refused to do; and, as he started retreating across the ice, Bagration pursued and defeated him. While the remnants of the Swedish garrison trickled back into Sweden, the Russians captured on and near the islands 2,000 prisoners, 40 guns, 10,000 rifles, and a flotilla of war vessels icebound in the harbors. After establishing himself in the archipelago, Bagration dispatched a cavalry vanguard composed of 400 men under General Kulnev to the Swedish mainland. This detachment took eight hours to cross the ice and, reaching the coast of Sweden, attacked and captured the small city of Grisselham some sixty miles from Stockholm. The utmost confusion reigned in the Swedish capital, where a revolution overthrowing King Gustavus had recently taken place, and the arrival of the Russians so close to Stockholm added to the panic. Three regiments were sent to Grisselham, but Kulnev held his own and returned to the Åland Islands only when so ordered.

In the meanwhile the second column, under Barclay de Tolly, proceeded to cross the Baltic directly from Vasa to Umea, a distance of some eighty miles. Fearing that the ice might break because of the approach of spring, Barclay had decided not to wait for the completion of his preparations but to move with the troops he had on hand. Therefore on March 20 he left with a force of 3,500 men and eight guns, taking with him ammunition boxes on sleighs, provisions for only ten days, and forage for only four days. All other baggage and transports were left behind. Nevertheless the march was perilous and difficult, owing to the appearance of great gaps of water where the ice had been broken by a storm and piled into huge blocks which had to be negotiated one by one. By night the detachment reached an uninhabited island, where it camped, and, pursuing its march the following day, reached Umea and captured it.

The third column, under General Shuvalov, proceeded via Torneo. Meeting stiff Swedish resistance, Shuvalov was forced to detach a column, under the command of General Alexeiev, to go around the Swedish positions by crossing over the ice. Alexeiev had the most difficult time of the three, for the ice was cracking under the weight of his artillery and gaps of water had to be bridged with planks. Furthermore, he discovered that the ice had receded from the shore and that a mile of sea separated him from the coast. Only after a detour of sixteen miles was he able to get back to the mainland. But the maneuver was successful, and General Grippenberg, by the capitulation of Kalix (March 25), surrendered 7,000 men, 22 guns, and 13 standards. These successes so demoralized the Swedish regency that it asked for an armistice, which Knorring, fearing the breaking of the ice, signed, thereafter ordering his forces back to Finland. Alexander was not pleased with the armistice and appointed Barclay de Tolly as Commander in Chief in place of Knorring. Desultory fighting on Swedish soil by Russian forces which had gone around the Gulf of Bothnia was carried on throughout the summer, until the final signing of the peace treaty; but for all practical purposes military operations came to an end with the expeditions across the ice.

It was the overthrow of King Gustavus on March 22 which made possible the opening of direct negotiations for peace between the two countries. Indeed, prior to this event in February, Alopeus had been sent to Abo especially to consult with the Russian High Command in Finland with regard to the minimum Russian conditions of peace. These were set as the cession of the whole of Finland up to the river Torneo, and the closing to British shipping of all Swedish ports except those on the Kategat. When the news of the Swedish *coup d'état* was received in St. Petersburg, Alopeus was ordered to proceed to Stockholm. Upon his arrival in the Swedish capital, the Russian minister presented himself to the Regent, the Duke of Sudermanland, and was convinced that the latter was anxious for peace. On the Swedish side Baron Stedingk was appointed negotiator, and on April 6 Baron Lagerbjelke, the newly appointed Foreign Minister, notified Rumiantsev of his wish to see the war end. On May 12 Lagerbjelke wrote a second time to ask for a passport for Baron Stedingk so as to permit the latter to proceed to St. Petersburg for the negotiations. To this Rumiantsev replied that prior to the opening of the negotiations Sweden was to accept the following conditions: peace was to be made with the allies of Russia as well, Sweden was to join the Continental System, and the new frontier between Russia and Sweden was to be the Gulf of Bothnia and the river Kalix. Early in July the Russians had won an engagement on Swedish soil at Gernefors, and this undoubtedly induced the Swedish Government to accept these preliminary terms. Accordingly Baron Stedingk, accompanied by Colonel Skjoldebrand, was ordered to go to Friedrichsham, where he met the Russian delegation headed by Rumiantsev and Alopeus.

The conference was formally opened on August 15, and the Swedish envoys immediately raised the question of the Åland Islands, declaring that Sweden could not abandon them after the loss of Finland. Rumiantsev suggested discussing each question in turn, and asked whether Sweden was prepared to conclude peace with France and Denmark as well as Russia, to which the Swedes replied affirmatively. When the question of the Continental System was raised, Stedingk replied that Sweden could not join it without becoming involved in a quarrel with Britain. Rumiantsev said that in that case Russia would be forced by her allies to renew military operations against Sweden, and the Swedes yielded. The greatest resistance was met on the question of the Åland Islands, which, according to Stedingk, were the guardians and the signal post of Stockholm. Should they be ceded to Russia, he said, the inhabitants of Stockholm would not be able to sleep quietly a single night, for fear of a sudden attack—to which Rumiantsev replied that should Russia content herself with Finland alone it would be like taking a trunk and then throwing away the key. Seeing the Russians adamant, Stedingk and Skjoldebrand tried vainly to obtain a pledge of neutralization of the islands, but Rumiantsev insisted that the Czar demanded their unconditional cession. Having yielded on this point, the Swedes raised the issue of the frontier of Finland, suggesting the river Kemi as the border, and asked Rumiantsev to appeal to the Czar to this effect. The reply came on August 29, and Alexander authorized drawing the border on the river Torneo, midway between the Kalix and the Kemi rivers. Thus all the issues were settled; and the Treaty of Friedrichsham was signed in September, 1809, under which (Article IV) Sweden ceded to Russia unconditionally the whole of Finland up to the river Torneo and the Åland Islands.

VI

As a *quid pro quo* for Russia's action against England and Sweden, Napoleon sent a French officer, Commandant Guilleminot, to the Russian Headquarters in Wallachia to negotiate an armistice with Turkey, which was duly concluded on August 24, 1807, at Slobodzia. But thereby thorny issues arose between the two allies of Tilsit, and the Turkish question became inextricably tangled with the much more dangerous Prussian question. Indeed, the armistice provided for the evacuation of the Danubian Principalities by the Russians, and accordingly the Russian Army started to retreat toward the Dniester. But the march was countermanded by special orders from St. Petersburg, the Russian columns reoccupied the lines previously held, and at the same time Czar Alexander refused to ratify the armistice, merely pledging himself not to resume hostilities against the Turks for the time being. Napoleon, who received information of these events in October, was profoundly incensed by what he termed Russia's duplicity. His policy in dealing with his new ally was never to cede a point to Russia without receiving a corresponding advantage for France, and in his view Russia was maintaining her hold on the Principalities without France's having obtained a corresponding benefit. Furthermore, the Russian conquest of Moldavia and Wallachia appeared to him to be the beginning of the partition of the Turkish Empire. He considered the crumbling of this empire inevitable, but he wanted this event to occur at an opportune moment for himself and not as a result of Russia's unilateral action. Moreover, at present England was in a position to seize the territories of Turkey on the eastern Mediterranean coast before France would be able to move.

But Napoleon failed to apprehend the correlation of Russia's stand in Wallachia with his own stand in Prussia. To be sure, after Tilsit the Grand Army had recrossed the Passarge River and had evacuated Königsberg; but the rest of Prussia had remained under French occupation, and the French Army was quartered between the Elbe and the Vistula. Furthermore, having imposed upon Prussia a contribution so enormous that the country could not pay it, Napoleon was citing the nonpayment of this debt as the reason for the seizure of Silesia, which would cripple Prussia and keep her separated from Austria. With Silesia in his hands, adjoining the Grand Duchy of Warsaw on one side and the lands of the Confederation of the Rhine on the other, Napoleon would have been in control of a strip of territory stretching from France to Russia and cutting Central Europe in two. Thus Napoleon thought that Silesia was to be the compensation which France would obtain for the cession of the Danubian Principalities to Russia, but Alexander had outwitted his partner by keeping the Principalities. So long as the French remained in Prussia, the Russians would remain on the Danube.

The exchange of formal ambassadors between France and Russia for the first time since the war was to facilitate the pursuit of official negotiations. General Caulaincourt was appointed ambassador to St. Petersburg, and Count Tolstoy was to represent Russia in Paris. Tolstoy, a diplomat of the old school who hated the French Revolution and distrusted Napoleon, brought with him a mood of suspicion which could not be overcome by the cordiality of the Emperor toward him. One of his first moves was to raise the Prussian question. Napoleon, however, remained evasive in his replies. Finally the Emperor made it clear that he would not evacuate Prussia as long as the Russians remained in possession of the Principalities. Caulaincourt on his side had been told by Alexander that there could be no question of the dismemberment of Prussia serving as compensation to France for Russia's conquests in Turkey.[15] Thus from the outset the alliance had hit a snag, and the deadlock was growing into a crisis.

When it became clear to Napoleon that Russia would not accept the cession of Silesia in return for the Principalities, a new trend of thought began to develop in his mind—the only way to satisfy Russia and at the same time to compensate France would be to proceed in common to the partition of Turkey. Vague but gradually more precise instructions to this effect began appearing in Napoleon's diplomatic correspondence. This partition could be made to serve his ulterior purposes, and through Thrace, Constantinople, and Asia Minor would he not be in a position to strike at India? If he could obtain from Russia, in return for the territories ceded to her in the Balkans, her co-operation in a joint Russo-French expedition against British India, the dream he had nourished during his Egyptian expedition might still become a reality and Britain might be defeated. It would be easy for Russia to move an expeditionary force through Persia to join a French army coming through Asia Minor, and both armies moving through Afghanistan could deliver a crushing blow at England's domination in India. These ideas seemed to have matured in his mind during the last months of 1807, and he asked his agents in Turkey to provide him with necessary information concerning the territories over which his armies would have to pass.

At the same time, to secure himself against Russia should she prove hostile to his schemes, Napoleon approached Austria. On January 22, 1808, in an interview with Metternich, then Austrian ambassador to France, he stressed the dangers to Austria of Russia's expansion in the Balkans and stated that should Russia come into possession of Constantinople, France and Austria would need each other to counterbalance such a move, and should Turkey be partitioned France would take into consideration the legitimate interests

[15] Caulaincourt's report December 23, 1807 (Vandal, *op. cit.*, I, 207).

of Austria along the valley of the Danube. Thus having prepared the ground all around and having laid the foundations for a subtle scheme to use Austria to stop Russia and vice versa, he decided to come out definitely into the open. In a letter addressed to the Czar dated February 2, 1808, he officially raised the issue of Franco-Russian co-operation in the Near East. In this important letter he said that, negotiations with England having failed, it was only by "great and vast measures" that peace could be attained. Hence Russia was to proceed actively against Sweden in the north, while an army of fifty thousand, composed of Russians, French, and possibly some Austrians, would advance toward India, the French coming from Dalmatia and the Russians from the Danube. Napoleon estimated that by the time this army could reach the Euphrates, British resistance would collapse, and he set May 1 as the date for his operation, to be carried out simultaneously with the occupation of Stockholm by the Russians. Thus menaced in the north, in the Levant, and in India, Britain would sue for peace. He further suggested that the details of the plan should be worked out in St. Petersburg with Caulaincourt, who was given full powers to negotiate the matter, thus obviating the necessity of working with the obviously inimical Tolstoy. The sending of this letter coincided with vast military and naval concentrations carried out by Napoleon in the Mediterranean, which indicated to what an extent the plan had gripped his imagination.

Indeed, the French army in Dalmatia was strengthened very considerably, while Corfu became the great naval and military base and a point of concentration for the French squadrons. All the French naval forces in the Atlantic and the Channel received orders to proceed immediately to the Mediterranean; and the French squadrons at Brest, Lorient, and Rochefort were to move toward Toulon. From there, in January, they proceeded under Admiral Ganteaume to Corfu, whence a part of the French forces were to be diverted for the occupation of Sicily (recently evacuated by the British); after this, having secured his flank, Napoleon seems to have had in mind a second expedition to Egypt, coincidental with the advance of the French Army through the Balkans toward Asia Minor. This gigantic operation was to be directed by Napoleon himself from a central point in Italy, whereas, in faraway Scandinavia, the Russian advance on Sweden was to coincide with an advance of Bernadotte's corps from Pomerania, in order to divert British attention to the North Sea and the Baltic.

When Napoleon's letter of February 2 arrived in St. Petersburg, Alexander was puzzled. He was beginning seriously to distrust Napoleon's policy in Germany, and the idea of diverting his own forces to a distant adventure in Asia did not appeal to him. Moreover, he had the wars with Turkey, Sweden, and England on hand; and besides, had he not done his share toward fulfilling the pledges he had given at Tilsit? But as Napoleon suggested negotiations through an intermediary, Caulaincourt, Alexander authorized Count Rumiantsev to open discussions with Caulaincourt, thereby setting one of the most amazing examples of bargaining in diplomatic history. According to the verbatim reports of these conversations sent by Caulaincourt, the French ambassador said outright: "Let us find out what concerns you—what the Emperor [Alexander] desired at Tilsit."[16] Rumiantsev replied that Russia would like to have Moldavia, Wallachia, and Bulgaria, leaving Greece, Albania, and Crete to France, while Austria could receive Croatia and Bosnia. However, Caulaincourt wanted Bosnia for France. The fate of Serbia remained in the balance, Rumiantsev suggesting a joint Franco-Russian protectorate. Caulaincourt objected, stating that this would lead to quarrels between the two powers. Rumiantsev then suggested that an Austrian archduke chosen by Napoleon might be made ruler of that country. Caulaincourt raised the general objection that whereas Russia was obtaining regions closely bound to each other by racial and geographic ties, France would get scattered territories populated mostly by Turks. When Rumiantsev further demanded Constantinople and the Straits, Caulaincourt objected, saying that Russia would thus hold the keys to both the Black Sea and the Sea of Marmara, which was asking too much. Rumiantsev then offered France the Archipelago, Egypt, and Syria in addition to the earlier offers, but reserved Serbia for Russia. In subsequent conversations he suggested that France should take also Rumelia and Macedonia, Austria should have Serbia, but Russia retain Constantinople and the Straits. Caulaincourt replied that Constantinople alone was worth all the territories offered to France, and suggested that France should

[16] *Ibid.*, I, 285-295.

have the Dardanelles in compensation for Constantinople. Rumiantsev remained firm and referred the matter to the Czar. In an interview with the French ambassador, Alexander fully endorsed his minister; he insisted upon the possession of both the Straits and opposed all the arguments of the Frenchman with regard to the cession of the Dardanelles to France, but offered as a last resort the neutralization of Constantinople. This brought the conversations to an end. Both sides then drew up a memorandum stating their points of view. Caulaincourt's project, with reservations for the approval of Napoleon, claimed for France the whole of the Balkan Peninsula south of a line between the Ionian Islands and Salonica, leaving to Russia Bessarabia, Moldavia, Wallachia, and Bulgaria. An intermediary zone comprising Serbia and northern Macedonia was to be given to Austria. Constantinople and the Straits were to be made an autonomous principality. An alternate suggestion gave France the Dardanelles and a strip of Macedonia connecting it with Salonica, Austria losing the seacoast and obtaining Croatia, Bosnia, and a section of Macedonia. Furthermore, in Asiatic Turkey, France was to have Syria, Anatolia, and Egypt, while to Russia would go Trebizond.

In the Russian project Russia claimed the Danubian Principalities, a part of Serbia, the whole of Bulgaria, and a frontier running from the Carpathians to the Danube and the Maritza, whence, engulfing Constantinople and the Straits, it swerved toward the Black Sea. Beyond the intermediate zone reserved for Austria along this border, France was offered Albania, Epyrus, Thessaly, Greece proper, the Archipelago, Egypt, Syria, and Asia Minor. Russia offered an army to help France obtain these territories as well as to conquer India. An interview between the two emperors was to take place to work out the details, conditional however upon France's accepting the Russian offer in principle. But Constantinople and the Straits remained the stumbling block to such an acceptance.

When in March the Spanish crisis suddenly broke out, Napoleon, entirely absorbed by his Oriental plans, regarded it merely as a temporary delay and nuisance, and continued preparing for the interview with Alexander which he expected to take place in the spring. As for Russia, her war with Sweden was dragging on, and the aid promised by Napoleon did not materialize. Bernadotte advanced his corps cautiously to the coast of Holstein, but did not cross the sea into Sweden. This lack of support on the part of Bernadotte was attributed in St. Petersburg to Napoleon's duplicity in dealing with his ally.

While Russia was facing these difficulties, the situation in Spain was leading up to a crisis, and these factors necessitated the postponement of the interview between the two emperors, as well as of the realization of the great Oriental scheme. However, Napoleon was still under the impression that the events in Spain were causing a mere temporary delay, and as late as the end of June he was still actively pursuing his preparations for the vast enterprise. But in July the situation in Spain became so alarming that Napoleon had to postpone further his plans in the Orient; and then came news of the disastrous capitulation of Dupont's army at Baylen. The whole of Europe was electrified by the news of the French defeat, and Austria, anxious to avenge her past humiliations, began feverishly arming for a new war. Faced with two serious wars, in Spain and in Austria, Napoleon had to abandon definitely his project for the Indian expedition and concentrate on his immediate problems. He adopted a much more conciliatory attitude toward Prussia, promising to evacuate that country, and he decided to use all the force of his diplomatic ability to avoid war with Austria. Here he could make use of Russia. If Russia could be induced to threaten Austria and force her to remain neutral, Napoleon would be in a position to concentrate his undivided attention on Spain and solve that vexatious problem. Hence the proposed interview with Alexander was acquiring a new importance. He would use that interview to force Alexander to adopt a stern attitude toward Austria. Thus far the attitude of Russia toward Austria's arming had been extremely hesitant; she did not want to see a war so close to her borders, but on the other hand she was beginning to fear Napoleon's ambitions more and more. In the words of Tolstoy, the ambassador in Paris: "The destruction of Austria would be the forerunner and the means of our [Russia's] own destruction."[17] Was it therefore in Russia's interest to keep Austria from arming? Hence the notes presented by the Russian ambassador in Vienna, Prince Kurakin, were written so

[17] *Ibid.*, I, 375.

cautiously in the name of peace that they could be interpreted by Austria as encouraging her aggressiveness.

To complicate the situation, a revolution had broken out in Constantinople, forcing the Eastern question once more to the fore. Mustapha IV, having dethroned Selim III, was faced with a rebellion of the Pasha of Rustchuk, who was aiming at re-establishing Selim III on the throne. Mustapha had ordered Selim killed, but perished himself instead. This question also had to be settled at the coming interview; hence Alexander notified Napoleon that he would be willing to meet him halfway between the two capitals, at Erfurt, on September 27, 1808.

In going to Erfurt, Alexander was prepared to drive a hard bargain. He considered that by his wars with England and Sweden he had fulfilled his share of commitments under the Treaty of Tilsit, whereas France had not declared war on Turkey and had merely repaid him with empty words and schemes. Even the sudden change of attitude on the part of Napoleon toward Prussia, which at first Alexander thought to be the belated result of the meeting at Tilsit, had proved merely to be the consequence of the events in Spain that had made it necessary for Napoleon to withdraw troops from Prussia in order to send them to the Spanish front. Besides, the withdrawal was not complete. France had agreed to have the Prussian administration reintroduced over the greater part of Prussian territories, but retained the three strategic fortresses on the river Oder—Stettin, Glogau, and Küstrin. Napoleon had furthermore increased his forces in the Grand Duchy of Warsaw, and thus was maintaining unbroken his line of communication towards Russia. The question of Napoleon's hold over Prussia was becoming of prime importance to Russia, and was the first major issue which Alexander was anxious to settle at Erfurt. The Turkish question, with the dangerous potentialities growing out of the revolutions in Constantinople and the necessity of taking a firmer and more active stand in the Balkans, was the second issue. These questions, coupled with those which interested Napoleon, namely, the problems of Spain and Austria, formed the four major issues on the agenda of the meeting.

Napoleon, however, wanted to get the most for himself while promising the least possible to his ally. He was anxious to obtain from Russia freedom of action in Spain and unreserved and active Russian support against Austria, in return for which he was prepared to grant Russia the Danubian Principalities—not immediately but in principle, at a later date and if Russia's services were sufficiently valuable to him.

The importance of this meeting at Erfurt was sufficiently realized in Europe to bring many crowned heads and leading statesmen to this little German city. Indeed, the kings of Saxony, Württemberg, Bavaria, and Westphalia, the dukes of Oldenburg, Weimar, Mecklenburg-Schwerin, and many others were present. Alexander was accompanied by his brother, the Grand Duke Constantine, his ministers Count Speransky, Count Rumiantsev, and Prince Golitsin. In the very large retinue of Napoleon the most important single adviser was Talleyrand, whom Napoleon had brought with him for the specific purpose of charming and impressing Alexander. In this he made a grave mistake. He did not know that Talleyrand had been intriguing with Metternich in Paris and encouraging Austria in her anti-French policy in the secret hope of putting a brake on Napoleon's ambitions, and that he was now prepared to betray Napoleon to Alexander. Indeed, in the first audience he had with the Czar, Talleyrand nonchalantly observed, "Sire, what are you coming here to do? It is for you to save Europe, and you will succeed only if you oppose Napoleon. The French nation is civilized; its sovereign is not. The ruler of Russia is civilized, but the people are not. Therefore it is for the sovereign of Russia to ally himself with the French nation."[18] Talleyrand also worked hard trying to win over the experienced and distrustful Rumiantsev, and he did succeed in firmly impressing the Russians with the idea that the French people were not in sympathy with Napoleon's ambitions.

When the conversations opened, the two emperors discussed general principles, while Talleyrand and Rumiantsev worked out the details. The negotiations proceeded far from smoothly. Napoleon insisted that Prussia should accept his terms and ratify a treaty to that effect before he would evacuate the three fortresses. Alexander pledged Prussia's good behavior and promised to put pressure on that kingdom, but he also raised the issue of the presence of French

[18] Chevalier de Metternich, *Mémoires, documents et écrits divers laissés par le prince de Metternich* publiés par son fils le prince Richard de Metternich (Paris, 1880-1884), II, 248.

forces in the Grand Duchy of Warsaw. Napoleon promised to withdraw his troops from Poland and not to reoccupy it, but as he never kept his word in that respect, this issue became the main cause of subsequent distrust between the allies. Though originally the conference had been called to discuss the question of the partition of Turkey, Napoleon was anxious to subordinate this issue to the more burning question of Russia's stand against Austria. But Alexander insisted that the fate of the Danubian Principalities be settled first. Thus it was decided to postpone the Oriental question until another conference. As for Moldavia and Wallachia, Napoleon had conceded them to Russia in principle, but was nevertheless anxious to use them as a bargaining card. He demanded that a joint letter by the two emperors be addressed to King George, inviting Britain to conclude peace, and hinting at vigorous action in the Mediterranean and the Orient should Britain refuse to do so; with regard to Austria, Napoleon wanted France and Russia to force the Court of Vienna to line up with them and declare war upon England, should that power refuse to conclude peace. Furthermore, Austria was to disarm and to recognize the new conditions in Spain. On these points he met the most obstinate resistance on the part of Alexander, and finally, exasperated, he observed sarcastically to Caulaincourt, "Your Emperor is stubborn as a mule and is deaf to what he does not wish to hear."[19]

After insisting vainly for several days, he lost patience and had an outburst of temper, upon which Alexander said calmly, "You are violent. I am stubborn, and anger will achieve nothing with me. Let's talk and discuss or I will leave."[20] Thus a crisis had been reached between the two allies, and "this emperor [Alexander] who was said to be weak and hesitant was showing a surprising firmness of character veiled by an unalterable serenity."[21]

Eight days passed in futile discussions, and finally Napoleon gave in, abandoning the scheme of a joint move against Austria, and merely accepting a pledge that should war come Russia would aid France. In return, however, he overrode the protests of Russia and kept the Prussian fortresses, on the ground that they flanked Austria and therefore had become a strategic necessity. On this compromise basis Talleyrand and Rumiantsev were instructed to work out a

[19] Vandal, *op. cit.*, I, 435. [20] *Ibid.*, I, 435. [21] *Ibid.*, I, 434.

convention, which was duly signed on October 12, 1808. This convention stipulated that a joint offer of peace should be made to England and that the two powers would act jointly in negotiations resulting from this offer. France and Russia respectively guaranteed their mutual conquests accomplished since Tilsit (Articles I-III), and each retained whatever it had occupied (Article IV). France not only accepted the annexation by Russia of Finland, Moldavia, and Wallachia, but promised in the coming negotiations with England to obtain recognition of these annexations by Great Britain (Articles V-VIII). Russia obtained the right to negotiate directly with Turkey without French mediation, but in return promised not to set her forces in action in Rumania before January 1, 1809 (Article IX). Should Austria attack Russia, France would come to the aid of her ally, and conversely Russia would aid France in the event of a Franco-Austrian war (Article X). A new meeting would be arranged within a year in the event of failure of the peace negotiations, and also the contracting parties pledged to respect and guarantee the remaining possessions of the Turkish Empire (Articles XII-XVI). Thus compromises veiled the mutual incompatibilities and suspicions which made this meeting very different from the meeting at Tilsit.

The world at large, however, knew nothing of these underground fissures, and the awesome spectacle of the two Caesars deciding the issues of the world was the more impressive because of their public show of friendship. The two emperors rode out to Weimar together, where the Duke of Saxe-Weimar had arranged a reception in their honor with Goethe and Wieland present. Even more spectacular was the gala performance at the theater, where Napoleon and Alexander sat in the front row with the seats behind them occupied by thirty-four crowned heads. When on the stage in the play of Voltaire these words were uttered: "The friendship of a great man is a benefaction from the gods," Alexander rose and ostentatiously shook the hand of Napoleon. But these spectacular gestures, as well as the gifts which each of the allies was showering on the other, were lacking in sincerity.

VII

With Napoleon becoming more and more entangled in Spain and Austria preparing feverishly for war, Alexander's policy after Erfurt became increasingly cautious. He already had three wars on hand, one with England, one with Sweden, and one with Turkey; and he had no desire to become entangled in a fourth. Moreover, he was contemplating a grandiose scheme of internal reforms; and the liberal statesman Speransky was now rapidly gaining in power and influence. Under these circumstances his plans did not go beyond the immediate interests of Russia, which were to terminate the Swedish and Balkan wars in such a way that Russia would obtain Finland and the Danubian Principalities. Though on both fronts there was a truce, Alexander realized that further fighting would be necessary to achieve this end. With regard to his treaty obligations toward Napoleon, he would attempt to give Napoleon more tokens of moral encouragement than actual support. As Vandal puts it tersely, he was prepared to give Napoleon "the friendship of the Czar rather than the support of Russia."[22] The tempting vision of the great scheme of partitioning Turkey was definitely relegated by him to the realm of dreams and romanticism, and was not to be considered as a practical policy. This and the increasing distrust of Napoleon which was growing in the mind of Alexander made one thing clear to him: Austria and Prussia, both potential allies in the future and barriers to Napoleon's ambitions, must not be further weakened. Hence, although Napoleon was using all his persuasive powers to bring Russia to adopt a clear-cut stand against Austria's armament, the Czar preferred a definitely ambiguous policy, limiting himself to mild and friendly remonstrances. These were quickly interpreted in Vienna as revealing Russia's secret sympathy with Austria's cause, the more so that there were other tokens of the same nature. Count Tolstoy, the former Russian ambassador in Paris, passing through Vienna after Erfurt, was royally received and expressed freely his bitter anti-French feelings. Too, there was in Vienna a large colony of Russians of the highest social rank who had established themselves there in protest against the pro-French tendencies in St. Petersburg. This group was led by Count Andrei Razumovsky, former Russian ambassador in Vienna, who had quit his post after Tilsit but remained in the Austrian capital to carry on his private war against France. In these Russian circles one salon in particular predominated—that of Princess Bagration, who unquestionably ruled Viennese society. She already had by this time the

[22] *Ibid.*, II, 9.

leading salon in Vienna, in which congregated not only members of the Austrian aristocracy, but all who were influential in government and politics. Here fashions and political opinions were made, and the latter were bitterly anti-French. The influence of Princess Bagration may be seen in the fact that even after Napoleon had married Marie Louise, Princess Bagration decreed that it was not good form to be seen too frequently at the French Embassy, and the French diplomats remained socially ostracized.

The influence of these social groups, serving as a link between the two countries and revealing the true sympathies of Russia, canceled any effect which the mild and hesitating warnings of the Czar might have had on Austria. A further incident was inevitably interpreted in the same way. In January, 1809, the King and Queen of Prussia made their return call to St. Petersburg, and were received with a warmth of hospitality and a magnificence not at all in keeping with the reduced status of the royal couple, and though no politics intruded in the splendid festivities which were arranged for the guests, this visit was interpreted as a tacit but hostile demonstration against France.

Thus encouraged, Austria proceeded with her bellicose plans; and, as the danger of war was growing hourly, Napoleon made feverish efforts to obtain the aid of Russia. He concentrated his efforts on Count Rumiantsev, the Russian Foreign Minister, who had rejoined him in Paris after the Erfurt meeting. Rumiantsev, a man of wide political experience and great vision, was a staunch supporter of the Franco-Russian alliance, which he deemed a necessity owing to the geographical position of the two countries. But he too came to distrust the excessive ambitions of Napoleon; and finally, pressed by Napoleon, he evaded the issue by returning to Russia in the midst of the crisis. Having obtained nothing from the minister, Napoleon turned to the Czar, and through his ambassador, Caulaincourt, tried to influence him to take a definite stand. At first he wanted Russia to intervene on behalf of peace by a military demonstration; then as war loomed nearer and nearer, he wanted Russia to give definite assurances of military co-operation. He argued that Russia could detach eighty thousand men for use against Austria without weakening her position in the Swedish or Turkish wars. He wanted Russia to concentrate her forces in Poland, to detach a part of the Danubian

Army in order to threaten Transylvania, and to send a corps to occupy Dresden so as to cut the communications between Austria and Prussia. Such was the tenor of the increasingly urgent messages Napoleon addressed either directly to the Czar or through Caulaincourt on March 5, 11, 18, 22, 23, 24, 26, and 29. But Alexander remained evasive, playing the same game that Napoleon had played when the Czar wanted to obtain from him the cession of the Danubian Principalities—a policy of indefinite promises and postponements. When on April 9 the Austrian armies crossed into Bavaria and the war started, Napoleon still did not know what his Russian ally was going to do. As a precautionary measure Alexander had assembled on his Polish frontier facing Galicia some sixty thousand men under Prince Golitsin, including four divisions of infantry and some cavalry, but he obstinately refused Caulaincourt's demands to enter Galicia should the Austrians advance into the Grand Duchy of Warsaw.

However, after an Austrian army fifty thousand strong under Archduke Ferdinand did in fact invade the Grand Duchy of Warsaw, his attitude stiffened somewhat; and, with Napoleon insisting on the *casus foederis*, he finally on May 15 issued an order for Golitsin's army to advance into Galicia. But in the meanwhile the Austrians had defeated the Polish Army under Prince Joseph Poniatovski, had occupied Warsaw, and were advancing down the Vistula toward Thorn and Danzig. Poniatovski, being cut off from his capital, upon the advice of Napoleon decided upon a daring maneuver. Following the Vistula upstream and working his way in the opposite direction to the Austrians, he invaded Galicia early in May and raised a rebellion among the peoples of Austrian Poland. By May 23, with Austrian garrisons capitulating at his approach, Poniatovski entered Lemberg in triumph, after which he set himself the task of organizing a Polish government, and in the name of the King of Saxony he appealed to all Poles to unite in the task of liberating Poland. These events and this agitation had dangerous repercussions across the Russian border, where the Polish elements, particularly in Podolia and Volhynia, were showing definite signs of unrest. Thus the situation had altered very significantly—the Russian army entering Galicia was facing not the Austrians but the Poles, and moreover it was encountering a dangerous agitation in its rear. Just as the Russians were getting under way came the news of the battle of Essling, in which the French had suffered a bad defeat. Thus events themselves were forging a community of interests between Russia and Austria; Russia had apparently bet on the wrong horse. Under these circumstances Alexander waited and temporized, to the increasing exasperation of Napoleon. "Compliments and phrases are not armies, and it is armies that the situation demands," wrote Champagny to Caulaincourt on June 2.[23] However, the next day, June 3, fifty-three days after the beginning of hostilities, three Russian divisions with their cavalry, forming a total of forty-five thousand men, crossed into Galicia and faced the Polish Army of Occupation. Archduke Ferdinand, having received news of the events in Galicia, abandoned his advance, evacuated Warsaw on June 2, and was marching back upstream toward Galicia.

Thus an odd situation was developing where the Russians and Austrians, officially at war with each other, were both facing the same enemy, i.e., the Poles, who were the official allies of the Russians. The Austrians, moving upstream, menaced Sandomir on the Vistula at the point where the river San flows into it. Poniatovski hurried to the rescue of this key city, and sent urgent requests to Golitsin to come to his aid. But the latter moved so slowly that by the time his troops reached the San, Sandomir had fallen. At a conference between the commanders of the two armies, after the Poles and the Russians had established contact, it was agreed that Poniatovski should cross to the left bank of the Vistula, whereas Golitsin would remain on the right bank, so that the broad river would serve to separate the two armies and they might thereby avoid the possible occurrence of dangerous incidents. At the same time an emissary of Archduke Ferdinand, Major Fiquelmont, had reached Russian Headquarters, where he was received with more cordiality than was due an enemy; and in the course of the negotiations Golitsin let it be known that the Russians would not go beyond the Vistula to the west, nor beyond the Visloka, another confluent of the river, to the south. Thus a definite pact had been concluded with the Austrians; and upon reaching the line of the Visloka, the Russian Army stopped.

Freed from the Russian menace, the Austrians speedily reoccu-

[23] *Ibid.*, II, 94.

pied Lemberg. Meanwhile the relations between the Russian and Polish headquarters were becoming acrimonious. The Poles accused the Russians of restoring the Austrian colors and Austrian administration in the territory they had occupied, and the Russians countered with the charge of Polish revolutionary propaganda and activities. Presently the inevitable clash occurred. While Archduke Ferdinand was at Lemberg, Poniatovski made a dash to occupy the medieval capital of Poland, Cracow, where only small Austrian forces were concentrated. But the Russian Headquarters saw the importance of this move and sent a flying Russian column under General Suvorov (a relative of the Field Marshal) to occupy the city in place of the retreating Austrians. Suvorov's cavalry reached Cracow on July 14, a few hours ahead of the Polish Army, and when Poniatovski entered the city he found Russian Hussars barring his way. An armed clash was averted only by the decision of the commanders of the respective forces to divide the city into two zones, one Russian and the other Polish. These incidents caused considerable emotion in St. Petersburg, and Rumiantsev forwarded a note to Napoleon in which Russia's complaints against the Poles were enumerated. Thus for the first time the question of Poland was officially raised between the allies, and Alexander declared to Caulaincourt that the Polish question was the one issue upon which he would remain adamant and that there could be no question of the restoration of Poland. "I want to be reassured at all costs," he added significantly.[24] Under these circumstances Napoleon's victory at Wagram brought little rejoicing in St. Petersburg, but the subsequent armistice, by immobilizing all the armies, brought relief to the growing tension.

But the thorny question was to be revived in the peace negotiations. Having decided to detach Galicia from Austria, Napoleon was faced with the problem of what to do with this Polish province. He had first thought of making it an independent state to be given to the Grand Duke of Würzburg, the brother of Emperor Francis, upon whose devotion he could depend. But he abandoned this scheme, fearing that, because the Grand Duke was a Hapsburg, the link with Austria would remain too close. The alternate solution was to divide the province between Russia and the Grand Duchy of

[24] *Ibid.*, II, 113.

Warsaw. Just as Napoleon was pondering this problem, he received a letter from Alexander I in which the latter placed the Polish question squarely in his hands, reminding him at the same time that Russia had participated in the war while she had three other wars on hand, of which two were the result of the French alliance. This letter indicated that Russia was not going to participate in the peace negotiations. The far-seeing Alexander thus placed in the hands of Napoleon the responsibility for the successful maintenance of the alliance, and avoided the hostility which the active participation of Russia in the partition of Austria might produce in that country. On the Austrian side the negotiators fought bitterly to retain the provinces demanded by Napoleon, particularly Illyria and Lower Austria, but were willing to agree to the cession of Galicia in the hope that the latter would prove the cause of subsequent discord between France and Russia. There was a further consideration which was of importance to Napoleon: whereas Russia had been only lukewarm, the armies of the Grand Duchy of Warsaw had fought with a somewhat self-interested but nevertheless very real zeal.

But the Austrians adopted a policy of temporizing, and the negotiations did not progress. Napoleon, exasperated, played a game of diplomatic bluff and, without having previously consulted Russia, announced that he was referring the whole matter for settlement to the Emperor of Russia. At the same time he ordered troop movements. This double threat of a war and of the revival of the dreaded Franco-Russian alliance was sufficient to make the Austrians capitulate, and the Peace of Vienna was signed on October 14, 1809. Having received the territories he had asked for, including Galicia, Napoleon decided to cede practically all of it to the Grand Duchy of Warsaw, with the exception of the district of Tarnopol, a small section of Eastern Galicia, which he allotted to Russia. In a letter to the Czar written the same day and explaining his decision, he pledged himself not to aid the renascence of Poland and promised to see that the very name of Poland should disappear from history. These guarantees did not satisfy Alexander, and the news of the signing of the Treaty of Vienna produced a genuine dismay when it reached St. Petersburg. To understand this we must remember that, in the three partitionings of Poland, Russia did not acquire any Polish territories but instead received the non-Polish border provinces of the republic, whereas Poland proper went to Austria and Prussia. The Prussian share was converted after Tilsit into the Grand Duchy of Warsaw, and now, by the Treaty of Vienna, the Austrian share was adjoined to it. To all effects a united Poland was re-created with the single exception of the insignificant district of Tarnopol. Thus even though Napoleon's decision was a fair and logical one—"They got more than they earned," he grumbled, speaking of the cession of Tarnopol to Russia—still it was not a wise one. Caulaincourt kept him well informed about the mood of Russia, and he must have seen in this veiled re-creation of Poland a dangerous cause of inevitable future discord between the allies. The Russian reply was prompt and came in the form of a demand that Napoleon's pledges with regard to the nonrestoration of Poland should be put in treaty form, Napoleon to guarantee the borders as delimited by the two powers and to give formal assurance never to restore Poland. As for Napoleon, he raised an issue which was destined to put the alliance to a further severe test.

The issue in question had first appeared in the form of a rumor during the meeting at Erfurt. Alexander had been sufficiently disturbed to order his ambassador in Paris to make a confidential inquiry, but the latter had reported that it was nothing more than a rumor. It concerned Napoleon's divorce and his intention of asking for the hand of a Russian grand duchess. Now, however, after the Treaty of Vienna, since the divorce from Josephine was becoming a reality, the matter was revived. It was natural that Napoleon, desiring a union with one of the leading dynasties of Europe, should think first of capitalizing on his alliance. Hence in secret instructions given to Caulaincourt on November 22 he ordered his ambassador in St. Petersburg to talk the matter over frankly with the Czar and prepare the ground for an official demand for the hand of Grand Duchess Anna Pavlovna, the Czar's younger sister. Earlier rumors had credited Napoleon with the intention of proposing to Grand Duchess Catherine, the elder sister, but the latter had, somewhat hastily, been married to the Duke of Oldenburg. Just as this letter was about to be sent, Napoleon received word of Russia's insistence upon concluding the treaty of guarantee concerning Poland. In his haste to have the marriage issue settled favorably, Napoleon ordered that a second letter should be inserted for the use of Caulaincourt, informing him that he was prepared to meet Russia's demand. To emphasize still further his feelings toward Russia, Napoleon made a notable remark in the throne speech at the opening of the *Corps Législatif* on December 3: "My ally and friend, the Emperor of Russia, has united to his vast Empire Finland, Moldavia, Wallachia, and a part of Galicia. I am not jealous of anything good which might come to this Empire, my sentiments for its illustrious sovereign being in conformity with my policies."[25] Thus he stressed his acceptance of the union of the Danubian Principalities, anticipating an event which had not yet occurred. Finally, in a further message to Caulaincourt he emphasized that no difficulties of any kind, religious or otherwise, should be raised which might interfere with his marriage scheme. The rumor of these nuptials having spread over Paris, the project was spoken of as the union of Rome and Byzantium—of Charlemagne and Empress Irene. But there seemed to be little response to this enthusiasm in Russia, and as Napoleon impatiently read the diplomatic mail from St. Petersburg, he found in it only complaints—that Marshal Berthier had used the name "Poles" in an official document, that the French consul in Bucharest had adopted an anti-Russian attitude, and so forth. Napoleon began to understand that his plan might not materialize, and, anxious that there should be no delay between his divorce and remarriage, he ordered his ambassador in Vienna to start subsidiary negotiations for a possible union with a Hapsburg princess. Thus the two sets of negotiations were running parallel. Further to stress his willingness, Napoleon offered to grant a loan to Russia of thirty to fifty million francs, and authorized the sending of several French naval experts to Russia to aid in the construction of naval craft of a highly specialized type. Cashing in on these good feelings, Rumiantsev lost no time in drawing up a treaty of eight articles concerning Poland, of which the first article emphatically declared that "the Kingdom of Poland will never be re-established."[26] In accordance with the instructions received, Caulaincourt signed the treaty and sent it to Napoleon for ratification.

In the interval, with regard to the marriage project, not only was there unanimous opposition to it in Russian society but, more im-

[25] *Ibid.*, II, 190.

[26] *Ibid.*, II, 222.

portant, it was vetoed by the Dowager Empress, who, according to the will of Emperor Paul, was to have the final word in the question of the marriage of her daughters. Alexander himself drew a distinct line between having Napoleon as a political ally and as a brother-in-law. But in view of the delicate negotiations over Poland it was important not to antagonize Napoleon; hence a policy of postponement and elusive replies was adopted. Under repeated instructions from Paris, the French ambassador kept pressing for a definite reply. Alexander evaded an answer by referring him to the Dowager Empress, who in turn replied that no definite answer could be made without the consent of the eldest daughter, Grand Duchess Catherine, who was absent. Thus the situation dragged on till February, 1810. Finally an answer had to be given when Napoleon asked categorically for a yes or no. Alexander, putting it as tactfully as he could, refused the hand of his sister, stressing her youth. When the news of the Russian refusal reached Paris, Napoleon, in his spite, refused to ratify the treaty concerning Poland, though he left the door open for future but increasingly futile negotiations.

In Austria the response to Napoleon's matrimonial projects had been very different, the Austrian government hoping to retrieve the disastrous Treaty of Vienna by a Hapsburg marriage—hence the announcement of Napoleon's engagement to Marie Louise came practically simultaneously with the Russian refusal. However much both parties in Paris and in St. Petersburg continued their protests of friendship, Napoleon's vanity had been bitterly hurt, and a further element of discord was introduced into the moribund Franco-Russian alliance. How far the two countries had drifted apart became immediately noticeable at the ceremonies of the celebration of Napoleon's marriage in Paris. The Russian ambassador, Prince Kurakin, who, so far, had been the most influential member of the diplomatic corps and who had been receiving the major portion of Napoleon's favors and attention, found himself during the various ceremonies and celebrations of the marriage relegated to second place and somewhat cold-shouldered. His place was now occupied rather too ostentatiously by Count Metternich. Finally, the loan which Napoleon had promised Russia was diverted to Austria.

These unmistakable signs, which did not miss the eye of Alexander, resulted in a very important shift in Russian policy with regard to Poland. Napoleon had, as we have seen, rejected the treaty his ambassador had signed; but he had sent a counterproposal, thereby leaving the door open. To this counterproposal Russia replied by another counterproposal, but it would be futile to go into the details of these negotiations, which continued to drag on and led nowhere. The important thing was that though Napoleon was undoubtedly motivated by spite in refusing to sign a treaty which he had been ready to accept, there was also a political reason caused by the change in the status of the alliance. Although he had been ready to sacrifice Poland for the sake of the advantages he hoped to get from Russia, when these were not forthcoming in the degree he expected, he began to look upon Poland with a different eye. Poland was assuming a strategic importance which he could not overlook in the now not improbable event of a war with Russia. And now that he had secured Austria through his marriage, Poland would become even more important strategically, for the Austrian Army could use that country as a base for operations against Russia, just as his own French Army had used it. Under these circumstances it was important for him to strengthen Poland rather than weaken it.

By a curious parallel evolution of thought, just as in the days preceding Tilsit, only in reverse, Alexander was beginning to contemplate a similar policy. To understand Alexander's diplomacy one has to bear in mind his complex personality. On more than one occasion we find that while one idea dominated his mind, at the same time a contrary trend was nurtured subconsciously, which, when the circumstances became favorable, emerged and replaced the previous idea. Such was the case, for instance, when he was oscillating between his liberal views and the Holy Alliance. Such was now his attitude toward Poland. While he had been working to crush Poland so as to prevent it from becoming the tool of Napoleon, we also find a contrary attitude gradually gaining strength in him. It existed throughout his reign, and by going back to his early youth we can find the inception of this idea in his friendship with Prince Adam Czartoryski. The next stage occurred when Alexander visited Poland on his way to participate in the campaign of Austerlitz and was enthusiastically received by the Polish nobility, while he himself made certain pledges with regard to the future of Poland. Dormant through the Tilsit period, this pro-Polish trend came to new life in the face of the crisis in the Franco-Russia alliance.

The basis for such a policy was a factor which was to play an important part in Alexander's calculations, namely, the existence in the Grand Duchy of Warsaw of a definite pro-Russian party, which visualized the salvation of Poland in the support of Alexander rather than in the support of Napoleon. This party, though small, was influential, composed as it was of the great landed nobility of the country. When the Russian Army was concentrating against Austria in 1809, a delegation representing this party secretly reached the headquarters of Prince Golitsin and made a definite offer: Should Alexander reunite Poland under his scepter and give it back its ancient frontiers, many nobles would be willing to recognize him as their king. Golitsin transmitted this offer to the Czar, suggesting that a Kingdom of Poland should be re-created, which would be composed of all the territories of the former Kingdom, with the exception of White Russia and the governments of Kiev and Podolia.[27] In reply, by order of Alexander, Rumiantsev wrote a carefully worded letter[28] in which he compared the relations of Poland and Russia with those of Ireland and England, and instructed Golitsin to encourage secretly the Polish magnates to ask for a union of Galicia and Poland under the scepter of the Czar. Thus the idea continued to be nourished and was germinating. After the news of Napoleon's refusal to ratify the Polish treaty, followed by the announcement of his Austrian marriage, the next stage was reached. Czartoryski had just returned to St. Petersburg from a self-imposed exile of several years abroad. Alexander saw him several times in January, March, and April, 1810. Somewhat constrained at first, Alexander soon renewed his friendliness and became more outspoken. In March he definitely suggested to Czartoryski that the latter should work out a plan "to reunite Poland to prevent Bonaparte from doing it."[29] Czartoryski, somewhat mistrustful, drew up a memorandum which he read to the Czar, after which the matter re-

[27] Letter of Golitsin to Czar Alexander dated 4-16 June, 1809 (Vandal, *op. cit.*, II, Appendix II).

[28] Letter of Golitsin to Czar Alexander dated 15-27 June, 1809 (Vandal, *op. cit.*, II, Appendix II).

[29] Vandal, *op. cit.*, II, 339.

mained in abeyance, the time not being ripe for any further action. But the idea kept gaining strength in Alexander's mind.

However, an issue of more pressing importance linked with the Polish question demanded immediate attention. Prussia was receiving intelligence both from Paris and Vienna to the effect that the marriage of Empress Marie Louise to Napoleon had resulted in an alarming swing of Austria's foreign policy toward France. Indeed, Metternich, now in Paris with the Empress, was an ardent partisan of an alliance with France, and his influence dominated both the Court and the Government. In Vienna, France had suddenly become fashionable; and the Russian clique, previously so influential in society, was rapidly losing ground. Alexander was quick to see that, in the event of a war between Russia and France, not only would Poland act as a spearhead for the invading armies, but the Austrian Army might become the right flank of Napoleon's Grand Army. To offset this danger Austria had to be won back to Russia. But the problem was too delicate a one to be handled by the official Russian ambassador in Vienna, Count Shuvalov. Hence a secret envoy was sent to Vienna to work in co-operation with Shuvalov. He was Alopeus, ostensibly appointed minister to the Court of Naples, but with secret instructions not to proceed beyond Vienna. Having arrived at the Austrian capital, he delayed his departure under various pretexts and proceeded at once to get in touch with the Russian salons and through them to make his way into influential Austrian circles. The instructions given to him by Rumiantsev were a masterpiece of diplomatic dexterity. He was to say that the natural sympathy which Russia had always had for Austria was now enhanced by the marriage of Marie Louise, since this had led to a friendship between Austria and France, and France was an ally of Russia. With the increase in power Austria had thus acquired she might be tempted in the future to regain her lost possessions in Germany and Italy, and Russia was the only power which would look upon this with equanimity, as her interests lay elsewhere and did not conflict with those of Austria. The support of Russia would be invaluable for Austria should she contemplate any such schemes. Thus it would be in Austria's interest to come closer to Russia. So with Machiavellian cunning Russia was playing the role of temptress and sowing the seeds of discord with France, since the territories lost by Austria were in Napoleon's possession.

Alopeus, powerfully supported by the pro-Russian circles, succeeded in swaying the Austrian Government to a point where Metternich, alarmed, rushed back to Vienna from Paris to block this dangerous drift. In Paris, Metternich had been working to strengthen his relations with Napoleon with the obvious intention of displacing Russia completely, and he predicted to Napoleon the inevitability of an armed conflict between Russia and France. The pledge Napoleon had given to Russia in the Polish treaty, not to re-establish Poland, irritated Napoleon profoundly. Metternich added fuel to the flames by indicating the dangers both to Austria and to France in Russia's aggressive policy in the Balkans, and he went so far as to suggest that Napoleon should denounce the Convention of Erfurt. Napoleon was not prepared to take such an overt step; but, with Austria coming to him, he needed the Russian alliance less and less. Hence his attitude on Poland began stiffening, and as the negotiations with Russia on this issue had been dragging on futilely, he finally made a definite break in July by not replying to a Russian note. Thus the first step toward war had been taken.

It was at this time also that the first military measures were taken on both sides. Napoleon, so deeply involved in Spain, could not spare any forces, but he secretly delivered thirty thousand rifles to the Polish Army and instructed the Grand Duke of Warsaw to fortify Praha, a suburb of Warsaw, and Modlin; concurrently Russia started building a line of fortifications along the Dvina and the upper Dnieper, and brought several army corps up to the Polish border. Presently new and graver issues were to arise between the allies. The election of Bernadotte as Prince Royal of Sweden was viewed in St. Petersburg with open hostility as a move on the part of France to reach out toward Russia through Sweden as well as through Poland, and the proximity of St. Petersburg to the Swedish border made Russia particularly sensitive to any threat from that direction.

But it was the Continental System which was becoming the main cause of friction between the two countries. In an attempt to enforce the closing of the North Sea ports, Napoleon was induced to start a series of annexations to his Empire—first Holland, then the

Hanseatic cities Bremen, Hamburg, Lübeck. Russia was watching with alarm this rapid extension of the French Empire along the North Sea, stretching out like a third finger between Poland and Sweden, toward the Russian frontier. But, to obtain a continuous stretch of French possessions, Napoleon had to annex the intermediate territories as well, and here between Ost-Frisia and Hanover lay the Duchy of Oldenburg. The reigning Duke of Oldenburg was an uncle of the Czar, and the house was doubly related to the Romanovs by the recent marriage of the Grand Duchess Catherine. For this reason Napoleon hesitated for a while, but on January 22, 1811, he signed a decree officially annexing Oldenburg. The Duke was to be compensated by the transference of his family rights to Erfurt. This was a flagrant violation of the Treaty of Tilsit, which specifically mentioned the inviolability of the duchies of Oldenburg, Saxe-Coburg, and Mecklenburg-Schwerin. Alexander, rightly indignant, took this as an open insult; and the Oldenburg issue became the gravest problem between him and Napoleon, becoming later the actual *casus belli.* Napoleon, however, countered with equally indignant accusations that Russia was not living up to the promises she had given with regard to the application of the Continental System. The closing of the North Sea ports, rigidly applied since the French had taken possession, forced British trade to seek an outlet farther east. Neutral vessels carrying British cargoes, failing to discharge their cargoes at Hamburg, Lübeck, or Danzig, made for the Baltic ports of Sweden and Russia. The Russian Government permitted these vessels to unload provided a certificate was shown establishing the non-British origin of the merchandise. Napoleon contended that these certificates could be easily obtained, and that they covered British merchandise. He therefore wrote a personal letter to Alexander complaining about this. At the same time Caulaincourt was instructed to bring up the matter in St. Petersburg. Alexander replied that he would scrupulously fulfil his obligations with regard to the Treaty of Tilsit, but that to extend these agreements to neutral trade would be to go beyond the stipulations of the treaty and hence could not be considered a requirement. Napoleon had further approached Russia (September 7) with a demand that she should raise her tariffs on imports of colonial products, and the two issues became inevitably intertwined; to both of these Rumiantsev was instructed to give a courteous but negative reply.

Presently a third economic issue arose. By the Treaty of Tilsit (Article XXVII) the contracting parties had agreed to regulate their trading relations along prewar lines, which entailed putting into effect the Franco-Russian treaty of commerce of January 11, 1787, pending the signing of a new treaty. But the Continental System had completely upset the trade relations of Russia. British trade had come to a standstill, whereas French importations protected by the treaty had increased tremendously, mostly in high-priced luxury products drawing large amounts of money out of the country and thereby causing the fall of Russian currency. In an effort to restore the trade balance a ukase was issued on December 31, 1810, introducing prohibitive tariffs on merchandise coming in by land, most of which was of French origin.

Thus both Alexander and Napoleon had taken steps toward open hostility. The quarrel which could no longer be concealed now came out into the open.

Chapter VII

Napoleon's Invasion of Russia in 1812

I

A war with France appearing more and more imminent, Alexander in the beginning of 1811 seems for a while to have entertained the thought of striking first. His calculations were based on the fact that Napoleon, absorbed in the Spanish war, had only 60,000 French troops in Germany, whereas Russia had 240,000 men ready for action.[1] If these forces invaded Germany and reached the line of the Oder, Alexander hoped for the uprising of the Germans, particularly the Prussians, and possibly the Danes, against Napoleon, and the eventual participation of Austria on his side. But the Grand Duchy of Warsaw was so situated that if it remained loyal to France it might take the Russian armies in Germany in reverse or in flank, and endanger the whole scheme, or, again, by resisting a Russian invasion of Polish territory give Napoleon time to strike back. Thus Poland once more became the crucial factor in his calculations. Hence in January, 1811, a secret correspondence, carried on by messengers smuggling themselves across the Russian-Polish border, was resumed between the Czar and Prince Czartoryski, who was residing on his palatial estate of Pulawi near Warsaw. Czartoryski wrote to the Czar that he would be willing to work for Alexander's scheme of restoring Poland, provided the Czar gave some guarantees concerning a constitution for Poland along the lines of the Constitution of 1791, granting autonomy and liberty to the Poles, and agreed to the restitution to Poland of the provinces she had lost in her partitions. In a long letter written on January 30 in reply, Alexander pledged himself to restore Poland to the limits of her ancient possessions, that is to say with borders along the Dvina, the Berezina, and the Dnieper, to give complete self-government and autonomy

[1] Figures given by Czar Alexander to Prince Czartoryski (Vandal, *op. cit.*, III, 34).

with a national administration and army, and to grant a liberal constitution. In return he demanded the military co-operation of the Poles against Napoleon, and he furnished Czartoryski with the secret information concerning his plans and the state of his army, as already mentioned.

At the same time Rumiantsev was instructed to sound out the courts of Prussia, Sweden, and particularly Austria. And while his instructions to Count Stackelberg, now Russian ambassador in Vienna, stressed the dangers of the continuous expansion of Napoleon's Empire, the Czar, going over the head of his chancellor, wrote on February 13 a personal and more explicit letter to Emperor Francis, in which he argued that Poland would be re-created by Napoleon and thus Galicia would be lost to Austria anyway. It would therefore be in Austria's interest to come to terms with Russia on the question of re-creating Poland and giving to it Galicia, thereby working for the cause of Europe as a whole. As an additional lure, Alexander promised to cede the Danubian Principalities to Austria in return for Austria's co-operation in the coming struggle.[2]

Last but not least, the Russian Embassy in Paris was endeavoring to establish contact with and to merge the efforts of all discontented elements in the French capital, and for this purpose one of the secretaries of the embassy, the young and promising Nesselrode, was specially accredited as unofficial envoy to Prince Talleyrand.

Napoleon also began preparing for the coming struggle. He gradually increased the strength of Davout's corps stationed in Germany, bringing it up to a total of five divisions; he ordered repairs on the military roads leading toward Russia, an increase in the garrison of Danzig, the storing of huge military supplies at Hamburg and Magdeburg, and the consignment to the Grand Duke of Warsaw of sixty thousand rifles bought in Austria. But he kept on denying that these military preparations had any significance, and insisted on maintaining strictly the outward appearance of the alliance. As Alexander responded with a punctilious observance of proprieties, few were the observers who could see the underlying causes of the coming war.

In March the first important troop movements were ordered in Russia. With great secrecy and marching in separate columns, units

[2] Martens, *op. cit.*, III, 78-79.

of two armies marched toward their points of concentration at Vilno, Grodno, Bialystok, and Brest-Litovsk. A few divisions were also detached from the army operating in Moldavia and marched north. Thus an imposing military force was assembled along the Russo-Polish frontier ready to open an offensive or act as a defense barrier, according to circumstances. These circumstances decided the issue, for the time being, in favor of the latter course. Indeed, from Warsaw Czartoryski reported the complete failure to win over the cause of Russia the influential circles of the Polish capital—they remained faithful to their alliance with Napoleon. The overtures made by Alexander to Austria met with the same fate, because of the attitude of Metternich. Not only did Metternich block the pro-Russian intrigue in Vienna, but he also declared that any violation of Austrian territory by Russian troops would lead to war and that the concentration of Russian armies along the borders of Galicia and Bukovina would force Austria to mobilize. In Prussia and in Sweden the attitude toward Russia was hesitant. Thus the moment was not propitious for a forward policy.

In the meanwhile Rumiantsev was striving desperately to save the crumbling alliance by finding a solution to the main issues which were causing the cleavage: on the Russian side the Polish policy of Napoleon and his annexation of the Duchy of Oldenburg, on the French side the prohibitive ukase of December 31, 1810, which continued to elicit from Napoleon the bitterest protests. As the French Emperor had suggested compensating the dispossessed Duke of Oldenburg with a territory around Erfurt, Rumiantsev very cautiously and diplomatically put forward another solution: namely, that the Duke should be compensated by the cession of a part of the Grand Duchy of Warsaw which would both settle the acute Oldenburg question by giving sufficient compensation, and at the same time weaken the Grand Duchy of Warsaw by a partition and the creation of a new pro-Russian Polish state.

Meanwhile alarming reports about Russian troop movements reached Napoleon from Warsaw, Turkey, and Sweden almost simultaneously early in April. Then came a succession of reports from the French minister in Warsaw, Bignon, to whom Prince Joseph Poniatovski had revealed the full content of Alexander's correspondence with Czartoryski. Napoleon immediately ordered the King of

Saxony to mobilize the Polish Army, and speeded up further troop movements to Germany. These measures caused a panic all over Europe, particularly in Paris, where stocks fell violently. But Alexander did not move, and Napoleon was not yet prepared to face a war with Russia; hence the alarm gradually subsided. But to the Russian hint of compensations in Poland for the Duke of Oldenburg, Napoleon opposed an angry "no." Finding that Caulaincourt had become too pro-Russian, Napoleon recalled him and sent in his stead General Lauriston. Upon his return to Paris in June Caulaincourt had a seven-hour interview with Napoleon in which he stated bluntly that the Emperor could follow one of two courses: either give up Poland and retain the alliance with Russia, or rely on Poland and face a war with Russia. The Ambassador added that there was no danger of an attack coming from Alexander, but should Napoleon invade Russia, he would meet a very stiff resistance from a united nation. This clear-sighted analysis seems to have impressed the Emperor, and he pondered over the problem for the next two months. He stored up his resentment until finally, on August 15 at a reception of the diplomatic corps in honor of his birthday, he burst forth in a violent diatribe against Russia to the Russian ambassador, Prince Kurakin. These calculated outbursts of rage were always a sign of coming war and were immediately interpreted as such by the diplomats, and particularly by the Austrians, who themselves had undergone a similar scene prior to the war of 1809. The next day Napoleon closeted himself with his secretary and dictated a long document in which he examined all the pros and cons of the Russian war menace. He was prone to do this to clarify his own ideas before taking an important decision. In this voluminous memorandum he came to the decision that a war with Russia was inevitable —it may therefore be said that the fatal decision to invade Russia was made on that day, August 16, 1811.

War therefore had been decided upon in principle, but both Napoleon and Alexander were eager to postpone it for a while. Napoleon needed six months more to prepare for it and desired to be able to select his own time to strike, and Alexander had definitely given up the idea of an offensive warfare and was leaving the next move to Napoleon. Indeed, he had come under the influence of military experts who pointed out Wellington's successful strategy at Torres-Vedras as the example to be followed, and contended that the only chance of success for Alexander lay in drawing the enemy deeply into Russia and then withering away his forces by constant rear-guard actions. Thus the disparity in size of the respective armies would tend to disappear. This strategy was advocated by the foreign experts in Russian service, of whom the most famous was General Pfuhl, and also the Russian generals, of whom the strongest advocate of this Fabian policy was Barclay de Tolly, who after Eylau had expressed his views on the subject in no uncertain terms. "If I were commander in chief I would avoid a decisive battle, and would carry out a retreat in such a way that the French would find in place of victory, a second Poltava."[3]

Thus for the next months the conflict was to remain in a frozen state with neither side anxious to bring matters to a head. Napoleon was pursuing steadily and systematically his preparations for the greatest war in his career. Danzig was becoming the great base, with stores, foundries, and workshops to meet the needs of the entire army. It was protected by an army composed of French, Polish, Westphalian, Hessian, and Baden troops. The Polish Army in the Grand Duchy of Warsaw had been brought up to the largest possible complement. In the second line, on the Elbe and the Oder, purely French troops some 200,000 strong were supported by the German battalions of the Confederation of the Rhine; farther in the rear in Holland and in northern France a third army was being formed; while in Italy, Neapolitan and other Italian units under Prince Eugene were being concentrated between Brescia and Verona. Swiss, Croatian, Portuguese, and Spanish units were marching to the various centers to join these armies. At the same time Napoleon paid the greatest attention to technical details, assembling guns, creating three special pontoon regiments, and in his love for detail providing not only for winter clothing, but for 28,000,000 bottles of wine and 2,000,000 bottles of brandy.[4] These formidable preparations foreshadowed the creation of an army of 1,300,000 men, of whom some 600,000 could be earmarked for the invasion of Russia. Against these the Russian Army, already on war footing, represented 27 divisions composed of 540 battalions, 410 squadrons, and 1,600 guns,

[3] Vandal, *op. cit.*, III, 165.
[4] *Ibid.*, III, 233.

totaling between 250,000 and 300,000 men. That was the absolute limit which Alexander could muster in view of the requirements for the wars on other fronts—in Moldavia, in the Caucasus against Persia, and finally in holding Finland. Under these circumstances the question of obtaining the co-operation of allies became of paramount importance; to release the Moldavian Army by a peace with Turkey became another objective.

The outlook in this respect appeared by no means hopeless at the close of the year 1811. A smashing defeat inflicted upon the Turks at Rustchuk by Kutusov seemed to promise the end of that long-drawn-out war. In Sweden, Bernadotte, having failed to obtain the promise of the cession of Norway from Napoleon, was willing to turn to Russia at this price. And though Austria had turned down all Russian advances, Prussia was looking once more toward Russian assistance and had succeeded in building up a military strength which could not be overlooked. The most promising partner seemed to be Prussia.

The imminence of the war with Russia produced a panic in Berlin. Not without logic did the Prussian Government argue that any invasion of Russia by Napoleon had to be preceded by a complete subjugation of Prussia by the French. Prussia started rearming feverishly and, notwithstanding the close supervision of French agents, succeeded in building up a well-equipped army of 100,000 men. On the diplomatic front and in conjunction with this rearming, Prussia once more turned to Russia. General Scharnhorst, the great reorganizer of Prussia's military system, was sent to St. Petersburg on a very secret mission. Traveling under an assumed name, he reached St. Petersburg and on October 4, 1811, had an interview with Alexander at Tsarskoye Selo. He had come to offer a military convention according to which the Prussian Army would fight side by side with the Russians provided that, at the opening of hostilities, the Russians would advance beyond the Vistula toward the Oder and join the Prussians, who would operate in Pomerania and Silesia on the flanks of the Russian Army. Here, supported by the fortresses of the Oder, the allied armies would offer battle to Napoleon.[5]

Alexander was puzzled. The proffered help of 100,000 Prus-

[5] Martens, *op. cit.*, VII, 24-37.

sians was not to be scorned; on the other hand it meant the abandonment of the carefully worked out plan of drawing the enemy into Russia. Furthermore, Scharnhorst hinted that should Russia refuse to support her, Prussia would have no alternative but to join Napoleon. With this formidable menace arising, Alexander began to yield. In a series of conferences between Scharnhorst on one side and Chancellor Rumiantsev and the Minister of War Barclay de Tolly on the other, a compromise plan was evolved whereby the Russians would advance toward the Vistula while the Prussians would fall back toward that river, and the junction of the two armies would be carried out along the Vistula. A military convention was duly signed on October 17 embodying these plans.

In the meanwhile Napoleon had not remained inactive. In view of the persistent rearming of Prussia signaled to him by his spies, to wipe Prussia out of existence he had merely to order the troops of Davout, the garrisons of Danzig, Westphalia, and Warsaw to converge on Berlin. The French minister in Berlin, Count de Saint Marsan, presented a virtual ultimatum to Berlin, and just as the panic in that capital had reached a climax, Napoleon made an offer of alliance. Friedrich Wilhelm, hesitant, terrified, could not make up his mind which way to turn. He sent Scharnhorst, upon his return from Russia, to Vienna to attempt to line up Austria in the new coalition, but here Scharnhorst's mission failed completely. Finally on January 29, 1812, the Prussian Government informed the Count de Saint Marsan that it was ready to accept Napoleon's terms, and Prussia not only joined France but pledged herself to give a Prussian contingent twenty thousand strong to the Grand Army. In the meanwhile on December 17 Napoleon officially raised the question of an alliance with Prince Schwarzenberg, the Austrian ambassador in Paris, and here he met with no difficulties. Austria pledged herself to fight on the side of France, for which she would obtain the return of Galicia and possibly Silesia, should Prussia be unfaithful. She might further compensate herself at the expense of Turkey in the Danubian Provinces.

In February the Grand Army was set in motion. Davout began a slow advance toward the Vistula with a screening force of 100,000 men, followed by 120,000 German troops of the Confederation and the other French corps. The Italian divisions, assembled at Verona, crossed the Alps and entered Bavaria, while the Imperial Guard stationed in northern France and Belgium moved up as general reserve. Eager to avoid a premature Russian attack, Napoleon ordered the greatest secrecy to be maintained, and many a commander had to regain his unit without saying goodbye to his family. Further to lull the Russians, Napoleon initiated last-minute negotiations for peace through the agency of Alexander's confidential agent in Paris, Colonel Count Chernyshev, to whom he put his conditions for avoiding war: (1) the strict observance by Russia of the Continental System, with exclusion of neutrals from Russian ports, (2) a treaty of commerce favorable to France, and (3) the settlement of the Oldenburg question, either by a monetary indemnity or by Russia's waiving her claims. As the Grand Army approached Prussia, Napoleon had his agreement with that country converted into a formal treaty, which was duly signed on February 23; and three weeks later on March 14 he signed a treaty with Austria. When the Grand Army passed through Prussia it was accordingly increased by 20,000 Prussians under General Yorck, while 30,000 Austrians under Prince Schwarzenberg began moving through Galicia towards the Ukraine.

Thus Napoleon had arrayed the whole of Europe against Russia —if he could obtain the alliance of Sweden and Turkey, he would be in a position to develop two formidable flank attacks which would threaten his enemy through Finland and from the Black Sea—a colossal encircling maneuver. Accordingly in February his ambassador to Constantinople, Latour-Maubourg, proposed an alliance to Turkey. Turkey was to assemble 100,000 men on the Danube for an advance into southern Russia, and to raise the Standard of a Holy War among the Moslems of Russia, the Caucasus, and the East. As recompense, Turkey was promised the return of the Crimea and the whole coast of the Black Sea. But the Turks, exhausted by the long-drawn-out war with Russia, showed little enthusiasm for this scheme. Similarly, Napoleon offered Sweden the return of Finland and a subsidy of twelve million. This offer was transmitted through the Princess Royal of Sweden, the wife of Bernadotte, the former Désirée Clary, with whom in his youth Napoleon had had a romantic affair. Désirée, who had been in Paris, left abruptly for Stockholm to persuade her husband to accept these terms, but she was too late. Sweden was negotiating with Russia for an alliance which would fulfil her ambitions.

II

When Marshal Bernadotte, on August 21, 1810, was elected Crown Prince of Sweden, it was believed in Sweden that this move would result in the recovery of Finland. It was even on this belief that Bernadotte's popularity rested, and the French Marshal was given preference over the Duke of Oldenburg, the candidate proposed by Count Adlerkreutz. Adlerkreutz's theory was that Oldenburg, having married the sister of Alexander, would be in a position to recover Finland, since the Russian Grand Duchess would become Crown Princess of Sweden. But feeling against Russia was running too high in Sweden to make possible the election of a pro-Russian candidate. However, the Swedes miscalculated with regard to Bernadotte, at least in one respect: instead of becoming the enemy of Russia, he became on the contrary her only ally in the greatest crisis of that country's history. This was due to the fact, not sufficiently realized in Sweden, that Bernadotte had been a personal enemy of Napoleon, and that once Napoleon had turned against Russia it was natural to find Bernadotte siding with Alexander.

However, the new Crown Prince of Sweden, known henceforth under the name of Charles John, had to find some compensation for Sweden if his popularity was to survive. Thus he turned the attention of the Swedish people to Norway, which the Swedes had coveted for a long time. This acquisition would be a signal increase in Swedish territory, and at the same time would materially weaken Napoleon's one trustworthy ally in Scandinavia—King Frederick VI of Denmark. When, because of the illness of the elderly King Charles XIII, Prince Charles John was put at the helm of state affairs, his decision had apparently been made, for the efforts of Baron Alquier, the French minister, to entice him into an alliance with France against Russia failed completely. On the other hand, the basis for a friendship with Russia was strengthened by the occupation in January, 1812, of Swedish Pomerania by the French. This incident gave Charles John the opportunity of writing to Alexander on February 6, 1812, stating that this violation of Swedish territory had so affected the elderly king that he was sending Baron Löwenhielm to St. Petersburg to discuss the possibilities of an alliance with Russia. Thus the first move was made by Charles John.

Upon arriving in St. Petersburg, Löwenhielm got in touch with a Swedish *émigré,* Gustave Armfelt, now a Russian citizen, who coached him in the best way to approach the Czar. At the first audience with Alexander, Löwenhielm made it plain that Sweden had the choice of siding with Napoleon to regain Finland, or of siding with Russia to gain Norway. According to Löwenhielm, Alexander said: "Let us not speak of Finland; it is not the most beautiful page of my history," and he solemnly promised Norway to Sweden.[6] A secret treaty was drawn up by which Russia promised to aid Sweden in conquering Norway with a contingent of fifteen to twenty thousand men, in return for Sweden's aid to Russia in the event of a war with France outside Russia. Denmark was to be invited to join the alliance, and in return for the cession of Norway would receive compensation in Germany. Should Denmark refuse, an expedition would attack Zealand; the Swedes were to provide the transportation for the expeditionary force, and the Russian contingent was to be ready by May, 1812. Furthermore, Sweden would put pressure on Turkey to bring her to make peace with Russia.

Meanwhile, parallel negotiations were proceeding in Stockholm between Charles John and General Suchtelen, sent by Russia as special envoy; and a second version of the treaty was drafted, slightly more favorable to the Swedes, with Russia promising to take charge of the transportation of her own troops as well. This version was accepted as definitive and signed on April 15, 1812. The invasion of Russia in June by Napoleon, however, forced the Czar to postpone indefinitely the sending of the promised expeditionary force, and the treaty remained a dead letter. But the alliance produced one immediate result. Edward Thornton, the British envoy to Sweden, signed at Örebro on July 18, 1812, identical treaties of peace for England with both Sweden and Russia.[7]

[6] Carl Gustaf Löwenhielm, *Min lefvernes beskrifning* (Stockholm, 1923), p. 138.

[7] After Napoleon's invasion had begun and the Russian Army was retreating toward Moscow, Russia further improved her position by an agreement signed on August 27, 1812, at Abo, Finland, at a meeting between Charles John and Alexander arranged at the suggestion of the British Admiral Betinck. Here Alexander reiterated his promise to give support to Sweden, who had been preparing for the expedition against Denmark, by sending thirty-five thousand men during September and November. In the new treaty there drawn up Russia recognized future Swedish possession of Zealand and Bornholm, should these be taken

Just at the time the treaty of St. Petersburg had definitely brought Sweden over to the Russian side, Chernyshev arrived in St. Petersburg, bringing with him Napoleon's terms. Strengthened by his treaty with Sweden and seeing through Napoleon's scheme for gaining time, Alexander replied on April 8 with counter conditions of peace which were a virtual ultimatum: Napoleon was to evacuate northeastern Germany, including Prussia and Swedish Pomerania, and to reduce the garrisons of Danzig and the fortresses beyond the Elbe, and thus cease to menace Russia. Only after these steps had been taken could negotiations start along the lines suggested by Napoleon. However, there would be no question of barring neutral shipping from Russian ports. Thus Alexander had burned his bridges. Upon presentation of this note the Russian ambassador in Paris, Prince Kurakin, failing to obtain satisfaction, asked for his passports. Nothing could have been more unwelcome to Napoleon, whose troop movements had not yet been completed. Hence he dispatched General Narbonne to Russia on a mission of last-minute negotiations with the main object of gaining time. He further instructed his Foreign Office to delay the open break with Russia by retaining Kurakin in Paris by any means possible. At the same time he speeded up his departure for the Grand Army and left Paris on May 9, never again to return as a victor. Three weeks earlier, on April 21, Alexander, after a solemn religious service at the Cathedral of Kazan, had left for Vilno, the General Headquarters of his armies. Napoleon on his way to the front held his last great court at Dresden as guest of the King of Saxony in the presence of Emperor Francis of Austria, the King of Prussia, and all the princes of the Confederation of the Rhine. It was a second Erfurt, with all the splendor and pageantry, but with Emperor Francis taking the place of Czar Alexander. On May 28 Napoleon left Dresden and set out for Poland.

In the meanwhile, before clearing his decks for action, Alexander had to make peace with Turkey. Military operations on the Danube had been languishing since the recall of the divisions and since the

---

by Sweden, in return for Sweden's recognition of an extension of Russian territory in Poland. A welcome result for Russia of this treaty was the removal of Swedish troops from the borders of Finland, which gave Russia security on her northern frontier. Since, however, subsequent events in the campaign of 1812 made it impossible for Russia to send the troops at the specified time, Sweden demobilized her expeditionary force against Denmark.

defeat of the Turks at Rustchuk. Eager to put an end to them, Alexander had instructed Kutusov to offer more moderate terms to Turkey—instead of demanding Moldavia and Wallachia he was merely to ask for Bessarabia up to the river Pruth, coupled, however, with a military alliance with Turkey. On this basis the preliminaries of peace were signed on May 28 at Bucharest. The question of alliance was to be discussed subsequently in Constantinople. The peace was a hasty one, and, aside from the cession of Bessarabia to Russia and the retrocession of the Danubian Principalities to Turkey, it left all issues undefined and open for further conflicts; but its main purpose, that of releasing the Moldavian Army, had been achieved, and it thus marked a diplomatic defeat for Napoleon: his great encircling scheme through Sweden and Turkey had fallen through.

And now it was Russia who began contemplating a similar scheme in reverse. While the negotiations for the ratification of the treaty were being pursued in Constantinople, Admiral Chichagov came forward with a daring plan. The Turks were to be lured into an alliance by a promise to return Illyria and Dalmatia. If they refused active co-operation, they were then merely to pledge the free passage of Russian troops through their territory. Chichagov, backed by the remaining units of the Moldavian Army, would raise a rebellion among the Balkan Slavs and form guerilla bands. Crossing the Balkan Peninsula, he would make his way into Dalmatia, march up the Adriatic, and threaten Trieste and Venice, and if all went well even push into Switzerland, raising everywhere the standard of rebellion of the oppressed peoples against Napoleon; at the same time an Anglo-Russian squadron would attack the coast of Naples. To achieve these ends he was secretly to promise the Balkan Slavs emancipation from the Turkish yoke and to hold out to them as a future possibility the creation of a great Slav empire in the Balkans under the protectorate of Russia. Thus the earliest potentialities of Pan-Slavism were being exploited. At the same time such a rebellion flaring up along the southern borders of Austria would probably carry the agitation to the Slavs of Austria and paralyze that country's endeavor to unite with Napoleon. However romantic such a scheme may have been, it had sufficient practical possibilities to enable Chichagov to obtain instructions to proceed with the plan.

The idea bore fruit at least in one direction. At the end of April Metternich secretly informed the Russian cabinet of the existence of the French alliance, at the same time informing Russia that Austria had no serious intention of carrying out her pledges to Napoleon and that Schwarzenberg had been instructed not to penetrate far beyond the frontier and not to fight the Russians. This started secret negotiations between Vienna and St. Petersburg, during which time Chichagov was ordered to proceed actively with his plans to impress Austria, and Metternich was discreetly told that Russia had the means of raising a rebellion not only among the Southern Slavs in Austria but among the Hungarians as well. Metternich apparently was sufficiently impressed to offer a more concrete basis for relations between the two countries in the coming war. Austria would reduce her corps in the Grand Army from thirty thousand to twenty-six thousand and would remain passive after Schwarzenberg had penetrated into Russia, keeping the bulk of her forces in reserve. The Russians for their part would localize the war against Austria entirely to the front occupied by Schwarzenberg, and abstain from any military activities on any other Austrian frontier. A verbal guarantee to this effect was given by both parties, which put an end to Chichagov's scheme but also gave Russia the valuable assurance that Austria would not be more dangerous to Russia now than Russia had been to Austria in the war of 1809. At the same time the King of Prussia wrote to the Czar explaining his policy and apologizing for his defection. Intelligence came to Russia from Bavaria and from various other states of the Germanic Confederation indicative of sympathy, and it became clear that the isolation of Russia was more apparent than real.

From Dresden Napoleon went to Posen, where he was rapturously received by the Polish population, and then proceeded on his way to the Nieman. On June 16 at Königsberg, timing this act so that it would become known in Russia at the very moment his army was crossing the river and entering Russia, he finally permitted Kurakin to receive his passports and recalled Lauriston from St. Petersburg. Five days later he issued a proclamation to his armies calling them to action in the "second Polish war." But when the last negotiations were conducted, hostilities had already begun. Alexander had received the news of Napoleon's invasion as he was attending a ball given by the nobility in the manor of Zakrety near Vilno. He immediately left the dance, secretly, and passed the night working. He drew up a diplomatic note refuting point by point the allegations of the French manifesto of war, and sent his Minister of Police, General Balashov, as emissary with a personal letter to Napoleon. He put as conditions for the renewal of peace negotiations the complete evacuation of Russian territory by the French, after which he would be ready to negotiate on the basis of his ultimatum of the month of April. It was apparent that he had not the slightest hope of seeing Napoleon comply with these terms, but he had in mind the effect on public opinion in Europe produced by this last gesture of peace made after the enemy was already in his territory. Balashov crossed the French lines near Vilno and arrived at Davout's headquarters. Here he was kept a virtual prisoner until Napoleon saw fit to receive him on July 1. By this time Napoleon was in Vilno; he made a point of receiving the Russian emissary in the very room that Alexander had occupied during his stay in the palace. For several hours Napoleon soliloquized before the Russian, recounting his grievances and attempting to terrorize him into a submission by proxy. "Tell the Emperor Alexander that I give him my word that I have 550,000 men on this side of the Vistula," he said as a last argument.[8] The same evening he invited Balashov to dinner, where a famous conversation ensued, the Russian showing himself the equal of the Emperor in the art of repartee. To Napoleon's question of how many churches there were in Moscow, Balashov answered that there were more than 340. Napoleon asked why there were so many. "Because our people are religious." "Nobody is religious nowadays," said Napoleon. "I beg your pardon, Sire, people are not religious in Germany or in Italy, but they still are in Spain and in Russia," Balashov retorted mischievously. Changing the subject, Napoleon asked which was the best way to Moscow, to which the Russian replied that one could take whichever road one preferred. "Charles XII took the road by Poltava," he added.

Balashov was sent back to Alexander with a letter in which Napoleon reiterated his grievances and enclosed a copy of his proclamation to the Grand Army. This brought all further negotiations

[8] Vandal, *op. cit.*, III, 522.

to a standstill. Summing up the situation, Napoleon said to Berthier, Caulaincourt, and Bessière:

> Alexander is laughing at me. Does he believe that I have come to Vilno to discuss commercial treaties? It is time to finish with the Northern Colossus, to push him back and to place Poland between him and civilization. I will not object to the Russians' receiving the British at Archangel, but the Baltic must be closed to them. The time is gone when Catherine made Louis XV tremble. . . . Civilization rejects these inhabitants of the North.[9]

Destiny, however, was to reject Napoleon.

III

No war has been more generally misinterpreted in history than Napoleon's campaign in Russia. Too readily it has been dismissed with the statement that Napoleon was driven out by the cold. In saying this, historians forget that they thereby merely endorse Napoleon's "war propaganda"—the official explanation which Napoleon gave Europe to account for his defeat and make it appear an "act of God" for which he could not be responsible. Thus accepted, the legend of the defeat of the Grand Army by the cold in Russia has crept into history, and this superficial view has been repeated glibly ever since. If Napoleon were defeated merely by climatic conditions, however, it becomes impossible to explain the importance that the war had as a milestone in the development of relations between Russia and the West. To get a more accurate and balanced view, one must study the three factors which came into play in the course of this great struggle. These were, in order of importance, the military factor, the national factor (the nation at arms), and the geographical factor, which includes both the terrain of the theater of operations and the climate. Let us analyze first the military factor.

That Napoleon was aware, by the experience gained in the Polish-East Prussian campaign of 1807, that a crucial and difficult struggle lay ahead of him may be seen in the very magnitude and thoroughness of his preparations for this war. The Grand Army was expanded to become the greatest fighting force ever recorded in European history—a grand total of 1,187,000 men, of whom about

[9] *Ibid.*, III, 516.

600,000 were detailed for the invasion. With the sole exception of Sweden, Russia found herself alone, facing the crushing impact of virtually the whole of continental Europe, to which formidable menace she could oppose a mere 200,000 men. But here lay the first error in Napoleon's calculations—with his mathematical mind he was prone to attribute too much importance to numerical factors alone. The Grand Army, with its 850,000 Frenchmen and 337,000 foreigners, could not have the moral cohesion of a national army; and such diverse contingents as the Neapolitan Corps, the Swiss, the Polish, Portuguese, Spanish, Croation, Belgian, and Dutch contingents could not blend effectively. Thus the very numbers tended to weaken the military value of the invading army, whereas the smaller but morally united and compact Russian Army had a distinct advantage over its foe in this respect. This advantage might have been offset by a careful management of the plan of campaign; and we find, if we believe Metternich, that Napoleon was all for caution at first. Indeed, Metternich states in his *Mémoires* that when at Dresden in May, 1812, the Grand Army marched past the assembled rulers of Europe, revealing such formidable power, Napoleon divulged his plan for a long-drawn-out war:

> My undertaking is of the kind that is solved by patience; triumph will come to the most patient. I am going to open the campaign by crossing the Nieman and will terminate it at Smolensk and Minsk. There I will halt. I will fortify these two places, and from Vilno, where I will establish the General Headquarters during next winter, I will organize Lithuania. . . . We will see who will get tired of it first, I to let my army live at the expense of Russia, or Alexander to feed my army at the expense of his country.[10]

But in a desperate resolve to obtain a quick and decisive battle Napoleon had to push as far as Vilno, then to Smolensk, and finally to make the fatal move of marching on Moscow. Thus we must from the very outset make this important point. The greatness of Napoleon as a military leader was based, as may be seen in all his previous campaigns, on the fact that he knew how to keep the initiative in his own hands throughout the struggle by constantly imposing his will on the enemy. And yet in this war we find the initiative slipping away to the elusively retreating Russians, whose

[10] Metternich, *op. cit.*, I, 122.

plan of campaign was imposed upon him. From the outset he was not the master of his moves. How and why did this occur? The explanation lies in the very nature of the situation in which the Russian Army found itself, and in its special character on the one hand and the character of the country and the people on the other.

At the opening of the war the Russian forces were divided into three armies stretched out along the border in anticipation of a possible attack by Napoleon, which could come from East Prussia or from Poland or from Austria. Thus the First Army of the West under Barclay de Tolly (90,000 men) had its headquarters at Vilno and was covering the Nieman. The Second Army of the West under Bagration (60,000 men), with headquarters at Volkovysk covering Poland, was separated from the First Army by several hundred miles. The Third Army, known as the Army of Reserve, commanded by Tormasov (45,000 men), was again several hundred miles farther south in Volhynia with headquarters at Lutsk.[11] The so-called Moldavian Army under Admiral Chichagov (50,000 men), which had been fighting the Turks on the Danube, freed by the peace of Bucharest, was able to come up during the last phase of the war. With this disposition of forces, when the main line of Napoleon's attack along the Nieman became clear, the strategy which the Russian command had to adopt was imposed upon it by the logic of the situation. Indeed, on June 24 Napoleon crossed the Nieman with 220,000 under his own command, 80,000 under the Viceroy of Italy on his right and 40,000 under Macdonald on his left flank, with Schwarzenberg farther south on the Bug, three other corps in Poland proper, and finally 100,000 in reserve. Thus at the lowest estimate Barclay's 90,000 faced 350,000 men. Under these circumstances Barclay fell back, ordering Bagration to do the same and to unite with him, since his task of observation had been completed now that Napoleon had shown his line of attack. Accordingly, Barclay started his retreat on the twenty-sixth and Bagration on the twenty-ninth. Napoleon naturally wished to prevent the union of the two Russian armies; hence he drove a wedge between them by

[11] Clausewitz gives the following figures: Barclay de Tolly, 90,000 men, Bagration, 50,000 men, Reserve Army, 30,000 men, Cossacks, 10,000 men, grand total, 180,000 men (General Karl von Clausewitz, *La Campagne de 1812 en Russie*, Paris, 1900, p. 3).

detaching Davout for the purpose of keeping Bagration separated from Barclay.[12]

As the First Russian Army passed Vitebsk in its retreat, Barclay, not being sure of the goal set by Napoleon, detached Wittgenstein with 25,000 men to proceed north and cover St. Petersburg by holding Riga and the line of the Dvina (July 23). Napoleon sent Oudinot with 40,000 after Wittgenstein, while farther to the north-west, Macdonald with 30,000 men faced Riga and Jacobstadt. Thus a new front came into existence, forming the extreme left flank of the French advance. Wittgenstein attacked Oudinot at Polotsk (August 17), but was repulsed the next day by St. Cyr, who had replaced Oudinot, wounded the preceding day. After this the two opposing forces here neutralized each other and did not participate in the main operations until the very last phase of the war. On the extreme right flank Schwarzenberg with 35,000 men and Reynier with 17,000 faced Tormasov's Reserve Army, which inflicted a heavy defeat on Reynier by capturing an entire brigade of 6,000 men (Klenzel) and repulsing Reynier at Slonim. This forced Schwarzenberg to disobey Napoleon's order to rejoin the main army advancing on Moscow, and he remained where he was. Thus both flanks were immobilized for the time being. In the meanwhile Barclay, anxious to unite as quickly as possible with Bagration, marched past Vitebsk, contenting himself merely with a rear-guard action against Murat before that city, which lasted three days. Upon reaching Smolensk (August 2), Barclay stopped to await Bagration, who came up two days later.

Thus the first task set by the Russian Command, that of getting the First and Second Armies united, had been successfully achieved; and Napoleon's attempt to drive a wedge between the two armies had failed. To achieve their junction the two Russian armies had to retreat faster than the enemy advanced. An orderly retreat has always been considered by military experts as the stiffest test for an army, for it demands two qualities: successful co-ordination of staff work and iron discipline, without which demoralization sets in, turning the retreat into a rout. The testimony of the enemy and the number of prisoners lost are the surest gauge of the condition of the retreating army. "The Russian army," writes Caulaincourt, "marched

[12] *Ibid.*, pp. 37-38.

in good order, without undue haste, like men intent on abandoning nothing and prepared in case of necessity to stand their ground";[13] as for prisoners ". . . [Napoleon] needed prisoners at any price, they were the only source of information about the Russian army. . . . While we were following the Russian army, powerless to obtain the least information about it, great changes were taking place in its formation,"[14] and he exults over the capture of a Cossack whose horse had been killed, and of a Negro cook.

Turning for comparison to the French Army, we find it from the very beginning of the advance suffering from lack of organization, bad discipline, and increasing demoralization. When Napoleon occupied Vilno he issued orders for the organization of the conquered territory of Lithuania into prefectures and subprefectures and appointed inspectors, tax collectors, and police commissioners. He issued grandiloquent appeals to the population, reminding the Poles of their past glory and promising the Lithuanians liberation from the Russian yoke and from serfdom. But all these measures were nullified by the bad conduct of the Army, which resulted in the hostility of the population from the outset. We have a graphic account of both the disorganization and the lack of discipline of the Grand Army from Labaume, who, as staff officer under the Viceroy of Italy, Prince Eugene, gives us a detailed account of the events he witnessed with the Fourth Corps.[15] He notes that scarcely had the Army crossed the Nieman when, in the first five days of heavy rains, horses were lost. Near Pilony he saw hundreds of dead horses, carriages overturned, baggage scattered, and this was in the last days of June.[16] At Novo Troki (July 4) the soldiery was "robbing or destroying everything which came into their hands," and Labaume already speaks of the army "subsisting only by looting the inhabitants; as a result of which extreme confusion reigned and that fatal lack of discipline which is always a sign of the sure ruin of an army."[17] The subprefect of Novo Troki, traveling from Vilno to regain his post, was stopped by stragglers who robbed him and his escort, ate

[13] Marquis Armand Augustin Louis de Caulaincourt, *With Napoleon in Russia: The Memoirs of General de Caulaincourt, Duke of Vicenza* (New York, 1935), p. 82.

[14] *Ibid.*, pp. 86-88.

[15] Eugène Labaume, *Relation circonstanciée de la campagne de Russie* (Paris, 1814), *passim.*

[16] *Ibid.*, p. 32.

[17] *Ibid.*, p. 35.

up his provisions, and went off with his horses, leaving the unfortunate official to return to Novo Troki on foot.[18] Again, approaching Smolensk, when the columns of the Grand Army effected their junction near Rasasna:

> This immense uniting of men at one point increased our misery and redoubled the confusion and disorder on the main highways; straying soldiers looked in vain for their regiments, others, with urgent orders, could not execute them because of the overcrowding on the roads, and consequently a dreadful noise was heard on the bridges and narrow defiles.[19]

At Smolensk, Barclay received eight thousand men in reinforcements and, moreover, having taken command of both armies, became Commander in Chief, with Bagration under his orders; and the retreat became now a straightforward march in a single column. However, on August 8 he made a timid attempt to counterattack and inflicted a severe defeat on the French vanguard under Sebastiani at Jukovo. This second spurt of Russian activity gave Napoleon hope that the Russians were intending to defend Smolensk to the last ditch and thus fight the great battle which Napoleon was so anxiously seeking.

Accordingly Napoleon crossed the Dnieper at Rasasna and lost valuable time in preparing his whole army for an attack on Smolensk. In the meanwhile Bagration had thrown the division of Rayevsky into Smolensk, while he himself retreated toward Dorogobuzh; Barclay decided to sacrifice the division of Neverovsky, which for three days (August 15-17) heroically held back the much greater forces of Murat, thus permitting Barclay's army to get away. When Napoleon, after virtually destroying Neverovsky, made his way into the burning city thinking he had achieved a major victory, he found that Barclay was out of reach. It is true that in an effort to come out on the Moscow road with Bagration, Barclay had to make a perilous flank march and to fight another rear-guard action at Valutina Gora, where he had to engage a third of his forces, but once more he foiled Napoleon's plans and escaped.

This series of engagements around Smolensk cost the French, according to Clausewitz, twenty thousand men, and the Russians the same number or more. So ended the first phase of the war, and

[18] *Ibid.*, p. 40.
[19] *Ibid.*, p. 89.

Napoleon's intention to terminate the war at Smolensk had not materialized. Caulaincourt says of him at Smolensk: "The Emperor was puzzled and at once became annoyed at having to march on and on and move yet farther from his goal. . . . He tried to make me say that the Russians would hold and fight a battle, which was what he wanted. He was like a man in need of consolation."[20]

The second phase of the campaign opened with Napoleon's decision to advance on Moscow, making Smolensk his main base of operations. A constant series of rear-guard engagements took place, but were of relatively minor importance, the Russians always eluding Napoleon's armies. Indeed, on August 23, a rear-guard action took place at Dorogobuzh, and four days later Murat forced the crossing of the Osma in the face of resistance put up by the enemy's rear guard. The next day the French occupied the city of Viazma, to which the Russians had set fire; and on September 1, after another brush with the Russian rear guard, the city of Gshatsk, also aflame, was captured. Two days earlier, on August 29, Kutuzov was appointed Commander in Chief of the Russian armies, with Bennigsen acting as Chief of Staff. Both Barclay and Bagration remained in charge of their respective armies under the orders of Kutuzov, who was appointed with the specific understanding that he would stop the retreat and fight a battle to defend Moscow. Kutuzov selected for this purpose a position on the Kolotcha, a tributary of the river Moskva, some seventy miles from Moscow near the village of Borodino. While the army was fortifying and taking up this position, the rear guard was offering stiffer and stiffer resistance to hold back the enemy as long as possible. The French resumed their advance from Gshatsk on September 4, and at Gridnevo had a very hot engagement with the Russian rear guard, which fell back to Kolotskoye, whence the enemy obtained his first view of the battlefield of Borodino.

Napoleon arrived in person at this point on September 5 at 2:00 P.M. and noticed the redoubt of Shevardino, which the Russians had erected ahead of their positions, on a plateau overlooking a ravine. This redoubt covered the approach to the main Russian line and protected the Russian left flank. Napoleon decided forthwith to take it, using those troops he had on hand—the cavalry of Ney,

[20] Caulaincourt, *op. cit.*, p. 75.

the division of Compans, and Poniatovski's Polish division. The assault started at 4:00 P.M., and the French, after climbing the ravine, were stopped in their advance and contented themselves with opening a murderous fire on the defenders at extremely short range. The Russians stood their ground, and the French had to bring up their reserves and more artillery. Only after these had been engaged did they succeed in capturing the redoubt, the engagement costing the Russians some six thousand and the French some four thousand men. After the preliminary action had eliminated for the French a dangerous salient in the Russian line, the following day (September 6) was spent by both sides in preparing for the battle. It is to be noticed that whereas there was revelry going on in the French camp, on the Russian side a deeply religious mood prevailed, and a miraculous ikon of the Virgin was carried through the ranks of the army, blessing the troops for the forthcoming action.

Kutuzov had taken up a very strong position roughly north-south facing west, and extending somewhat over three miles, while the enemy approached along the new Smolensk highway. On Kutuzov's left, this position was covered by a large forest around the village of Outitsa. To the center and immediately back of the redoubt of Shevardino was the fortified village of Semenovskoye, and about half a mile farther to the north the Grand Redoubt. These two points were the keys of the whole defense. Semenovskoye was defended by trenches housing artillery and preceded by three flèches, smaller fortifications on the heights beyond, whereas the Grand Redoubt was defended by a battery of twenty-one cannon. Farther to the north the Russian line extended to the river Kolotcha, on the banks of which was located the village of Borodino. From Borodino the line turned at right angles and ran due east along the river to the village of Gorky. Contrary to the advice of Bennigsen, Kutuzov insisted on holding this sector of the line with very heavy forces—two army corps (Baggovut and Ostermann) covering Gorky, and the cavalry of Platov, Korff, and Ouvarov observing the course of the Kolotcha—in fact, the major portion of Barclay de Tolly's forces. This he did out of fear that the French following the new Smolensk highway running parallel to the river would attempt an enveloping movement from this side. Linking up with the center through the village of Borodino was the corps of Dokturov. The center proper was held by Bagration's army, with the corps of Rayevsky extending from the Grand Redoubt to Semenovskoye, and the corps of Borosdin defending the positions around that village. Farther to the south the corps of Tuchkov, composed mostly of militia, formed the extreme left flank holding the village of Outitsa. The general reserve under Kutuzov was formed of two cuirassier divisions, the remnants of the rear-guard forces of General Konovnitsin, and militia. All told, according to Bennigsen, the army numbered 120,000 men (of whom 17,500 were cavalry) and 640 cannon.

Pitted against these forces Napoleon had about 125,000 men with 580 cannon. His plan of attack followed his usual line. Poniatovski with the Fifth Polish Corps was to outflank the Russian positions from the south in order to draw the enemy forces from the center toward Outitsa, whereas Prince Eugene with the Fourth Corps was to attack the other flank at Borodino, thereby pinning Barclay's forces to the Kolotcha sector. In the meanwhile the main attack was to be directed by Davout and Ney against Semenovskoye, after the capture of which these forces would veer north and attack the Grand Redoubt from the flank and the rear, while Prince Eugene was to fall upon it from the north. Poniatovski in turn, after capturing Outitsa, was to proceed north to the support of Davout. Such was the plan—a double pincer movement on the flanks, while the main attack would dispose first of one and then of the other key positions. The reality was to fall somewhat short of these expectations.

The battle started at 6:00 A.M. (September 7) with the French artillery opening up against the Russian positions; Poniatovski started his flanking movement but met such determined opposition on the part of the half-trained militia at Outitsa that he was unable to make headway and therefore could not give Davout the support upon which the latter was counting. This attack therefore miscarried, and it was only at the very end of the battle that Poniatovski finally succeeded in getting beyond Outitsa, after Tuchkov had been mortally wounded; but by that time this maneuver had lost its significance.

On the opposite flank Prince Eugene, moving along the left bank of the Kolotcha, captured Borodino easily, for it was held only by Russian patrols; but when he proceeded further he ran into trouble.

His attempt to cross the river finished in disaster—his infantry was thrown back across the river, and General Plausonne, leading the attack, was killed. Prince Eugene had to content himself with holding Borodino on the left bank of the river until the French counterattack permitted him to try a second crossing. Thus he had failed to pin down Barclay de Tolly, and the latter's forces were moved up freely to the danger points in the central sector. Thus both flanking movements, upon which Napoleon's strategy so heavily relied, miscarried; and the battle degenerated into a frontal clash of the two armies around Semenovskoye and the Grand Redoubt, with little scope for maneuvering. Indeed, the main attack led by Davout was first directed against Semenovskoye. The division of General Compans assailed the south flèche. Compans was wounded and replaced by Rapp, who was wounded in turn. Davout, also injured, was replaced by Murat. Ney came to the support of Murat and attacked the north flèche, which his troops captured, only to be immediately driven out by a violent Russian counterattack. A second French attack supported by a cavalry charge gave the flèches once more to the French, and by ten o'clock they were finally in possession of them. Thus four hours of violent fighting had given them possession of only the outer defenses of Semenovskoye, and therefore the real battle was just beginning. Kutuzov, having sized up the threat of Prince Eugene's flanking movement and found it not dangerous, had had time to withdraw the greater part of Barclay's army to feed the defenses of the center. Had Poniatovski been successful in his flanking movement and threatened the plateau of Semenovskoye from the south, the Russian position would have been more dangerous. His failure left the whole task to the corps of Ney and Murat, who after 10:00 A.M. began the main attack. Indeed, Murat launched the cavalry of Latour-Maubourg into the gap between Semenovskoye and the Grand Redoubt, while Ney attacked the plateau. At the same time Prince Eugene finally succeeded in throwing a division across the Kolotcha, which broke into the Grand Redoubt from the north, and fierce hand-to-hand fighting took place between the French and the division of Paskevich holding the Redoubt.

But the Russians counterattacked with fierce energy. The French were driven out of the Grand Redoubt, and General Bonnamy, heading the French attack, was captured. Latour-Maubourg's cavalry in turn was thrown back, and Murat and Ney were so vigorously blocked in their advance that they sent urgent appeals to Napoleon for reinforcements. But while Napoleon sent the division of Friant to reinforce Murat, the corps of Baggovut, followed by that of Ostermann of Barclay's army, led by Barclay himself, was coming into the line; and, thus strengthened, the Russians launched a formidable counteroffensive while their cavalry crossed the Kolotcha and fell upon Prince Eugene's rear. The two armies clashed in furious and confused hand-to-hand fighting, interspersed with savage cavalry charges. At this moment, a critical one for the French, as they had been driven back from their positions, Ney and Murat threw in their last reserve, their cavalry, in a futile attempt to break through the Russian lines. Most of the French divisional commanders were wounded, including Friant, Nansouty, and Dessaix; and Montbrun was killed. Ney and Murat sent desperate appeals to Napoleon to use his last reserve, the Young Guards, but the Emperor refused, declaring, as he explained later, that he could not use his last card so far away from home.

Meanwhile the Russian attack had spent itself, and the Russians began falling back to their lines with ranks unbroken. Seeing this, Napoleon sent his Guards Artillery to form a battery of eighty cannon and to crush the defenders of the Grand Redoubt. At the same time he ordered Prince Eugene, whose forces had thus far suffered least, to renew the attack on the Redoubt. While Prince Eugene's infantry advanced, Murat sent the cavalry of Montbrun, now commanded by Caulaincourt, brother of the former ambassador, in a great charge which clashed with a countercharge of Russian cavalry. Caulaincourt was killed and the French charge was broken, but Grouchy charged with the cavalry of Prince Eugene's corps and pushed back the Russian cavalry of Korff, opening the way for the divisions of Gérard and Morand, who finally broke into the Grand Redoubt at 3:00 P.M.

> The Great Redoubt belched out a veritable hell on our center [writes the historian, Caulaincourt]. In vain did Marshal Ney and the Viceroy combine their forces to attack it; they were repulsed. . . . shortly before this a lieutenant general and some fifteen prisoners taken in the redoubt were brought to him [Napoleon]. This capture gave the Emperor great

pleasure. . . . It was quite inexplicable to him that redoubts and positions so audaciously captured and so doggedly defended should yield so few prisoners. . . . Several times he said to the Prince of Neuchâtel and to me: "These Russians let themselves be killed like automatons; they are not taken alive, this does not help us at all."[21]

And Labaume adds the following touch: "The interior of the redoubt presented a terrifying picture: corpses were piled one on the other and among them were many wounded. . . . All the Russian soldiers who were in the redoubt perished, preferring not to surrender. . . ."[22]

After the capture of the redoubt, the battle died out from sheer exhaustion of the armies. Napoleon at 4:00 P.M. merely ordered the opening of a cannonade of his massed artillery of four hundred guns against the unbroken lines "of the admirable Russian army massed in silence and still threatening,"[23] holding a line a few hundred yards back of the lost positions. By six o'clock this cannonade stopped, and the battle came to an end.

The losses were terrific. The French lost, according to Thiers, 30,000 men, including 49 generals. The Russian losses were 18 generals, 1,732 other officers, and 35,000 men. Among the generals, Bagration and the two brothers Tuchkov were killed or mortally wounded.[24]

After the battle the Russian Army took up a position just behind the one the French had captured, and so little had its power of resistance been weakened that at the council of war held at Fili the same night the discussions ended in a draw—seven votes to continue the battle the next day, seven to retreat; and the decisive vote was cast by Kutuzov himself. The retreat proceeded in orderly fashion in four columns along the Moscow road, showing, as Clausewitz states, "an order and a fighting capacity which was not usual after a lost battle." The rear guard under Miloradovich offered an increasingly stubborn resistance. Colonel Combe writes in his memoirs, "We were advancing on Moscow but slowly, the Russian army not falling back any longer as before the capture of Smolensk, but

[21] *Ibid.*, pp. 98-99.
[22] Labaume, *op. cit.*, pp. 141-142.
[23] Bourdeau, *op. cit.*, II, 198.
[24] Comte Feodor Vasilievitch Rostopchin, *La Vérité sur l'incendie de Moscou . . . suivi de ses Mémoires écrits en dix minutes . . .* (Paris, 1823), p. 37.

defending the ground inch by inch and inflicting upon us heavy losses with their cannon. . . ."[25]

Indeed, the Grand Army resumed its march on September 8, leaving Junot with his corps at Kolotskoye and advancing in three columns: Murat in the van of the main column marching by the highway to Mozhaisk, Poniatovski on his right marching on Vereia, and Prince Eugene on the left heading toward Rouza. On the ninth Murat was halted before Mozhaisk by the stubborn resistance of the Russian rear guard under Miloradovich. Only after a heavy attack by the French did Miloradovich abandon the city, after setting fire to it. Subsequently he took up a good position behind the river Nara and inflicted a loss of over two thousand men on the division of Friant, which Murat had launched against the Russian positions. Mortier, furious at this loss inflicted on a division of his corps, reported to Napoleon that henceforth he refused to take orders from Murat. This heavy rear-guard action permitted the main Russian forces not only to withdraw, but also to proceed to the evacuation of Moscow as well.

Indeed, by order of the Governor of Moscow, Count Rostopchin, the city was to be evacuated by its population. While the Russian columns were passing through the city in good order, with bands playing, to take up a position to the east of the city, a furious panic had gripped the civilian population and more than 200,000 people fled in two days. Amid great confusion the police set fire to whatever provisions could not be taken away, the prisons were thrown open, and the prisoners, joining the riffraff of the population, proceeded to break open casks of wine and to loot houses. In the meanwhile the French on the thirteenth having reached Sparrow Heights overlooking the city, Miloradovich agreed upon a suspension of arms for the next day to spare the city. Napoleon, who had stopped at Mozhaisk, came up in order to make a triumphant entry into the historic Russian capital. On September 15 he gazed with exultation over the city from Sparrow Heights, and it is said that he murmured: "There it is at last—that celebrated city. Now the war is finished." He sent Murat into the city to prepare his entrance, but the latter roamed about vainly in the empty streets in search of

[25] Colonel Michel Combe, *Mémoires de colonel Combe sur les campagnes de Russie, 1812; de Saxe, 1813; de France, 1814 et 1815* (Paris, 1896), p. 98.

authorities and welcoming deputies. Some ten thousand people, mostly vagabonds and criminals, were the sole remaining inhabitants. Finally Murat found a French bookseller, who was brought before the Emperor. "Where is the Senate?" asked Napoleon. "It has gone away." "And the Governor?" "He has gone away." "Where are the people?" "There are no people." "Who is there in the city?" "Nobody."

Napoleon entered the empty city while the last Russian columns were leaving the eastern suburbs, and the French were even subjected to fire from some concealed sharpshooters. The following day, September 16, Napoleon took up his residence in the Kremlin while his troops were scattered throughout the city. They found, so reported the Ordnance Service, enough food to last them six months. But their exultation over this fact was to prove shortlived. The same evening fires broke out in various parts of the city and, carried by a high wind, had soon converted the city into a sheet of flames.

A recapitulatory analysis of the Russian retreat and Napoleon's advance up to this point will help considerably in understanding the subsequent developments of the war, and will give us an important clue to Napoleon's defeat. Throughout the retreat, deducting the forces engaged elsewhere, i.e., Wittgenstein's, Tormasov's, and Chichagov's corps, the Russians had engaged 153,000 men against the main French Army. In this figure are included the reinforcements which the army received from the interior, i.e., the 8,000 men already mentioned, 15,000 men brought by General Miloradovich on August 27, and 10,000 half-trained militia brought up to the battlefield of Borodino on September 4. The total losses of the Russian Army during the whole retreat, including therefore the Battle of Borodino and the minor rear-guard engagements which were to follow, amounted to 80,000 men, or 55 per cent of the total effectives.

On the French side, if we deduct the detachments facing Wittgenstein and Tormasov, we find the Grand Army advancing on Moscow proper amounting to 365,000 men and composed of two groups: left center under Napoleon, 297,000 men (First, Second, Third, Fourth, Sixth Corps, Guards Corps, and Murat's cavalry), and right center under Jerome, 78,000 men (Fifth, Seventh, Eighth

[26] William Richard Morfill, *A History of Russia from the Birth of Peter the Great to Nicholas II* (London, 1902), p. 304.

Corps and cavalry of Latour-Maubourg). On September 3 Victor, crossing the Nieman from Germany, brought up the Ninth Corps of 34,000 men, to be held as general reserve at Smolensk. With 74,000 men under Macdonald, Schwarzenberg, etc., detached for special assignments, and two more divisions totaling 27,000 men brought up from the rear (Durutte and Loison), the grand total of troops engaged in the campaign by Napoleon amounted to 610,000 men, including all technical services, replacements, etc.[27] After his failure to keep Bagration separated from Barclay, Napoleon ordered the two portions of his army to unite at Vitebsk and henceforth, excluding the units on the extreme right and left flanks, to advance in a single column. Having been forced to detach Oudinot and St. Cyr to reinforce Macdonald, and Reynier to go to the support of Schwarzenberg, Napoleon, in the period between the crossing of the Nieman and the capture of Vitebsk, that is to say between June 24 and August 8, theoretically had remaining with him 285,000 men. But in reality he had only 185,000, indicating that the army had lost 100,000 men, or one fourth of its complement, before any real fighting had begun. This loss was primarily due to desertions, stragglers, and disease—particularly a bad epidemic of dysentery—and the breakdown of the supply service which left the advancing army without bread or meat. For the subsequent period of five weeks, which included both the fighting around Smolensk and the Battle of Borodino, we find the French losses numbering 82,000 men and after the Battle of Borodino, at the time of Napoleon's entry into Moscow, the French Army totaling only 103,000. According to the calculations of Clausewitz the units of the army entering Moscow originally numbered 288,000 men—thus the loss sustained by the army amounted to 185,000 (excluding the stragglers, who were rounded up and put to garrison the rear).[28]

Thus, comparing the two sets of figures, we find the French losing 105,000 more men than the Russians during the period of actual fighting, though it is usually contended that the losses of a retreating army are far greater than those of an advancing army. Assuming that the climatic factor affected both armies equally (after the first eight days the weather was warm and fine), it is true that

[27] Clausewitz, *op. cit.*, p. 77.

[28] *Ibid.*, p. 79.

the Russians had the advantage of marching through a country untouched by war, whereas the French found desolation and waste; but this did not apply to all regions which they crossed, and a more efficient supply service could have remedied the difficulty. We have therefore to deduce that the difference between the two armies was one of morale. On the Russian side there was still the tradition of Suvorov mingled with a religious spirit and the feeling that the very existence of the nation was at stake. On the French side the cosmopolitan soldiery was not inspired by any higher motives than looting and the promise that a quick victory would end the war; the magnetism of Napoleon and the magnificent traditions of the Grand Army were not sufficient to counteract the looseness of discipline and the demoralization which had set in, and the memoirs of the participants, particularly those of Labaume and Ségur, stress continuously the disgraceful scenes of looting and vandalism which sapped the spirit of the army throughout its advance.

In the light of these factors the Battle of Borodino gains a new significance. Technically, Napoleon was victor and had opened the road to Moscow, but he failed in his main purpose—namely, to crush the enemy in one decisive battle and secure peace. Tactically also he failed to achieve results from the application of his favorite maneuver, which had given victory in all his previous battles—and this failure for the first time in his career was not due to an act of God, like the blizzard at Preussich-Eylau, but to the stubbornness of his adversary. Thus it may be said that through the interaction of all the factors examined, including the Battle of Borodino, Napoleon's position was already becoming critical at the moment of his greatest triumph—his entry into Moscow. Had he been given a chance to recuperate in Moscow from the losses incurred and to bring up reinforcements, the subsequent story might have been very different. But the great conflagration which reduced the city to ashes in the moment he took possession of it killed the last hope he had for redeeming his fortunes.

IV

From this point of view the importance of the fire of Moscow cannot be overemphasized, not only as a spectacular event in history but as a cause of Napoleon's defeat. It was this fire that definitely turned the tide of war against the French. We have already seen how the overwhelming preponderance of the Grand Army at the beginning of the campaign was brought down from a ratio of three to one (if we include reserves on both sides) to a point where the forces were even at Moscow. Still more grave was the failure, because of the misbehavior of the French troops and of the failure of the policy of Napoleon to win over the local populations as he advanced; the ominous remark of General Balashov that Napoleon was fighting not an army but a nation was becoming increasingly true. The fire of Moscow was to augment these two unfavorable trends. Discipline among the French troops vanished when the city was reduced to ashes, forcing the troops to loot for subsistence and thereby bringing the temptation to steal anything valuable which was to be found in the ruins of the few remaining houses. Even more important, the troops now had to be quartered wherever possible, and since the stone churches had withstood the ravages of the flames, these were used for the purpose. In some cases they were converted into stables for the cavalry. Tales spread all over Russia not only of the destruction of Russia's finest city, which was attributed to the French, but of the horrors committed—the looting and, above all, the profanation of the churches. These accounts enflamed to fanaticism the hatred of the population, and prepared the way for the ruthless guerilla fighting of the last stage of the war.

In the meanwhile the Russian Army, having passed through Moscow, took up a position on the Riazan road, where it was given a complete rest, re-equipped, and reinforced up to 110,000 men by the pouring in of militia and new levies. Thus, whereas the Russians profited by the respite to bring their army into good shape again, Napoleon's forces were getting more and more disorganized, and numerically the Russians were gaining the advantage. Other things being equal, Napoleon was losing, and if we add to these other factors the popular resistance and later the weather conditions, defeat becomes a foregone conclusion.

The fire of Moscow thus forms the turning point of the war. There are three versions of the origin of the conflagration: the French accused Count Rostopchin, Governor of Moscow, of deliberately setting fire to the city for patriotic reasons; the Russians threw the blame on the French; and finally, Tolstoy holds the view generally accepted today that the fire was accidental—a wooden city left empty without police or authorities was bound to burn. Let us see what Rostopchin himself has to say on the causes of the fire (and it may be noted that Rostopchin was not the ruthless brute depicted in French war propaganda, but a man of high culture and refinement with a delightful sense of humor, as witness his witty *My Memoirs or Me Unadorned, Written in Ten Minutes*,[29] first published posthumously in *Le Temps*. Rostopchin acknowledged that when the city was evacuated by its population, civil authorities ordered the departure of the fire department of Moscow, composed of 96 engines and 2,100 firemen and officers. Thus the city had no equipment to fight fires except the improvised army equipment of the French. On the first night of the occupation of Moscow fire broke out in the bazaar facing the Kremlin, followed by other outbreaks in various sections of the city; by the fifth day a strong wind had carried it over the whole city, which was ravaged for three days more, destroying 7,632 houses, or three fourths of the city.[30] The population of Moscow (240,000) had been evacuated by Rostopchin in the twenty-three days between the fall of Smolensk and the coming of the French, and all in all only 12,000 to 15,000 remained in Moscow. These were foreigners, small bourgeois or peasants, and a few prisoners from the jails, allowed to stay because, as the lowest classes did not speak French, no contact useful to the enemy could be established.[31]

Rostopchin flatly denies Napoleon's statement made in his bulletins to the Grand Army—that Rostopchin had engineered the fire and that the French had caught and executed three hundred persons accused of arson who were acting under orders of the Governor of Moscow. Upon his return to Moscow after Napoleon's departure, he investigated the causes of the fire and interviewed one man who had escaped execution by the French. He said he had been arrested on charges of arson, marched with a party of thirty to Devitchye Pole, where thirteen of the party were executed and the others released. Neither he nor the others knew what their crime had been. As for the fire itself, it was caused, according to Rostopchin, partly by drunken French soldiery running wild, and partly by the remaining inhabitants setting their houses on fire. He cites two cases in particular: one of a carter who set fire to his establishment when

[29] Rostopchin, *op. cit.* [30] *Ibid.*, pp. 15-19. [31] *Ibid.*, pp. 29-35.

the French came to requisition his carriages, and the other of a merchant who, seeing French soldiers break into his cellar where they soon lay in drunken stupor, set the house on fire so that these enemies should perish.

To what extent the burning of Moscow demoralized the already unruly soldiery of Napoleon may be seen in the graphic account of Labaume, who states that when the French entered they found the city empty except for a few vagabonds and, in the churches which the French scouts immediately inspected, a few "children, old men, or Russian officers wounded in preceding battles." But in the churches "the altars were decorated as for a holiday, thousands of candles burning in honor of the saint protecting the country; . . . this imposing and religious apparel made the nation we had defeated powerful and worthy of respect, and infused in us a terror caused by the feeling of a great injustice; we dared not advance save with a timid step in the midst of this frightening solitude. . . ."[32] But already upon approaching the bazaar he found French soldiers looting the great stores and selling the proceeds of their loot, or "carrying away on their backs pieces of cloth, heads of sugar, and bales of merchandise." At the Exchange was worse confusion—"the street was covered in an instant with quantities of goods,"[33] while the building was burning. But the real looting started with the spread of the flames:

> How to paint the confusion which arose when looting was tolerated all over this immense city; soldiers, vivandières, convicts, and prostitutes ran wild in the streets and penetrated into abandoned palaces, taking whatever appealed to their cupidity. Some covered themselves with gold brocades and silks, others put on their shoulders, without discrimination, the most costly furs. . . . The remainder broke into wine cellars in crowds, and, drinking the most precious wines, in an unsteady gait carried away with them their immense loot.[34]

The houses which were still inhabited were not spared, and in some, where French officers had taken up quarters, the owners appealed to them for protection, but in vain. When the generals received the order to take up quarters outside of Moscow,

> the license became frightful and the soldiers, no longer restrained by the fear inspired by the presence of their chiefs, let themslves go in all the

[32] Labaume, *op. cit.*, p. 191. [33] *Ibid.*, pp. 192-193. [34] *Ibid.*, p. 206.

excesses one can imagine; no retreat was safe enough, no place holy enough to be saved from their avidity. But nothing excited their cupidity so much as the church of St. Michael, where the Emperors of Russia were buried. . . .[35]

and Labaume goes on to relate how the church was looted by the grenadiers.

After giving in detail the picture of the fire of Moscow, he adds:

I will content myself with painting the frightful confusion which took possession of our army when the fire had burned all the quarters of Moscow. . . . A long train of carriages loaded with loot was to be seen through the thick smoke. Forced by the traffic to stop at each moment, one heard the shouts of the drivers who, fearing to be burned, issued frightful howls in advance; everywhere armed men, who, though departing, broke through doors in their anxiety not to leave a house untouched; and if any new object was preferable to the one they had taken, left the first one to carry away their latest loot. Many, not having any carriage, carried their loot on their backs.[36]

Others wandered from street to street in a labyrinth of flames, and thus "perished, the victims of their cupidity." And as the Fourth Corps made its way out of Moscow, Labaume saw "the unfortunate inhabitants pull in dilapidated carriages all they had saved from their burned homes. And as the soldiers had taken their horses, one saw men and women pulling those carriages in which a sick mother or a paralytic old man was sitting."[37] Thus the French were sowing the seeds of a ruthless guerilla warfare which was to be fanned by the violent hatred of the people; and Napoleon, at a time when he no longer possessed a numerical superiority over the enemy, allowed this demoralization to affect the fighting power of his army. Caulaincourt gives us the same picture:

His [Napoleon's] departure from Moscow was the signal for outbreaks of gravest disorders. Such houses as had been saved from the fire were pillaged. Such unfortunate inhabitants as had remained were ill-treated. Shops and wine cellars were forced open; and thence flowed every excess, every crime that can result from the drunkenness of soldiers who have gotten out of the superiors' control.[38]

[35] *Ibid.*, p. 207.
[36] *Ibid.*, p. 213.
[37] *Ibid.*, p. 214.
[38] Caulaincourt, *op. cit.*, p. 124.

Napoleon stayed five weeks in Moscow. He felt he could not continue the war with the forces he had on hand, and therefore he hoped to profit by his occupation of Russia's second capital to impose peace. Hence he sent Lauriston to Kutuzov's headquarters with a message proposing peace on October 4 and again on October 14. The first time Kutuzov took the message without receiving Lauriston; the second time he received him and forwarded the message to St. Petersburg without committing himself. He refused an armistice and merely agreed to a suspension of firing, reserving his freedom of action on the flanks. In St. Petersburg Alexander maintained a haughty silence. Napoleon lost valuable time waiting for these replies. He was, moreover, also lured by the feeling of false security inspired by the unseasonably warm weather. Writes Caulaincourt concerning the first week in October: "Every day His Majesty remarked very pointedly when I was present, that the autumn in Moscow was finer and even warmer than in Fontainebleau."[39] During his stay Napoleon had increased his forces by thirteen thousand men, with replacements, stragglers, and convalescents who had reported for duty. Thus the two armies were of equal size, but the morale was very different. The main asset the French still possessed was the fear which the genius of Napoleon inspired in his adversaries, and which forced Kutuzov to be overcautious.

While Napoleon was wasting his time in Moscow, undecided as to the next move to make, important developments were occurring on the outlying fronts. On the extreme left flank of the French, while Macdonald was held at bay in front of Riga, Wittgenstein, reinforced to forty thousand men, suddenly attacked from Polotsk the combined corps of St. Cyr and Oudinot, inflicting a heavy defeat and forcing them back. Victor, in reserve at Smolensk, hurried to the assistance of St. Cyr, who was falling back towards him.

Even graver was the news coming from the extreme right flank of the French. Admiral Chichagov with the Moldavian Army, thirty-five thousand strong, released by the signing of the Treaty of Bucharest, had effected his junction with Tormasov's corps on September 18, and, taking the offensive against Schwarzenberg, had driven him beyond the Bug on the road to Warsaw. Thus by these virtually simultaneous offensives on the flanks, Wittgenstein and Chich-

[39] *Ibid.*, p. 139.

agov were preparing the pincer movement which was to affect the French retreat in its last period. That the Russian command seems to have had something of this sort in mind while Napoleon was still in Moscow may be seen by the order given to Chichagov, after his offensive against Schwarzenberg, to march toward the Berezina to cut Napoleon's retreat on that river. Accordingly Chichagov took up temporary quarters until the end of October, awaiting his turn to act.

In the meanwhile Kutuzov suddenly took the offensive, falling upon Murat's vanguard corps of 20,000 at Tarutino, inflicting losses of some 3,000 to 4,000 men and capturing 36 guns (October 18). The same day, apparently frightened by this action, Napoleon ordered his army to leave Moscow. He himself left the next day, the nineteenth, leaving behind him Mortier with 10,000 men of the Young Guards to blow up the Kremlin, an unnecessary and fortunately unsuccessful act of vandalism which served only further to infuriate the Russians. In selecting his line of retreat, Bonaparte had to take into consideration the fact that Kutuzov, having taken up his position at Tarutino, was three marching days nearer to Smolensk, Napoleon's main base, than he himself. Under these circumstances he selected the general direction of Kaluga in order to draw Kutuzov away from his main line of retreat and, further, to have a region, warmer in climate and untouched by war, where supplies would be plentiful and conditions propitious for his army to winter, if need arose.

Kutuzov, learning of the direction taken by Napoleon, which menaced his left flank, moved towards Maloyaroslavetz, his advance guard falling upon Prince Eugene just as he was crossing the Luzha River in sight of the city. An extremely bloody engagement followed on October 24 in the city itself, and, though Prince Eugene held his positions, he dared not advance further. The next day Napoleon, who had brought up his main army to Maloyaroslavetz, saw that as a result of the battle of the previous day the Russians were turning his right flank in a march towards Viazma. He gave the order to retreat along the route whence he had come, namely, through Borovsk and Vereya onto the highway from Moscow to Smolensk, the road that his own army had devastated during its advance. Thus the battle of Maloyaroslavetz, by forcing Napoleon back on the old road, decided the issue of the campaign. Also on the same day Platov's Cossacks in a daring raid fell upon the Imperial Headquarters, capturing eleven guns and endangering Napoleon himself. From this time on the Cossacks were gradually to become the terror of the French by their constant, swift, unexpected attacks.

While Napoleon was making his way back on the main highway, Kutuzov marched on Viazma, and Miloradovich with twenty-five thousand on Gzhatsk, thus marching parallel to the French Army, while Platov's Cossacks followed behind the French, mopping up their stragglers and transports. On November 3 Miloradovich and Platov attacked the enemy's forces assembled at Viazma, where they had stopped to await the arrival of Davout, who was in the rear guard. Another bloody but inconclusive engagement followed. This started the series of rear-guard actions which were to become increasingly disastrous for the French. Indeed Ney and Miloradovich came to grips at Semlevo and Dorogobuzh, while Prince Eugene, in attempting to cross the Vop, lost 60 cannon and a brigade of 2,000 men taken prisoner by the "Partisans" (guerillas) under Orlov-Davydov. The cost of these various engagements to the French in the three weeks from the time they left Moscow amounted to 61,000 men out of a total of 103,000 men. The weather thus far had been dry and exceptionally fine.

On November 9 Napoleon completed the first lap of his retreat by reaching Smolensk (Smolensk lying approximately halfway between Moscow and the Nieman). On the sixth, three days earlier, the first snow of the season fell, forecasting the rigors of the coming winter. But at this time Napoleon had remaining with him only 42,000 men of the 300,000 he had taken to Moscow, and consequently the tale so often told of the army's perishing from cold in the steppes of Russia applies only to this handful of survivors of earlier battles and retreats, and even then, it must be pointed out, of these about three fourths were to perish in subsequent battles.

With the coming of the snow, Labaume says, ". . . the army lost its power and military attitude. The soldier ceased to obey his officer, and the officer detached himself from his general; disorganized regiments marched as they chose—in search of food, they spread out over the plain, burning and destroying everything they found."[40]

The retreating army had pinned all their trust upon Smolensk, where they hoped plentiful supplies were awaiting them, and where they had been promised the retreat would stop. But in Smolensk, through maladministration, the food supplies had been eaten up and the garrison came out to meet the retreating army in the hope of getting supplies itself. Under the circumstances, with the temperature having fallen, according to Labaume,[41] to twenty-two degrees centigrade (fifteen below zero Farenheit), and the Russians pressing hard, there was nothing to do but continue the retreat. Napoleon left Smolensk on the fourteenth, taking with him the five thousand men he had found in the city and thereby increasing his forces to forty-seven thousand men. He was in a hurry to get away before the pincer movement, foreshadowed earlier by the movements of Wittgenstein and Chichagov, could cut his retreat. Although this Russian maneuver failed in its main purpose of capturing Napoleon and his army, through the superior maneuvering of Napoleon, it did nevertheless virtually destroy his forces.

On leaving Smolensk, Napoleon had found that Kutuzov had gained upon him in his retreat and was waiting for him at Krasnoye. Here Kutuzov had a chance to cut the enemy line by giving a major battle, but either out of fear of Napoleon's genius or out of a conviction that the war had been won already, Kutuzov selected the more economical and less heroic method of continuous harassing attacks on the enemy, which resulted in ten separate engagements around Krasnoye, but no general battle. These bloody engagements fought between November 14 and 18 inflicted formidable losses on Napoleon's diminished forces, estimated by Clausewitz at about 20,000 men, or two thirds of the French losses at Borodino. Moreover, the army had been further reduced by some 10,000 stragglers, most of whom were captured by the Russians in their mopping-up operations. Lastly, the Russians took from the French 230 guns in the four days of fighting at Krasnoye. On the eighteenth Ney with his rear-guard corps was in the greatest danger of capture. He managed to evade the Russians by a daring march in the darkness of the night, but he escaped with only 600 men, leaving the rest

[40] *Ibid.*, p. 289.
[41] Labaume, *op. cit.*, p. 314.

of his corps of 6,000 and all his artillery in the hands of the enemy. After Krasnoye, Bonaparte had only 12,000 men remaining, not including the corps of Oudinot, Victor, Reynier, and Schwarzenberg now maneuvering to rejoin him.

With the exception of the cold spell at Smolensk, during this period the weather remained reasonably seasonal. Ney, after his escape from Krasnoye, crossed the Dnieper on thin, newly formed ice, taking great risks as he saw the ice break under him. Approaching the Berezina, Caulaincourt spoke of the possibility of a thaw. But to the undernourished and thinly clad French, this weather seemed much colder than it really was—hence the hundreds of bodies of those who had died from exposure which strewed the road; hence also the pitched battles between groups of soldiers for shelter, for the meat of fallen horses, or even for a pair of shoes.

VI

The maneuver of Krasnoye was very nearly disastrous for the retreating French, and a much greater danger was now confronting them. Wittgenstein had followed the retreating Oudinot and on October 31 had attacked and dislodged him at Tchachnik, inflicting a loss of some 800 men. Victor's corps came to the aid of the hard-pressed Oudinot and effected a junction with him, bringing the total French force opposing Wittgenstein to thirty-two thousand men. On November 14 the two marshals attacked Wittgenstein at the village of Smiliantsy, near the river Oula; the village changed hands repeatedly during a very hot engagement, finally remaining in Russian hands. Having lost two thousand men, Victor was afraid to renew the struggle and remained inactive while Wittgenstein captured Vitebsk, which was a French supply center second only to Smolensk. The capture of this city was a double disaster for Napoleon, for it permitted Wittgenstein to approach the line of the Berezina from the northeast, that is, along its right bank. Worried about his line of retreat, Napoleon urgently dispatched Oudinot on November 19 with the Second Corps to occupy and hold the crossing at Borisov, while Victor was to attempt to keep Wittgenstein occupied by marching abreast of him. Thus, according to his plans, the Emperor would be in a position to cross the river between the positions occupied by both marshals, and then to turn and offer one more battle. But on November 22 he learned of the fall of Minsk, the next most important supply center toward which he was heading, and soon after of the arrival of Chichagov's army at Borisov. Chichagov on September 18 carried out his junction with Tormasov near Lutzk in Volhynia, and, now sixty thousand strong, the two corps crossed the Styr and by October 4 had pushed the Austro-Saxon troops of Schwarzenberg and Reynier out of Brest-Litovsk on the Bug. Leaving Sacken with twenty-eight thousand men to watch Schwarzenberg, Chichagov marched on Minsk. Schwarzenberg stopped, wasting time in indecision and countermarches. Chichagov profited by this to push forward and, crushing the Poles of Dombrovski, captured Minsk on November 17. From here, after some hesitation, the Admiral decided to march toward the Berezina, sending the corps of Lambert and Langeron toward Borisov and spreading his other corps to the right and to the left of Borisov. Lambert occupied Borisov on November 21 after a hot engagement with Dombrovski, who had gone there through Bobruisk. In the meanwhile Schwarzenberg finally made up his mind to pursue Chichagov and marched on Volkovysk, but by doing this he exposed Reynier to the danger of being crushed by Sacken. Accordingly, Schwarzenberg changed his mind once more and retreated, going to the aid of Reynier and abandoning the idea of following Chichagov. Finally the main Russian army of Kutuzov came up, somewhat sluggishly passing Lanniki on November 22, Morozovo the following day, and Kopys (on the road to Orsha and Borisov) on November 24. Thus Kutuzov on the twenty-fifth was some eighty miles to the east of Borisov and, having abandoned the main highway between Smolensk and Borisov, had turned slightly to the south. He was to reach the Berezina at Orsha with his main army on the thirtieth, while he pushed his advance guard forward. Napoleon, as he approached the Berezina, was therefore faced with Chichagov ahead of him holding the left bank of the river and the crossing at Borisov, Wittgenstein to the north on his right flank, and Kutuzov in his rear with the opportunity of encircling him from the south.

It required all the genius and all the inhuman ruthlessness of Napoleon to get out of such a trap. After hesitating between facing Wittgenstein and Chichagov, Napoleon decided to attempt the crossing by attacking Chichagov, who was marching to a junction with Wittgenstein. Oudinot struck unexpectedly at the vanguard of Chichagov under Pahlen, which had crossed the river at Borisov and, after a heavy engagement fought on the twenty-third of November at Lochnitza, the Russians were forced to recross the river. Napoleon himself arrived at Lochnitza the following day and decided to attempt the crossing a few miles to the north of Borisov at Studianka. Here the French engineers built two bridges, one for the troops and one for the artillery and transports. The bridges were ready on the twenty-sixth, and the next day Napoleon crossed and supervised the crossing of what remained of the corps of Prince Eugene, Ney, Poniatovski, Junot, and Davout. But these were only the organized units and represented about half of the army. The stragglers, the wounded, the camp followers with other civilians who had attached themselves to the retreating army, and all the rear units, as well as the artillery and transports, had still to cross. To protect these, the corps of Victor and Oudinot remained on the left bank, and the division of Partouneaux occupied Borisov. As might have been expected, divided thus by the river, the army was to face attacks on both banks. Indeed Wittgenstein, after dislodging Partouneaux from Borisov and eventually forcing him to surrender with seven thousand men, threw two bridges across at Borisov and sought to establish contact with Chichagov. Napoleon's policy was to keep the two armies from uniting. Hence when on the twenty-eighth Chichagov started his advance toward the bridges, the French offered the most desperate resistance in the forests around Brillov, and though Chichagov succeeded in throwing the corps of Yermolov across the river at Borisov, the bulk of his army was held back and blocked on the highway a mile from the river, around Stakov. On the left bank Wittgenstein had joined forces at Lochnitza with the corps of Miloradovich, the vanguard of Kutuzov's army, and succeeded in approaching the causeway and the bridges over which the second half of the French Army was crossing. Though Victor made desperate efforts to hold the Russians back, he was unable to do so. The Russians shelled the bridges, causing the utmost confusion and panic among the crossing columns. In this panic many were crushed under the wheels of the heavy carriages, others were thrown into the water, and still others attempted to swim across the river and perished in its icy waters. Seeing that he could hold out no longer against the advancing Russian infantry, Victor, in the night of November 28-29, crossed the river himself and set fire to the bridges, leaving most of the army's artillery and baggage and all of the stragglers and wounded stranded on the causeway at the mercy of the enemy.

As for the army which had crossed, it set out to reach the Nieman by marching via Zemlin to Molodechno. How many men had Napoleon succeeded in rescuing? The figure varies from 9,000 according to Russians sources, to 20,000 and even 30,000 according to French sources.[42] Because of the extreme confusion which prevailed no count was possible, but perhaps 20,000 men would be the approximate figure, the rest being counted as lost. The Russians had lost in the three-day battle about 7,000 men. The operations along the Berezina had been the last serious engagement of the war, and only desultory and scattered fighting took place thereafter.

Though Napoleon had succeeded in getting away from the Berezina with about half his forces, it was nevertheless a phantom army which he now had. Without baggage and with most of the artillery and food supplies lost at the Berezina, the French were wandering aimlessly through the forests and the marshes of White Russia trying to reach the Nieman. The severe cold and hunger killed them off by the thousand. Only Ney with 700 men and Victor's corps of 4,000 offered some semblance of resistance at Molodechno (December 4). The following day Napoleon, having reached Smorgon, abandoned his army and rushed to Paris, leaving the command to Murat. The latter reached Vilno on the eighth, where disorder and confusion were at their height. The Bavarian corps of Wrede rejoined Ney and attempted to hold the Russians, but Murat was forced to evacuate the city on the ninth, and the Russians took 15,000 prisoners and the supplies which had been stored there for an army of 100,000 men.

Kutuzov's strategy after Berezina was to separate the French from Schwarzenberg's army. Accordingly he marched south and parallel to the French retreat, leaving Wittgenstein the task of disposing of the rest of the Grand Army. Murat reached Kovno, the last Russian city, on the eleventh, his corps having only a few hundred men remaining in them. The Russians were following so

[42] Bourdeau, *op. cit.*, III, 234.

closely on his heels that after a feeble defense, Murat abandoned the city and marched into Prussia, where at Gumbinnen he ordered the general re-assembling along the Vistula of the scattered remnants of the Grand Army. Davout was to proceed to Thorn, Prince Eugene and Victor to Marienwerder, the Second and Third Corps (Maison and Marchand) to Marienbourg, Ney to Königsberg, the Poles of Poniatovski to Warsaw, the artillery and engineers to Danzig. The invasion was over.

According to the official Russian *Gazette de St. Petersbourg*, the losses sustained by the French during the campaign were as follows: officers taken prisoner 6,000, soldiers 130,000, French corpses cremated 308,000, cannon captured 900, rifles 100,000, transport wagons, ammunition carriages, etc. 25,000. As for Kutuzov's army, it was reduced by the time it reached Vilno to 27,464 men and 200 guns, but the other corps of Wittgenstein, Essen, and Sacken brought it up to 110,000.[43]

As the corps of Macdonald, the only one still in fairly good shape, was falling back from Riga on Tilsit, Wittgenstein's vanguard was preceding him. A feeble Russian force under General Diebitch (1,800 men and six guns) had placed itself between Macdonald and the Prussian corps of Yorck. Yorck had in the meanwhile been maneuvering to join Macdonald. The result was that Yorck's vanguard under General Kleist had stumbled upon Diebitch's force. Diebitch opened negotiations with Kleist (December 25), and the same evening an interview took place between Diebitch and Yorck. The latter had already been in communication with the Russian General Headquarters and had received a letter from the Czar (December 18) promising the restitution to Prussia of her lost territories. But having no instructions from the King, Yorck was averse to taking any definite step—he therefore waited until the thirtieth. In the meanwhile the two armies, the Russian and Prussian, began fraternizing, and Diebitch withdrew his little force to Willkishken, giving Yorck a chance to simulate an advance on Tauroggen. Here Yorck, under the pretext that he was facing the main army of Wittgenstein and therefore was constrained to act by a show of force, signed a convention on his own initiative, by which it was agreed that the Prussians would cease all hostilities against

[43] Kazimierz Waliszewski, *Le Règne d'Alexandre Ier* (Paris, 1925), II, 164.

the Russians until March 1. This, the first defection of Napoleon's allies, was to be followed in due course by many others. Macdonald, having lost this important support, was faced with the necessity of continuing his retreat. He fell back to Königsberg, but was driven out of the city by Cossacks and by the inhabitants of the city, who took up arms, and finally stopped on the Passarge, holding a line between Danzig and Elbing with 14,000 men and 38 guns.

Early in January when the French forces made their first attempt to reorganize themselves and to hold a defensive line, they still represented, under the command of Murat, the imposing total of 136,000 men, including all allied contingents and reserves which had been left by Napoleon in Germany and had not participated in the invasion. Of these, 45,000 men were in the first line along the upper Vistula, while 20,000 men held the fortresses from Danzig to Plock; 40,000 were still in Poland, including the Austrians and Saxons of Schwarzenberg and Reynier, and a further 30,000 men were either garrisoning Berlin or coming up from the interior of Germany to hold the second line of the Oder. Murat, however, eager to regain Naples and assure the safety of his throne, abandoned the supreme command of the army to Prince Eugene, who, after making a futile attempt to hold the line of the Vistula, fell back successively to the Oder and to the Elbe in the new campaign which was about to begin.

Chapter VIII

The Campaign of 1813 in Germany

I

Once the French were expelled from Russia, there arose the question of what course to follow next. Two schools of thought prevailed in Russia. The one which may be called "isolationist" argued that, the task of liberating Russia having been achieved, Russia should, in view of the tremendous losses sustained and the devastation incurred, make peace with France and concentrate on reconstruction. As to what happened in Western Europe, that was of no concern to her. However, this school argued that Russia should gain some advantages for her victory and therefore should obtain the line of the Vistula from Prussia. Napoleon, defeated and exhausted, would be happy to make peace with Russia on these terms. This school of thought was headed by Rumiantsev and Kutuzov. What may be termed the "interventionist" school argued that the Russian problem could not be separated from the whole European problem, and the latter could be settled only by the overthrow of Napoleon. Western Europe, particularly Germany, crushed by the French, would arise only if the Russian armies carried the war into their territory and thereby gave them the incentive to do so. Urged on by Stein, Alexander held to this view, even though the situation did not look very hopeful. Although the King of Prussia opened negotiations for an alliance with Russia, he also offered new Prussian contingents to the French. Austria seemed to be well anchored in her alliance with France, and the King of Saxony remained loyal to Napoleon, even though he went to Prague to await events. The problem now, both military and diplomatic, was to turn these wavering allegiances to the side of Russia.

The Russian General Headquarters of Alexander and Kutuzov remained in Vilno until January 9. On that day the new campaign started. General Tormasov, with two corps and two cavalry divisions (18,000 men) set out together with the Imperial Headquarters and, crossing the Nieman on January 13, reached Plock by February 5. Two other corps (the Sixth and Eighth) remained in Vilno, where they were being refitted and completed after the losses sustained during the Russian campaign.

Two days later, on February 7, another Russian army, under Miloradovich and Sacken (30,000 men), entered Warsaw and disarmed the Polish militia. Schwarzenberg, with his army of 42,000, had evacuated Warsaw without fighting; and the Saxon corps of Reynier was retreating toward Kalish. General Winzingerode was sent to cut its retreat into Kalish, and on February 13 defeated it completely, capturing 1,500 prisoners, six guns, and two colors. The Saxon losses in killed and wounded amounted to 1,500 men; the Russian, 670.

A third Russian army, composed of the corps of Chichagov, Wittgenstein, and Platov (55,000 men), was to operate on the lower Vistula, and on January 13 attacked the headquarters of Prince Eugene at Elbingen, capturing fifteen guns and several hundred prisoners. Wittgenstein crossed the Vistula at Dirshau with 30,000 men, to whom were joined the Cossacks of Platov. Upon gaining the left bank of the river, he detached 12,000 men to march toward Danzig under General Levize, and sent partisan detachments under Chernyshev, Benckendorf, and Tettenborn to cut the communications of Prince Eugene. Chichagov with 17,000 men besieged Thorn, but relinquished his command to Barclay de Tolly. These movements forced the Viceroy to retreat beyond the Oder.

As soon as the Russian army reached the line of the Oder, the General Headquarters, with the Czar and Kutuzov, was moved up to Kalish, on February 24, where they remained until April 8. But the cautious Kutuzov decided to stop on the Oder, pending the clarification of the position of Prussia. However, partisan detachments under Chernyshev and Tettenborn with 6,000 men and 40 guns made a daring raid on Berlin, which was defended by Marshal Augereau. On February 21 they actually broke into the city and, though they were driven out, they forced Prince Eugene to concentrate 26,000 men for the defense of the Prussian capital. In the meanwhile the stand to be taken by Prussia was by no means clear, and General Yorck as late as February 20 was under secret orders from his government to remain in the rear of the Russian army during his advance toward the Oder, and not to open fire on the French.

As the Russian armies crossed the border into Prussia, a proclamation was issued to the Prussian people, written by the Czar but signed by Kutuzov. In this Russia pledged herself to bring

> peace and independence to those nations which are prepared to face sacrifices to achieve this end. It is essentially to Prussia that I issue this invitation, for it is the intention of His Imperal Majesty to put an end to the misfortunes which have fallen upon it and . . . to give back to the kingdom of Frederick the Great its former frontiers and luster.[1]

At the same time Alexander wrote a friendly letter to the King of Prussia informing him that Baron Stein had been appointed commissioner to administer such Prussian territories as had been deprived of their legal administration and that he would serve as intermediary between the Russian Army and the Prussian population. The hesitant King did not reply immediately, but finally wrote in February, excusing his silence by saying that he was waiting to see what position Austria would take. While he agreed to send General Knesebeck to open negotiations with the Czar for a "treaty of friendship and alliance which I hope will unite our nations forever as we are united personally in heart and in sentiment,"[2] nevertheless, at the same time Krusemarck, Prussian minister in Paris, was ordered to open negotiations with Napoleon. However, Alexander, writing through Stein, demanded a clear-cut reply on the part of the King—"Friendship, confidence, perseverance, courage," he said; "Providence will do the rest."[3]

He also appointed Anstett as special Russian delegate to deal directly with Hardenberg over the head of the slow-moving Knesebeck. Anstett, accompanied by Stein, went to Breslau and obtained from Hardenberg within twenty-four hours a treaty which, practically without modifications, followed the Russian draft submitted to Prussia. This treaty was signed by Kutuzov at Kalish on February 28; hence it took the name of the little Polish city in which were the Russian Headquarters at the time. By Articles II and V

[1] Martens, *op. cit.*, VII, 64.

[2] *Ibid.*, VII, 66.

[3] *Ibid.*, VII, 66.

of this all-important treaty, peace was restored between Russia and Prussia, and the former hostilities were replaced by a defensive and offensive alliance with the aim of reconstituting Prussia in such a way as to assure the tranquillity of both countries. To achieve this end, Russia was pledged to put 150,000 men in the field and Prussia as many as she could, including those raised by a national militia (Article III); the Russian Army was to co-operate immediately with the Prussian Army. Both sides were pledged not to sign a separate peace, and the treaty was to remain secret for two months; efforts were to be made to bring Austria into the alliance, and Russia was to aid Prussia to get subsidies and arms from England (Articles IV and XI). By secret additional clauses, Russia was to fight on until Prussia was reconstituted as of the year 1806, Russia pledging herself to turn over to Prussia all acquisitions of territory to be made in south Germany with the exception of the possessions of the King of Hanover. Furthermore, Russia guaranteed to Prussia her present borders, to which was to be added a territory which would make them contiguous to the province of Silesia.

On March 25, three weeks after the signing of the Treaty of Kalish, a joint proclamation by the Czar and the King of Prussia was once more issued to the German people. Inspired by Stein but signed by Kutuzov, this proclamation was much more explicit than the preceding one.

> Their Majesties, the Emperor of Russia and the King of Prussia, are coming solely for the purpose of aiding the sovereigns and the people of Germany to recover the hereditary possessions of the people which have been taken away from them, but which are their inalienable right: their liberty and their independence, honor and country. Every German still worth the name should join us promptly and with vigor, every one—prince, noble, or man from the ranks of the people—should aid with his property and position, body and life, spirit and heart, the goal set by Russia and Prussia. . . .

The proclamation goes on to say that the existence of the Confederation of the Rhine cannot be tolerated, and the Czar outlines his future relations with Germany by declaring, with regard to its constitution, that "the more the basis and the principles . . . will be modeled on the ancient spirit of the German people, the more will Germany, revitalized and strengthened, show itself to advantage among the peoples of Europe."[4]

This language, totally new in Europe in the relations of sovereigns toward the people, horrified Metternich, who declared it to be pure Jacobinism. But the proclamation also touched upon France, declaring that if France, "beautiful and powerful," will concern herself only with her internal development no foreign power will trouble her, and "no hostile enterprise will be directed against her legitimate frontiers. France should know that the other powers will lay down their arms only when the basis for the independence of all nations of Europe is established and assured."[5]

Thus by this proclamation Alexander was widening his scope beyond the confines of Germany alone and establishing his claim to the leadership of the European coalition; whereas Metternich was calling for the aid of the government against France, Alexander appealed directly to the people. In the meanwhile the first problem was to pursue the war against Napoleon on German soil.

II

The plan of allied military operations was worked out by the Prussian General Scharnhorst and received the approval of Alexander. Under this plan the armies were to be split in two—on the allied left flank was to be concentrated the bulk of the forces, which was to pin down the enemy, while on the right flank the allied forces were to attempt to turn the enemy's left flank by a converging movement from the north. According to this plan the left army, under the command of Blücher, composed of 27,000 Prussians and 13,000 Russians under Winzingerode, was to advance toward Dresden, and the right army with the 20,000 Russians and 30,000 Prussians of Yorck and Bülow respectively, under the supreme command of Wittgenstein, was to move on Berlin. The main Russian army (30,000 men) under Tormasov and Miloradovich remained in reserve on the Oder and around Kalish. The supreme command of all the allied armies was given to Kutuzov. Wittgenstein's army crossed the Oder on March 2; and two days later the Russian vanguard, under Prince Repnin, occupied Berlin, driving the Viceroy's forces out. Wittgenstein himself with the Russian corps of Berg made a triumphal entry into the Prussian capital on March 11,

[4] Sorel, *op. cit.*, VIII, 68-69.

[5] *Ibid.*, VIII, 68-69.

receiving the acclamations of the population, and was followed on the 17th by the Prussian corps of Yorck. The following day a light Russian force of 1,300 men under Tettenborn occupied Hamburg, and somewhat later another detachment under Benckendorff captured Lübeck.

The left, or Southern Army, under Blücher, after assembling around Breslau, proceeded to advance on March 20 toward the Elbe. The Russian corps of Winzingerode occupied Bautzen. Miloradovich with 10,000 men laid siege to Glogau and later, having been replaced by a Prussian force, marched toward the Elbe. As the army approached Dresden they found the city occupied by a corps of 3,000 men under Durutte. On March 20 a detachment of 700 Russian cavalry under Colonel Davydov reached the suburbs of Dresden. Davydov spread his force in a semicircle around Neustadt, the suburb of Dresden, ordered campfires to be lit all along the extended line, and then sent an emissary to ask for the surrender of Neustadt. The ruse succeeded; the French, believing that they had to deal with a much greater force, surrendered Neustadt and crossed the Elbe into Dresden proper, to retire a few days later beyond the Saale. Winzingerode on March 27 occupied the Saxon capital, and Blücher moved his headquarters to Altenburg.

Meanwhile the Viceroy, having abandoned Berlin, assembled the bulk of his army (52,000 men) around Magdeburg on the Elbe, thereby placing himself squarely between the Northern and Southern allied armies. It was for exactly this reason that Kutuzov had disapproved of Scharnhorst's plan—he wanted Blücher to cross the Elbe farther to the north, so as not to leave a gap between his own forces and those of Wittgenstein; but the next best thing to do was to force the French out of Magdeburg. Accordingly, Wittgenstein was ordered to proceed from Berlin southward to a junction with Blücher. On April 6 Wittgenstein attacked Prince Eugene at Magdeburg and severely defeated him, the French losing 1,000 prisoners. The Viceroy then proceeded to retreat toward the Saale, and Wittgenstein on April 10, leaving a part of his forces to besiege Magdeburg, crossed the Elbe, while the partisan detachments, operating in northern Germany near Bremen, inflicted a heavy defeat on the French. Lüneburg having rebelled against the French, General Moran with 2,500 men and eight guns marched into the city on April 1 and, having occupied it, proceeded to crush the rebellion with the severest penalties. The partisan force of Chernyshev, after a forced march of sixty miles in twenty-four hours, reached Lüneburg on the evening of the same day, and a mixed Russo-German force composed of one Russian and one Prussian infantry regiment and some Russian hussars attacked the French and drove them out of the city. Moran was mortally wounded, 80 officers and 2,200 men were taken prisoner; nine guns and three standards, as well as the transports, were captured. Having accomplished this, Chernyshev fell back to Boitsenburg.

In the meantime an important convention was signed in Breslau on March 19 between Russia and Prussia, Nesselrode and Stein signing for Russia, and Hardenberg and Scharnhorst for Prussia. It was decided by this convention to call upon all the rulers of Germany and their peoples to help the allies in their task of liberation, with the threat of deposing such rulers as should refuse to do so. This stern warning was due to the lukewarm or downright hostile reception accorded to the allied troops both in Saxony and in the Hanseatic cities of north Germany. Next, it was decided to form a Central Executive Council for the liberated regions, virtually an unofficial government. These territories, except for Prussia and Hanover, were to be divided into five military and civil districts extending from Saxony to Holland, and were to be administered by a military and civil governor; further, the Central Council was to have complete control over the raising and equipping of German troops in the regions within its jurisdiction, and lastly, all incomes and funds coming from the territories concerned were to be divided equally between Russian and Prussia, again with the exception of Hanover. The Central Executive Council was to have its seat in Dresden and was to be presided over by a Russian, Kosodavlev, with Count Kochubey and Baron Stein representing Alexander, and Shoen and Rediger representing Friedrich Wilhelm. Stein was to preside in the absence of Kosodavlev. Meanwhile on April 18 the Russian General Headquarters were moved to Bunzlau, and here the elderly Kutuzov caught a chill which took a turn for the worse; soon all hope for his recovery was lost. The Field Marshal died on April 28. Count Wittgenstein was appointed Commander in Chief, although there were four generals of superior rank in the army—

Blücher, Barclay de Tolly, Miloradovich, and Tormasov. Whatever the motives were in appointing Wittgenstein, the net result was that the command passed from the experienced if overcautious hands of Kutuzov to a much less able man at a most critical time; for Napoleon was once more taking the initiative at this point. Coinciding with this grave menace, however, came the news of the conclusion of an armistice between Austria and Russia on April 26. Schwarzenberg had fallen back into Galicia, Reynier and his Saxons had been driven out of Poland, and Poniatovski alone was clinging to the defense of his native land with the remnants of Polish units. After the conclusion of the armistice of April 26 he was forced to seek refuge in Austria, and on May 13 the Russians occupied Cracow. Later Poniatovski with some ten thousand Poles was released by the Austrians and permitted to rejoin Napoleon's Army, but for the time being the whole of Poland had been cleared of enemy forces and the left rear of the Russian Army made safe, just as Napoleon was about to strike.

Napoleon had hoped that Prince Eugene would hold Posen or the line of the Oder so that he might reconstitute the Grand Army in the rear and bring it up to Danzig and Thorn; but, as we have seen, under the circumstances Prince Eugene was forced to abandon first this line, then Berlin, and to fall back to the Elbe, holding a line from Dresden to Hamburg. At this time Prince Eugene had 17,000 men on the upper Elbe, between Dresden and Torgau, 18,000 in the center based on Wittenberg, and 35,000 in the lower Elbe, totaling 70,000 men in the first line, with reserves at Leipzig amounting to 20,000. Napoleon was furious at the retreat of Prince Eugene, whom he accused of indecision and of being hoodwinked by the Russian maneuvers. He wanted the Viceroy to hold back the enemy long enough to give him time to raise a new army of conscripts in France. This army was shaping itself rapidly, and by April 15 Napoleon was able to bring up to the river Main an army of 200,000 men and 450 guns (Third, Fourth, Sixth, and Twelfth Corps). Thus once more the genius and the will power of Napoleon had created a force numerically superior to the enemy. The Russians had now 110,000 men in line, and for replacements were drawing upon a reserve army under Prince Lobanov-Rostovsky, which was located between St. Petersburg and Yaroslavl. This Reserve army from January to July sent out to the front 67,000 infantry and 14,000 cavalry. The Prussians had about 90,000 men in line. Thus the French totaled about 300,000 men as against the allied 200,000 men.[6]

The new French army was composed of untrained men and was woefully weak in cavalry, of which Napoleon had only 8,000. His original plan was to march toward Stettin and Danzig, but the retreat of Prince Eugene to the Elbe had forced him to modify this plan and not to undertake anything until the army of Prince Eugene effected its junction with the army on the Main. Writing to Ney on April 28 he said, "I think the first point is to reach Leipzig. The Viceroy could emerge through Merseburg. . . . But the main thing at this moment is to form a junction."[7] This junction of the armies took place on May 7, the Viceroy, as foreseen by Napoleon, making his way through Merseburg, while Ney with the Third Corps was advancing through Weissenfels toward Lützen, followed by the Sixth Corps of Marmont and the Guards, with the Fourth Corps (Bertrand) and the Twelfth Corps (Oudinot) farther to the south. At this point Napoleon had rejoined the army and was ready to impart to it that singleness of drive and command which made it so formidable, whereas the allies once more suffered from the fatal weakness of a divided command. Wittgenstein had no authority over the senior generals and merely made suggestions to them, which they were free to accept or not. Alexander, forgetting the lesson of Austerlitz, closely supervised his Commander in Chief and interfered with his decisions. As Napoleon's main army reached the Saale and advanced on Leipzig, that is, on April 30, the Allies occupied the following positions: the corps of Yorck and Berg (18,000 men) were in the neighborhood of Leipzig, seeking to unite with Blücher, while Kleist and a force of 6,000 men were holding the city itself; as for Blücher's forces, 5,000 cavalry of Winzingerode's corps were at Lützen west of Leipzig, with the latter's 9,000 infantry at Eisdorf, some four miles back of Lützen; some twenty-five miles farther to the rear and due south of Leipzig, at Borna, were the main forces of Blücher (25,000 men), while on his left flank, farther to the south at Altenburg, was Miloradovich with 12,000 men; fi-

[6] Bogdanovich, *Istoria Tsarstovania Imperator Aleksandra I*, Vol. IV, appendix to Chapter XL, n.

[7] Camon, *op. cit.*, II, 51.

nally, 18,000 men of the main army had made their way through Dresden. Thus the allied forces, 54,000 Russians with 440 guns, and 38,000 Prussians with 216 guns, were scattered in a triangle south and west of Leipzig, between that city, Lützen, and Altenburg, with Lützen forming the apex of the triangle.[8] On May 1 Winzingerode's cavalry established contact with Ney's corps coming up to Lützen, and after a hot engagement along the course of the Rippach, fell back. In this engagement Marshal Bessières was mortally wounded. The allies decided to attack forthwith and ordered all available forces to move up to Lützen. Thus the next day, May 2, 50,000 infantry, 16,000 cavalry, and 400 guns with 6,000 men of the artillery were concentrated in the neighborhood of Lützen, of whom 39,000 were Russian with 314 guns, and 33,000 Prussian with 136 guns.[9]

Wittgenstein's plan, worked out by General Diebitch, was to let Ney start out on the road to Leipzig and then attack him frontally and on the flank by a converging movement from the south. Separated from the other French corps by the Saale, Ney would find himself in a precarious position, the more so because the French without cavalry could be taken by surprise. But for this plan to succeed, co-ordination and speed were necessary—two things woefully lacking with the allies. On the morning of May 2 Ney, with 40,000 men, had passed through Lützen and established his headquarters a few miles to the east at Kaya. Without knowing it he had established contact with the enemy, deployed on the banks of the Floss Graben. So little did Ney suspect any serious danger that he had left his headquarters to visit Napoleon, when at noon the allies suddenly opened the attack. Blücher was in the first line, followed by a second line composed of the corps of Berg, Yorck, and Winzingerode, with the Guards in reserve. Napoleon had thought the enemy to be closer to Leipzig than it was; hence he had ordered Lauriston and Macdonald to proceed toward that city, and already at 9:00 A.M. Lauriston had opened fire on Kleist's detachment. This early engagement had forced Napoleon to bring up the Guards to the aid of Lauriston, leaving Ney more and more isolated, when suddenly the violent fire which broke out in the direction of Ney's corps—and therefore in the rear of the forces facing Leipzig—in-

[8] Bogdanovich, *Istoria Tsarstvovania Aleksandra I*, IV, 42-43.

[9] *Ibid.*, Vol. IV, appendix to Chapter XL, n.

formed Napoleon of the allied attack. Taken by surprise, Napoleon acted with his customary vigor and speed. While Ney rushed to join his corps, the Emperor ordered Macdonald to turn back to join Ney, and Marmont, who was following Ney, to speed up his march. The Guards marched back to Lützen to back up Ney's position and act as reserve, and Bertrand was to flank the enemy on the right. But these movements took three hours to execute, and during this time Ney's five divisions had to bear alone the brunt of the allied attack. Had Wittgenstein acted with vigor, he would have crushed Ney, but he preferred to bring his corps into action one after another. Even though Blücher pressed hard and captured Ney's headquarters at Kaya, Ney held out, counterattacking vigorously. By four o'clock the allies had engaged all their forces, whereas Napoleon's reinforcements were just beginning to come up and the Emperor himself was directing the battle. At five o'clock Macdonald's corps reached the battlefield. The allies made a last desperate attack on Kaya, which had returned to French hands. During this attack Scharnhorst and Prince Mecklenburg-Strelitz were mortally wounded, the Prince of Hesse-Homburg killed, and Blücher wounded. Feeling that the allies had spent themselves, Napoleon at 7:00 P.M. launched his decisive counterattack with all the forces available.

In the meanwhile a desperate struggle was taking place for the possession of the village of Eisdorf, between Macdonald's corps and the Russian Second Corps; and Wittgenstein, seeing the Russians finally ousted from that key point, had thrown in his last reserve, the Grenadier Corps. Napoleon's counterattack dealt a formidable blow against the allied center at Kaya, and the allies fell back, abandoning that position. Threatened on the flanks by Macdonald and Marmont, the whole allied line gave way and the battle came to an end in the darkness, the French having regained all their lost ground and the allies still holding the village of Grossgörschen. The positions of the armies remained very much the same as in the morning, but the losses had been considerable—about 18,000 men for both the French and the allies. Ney's corps alone lost 12,000 men. The French had captured 2,000 prisoners, the allies five French guns. But Napoleon had 40,000 men to spare and the allies only 11,500 of the corps of Miloradovich. Moreover, the French threatened the Russian flanks. A council of war was held at 11:00 P.M. to decide the question of renewing the battle the next day; but Lauriston in the meanwhile had succeeded in occupying Leipzig, and with this new menace in his rear Wittgenstein decided to fall back to the line of the Elbe.

At the Battle of Lützen Napoleon was able to oppose 145,000 men to the 100,000 of the allies. This gave him the victory, but it proved sterile, for without cavalry he could not make use of his victory by pursuing the allies' columns, which were retreating in good order. He could not even find out where they had gone. There were obviously three possibilities: (1) the allies had fallen back jointly northeastward to defend Berlin, (2) the Prussians were covering Berlin while the Russians had marched toward Breslau to come closer to their own border and to maintain contact with Austria, (3) both armies had retreated together due east, via Dresden to Breslau and Silesia. Napoleon decided to provide against the first and second possibilities himself by marching with the main army to Dresden, while he detached Ney with 100,000 men to march on Berlin. On May 8 Napoleon reached Dresden, which the allies had abandoned, and established his headquarters there, pending clarification of the situation. On the thirteenth he wrote to Ney: "I still do not see clearly what the Prussians have done. It is certain that the Russians have retreated toward Breslau, but are the Prussians retreating on Breslau as the rumor goes, or have they thrown themselves upon Berlin to cover their capital, as would appear natural?"[10] It was only on the fifteenth that he finally obtained reliable information: the allies had been retreating in two parallel columns toward Breslau: the Prussians to the north through Colditz, Dobeln, and Meissen; the Russians to the south through Waldheim, Nossen, and Dresden. The two armies had converged at Bautzen, where they had stopped. Covering the retreat of the Russians was Miloradovich with his corps of eighteen thousand men. The latter had fought continuous and severe rear-guard actions. He held the French back at Dresden for three days and again fought a heavy engagement against Macdonald's corps at Bishofsverda, preventing Napoleon from finding out more about the march of the main columns, and also allowing the allies to retreat unmolested. For

[10] Camon, *op. cit.*, II, 58.

the important service he thus rendered, the Czar granted him the title of count.

The allies had decided to stop their retreat on the upper course of the Spree, but finding that line inadequate, fell back a few miles to Bautzen as their main line of defense. There was a political reason for deciding to offer another battle here. Their retreat was having a dangerous effect on Austria, who was vacillating between joining the allies and remaining faithful to Napoleon, and also was proving discouraging to the activities of German secret organizations (such as the Tugenbund) which were inciting the German people against the French. Furthermore, the allies had received reinforcements which made up for the losses sustained at Lützen. On May 16 the Russian corps of Barclay de Tolly (13,500 men) reached Bautzen, and 4,000 men came from the reserve army, while the Prussians received 8,000 men. Thus once more the allies had concentrated around 100,000 men for the battle, of which 70,000 were Russian with 474 guns, and 30,000 Prussian with 136 guns.[11]

The position selected was one of the strongest natural defense lines in Germany and had been effectively used by Frederick the Great during the Seven Years' War;[12] it was, strictly speaking, composed of two positions. The advance line ran along the Spree at the point where that stream came out of the Riesengebirge range to flow past the city of Bautzen and the small foothills into a wide valley. Thus the Russian left flank was protected by the towering mountains, and the center was on the high bluff upon which the city of Bautzen is located, while farther down stream toward the valley the Prussians held the small heights. But the line offered some disadvantages; hence it was to be held only by the detachments of the vanguard and the real resistance was to be offered on the second line of defense. The latter ran along a tributary of the Spree, the Blöser Wasser, which, coming out of the mountains and skirting the bluff back of Bautzen, fell into the Spree in the wider valley. Here the Russian left flank (Miloradovich) was once more protected by the mountains, the center (Guards and reserves) faced the city, and the Prussians of Blücher held the right flank.

Napoleon's plan was to have a battle in two stages—the first

[11] Bogdanovich, *Istoria Tsarstvovania Imperatora Aleksandra I*, IV, 63.
[12] The Battle of Hochkirchen.

day would be given to the capture of the advance line; then after a night's rest a direct onslaught on the second line was to be combined simultaneously with a flank attack by Ney, who, coming up the Spree, would strike at the end of the line and attempt to turn it. For this purpose Ney with 60,000 men had been engaged in a wide converging movement on Hoyerswerda, some twenty miles down the river. The allies, aware of this danger but underestimating the size of Ney's army, sent Barclay de Tolly with 13,500 men and Yorck with 8,000 men along both banks of the river to hold Ney back. This led to the bloody engagements of May 19, which would have been considered an actual battle had it not been for the greater one fought the following days. Barclay, working his way downstream, stumbled upon the advance guard of Ney's forces—the Italian division of Peyri—marching in the opposite direction from Hoyerswerda to Klix. The Italians, surrounded by the seasoned troops of Barclay, would have been completely destroyed if Ney had not sent his cavalry under Kellerman to their rescue. As it was, this division lost about half its men and a part of its artillery. Yorck, on the other hand, found himself engaged by the 20,000 men of Lauriston, and, after offering staunch resistance and sustaining heavy losses, rejoined Barclay. Realizing the size of the advancing column, both commanders fell back to the main army, and Barclay took up a position in the meadow beyond the Prussian army on the extreme right flank of the defense line facing the approaching Ney.

The next day (May 20) Napoleon launched his attack on the advance line. Although the Russians offered a strong resistance at Bautzen itself, where the struggle centered around the stone bridge crossing the river, and, farther down, Marmont met with extremely stiff resistance on the part of the Prussians, nevertheless, by evening the city of Bautzen and the whole advance line was in the hands of the French. At the same moment Ney had reached Klix, the springboard for his attack on the flank of the second line. The real battle, however, was still to be fought the next day on the second line, which had meanwhile been heavily fortified by the allies with redoubts and a powerful artillery.

It must be clearly understood that the Prussians still held the foothills beyond Bautzen. In this position their sector formed a promontory jutting out toward the enemy and separated from the rest of the allied line by the valley of the Blöser Wasser, which skirted these foothills from the rear side of the Prussian line and, meeting the Spree beyond, made of these foothills a kind of peninsula. It was this valley which attracted the attention of Napoleon. Ney was in an admirable position to make his way into this valley from Klix, and by reaching Hochkirchen, a village situated directly back of the Prussian sector, would be able to separate Blücher from the Russians. By pressing farther to his left over the slopes on the right bank of the Blöser Wasser, he would even be in a position to get into the rear of the whole allied line. This double danger was clearly seen by the allied command during the council of war held by the sovereigns during the preceding night; as Barclay de Tolly was facing Ney, it was to him that the all-important task of holding the entrance into the valley of the Blöser Wasser was entrusted. Alexander was much worried about Barclay's position and wanted to have him reinforced. Unfortunately, underestimating the size of Ney's army, he allowed himself to be persuaded that Barclay had enough men. Consequently Barclay, with some 10,000 to 13,000 men, was left to meet the impact of Ney's 60,000, and moreover was commissioned to hold a long front stretching out from the hills here to other hills across the stream. This meant that at no one point could he assemble more than 5,000 men, though he was amply provided with artillery and was supported by nearly all the Russo-Prussian cavalry held in reserve.

By the very nature of the situation, therefore, it was Ney upon whom the outcome of the battle depended. Realizing this, Napoleon ordered Ney to open the battle at dawn by crossing the Spree at Klix and advancing in the rear of Blücher, with the steeple of the church at Hochkirchen as the guiding objective. At the same time Napoleon was holding back his own forces until the sound of cannon would indicate that Ney had progressed into the valley near the villages of Preititz and Klein-Bautzen. Then he would deliver the smashing blow of a frontal attack on Blücher, synchronized with Ney's movements. Ney, having started his march on time, put as his first main objective a windmill located in the heart of the valley which Barclay had made his headquarters. At the same time, entering the valley, he dispatched one division of Lauriston's corps to his right to attack the Prussians from the rear, while two other divisions of the same corps were to climb the heights on his left near Gleine so as to get behind the Russian lines. With the rest of his forces he attacked Barclay. Barclay attempted to hold the French back with artillery fire, but, failing to do so and not having sufficient men, he dispatched General Müffling to Blücher to ask for more aid. In a precarious position himself, Blücher sent a few battalions of infantry, though he grumbled and scoffed at the danger of Ney's advance, misunderstanding its gravity.

Barclay, meanwhile, was forced out from the windmill on the floor of the valley and fell back to a position he could defend. His main idea was to keep the enemy from reaching Hochkirchen and getting into the rear of the whole allied line. This he succeeded in doing by taking up a position covering Gleine, on the heights over the right bank of the Blöser Wasser. Here he effectively stopped the advance of the two divisions of Lauriston's corps, which, it will be recalled, had moved in that direction. About this time the reinforcements sent by Blücher arrived and were thrown in to block the enemy's advance at Preititz; the Prussians attacked and recaptured the village. Upon hearing the firing at Preititz, Napoleon gave the signal for the main frontal attack. Bertrand, with three divisions, fell upon Blücher; and one of these divisions reached the village of Kreckwitz on the Blöser Wasser, and was thus able to lend a hand to Ney. Blücher, having exhausted his reserves, could not hold out any longer; and, with the Russians on the other side of the valley and Ney between, he was left to himself. Had Ney pursued his advance, Blücher would have found himself forced to surrender his twenty-five thousand men and two hundred guns. Jomini, the famous Swiss strategist who at this time was Ney's Chief of Staff, urgently advised the latter to press on to Hochkirchen and crush Barclay with his full strength, which he could have done; instead, Ney lost courage and stopped. Seeing the masses of Russo-Prussian cavalry arrayed in front of him in the valley, having practically no cavalry of his own, and realizing that he was between Blücher on one side and Barclay on the other, he decided that it was dangerous to venture any farther and merely contented himself with recapturing Preititz. Accordingly Blücher, when he had run out of reserves, saw the way open across the Blöser Wasser. Under cover of a screen of cavalry he literally slipped past Ney and rejoined Barclay.

Meanwhile at the other end of the battlefield the Russians scored a notable success—Miloradovich, counterattacking fiercely after hard fighting, succeded in driving Oudinot from the heights of Tronberg and pushing him back on Macdonald's left wing. But this success was of no value since with the retreat of Blücher the whole front gave way and Miloradovich was in turn forced to retreat. The battle had cost approximately fifteen thousand men on both sides, and Napoleon captured no prisoners but the wounded, and no guns but those put out of commission. His sanguine hopes of capturing Blücher, or even perhaps surrounding the whole allied army, did not materialize because of the blunder of Ney. Still, he had forced the allies out of the best defensive position they had and caused them to retreat into Silesia.

The allies fell back toward Gorlitz in two columns much in the order they had fought—Blücher and Barclay along one road; Miloradovich, Wittgenstein, and the Russian Guards along another. Napoleon, similarly advancing in two columns, marched on Schweidnitz and via Gorlitz to Breslau. During this retreat there was a bloody cavalry engagement at Reichenbach, and a few days later the French division of Maison (Ney's corps) inadvertently fell into a trap laid by the allied cavalry at Hannau. Attacked by massed cavalry, it loss over a thousand men and part of its artillery, and Ney himself was very nearly captured. The allies had decided to make another stand at Schweidnitz, where a fortified camp erected by Frederick the Great would give them the opportunity to reorganize their forces, but upon arriving there, they found that the camp had been destroyed by the French in 1807. Barclay de Tolly, now appointed Commander in Chief, advised retreating beyond Silesia into Poland, where the Russians would be secure to reorganize their badly shattered forces, while the Prussians could do the same in Silesia. Under these circumstances, and with Austria having already raised the issue of an armistice before the Battle of Bautzen, the meeting of the allied sovereigns at Schweidnitz decided upon the immediate conclusion of an armistice.

III

Before proceeding to discuss the events which followed the temporary cessation of hostilities as a result of the forthcoming armistice, it is necessary to trace in brief the role of Sweden in the campaign which had just ended. On April 22, 1813, Sweden adhered to the Treaty of Kalish, and Prussia in turn recognized the treaties of St. Petersburg and Abo between Russia and Sweden, which, it will be remembered, pledged Russia's aid to Sweden in the conquest of Norway. Furthermore, Prussia pledged herself, in a secret article, to place a corps at the disposal of Sweden in her struggle against Denmark for the possession of Norway. Sweden was to become a full-fledged member of the coalition and aid the allies in their struggle against Napoleon. But at the same time Alexander made an effort to detach Denmark from her alliance with France by offering her an alliance and promising, in return for her co-operation with Prussia and Russia, a position as a first-class power in the new Europe in the making. Indeed, Russia guaranteed not only the acquisition of the cities of Lübeck, Bremen, and Hamburg to Denmark, but even hinted at the occupation of Holland by Danish forces, contingent, however, on the renunciation of Norway by Denmark in favor of Sweden. England on her side offered to Denmark the return of her fleet and the possession of Holstein. Denmark, however, turned down these offers and remained faithful to her alliance with Napoleon. In reply to a personal letter sent to King Friedrich VI of Denmark by Alexander through Prince Dolgoruky, the Danish Minister Rosenkrantz stated that Denmark would consider an alliance with Russia only upon condition of retaining Norway. When Dolgoruky gave the impression that he was ready to accept these terms, he was hurriedly recalled and reprimanded. But these diplomatic maneuvers of Russia sowed such seeds of suspicion in the mind of Bernadotte that not only was Alexander forced to write to him saying that Dolgoruky had exceeded his instructions, but on April 17 Russia had solemnly to renew her pledge to Sweden maintaining the clauses of the previous treaties concerning Norway.

But the harm was done, and Bernadotte delayed landing his forces in Germany. Moreover, after the Swedes had landed at Stralsund they remained inactive, exposing the Russian column which had occupied Hamburg to a joint advance of French and Danish forces. When the Swedish General Döbeln, acting on his own initiative, proceeded to march to the aid of the Russians in Hamburg, he was summarily recalled by Bernadotte and court-martialed. Alexander, in turn, furious at this inactivity of the Swedes, particularly at the time of the battles of Lützen and Bautzen, made the cession of Norway to Sweden conditional on a more active participation by Bernadotte's forces in the general struggle when hostilities should be resumed.

The Battle of Bautzen made an armistice inevitable, just as the Battle of Friedland six years earlier had led to the armistice of Tilsit: both sides were anxious for a cessation of hostilities. Barclay de Tolly reported after the battle that he needed six weeks to reorganize his forces. Napoleon for his part was anxious to bring up reinforcements from Spain—particularly horses and the cavalry he needed so badly. Consequently Caulaincourt, whom Napoleon had selected as his negotiator because of his earlier associations with Russia, wrote to Nesselrode on May 25 requesting permission to pay his respects to the Czar. On May 30 the commissioners appointed by the respective headquarters assembled near Liegnitz—Caulaincourt for the French Army, Count Shuvalov and Kleist for the allies. The Russians insisted upon the exclusion of Hamburg from the zone of French occupation and upon the duration of the armistice for a period of a month. Napoleon, to whom these terms were submitted, compromised and agreed to give up Hamburg in return for Breslau, the armistice to last until July 20. These terms were signed on June 4 at Pleisswitz.

What the allies had gained was something more important than the respite necessary to re-form their armies—they gained time to bring to fruition the intricate diplomatic moves which transformed the Russo-Prussian alliance of Kalish into a European coalition. First and foremost their efforts were turned to winning Austria, which meant the accretion into their forces of 200,000 men. Already at the time of Kalish, Metternich, who even throughout the war of 1812 had kept in touch secretly with Count Stackelberg, Russian ambassador in Vienna, made overtures to him offering his mediation for a peace with France. At the same time Metternich reassured Napoleon of his faithfulness to the French alliance, and with extraordinary duplicity obtained from him the permission to increase the size of the Austrian Army, supposedly to defend the French Empire, but in reality, as later events showed, to be used against Napoleon.

With these brilliant but cynical diplomatic maneuverings of Metternich, whereby under guise of allegiance to France he gradually veered toward the allied camp, we are here concerned only in so far as they affect the relations with Russia. In a letter to Nesselrode early in February Metternich reiterated his proposal. In reply to the report of Count Stackelberg (January 26, 1813) concerning these overtures, Alexander instructed his ambassador in Vienna to accept the offer of mediation provided Austria broke away from Napoleon. If Metternich deemed it inadvisable to do this openly, Alexander suggested the conclusion of a secret convention whereby Austria would pledge herself to join the allies should the negotiations of peace with Napoleon prove to be unsatisfactory. Metternich, fearing to engage himself too far, refused this offer, pleading the bad condition of Austrian finances and of the Austrian Army. Nevertheless, he secretly pursued his negotiations with Russia and in March sent Lebzeltern to Russian headquarters, officially to conclude a convention dealing with the Polish troops in Galicia, but in reality to discover and report on Russia's disposition. Received by the Czar on March 8, Lebzeltern remained vague, but not so Alexander. "Is it possible," he said, "that while you remain vague and leave your intentions to be guessed at, we should throw ourselves into your arms, while you do not deign to tell us any of your thoughts?"[13] The Czar further offered to Austria the restitution of her frontiers, the possession of the Tyrol and Italy as far as Mantua, and the liberation of Germany from the French yoke. He suggested the calling of a European congress, and left Austria free to declare officially that she would not fight France, if she deemed it necessary.

But the issuance thereupon of the Manifesto to the German People, signed by Kutuzov on March 25, frightened Metternich, who considered the document a sign of Jacobin revival. As Sorel puts it, Metternich was aiming at forming a coalition of kings, whereas Alexander appealed directly to the people. Nevertheless, Lebzeltern went a slight step further toward Russia by signing a convention on March 29 concerning the disposal of the Polish corps

[13] Sorel, *op. cit.*, VIII, 66.

of Poniatovski, which was still in Galicia and was therefore regarded as a possible menace to the allied flank or rear. A masterpiece of diplomacy, this convention established a piece of intricate machinery to settle the problem: Russia was to denounce her armistice with Austria and the Russian Army was to advance along the Vistula, while the Austrian forces would cross to the right bank of the river. Thereupon a new convention for the cessation of hostilities would be signed, and the Poles would be permitted to evacuate the area occupied by the Russians and to regain Napoleon's army. Thus both Napoleon and Russia would be pleased.

Nevertheless, on March 28 Nesselrode wrote to Stackelberg to ask him to obtain from Metternich definite and clear answers as to the stand taken by Austria. Pinned down by this virtual ultimatum, Metternich replied on April 2 with a note in which he declared that there could be no question of an immediate rupture with France. Nevertheless,

> if France does not accede to an arrangement based on the principles which His Imperial Majesty believes necessary to the existence of his Empire and the well-being of Europe, His Majesty will use all the forces which Providence has put in his hands, to co-operate, in perfect accord with the allied powers in the establishment of such an order of things.[14]

Though Alexander deemed such wording rather vague and meaningless, he found in this note the first definite pledge of Austrian co-operation. Furthermore, this note was followed up by the arrival at the Russian headquarters of Count Stadion, known as an advocate of the Russian alliance.

On receiving the news of the Battle of Bautzen, Metternich wrote in his memoirs, "My decision was made; it was necessary to stop Napoleon in his forward march and to make clear to Emperor Alexander and King Friedrich Wilhelm the decision which the Emperor my master was about to take."[15] The evening after the Battle of Bautzen, Alexander ordered Nesselrode to proceed to Gitchin, whither the Austrian court had moved, to be closer to events. Nesselrode was instructed to tell Emperor Francis that, whatever happened, Russia was resolved to continue the struggle and to try to persuade the Austrians to join in. Metternich handed Nesselrode a note in which, always pursuing his idea of a mediation first, he

[14] Martens, *op. cit.*, III, 100.

[15] Metternich, *op. cit.*, I, 134-135.

outlined the conditions of peace which Austria deemed necessary to offer Napoleon. Nesselrode returned to the Russian headquarters with these conditions, which were submitted to careful scrutiny by a commission formed of Hardenberg, Stadion, and Nesselrode himself on June 10, 12, and 18. It was decided that Napoleon was to be given until July 20 to accept the offer of peace and, should he reject it, Austria would then join the allies. The conditions offered by Metternich as a *sine qua non* were the dissolution of the Grand Duchy of Warsaw, the re-establishment of Prussia within her former borders to include the Polish territories and Danzig, the restitution of Illyria to Austria, the restitution of the independence of the Hanseatic cities of Hamburg and Lübeck, the dissolution of the Confederation of the Rhine. Russia and Prussia acceded to these conditions as the basis for preliminary discussions of peace, provided England and Sweden were invited to participate in the actual negotiations. Having reached an agreement on these points, the three commissioners drew up a treaty which was signed at Reichenbach, whereby Austria was pledged to declare war on France after July 20, should Napoleon reject the conditions of peace offered to him (Article I); in that event Austria was to place 150,000 men in the field (Article VII). The other clauses of the treaty dealt with the aforementioned conditions of peace to be offered to the French.

In the meanwhile, upon Napoleon's invitation, Metternich had gone to Dresden to the historic meeting in which Napoleon tried in vain to restore his failing Austrian alliance. Just as Metternich, after a stormy meeting, was leaving Dresden on June 30, Napoleon agreed to the conditions of the allies provided the armistice were extended to August 10 and a congress were called at Prague to discuss the terms of peace, conditions which Metternich promised to get the allies to accept. Upon his return to allied headquarters, however, Metternich found the allies in anything but a co-operative mood. A conference was once more called, at Metternich's invitation, this time at Ratjiborzye, the palatial estate of the Duchess of Sagan; and in the words of Nesselrode: "This conference was one of the stormiest I ever attended, but the importance of rallying Austria was so great that it was necessary to accept all the conditions she had stipulated. The Sovereigns were no less irritated than their representatives at Ratjiborzye, at the idea of a congress and the delay it would cause in the resumption of hostilities."[16] Thus the allies had to accept the convocation of a congress.

Equally pressing was the problem of financing the war, and this inevitably resulted in negotiations with England. Diplomatic relations between Russia and England were re-established immediately after the signing of the Peace of Örebro, and Baron Nicolay took charge of the Russian embassy in London, as chargé d'affaires pending the arrival of a fully accredited ambassador. During Napoleon's invasion, England had shown her friendliness toward Russia by spontaneously offering 150,000 rifles for the Russian Army; too, charity funds were collected in London for the benefit of the victims of the fire of Moscow. Profiting by this good will, Nicolay raised the issue of a financial subsidy for fighting the war, but Castlereagh refused on the grounds of depletion of the treasury. A proposal of the Czar to mediate between England and the United States in the War of 1812 met with a similar refusal. The financial issue was reopened by the arrival of the new ambassador to London, Count Lieven, whose clever and intriguing wife was to leave such a mark on the diplomatic history of her time. This time the British Government agreed to negotiate, and raised the issue of the incorporation into the British Fleet of the vessels of the Russian squadron of Admiral Seniavin which were in British ports under the Convention of Lisbon of 1808.

Matters stood thus when the British Government took the initiative of appointing Lord Cathcart to the headquarters of Emperor Alexander, and Sir Charles Stewart to those of King Friedrich Wilhelm, with special instructions to start negotiations with the allied sovereigns. Both diplomats arrived in Dresden on April 24, 1813. The reason for this sudden change of attitude on the part of the British Government was that, as Lieven reported from London, it was haunted by the fear that Russia might sign a separate peace with France.[17] Russia had repeatedly stated that she needed money and armaments to continue the war, and it was obvious that if Prussia were not aided and Russia remained alone to fight, Russia could not carry on. On the other hand, by aiding Prussia and controlling

[16] Count Charles Robert Vasilievitch Nesselrode, *Lettres et papiers du chancelier Cte de Nesselrode, 1790-1850* [*-1856*], *extraits de ses archives* (Paris [1908-1912]), II, 99.

[17] Lieven's dispatch, dated April 6, 1813 (Martens, *op. cit.*, XI, 168).

her destinies through financial pressure England would obtain a hold on Russia as well, since both powers were united by the Treaty of Kalish. Therefore, in his negotiations with Prussia, Sir Charles Stewart guaranteed the Treaty of Kalish. A treaty between England and Prussia was signed at Reichenbach on June 14, and the following day a parallel treaty was signed with Russia, England pledging herself to pay Russia £1,000,000 plus £500,000 for upkeep of the Russian ships taken over by the British Admiralty. In return, Russia was to aid England by diplomatic means in obtaining additional territories for the Kingdom of Hanover. Article VII amplified the parallel clause of the Treaty of Kalish and stipulated that both contracting parties would act in perfect harmony with regard to military operations and diplomatic negotiations. They were pledged not to sign or negotiate separately a peace or a truce, except by common accord.[18] Thus was consummated England's accession to the coalition.

There remained Sweden. The sovereigns attributed an importance to Bernadotte's contribution to the cause which was not justified by subsequent events. Accordingly Pozzo di Borgo was sent to try to impress his former compatriot with the necessity of acting more energetically. Pozzo talked with the Prince Royal of Sweden at Carlscrona, and when, after much hesitation, the latter landed at Stralsund on May 17, four days before the Battle of Bautzen, the Russian diplomat resumed the interrupted discussions with him. Bernadotte had been annoyed, as already stated, at not receiving the promised aid from Russia for the conquest of Norway, and his annoyance showed itself in the recalling and court-martialing of the Swedish General Döbeln, who had captured Hamburg. This attack on a city which formed a part of the French Empire gave Napoleon a pretext for officially declaring war on Sweden, with the result that Bernadotte found himself rather unwittingly in the allied camp just as the armistice of Pleisswitz was signed. He complained to General Suremain on May 28, "The Emperor [of Russia] has betrayed me and the King of Prussia wants to betray me. I suspected at Abo that a trap had been set for me."[19]

[18] Sorel, *op. cit.*, VIII, 135.

[19] Léonce Pingaud, *Bernadotte, Napoléon et les Bourbons (1797-1814)* (Paris, 1901), p. 200.

Nevertheless he promised Pozzo for the time being to lay aside his ambitions about Norway and concentrate his energies on the struggle against Napoleon. To stimulate his sluggish enthusiasm, the allied sovereigns invited Bernadotte in June to visit them at the castle of Trachenberg in Silesia. Here Bernadotte's vanity was flattered by the honors accorded to him as a member of royalty, and he was invited to express his views on the plan of campaign to be adopted. Bernadotte's ambition to be appointed commander in chief of the allied armies could not be gratified because one of the conditions put forward by Austria in joining the coalition was that Prince Schwarzenberg should be given the supreme command. Bernadotte had therefore to be content with the command of the Northern Army, and with a promise that the Army of Silesia would also come under his orders, should military operations make this possible. A protocol was signed stipulating that all the allied forces would march against the greatest concentration of the enemy. Before the expiration of the armistice 90,000 to 100,000 men of the Army of Silesia were to join the so-called Bohemian Army of Prince Schwarzenberg, 220,000 strong. Bernadotte's Northern Army was to assemble on the lower Elbe and was to proceed immediately towards Leipzig. The Austrian Army and the allied forces which were to join it would, according to circumstances, advance along the Eger and the Ihof, or into Saxony or Silesia, or along the Danube. All the armies were to take the offensive.[20]

It will be noticed that the Austrian Army alone was left united and undivided under the single command of Schwarzenberg. The Prussian and the Russian divisions were scattered among the three armies. Again this concession was to win the good will of Austria. As for the task assigned to Bernadotte, he confessed to General Moreau, whom he met in Sweden, that he had no desire to go farther south than Pomerania and the lower Elbe for fear of lengthening his line of communications. The real reason for Bernadotte's hesitancy was his desire to concentrate his forces against Denmark, and also to avoid fighting his former compatriots. Had he been made commander in chief, he would have tried to win back the favor of the French by showing himself generous in victory. At Trachenberg he had vainly besought the allies to pledge themselves

[20] Sorel, *op. cit.*, VIII, 152.

to allow France to keep the frontier of the Rhine. So suspicious had his bearing become that Alexander appointed Pozzo di Borgo as special commissioner attached to Bernadotte. The secret instructions given Pozzo on August 12 were explicit: "You will see that the use of the forces placed under his command is not held back by any considerations of personal policy. The Prince must be made to understand that even in the event that he should aspire to become of interest for the French, the best way to achieve this purpose would be to destroy by force of arms the influence of their present ruler."[21] These suspicions were well grounded, as subsequent events were to show.

Meanwhile, in accordance with the promise made by Metternich to Napoleon in Dresden, the Congress of Prague opened its session. Its failure was a foregone conclusion: Napoleon had regretted the armistice the day he signed it; Russia and Prussia wanted the continuation of the war; and the result of the Congress was to permit Austria officially to break away from her French alliance and to reveal the ability and duplicity of Metternich, the only important statesman present. To show how little importance he attached to its proceedings, Alexander had himself represented by a minor official, D'Ansted, one-time chargé d'affaires in Vienna. On August 10, no agreement having been reached, the armistice came to an end and hostilities were resumed.

IV

At the opening of hostilities following the denunciation of the armistice of Pleisswitz, the Russian forces were distributed as follows: under Barclay de Tolly in the Bohemian Army, the corps of Wittgenstein (32,000 men and 92 guns), the Prussian corps of Kleist (42,000 men and 112 guns), and the Russo-Prussian reserves under Grand Duke Constantine—totaling 124,000 men and 402 guns, mixed Russians and Prussians; under Blücher in the Silesian Army, the Russian corps of Count Langeron (43,500 men and 176 guns), the corps of Sacken (17,800 men and 60 guns), and the Prussian corps of Yorck (38,000 men and 104 guns), totaling 100,000 men and 340 guns; finally, in the Northern Army under Bernadotte operating on the lower Elbe were the Russian corps of Winzingerode

[21] Pingaud, *op. cit.*, p. 218.

(30,000 men and 96 guns), the Russo-German legion of Count Walmoden, and the partisan detachments of Chernyshev and Tettenborn. In addition this army was composed of the Prussian corps of Bülow (41,000 men and 102 guns), Taunzien (39,000 men and 48 guns), the Swedish corps of Stedingk (24,000 men and 62 guns), Hanoverian and Hanseatic divisions, a British hussars regiment, the Prussian partisans of Lutzow (totaling 22,500 men and 53 guns).[22] Alexander himself proceeded to accompany the Army of Bohemia to the headquarters of Prince Schwarzenberg. As he reached Prague he received the request of two noted generals to enter the Russian service: the Swiss Jomini and the French revolutionary General Moreau. Jomini was accepted, but Moreau, who coveted the position of commander in chief of the allied forces, was merely attached to the Russian headquarters in a private capacity as a military expert, and was very shortly to meet an untimely death.

Though it was Blücher who opened the campaign, it was Bernadotte's forces which first scored some notable successes. On August 23 Bernadotte faced the corps of Bertrand and Reynier at Grossbeeren, and the Prussians of Bülow attacked without orders from headquarters and broke the French, who fled in disorder. During this battle, which was a Prussian victory, Bernadotte's conduct amply justified the suspicions of Pozzo di Borgo. He kept his Swedes out of the firing line and, except for the sending of one battery of artillery, studiously avoided giving any aid to the hard-pressed Bülow. He further showed such signs of agitation and indecision in having to fight his former compatriots that Metternich was fully justified in declaring that his actions revealed a constant preoccupation with his future status in the eyes of the French. Ney, to avenge the defeat of Grossbeeren, attacked Bernadotte at Dennewitz. Here again Pozzo reported, "The Prussian Army was left to its fate. . . . The Prince [Bernadotte] remained constantly with the Swedish forces, which were . . . kept a mile from the field where the action was taking place. The orders given to General Winzingerode were equally uncertain, and the latter complained to me repeatedly about this."[23] Thus this battle was once more a Prussian victory and not Bernadotte's.

[22] Bogdanovich, *Istoria Tsarstvovania Imperatora Aleksandra I*, Vol. IV, appendix to Chapter XL, n.

[23] Pingaud, *op. cit.*, p. 224.

Similarly, the daring raid of the Russian partisans of Chernyshev on Westphalia was an isolated incident in the otherwise sluggish campaign of Bernadotte, and does credit to the energy of the Russian general and not to his commander in chief. Knowing that a strong discontent existed in Westphalia against the rule of King Jerome, Chernyshev with a flying detachment of 2,300 men and six guns had marched on Cassel, and on the night of September 14-15 crossed the Elbe in boats, and, letting a rumor precede him that a powerful army was approaching, came up to Cassel by a roundabout way on September 27. Profiting by a morning fog, Chernyshev ordered Colonel Benckendorff with a regiment of Cossacks and some dragoons to march on Fulda to cut the road to Frankfurt, and sent Colonel Bedriaga with two Cossack regiments and two squadrons of hussars with two cannons to attack Cassel. King Jerome left his capital and fled to Frankfurt, but the inhabitants and the garrison of the city fought off the attack, firing from the windows of the houses, while two regiments of Westphalian cavalry struck from the rear. The attack failed, and Chernyshev remained quiet for a day in a suburb of Cassel. On September 30 he renewed his attack on the city and this time captured it, taking over a thousand prisoners, twenty guns, and much ammunition; his losses were only seventy men. On October 1 Chernyshev made his entry into the city and issued a proclamation declaring the rule of King Jerome at an end. After remaining in Cassel two more days, Chernyshev fell back to the Elbe to rejoin the army of Bernadotte.

As for Bernadotte himself, he showed the utmost inertia in moving to a junction with Blücher up the Elbe toward Leipzig—he complained that he was in a precarious position between the forts of the Elbe and the Oder with the corps of Davout and the Danish Army on his flank, even though Walmoden, who was observing the Danes, declared them to be too weak to do anything. Exasperated, Pozzo had a stormy discussion with Bernadotte on September 13, and repeated six days later his urgent appeal to cross the Elbe. Bernadotte finally yielded, but moved with deliberate slowness; and it was only when he finally effected his belated junction with Blücher during the Battle of Leipzig that his army formed an integral part of the allied operations—so far it had been acting entirely on its own initiative and was not doing its share.

In the meanwhile, as has already been stated, Blücher opened the campaign by advancing toward the Katzbach. Napoleon, having established himself in a central position in Saxony, had prepared for precisely such a contingency. He therefore left the Young Guards and the corps of Vandamme and Victor to cope with Schwarzenberg, and moved the bulk of his forces to the support of Ney and Macdonald, threatened by Blücher's advance. Indeed, by August 20 Sacken had occupied Buntzlau, Yorck was advancing on Goldberg, and Langeron was maneuvering to get around the French right flank. But these initial advantages were turned to a disastrous retreat by the coming of Napoleon. Blücher lost four thousand men in a two-day rear-guard action at Goldberg (August 23-24), and during his retreat demoralization set in. Both Russian and Prussian forces lost their discipline, falling back in disorder, and bitter quarrels broke out between the commanding generals. This failure was partly due to the lack of co-ordination between the armies. Blücher's forward movement was to coincide with Schwarzenberg's advance on Dresden, but the Bohemian Army moved so slowly that Napoleon was able to use his customary strategy of defeating each opponent separately. As the army of Schwarzenberg moved into Saxony in four bulky columns, overburdened with transports, it faced the corps of St. Cyr covering Dresden. Wittgenstein, with the First and Second Russian Corps and the cavalry of Pahlen, pursued him back to the city itself. Alexander urged an immediate assault on the city while St. Cyr was alone to defend it. But Schwarzenberg was afraid that Napoleon might invade his rear by a counteroffensive toward Prague through Lusatia into Bohemia. By the twenty-sixth of August the allies had 87,000 men menacing Dresden, with the rest of the army fifteen miles away at Dippholdiswalde. Jomini urged an immediate attack on the city, but Moreau took the view that it would cost 20,000 men and demoralize the troops. It was decided to postpone the decision for twenty-four hours. This delay proved to be fatal, for in the interval Napoleon had moved Vandamme, with 40,000 men, to Königstein to cut the rear of the Bohemian Army, and he himself with 80,000 men, responding to the appeals of St. Cyr, had marched to Dresden. By the time the allied attack got under way Napoleon was already in the city. Kleist attacked Grossgarten, and Wittgenstein followed in the sector between Grossgarten and the Elbe, whereas the Austrians advanced on the Prussian left. With the aid of the Prussians Wittgenstein captured the suburb of Pirna, but the assault was carried on too timidly and hesitantly when it became evident that the defense was in the hands of Napoleon. Jomini advised falling back on Dippholdiswalde, where the second half of the army was, and taking up a defensive position there. While the allied command was hesitating, Napoleon launched a counteroffensive with his full strength. Mortier, the Young Guards, and twenty squadrons of cavalry fell upon Wittgenstein, St. Cyr upon Kleist, and Ney and Murat upon the Austrians, who partly surrendered, partly fled. In the meanwhile Prince Eugene of Württemberg, holding Königstein with 13,000 Russians, was driven out by Vandamme with a loss of 1,500 men. Thus the battle came to an end with the allies thrown back along the whole line.

During the night the second half of the army (80,000 men) was brought up from Dippholdiswalde. The next morning in driving rain the French started the attack by falling upon the advance guard of Wittgenstein, and 5,000 Russians under General Roth had to face the 20,000 men of Mortier and Nansouty. After a hand-to-hand and bayonet struggle, Roth, who had held out four hours, fell back. Alexander at this point ordered Barclay de Tolly to counterattack, but the latter did not want to abandon the good position he was holding. It was at this time that General Moreau was mortally wounded by a French shell while he was standing in the Czar's suite.

In the meantime the Austrian army holding the left wing was being completely routed: four regiments surrendered, the front was broken through, and the Austrian losses amounted to fifteen thousand men and sixteen guns. At the news of this disaster Jomini counseled retreat to Dippholdiswalde. The Czar, however, insisted on carrying on the struggle; but Schwarzenberg, losing courage and fearing for his rear, followed Jomini's advice. He ordered a general retreat through Dippholdiswalde and Freiberg toward the Bohemian frontier. Barclay de Tolly with his Russian and Prussian forces was to follow the Pirna highway. However, this would have exposed him to a flank attack by Vandamme; hence Barclay took it upon himself to retreat on Dippholdiswalde. The result was overcrowding on this road and terrible confusion. Complete disorder, loss of discipline, and demoralization marked this retreat. The allies had lost in this disastrous battle about 40,000 men, mostly Austrian troops. Happily for the allies, the fatigue of the French and the ill health of Napoleon that day precluded any active pursuit of the retreating armies, whose withdrawal otherwise might have turned to a complete rout. But the tide, in this dark moment, was about to turn for the allies. A brilliant victory, the credit of which goes first to the Russian Army and second to the Prussians, changed the whole picture and, though only a local action, became the turning point in the whole campaign.

It will be recalled that during the first day of the battle of Dresden, Prince Eugene of Württemberg had a separate engagement with Vandamme at Königstein, and was forced back after suffering heavy losses. Barclay had dispatched to his aid a detachment under Count Ostermann composed of the First Russian Guards Division and two cavalry regiments. These forces found themselves dangerously separated from the bulk of the army, which was retreating to Dippholdiswalde. Accordingly, Barclay ordered Ostermann to fall back toward Maxen, which the latter did. As a result, however, Vandamme, with his corps of 30,000, secured access to the road to Töplitz in the rear of the disorganized allied forces, and would have been in a position to control the mountain passes through which the Bohemian Army would have to pass on its way to Bohemia. Seeing the danger, Prince Eugene of Württemberg conceived the idea of a flank march to Giesshufel, where he could cut the vital Dresden-Kulm-Töplitz highway, but to do this he had to march along the front of Vandamme's corps, twice as powerful as his own force. Ostermann, after some hestitation, decided to fall back to Peterswalde, farther down on the same highway. So it was agreed that while Prince Eugene and General Yermolov with the First and Second Russian Corps would attack the enemy around Kritswitz and Hausberg, to the east of the highway, and keep him occupied, Ostermann, with the First Russian Guards Division and the artillery and cavalry would slip past Vandamme to Peterswalde, to be followed by the Second Corps as rear guard. In this way the all-important highway, running south from Dresden to Kulm and Töplitz, on the left bank of the Elbe, would be secure.

Accordingly Prince Eugene with the crack units of the Russian Guards attacked Vandamme on August 28 at Hausberg and Kritswitz and captured these places. This kept Vandamme so occupied that the troops on the highway passed unmolested, but when the Russian forces reached Hallendorf, at the point where the road passes through a narrow defile, they were met with a withering artillery and rifle fire from the heights. The Preobrajensky Regiment made a bayonet attack on the French position and cleared the way. The Russian Guards, who had been leading the column, reached Peterswalde, followed by the artillery. But the French then fell vigorously upon the end of the column, composed of the units of the Second Corps, and dispersed it. The remnants of three infantry regiments were forced to make their way over mountain trails, while three others were forced off the highway and retreated westward, becoming cut off from their columns. Only twenty-five hundred men of the Second Corps reached Peterswalde, but it was an important achievement that the highway remained in the hands of the Russians and that the forces of Prince Eugene and Ostermann had broken through the defile. Vandamme followed the retreating enemy and stopped at Hallendorf. Upon receipt of orders from Napoleon to march on Töplitz, however, Vandamme the next morning at dawn attacked the remnants of the Second Corps. These, aided by two regiments of the Guards, attempted to hold back the enemy a few miles south of Peterswalde on the highway at Nollendorf, to give time for the main forces, the transports, and artillery to pursue the retreat. However, Vandamme drove the Russians off the Nollendorf plateau.

Meanwhile General Yermolov had found a good position covering Töplitz, on the highway between Kulm and Priesten, and thither the Russians hastened to retreat to make a stand. During the day this position was occupied first by the Guards, then by the Second Corps. A small rear-guard force was left at Kulm to cover the main position. By this time the combined forces of Prince Eugene and Ostermann, after the losses incurred the preceding day and at Nollendorf, did not exceed fifteen thousand men, and their ammunition was running low. On the other hand, Vandamme had thirty thousand men.[24] Vandamme now attacked the Russian left wing but was thrown back by the stout resistance of two Russian Guards regiments. Similar pressure was put on the left wing of Prince Eugene, but at

[24] Bogdanovich, *Istoria Tsarstvovania Imperatora Aleksandra I*, IV, 188.

2:00 P.M. the main attack developed on the center at Priesten. This passed from hand to hand in bitter fighting which cost the Semenovsky Guards Regiment nine hundred men. The French finally carried Priesten, and a second attack developed from Nollendorf on Kulm, where the Second Russian Corps had run out of ammunition and was giving ground. Whereas the French seemed to be putting fresh troops into action, the Russians, to stem these fierce drives, had by now thrown all available reserves into action; at this stage there were only two companies of the Preobrajensky Guards remaining in reserve.

Under these circumstances Alexander sent Jomini to ask for Austrian support. Reaching the headquarters of the nearest Austrian column, that of Coloredo, Jomini tried to persuade the latter to change the course of his march and go to the aid of the Russians. Coloredo, however, refused to do so without the authorization of Schwarzenberg. Alexander then appealed to Metternich, who finally persuaded Schwarzenberg to give the necessary orders to Coloredo. At the same time Alexander appealed to Kleist to change the direction of his march from Furstenwalde to Töplitz, and got more response from the Prussians than from the Austrians.

But all these negotiations meant delays, and Ostermann's forces were giving out. Priesten had been recaptured and lost for a third time, and the enemy had broken through the infantry lines and was reaching out for the artillery. A counterattack of Russian cavalry drove the enemy back, Priesten was recaptured once more and, when night put an end to the fighting, remained in Russian hands; but the day had cost the Russians six thousand men. It is true that during the night the units of the Second Corps which had been scattered in the mountains began coming up to the Russian lines. But on the enemy's side a fresh division and the remaining units of Vandamme's corps had come up. Thus both sides had been reinforced. Vandamme had once more thirty thousand men at hand with his right wing at Straden (twenty-three battalions), his center pushed back from Priesten towards Kulm (twenty-three battalions), and his left wing at Neudorf (eight battalions). The seventeen squadrons of Corbineau were lined up in front of the infantry line.

On the Russian side Barclay de Tolly, who had taken command of the operations, was ready for action but was awaiting the news of Kleist's movements. Austrian reserves having come up, the allied forces were now composed of 19,000 Russian infantry and 8,000 cavalry, 12,000 Austrian infantry and 500 cavalry, with a grand total of 107 guns. According to Barclay's plan the left wing (Prince Golitsin) and the center (Miloradovich) were to remain waiting, while the right wing (General Coloredo) was to drive the enemy back to Kulm. Accordingly at 9:00 A.M. August 30 Barclay gave the order to the Austrians of Coloredo to start the advance, and just as Coloredo had succeeded in driving back Vandamme's left, artillery fire from the French rear in the direction of Nollendorf indicated that Kleist with his Prussians had completed his flanking march. Vandamme, surrounded, decided to fall with all his might on Kleist, but this was the moment selected by Barclay for his main attack. Accordingly, the Russian center fell upon the two remaining French divisions and routed them completely. Pressing forward, the Russians captured the whole French artillery, and the Russian Guards Jäger Regiment captured Vandamme himself with his staff. Only scattered remnants of the French corps succeeded in escaping—the allies took 82 guns and the transports and baggage of the enemy and 10,000 prisoners, including four generals, not counting Vandamme. The French losses for the day were 5,000 killed and wounded; the Russians lost 1,000, the Prussians 1,500, and the Austrians 800. Had not the Russians on the preceding day held out to give time for the allied movements to mature, the result would have been very different.

The immediate result of the victory of Kulm was to bolster allied morale, which had sagged dangerously after the disaster at Dresden. The Austrians in particular were beginning to speak of abandoning the coalition, but now this danger was averted. As for Napoleon, from this time on he was to be on the defensive.

While Schwarzenberg now awaited the arrival from Poland of a newly formed Russian army under Bennigsen, Russian and Austrian partisans were active in the rear of the French. The Russian guerillas under General Tilleman operated around Chemnitz in Saxony, where they captured 4,000 prisoners and liberated 2,600 Russian prisoners. Napoleon was forced to detach a Guards cavalry division (General Lefebvre) against them, but with the aid of a detachment of 2,000 Cossacks of Platov, Tilleman inflicted a heavy defeat on Lefebvre at Altenburg on September 28, capturing 1,400 prisoners, five guns, and three colors. These local operations, as well as a victory of Blücher at Salzbach, did not interrupt a temporary lull. Napoleon was regrouping his forces and Schwarzenberg was awaiting Bennigsen. The latter arrived at Töplitz late in September and brought with him 57,000 men and 198 guns.[25] Now the allies took the offensive once more.

Blücher was ordered to cross the Elbe and to attempt to get in the rear of the enemy by marching toward Leipzig, or to a junction with Bernadotte, who was to come south following the course of the Elbe. Whereas Schwarzenberg was to advance north into Saxony on Chemnitz, Bennigsen's task was to protect the communications of the Bohemian Army and to serve as liaison with Blücher. This he was to do by taking up a position at Kulm and in the event of enemy pressure to fall back of the Eger River. Thus a concentric movement on Leipzig from the north (Bernadotte), from the east (Blücher), and from the south (Schwarzenberg) was outlined; and its success depended on the co-ordination of the movements of the various armies. Blücher started his advance on September 26 with 70,000 men against Ney's 34,000, and after much hesitation Bernadotte crossed the Elbe near Rosslau on the night of October 5. Yorck, in the van of Blücher's army, crossed the Elbe, throwing Ney back to Wittenberg with a loss of 1,000 prisoners and eleven guns. Ney, covering Leipzig, retreated due south to Delitzch. At a council of war on October 7 it was decided that Blücher should follow Ney to Delitzch and thence press on to Leipzig, whereas Bernadotte should take a parallel road farther to the west via Dessau, Zorbig, and Halle. But Napoleon started an advance to come to the aid of Ney and intended, should the occasion permit, to march due north toward Berlin and so force the allies to recross the Elbe. This maneuver so frightened Bernadotte that he stopped, but Blücher refused to be intimidated and marched toward Wettin. In the meantime the news of Schwarzenberg's advance from the south forced Napoleon to abandon the plan of marching north toward Berlin, and he decided to return to Leipzig and take up a central position there between the various advancing armies. The concen-

[25] *Ibid.*, IV, 244.

tric ring of the allies around that city could now be steadily tightened. It was to lead to the greatest battle of the campaign.

It must be emphasized that it is the Battle of Leipzig, and not Waterloo, which caused the downfall of Napoleon and his Empire, if any one battle can be singled out as decisive. The publicity given to Waterloo has tended to obscure the fact that Waterloo was merely the epilogue of a drama upon which the curtain had already fallen. Because of the importance of this great "Battle of the Nations" at Leipzig, and because so many armies participated in it, it is natural that each nation has claimed that its effort was essentially the cause of the victory. Some Swedish writers even emphasize Bernadotte's timid and half-hearted participation as the main factor which turned the fate of the battle. There is no need here to retell in detail the complicated story of the great battle; it is our purpose to single out and analyze the role played by the Russian armies as one of the important contributing factors to the final victory. This is not easy, for the allies adopted the principle of pooling their armies in such a way as to have all share the same danger; hence the Russian units were scattered among foreign divisions.

On October 14 Schwarzenberg approached Leipzig and forthwith undertook a major reconnaissance, using for this purpose 6,000 Russian cavalry of Count Pahlen and Cossacks, supported by the infantry of Kleist and the Russians of Prince Eugene of Württemberg and of Prince Gorchakov. Murat responded by sending out his whole cavalry (7,000 sabers), and a bitter clash ensued between the two cavalry forces. But the next day, whereas Schwarzenberg's army had assembled before Leipzig, Bennigsen, who was advancing on Dresden, was ordered to proceed to Leipzig. He left Dresden with 24,000 men and 64 cannon on the thirteenth, but his troops were so exhausted that he reached Leipzig only on the seventeenth. Blücher, on the other hand, moved on the fifteenth from Halle and was within sight of Leipzig the same evening with one corps (St. Priest) marching from Merseburg to Lindenau. Lastly, Bernadotte, who had a personal grudge against Blücher, stopped in Halle, notwithstanding the entreaties of Pozzo di Borgo, Sir Charles Stewart, and Vincent urging him to hurry, and moved finally with such deliberate slowness as to reach Landsberg, some fifteen miles from Leipzig, only on the evening of the sixteenth. Thus the concentration of the allied armies was by no means completed, but further delay would give time for Napoleon to concentrate his forces. The question therefore arose whether to wait for Bennigsen and Bernadotte, or to give battle immediately with only Schwarzenberg and Blücher at hand. The latter course was decided upon, and on the fifteenth signal rockets warned Blücher to be ready for battle the next day.

Afraid of risking a costly frontal attack, Schwarzenberg worked out a plan of enveloping the enemy's flank. His disposition gave the choicest sectors to the Austrians of Giulay, relegating the Russians to a marshy dead end between the rivers Pleisse and Elster. Furthermore, the corps of Wittgenstein would have found itself completely cut off at Wachau. Jomini on the contrary suggested a double flanking attack by Schwarzenberg from the south and Blücher from the north. This plan was supported by Barclay de Tolly and Diebitch. The issue was settled by Alexander, who, furious at Schwarzenberg's attitude, told him bluntly: "Very well, *Monsieur le Maréchal*, since you persist, you may do what you will with the Austrian Army, but as far as the Russian troops of Grand Duke Constantine and of Barclay are concerned, they will go to the right of the Pleisse, which is where they should be, and nowhere else."[26] Accordingly the Austrians of Meerveldt took over the disputed sector and the Russians of Barclay and Wittgenstein advanced on the right bank of the Pleisse in the center, with Gorchakov and the cavalry of Pahlen on the extreme right beyond the Prussians. In the second line was the Russian Grenadier Corps of General Rayevsky and back of him, as general reserve, the combined Russian and Prussian Guards under Grand Duke Constantine.

As for the distribution of French forces on this sector south of Leipzig, Murat, in command of three corps, held a line covering the city from Liebert-Wolkwitz to Wachau, and Mark Kleiberg with the Guards and the cavalry of Latour-Maubourg supporting him at Wachau. On Murat's right was Augereau and on his left Macdonald: all told these forces numbered 115,000 men.[27] Thus the center of the French defense and the most strongly held sector was Wachau. It was here that the Russians were planning to attack,

[26] *Ibid.*, IV, 267.

[27] Adolphe Thiers, *Histoire de consulat et de l'empire* (Paris, 1845-1884), XVI, 540.

and this soon became the crucial point of the battle. At 7:00 P.M. Barclay opened his attack simultaneously on Liebert-Wolkwitz, Wachau, and Crobern. Kleist with the Prussian division, the Russian Cuirassiers of Levashov, and a few Russian battalions, marched toward Crobern; Prince Eugene of Württemberg with the Russian and Prussian divisions attacked Wachau, which was captured by a Russian brigade, lost, recaptured by the Prussians, lost again, and once more taken by the Russians. Gorchakov with his Russian corps and a Prussian division was heading for Liebert-Wolkwitz, but, hearing the intense firing at Wachau, started to skirt the so-called University Wood to go to the aid of Prince Eugene. In so doing he dangerously exposed himself and was driven back. The French advanced upon him, but a successful charge of Pahlen's Russian cavalry supported by the Cossacks of Platov forced Sebastiani back.

Meanwhile the Austrians, who had engaged themselves in the triangular band of land between the Elster and Pleisse which Schwarzenberg had previously reserved for the Russians, suffered a disaster and fell back. But this was unimportant compared to the danger to which Wittgenstein was exposed when the massed French counterattack from Wachau developed. Napoleon, at noon, judging that the time had come to strike back, ordered Lauriston and Mortier to fall upon Gorchakov, and Oudinot and Victor to crush the feeble forces of Prince Eugene of Württemberg. Thus it was upon the Russians and the Prussians that the main blow fell. Alexander, seeing the peril, sent General Wolzogen to Schwarzenberg to ask him to cease the useless attack between the Elster and the Pleisse and to divert these forces to the aid of the threatened sector. Schwarzenberg refused, but finally yielded to the point of granting twenty thousand men of the reserve corps of Prince Hesse-Homburg. But because of his temporizing it took three hours for the latter to reach the firing line.

In the meanwhile Alexander and Friedrich Wilhelm were using up their last reserves trying to stem the French onrush. Murat had crushed Prince Eugene and captured his artillery, destroying a covering Russian battalion. The French then broke through the line of the Russian Second Corps. The 10,000 men of Rayevsky deployed in a line between the University Wood and Gulden Gössa were too thinned out to be effective, and a charge of Russian Cuirassiers was broken up by the massed French infantry of the corps of Lauriston, Victor, Mortier, and Oudinot formed in squares. However, Rayevsky's Grenadiers held Gulden Gössa against all French attacks, and there a stalemate resulted. Napoleon decided that the time had come to deliver a hammer blow and launched his entire massed cavalry (12,000 horses) on the decimated Russian lines. This resulted in the capture of 26 Russian guns, but a hundred-gun battery of the Russian Guards Artillery opened up on the French, while the reserves of Hesse-Homburg came up at this point and the Austrian cavalry struck from the flank. The Russians, under cover of their great battery, recovered all but six of the lost guns. This was followed by a massed charge of the Russian Guards Cavalry which drove the French back to Wachau, and the battle petered out at 5:00 P.M. approximately where it had started. Both sides had lost over 20,000 men.

A second battle was fought north of Leipzig at the same time. Here, covering Leipzig, was Marmont (20,000 men) at Möckern, with Ney, Souham, and the Polish division of Dombrovski coming up and taking their stand to the right of Marmont, in such a way as to establish contact with Murat to the south along the Partha River. Leaving the corps of Langeron to watch the road to Dölitzch, Blücher started his offensive at 10:00 A.M. with the corps of Yorck in the front line and Sacken in reserve. As soon as Blücher was sure that his left flank was not in danger from the main French army, he withdrew Langeron and directed him against Dombrovski. Whereas Yorck and Sacken attacked Möckern, Langeron with the corps of Kapzevich pressed on Dombrovski, who had been supported by Souham. Yorck broke through at Möckern; and Langeron, after fierce defense, drove Dombrovski back. The whole enemy line fell back, losing 2,000 prisoners, three colors, and 53 cannon (of which one standard and thirteen cannon were taken by the Russians). Yorck lost 6,000 men and Langeron 1,500. The following day Yorck was withdrawn into reserve and replaced by Sacken, who attacked Enterlitzch and Gohlis, but met with such strong resistance at the latter point that Yorck was once more called forth. Their combined efforts resulted in the capture of Gohlis, and Marmont and Ney fell back beyond the Partha to Pfaffendorf, where the action came to an end. Aside from this engagement, which was a follow-up of the fighting of the preceding day, there was a lull throughout the seventeenth; Schwarzenberg was awaiting the arrival of Bennigsen and Bernadotte, and Napoleon, awaiting the Saxons of Reynier, was undecided whether to retreat or not. Towards evening Bennigsen and the Austrian corps of Coloredo came up, and Bernadotte took up his position immediately back of Blücher. The allied armies had now grown to 282,000. Napoleon made up his mind to retreat the following day—unfortunately for him, too late.

As the third day of the battle opened, the French were holding a line from Dölitzch to Probstheyda, where it turned at a sharp angle northward toward the Partha. The sector from Dölitzch to Probstheyda faced the Bohemian Army and was held by about 90,000 men (Poniatovski, Augereau, Victor, Lauriston, Macdonald, the Guards, and four divisions of cavalry); the sector running from Probstheyda to the Partha faced Blücher and Bernadotte and was held by 40,000 under the general command of Ney (Marmont, Reynier, Souham, Margaron, Dombrovski); the corps of Macdonald at Stotteritz, beyond Probstheyda, linked the two sectors. Lastly Bertrand, supported by two divisions of the Young Guards of Mortier's corps, was assigned to the task of keeping the road to Weissenfels open. Thus for the French, Probstheyda was the key position, as its fall would endanger the flanks of both sectors; therefore it was here that Napoleon was to make his greatest effort, and here that he himself was to be during the whole battle, except for a short period when circumstances forced him to go to the Partha sector.

On the allied side the day opened with a converging attack of the Bohemian Army in three columns: the left column, composed of the Austrians of Prince Hesse-Homburg, Coloredo, Aloys Lichtenstein, supported by the cavalry of Nostitz, had Dolitzch as objective. The center column, composed of the Prussians of Kleist and the Russians of Barclay and Wittgenstein, with the Russo-Prussian Guards in reserve, marched from Wachau to Liebert-Wolkwitz and toward Probstheyda. Thus it was on this column that the major task of the day was to fall. Finally the right column, the Austrians of Klenau and the Russians of Bennigsen, moved against Macdonald, endeavoring to cut him off from Ney. This column moved from the University Wood and Seyfferlshayn on Zükelhausen and Holzhausen. The two columns had roughly 50,000–60,000 men each, and Bennigsen had about 70,000. On the northeastern sector Bernadotte had a meeting with Blücher at 8:00 P.M. and, notwithstanding the strong personal grudge he held against the Prussian, was persuaded to cross the Partha and advance against Reynier. This he did by the most circuitous route possible, crossing the river as far away from the enemy as he could, near Tauscha, due north of the city. Even so, Bernadotte insisted that his force should be increased for the occasion by 30,000 men, and Blücher was forced to lend him the corps of Langeron. This delayed Bernadotte's coming into action. As for Blücher, he advanced across the Partha due east of the city and marched against Marmont. Lastly, the corps of Meerveldt held the triangle between the Elster and the Pleisse, and Giulay was beyond the Elster. Such were in the main the concentric movements of the allies. And now it is necessary to see how these various attacks progressed and, in particular, how the Russians fared.

The main attack on Probstheyda was carried on at first by the three Prussian divisions of Kleist. Thrown back once by a terrible French fire, the Prussians renewed their attack and broke into the village, but were driven out by a bayonet charge of Victor's corps. While the Prussians fell back to re-form, Napoleon brought up his last reserves, Lauriston and two divisions of the Old Guards, and, leading them in person, placed them in support of Victor's hard-pressed corps. Whereupon the re-formed Prussian divisions united with the Russian divisions of Gorchakov and Prince Eugene of Württemberg, with the cavalry of Pahlen between them, and charged once more, capturing Probstheyda. Bitter hand-to-hand fighting took place in the streets of the village, but the French reserves were thrown into action and Probstheyda finally remained in French hands. Both sides lost so heavily that the battle here lapsed into an artillery duel which filled the rest of the afternoon with the heaviest cannonade ever recorded. Bennigsen in the meanwhile attacked Melckau with the aid of the Austrians of Bubna, driving Macdonald back; but Bennigsen had to regulate his movements to accord with the advances of Blücher and Bernadotte, with whose fate his army was linked. Blücher had come to grips with Ney at noon and forced his corps to fall back to maintain contact with Macdonald. But Marmont still held Schönfeld, the key position of that sector. When Bernadotte finally came up, Langeron's corps, which was advancing in the van, attacked Schönfeld but was thrown back. The Russians renewed their attack twice more, to be beaten off with very heavy losses.

But in the meanwhile Bernadotte indirectly had rendered a great service to the allied cause. Lying ahead of Sellershausen, to which Ney had retreated, on a strategically important salient, was a village named Paunsdorff. The possession of this village by the French would have severed the point of junction between the Silesian and the Bohemian Armies. For this reason Ney ordered Reynier to capture the village, with the Saxons' advance to be followed by the French division of Durutte. These same Saxons had been under the order of Bernadotte at the battle of Wagram. So Bernadotte with delightful ingenuousness sent the Russian General de Witz across the line to ask the commander of the Saxon batteries, according to Bernadotte's own words, "to render him the service of permitting the use of his artillery until the arrival of the batteries of the army [Bernadotte's] delayed in the defiles; to this the officer willingly complied."[28] The Saxon cavalry, then the infantry and the artillery, all passed over to Bernadotte, and the Saxon guns were turned against Durutte's division, which was following. The desertion of the Saxon Army has been overemphasized by French historians as causing the defeat of Napoleon. Actually some 4,000 Saxons with twelve guns on a secondary front could hardly turn the tide of the battle. But Durutte found himself in a critical position, and Napoleon rushed to his aid by personally leading the Guards Cavalry of Nansouty and ordering the latter to charge the divisions of Bülow, Bubna, and the Russian division of Paskevich of Bennigsen's army. This attack very nearly resulted in the capture of Bennigsen himself with his staff. Paskevich, however, managed to beat off the attack, as far as his sector was concerned, and pushed on to Zweinandorf. In the meanwhile Langeron's corps attacked Schönfeld once more; and the village, after changing hands seven times during the day, finally remained with the Russians. This battle came to an end at dusk with an artillery duel. During this time Giulay was fighting what amounted to a separate battle with Bertrand.

The result of the day was a net gain of territory for the allies

[28] Bulletin of Bernadotte after the battle of Leipzig.

all along the line, though the losses were severe, amounting to some 30,000 men out of a total of 282,000 engaged by the allies. The French losses were estimated probably conservatively at 20,000.[29] But whereas the allies were preparing to renew the battle the following day, Napoleon decided he could not hold out any longer and ordered a retreat along the road to Mainz. Against the better advice of his engineers he had not prepared any bridges across the Elster, and the only bridge available was the one at Lindenau, which was in reality a succession of bridges and causeways over the numerous branches of the Elster and the Pleisse and the marshy lowlands in between; it formed a veritable bottleneck foreshadowing a new Berezina. During the night the transports, artillery, hospitals, and a part of the army, including the Guards, crossed; but the confusion and the crowding was such that little progress was made. To cover this retreat, the corps of Macdonald, Marmont, Lauriston, the Poles of Poniatovski, and the divisions of Durutte and Dombrovski were ordered to hold the north and south suburbs of Leipzig against a possible renewed attack of the Silesian and Bohemian armies. Indeed, when in the morning the allies saw that the French were retreating, they immediately attacked. Advancing on Leipzig, Hesse-Homburg drove Poniatovski back through the Peter Thor, Kleist and Wittgenstein advanced through the Windmill Gate, and Klenau and Bennigsen via the Hospital Gate, while Bernadotte and Blücher's corps of Langeron and Sacken forced their way into the Halle suburb. Yorck was sent to impede the French crossing on the Elster. Fierce fighting occurred in the streets of the suburbs when, at 11:00 A.M., Bülow reached the city itself. The French resistance broke all at once, and a confused, disorderly retreat toward the bridge followed.

It was at this point that a French corporal, acting on his own initiative, set off the charge which blew up the span of the bridge over the main course of the Elster. Thus the corps defending the suburbs found themselves cut off with no way of escape. Some tried to swim the river, but for the most part drowned; others surrendered. Macdonald succeeded in reaching the other side by swimming the river on horseback, but Poniatovski, who tried to do

[29] Thiers, *op. cit.*, XVI, 608.

the same, drowned. Lauriston and Reynier and over twenty thousand men were taken prisoner.

Alexander, upon reaching the center of the city, was most gracious to Lauriston when he recognized the former French ambassador to his court. Similarly and with obvious diplomacy he showered Bernadotte with compliments on the role he had played in the battle. But he was ruthlessly uncivil to the unfortunate King of Saxony, who, hat in hand, was trying to attract his attention.

The losses during the four days' battle had been extremely severe on both sides: the French lost 60,000 men, 300 guns, and 33 generals captured. The Russians lost 22,000 men, the Prussians 16,000, the Austrians 12,000, and the Swedes 300. These losses give a measure of the importance of the respective armies in winning the victory. A Russo-Prussian garrison was left in Leipzig, and a Russian governor-general, Count Shuvalov, was appointed to take over the civil administration in place of the royal authority.

After the debacle at Leipzig there was nothing for Napoleon to do but fall back to the Rhine. By October 26 Schwarzenberg, having left Kleist in occupation of Erfurt, had reached Weimar; Wittgenstein was at Gotha, Blücher was approaching Eisenach, and Yorck linking himself up with Wittgenstein. Four days later Napoleon reached Hanau; the Silesian and Bohemian armies had gone relatively far apart at Fulda and Meiningen. Napoleon saw his chance to fall upon the isolated Austro-Bavarian corps of Wrede, whose "reserves" were composed of Russian partisans of Kaissarov, Chernyshev, and Orlov-Davydov. The French were already too demoralized to win a victory, however, and these partisans were employed to pursue the retreating enemy; Platov with his Cossacks and Chernyshev's men took over three thousand prisoners.

In the meanwhile Bernadotte had crossed the Saale and moved the corps of Winzingerode and Bülow towards the Rhine. But Bernadotte was looking elsewhere—anxious to obtain Norway from Denmark for Sweden, he turned north with sixty thousand men, including his Swedish troops and the Russian detachments of Count Vorontsov and Count Stroganov, to face the Danish Army and the corps of Marshal Davout. He left Vorontsov to observe Davout and moved on to occupy Kiel and Einsdorf. Winzingerode occupied the Grand Duchy of Berg, Hamburg was besieged by Stroganov and

Vorontsov, Friesland and Oldenburg were overrun by the flying detachments of Benckendorff, Chernyshev, and Narishkin. When a rebellion occurred in Amsterdam, driving the French garrison of General Molitor out of the city, Benckendorff moved up with six thousand Russians on boats and took possession of the city.

Napoleon, falling back to Frankfurt on October 31 and to Mainz two days later, abandoned the whole right bank of the Rhine. As the allies occupied the liberated territories, they set up an administration according to the plan worked out by Stein and Humboldt. A central committee under the presidency of Stein became the supreme administrative organ of the occupied regions. The latter appointed the Russian Prince Repnin as Governor-General of Saxony with seat at Leipzig, in place of the dispossessed King of Saxony.

But a more important issue for the allies was to decide what course to follow next. A definite phase of the war had come to an end, and Germany had been liberated. The situation was developing so rapidly that past agreements were becoming obsolete. On the ninth of September, a month after the resumption of hostilities, Austria and Russia on one hand, and Austria and Prussia on the other, had signed identical treaties further tightening their co-operation and clarifying their war aims. These treaties stipulated once more that no peace should be negotiated separately by either party but only in common, and in secret articles they stated their joint war aims as follows: (1) the re-establishment of Austria and Prussia within the borders of 1805; (2) the dissolution of the Confederation of the Rhine and the complete independence of the states located between the Rhine, the Alps, and the borders of Austria and Prussia; (3) the restitution of Hanover and its other Germanic possessions to the reigning house of Brunswick-Lüneburg; and (4) the disposal of the Grand Duchy of Warsaw by mutual consent of the three allied powers. Additional clauses provided for the restitution to Germany of German territories under the rule of French princes or forming part of the Thirty-second French Military Division, i.e., Westphalia and the Rhineland. These treaties further stipulated that they in no way infringed upon previous treaties, such as the agreements of Kalish and Reichenbach, or such agreements as might have been concluded with other powers. The conclusion of these treaties was followed by the signing of an Austro-British treaty of alliance, and a new financial convention between Great Britain and the allies.

Thus on paper the coalition was made more and more solid; but in reality when the fulfilment of these war aims had been achieved, a deep rift began to develop between Russia and Austria on the question of the next move. It is impossible to understand the subsequent events without clearly comprehending that from now on Alexander would have to conduct two wars—an open military campaign against France and a camouflaged diplomatic war against Austria. The reason for this lay in the role assumed by Alexander.

> Alexander now became a superior personality. It is now that he shows himself the real regulator, or as one was beginning to say in the classical jargon of the time, the King of Kings, the Agamemnon of the new Iliad. He did not lose sight for one moment of the plans of his reign conceived in his youth, the reality of his mature days: to reconstitute Europe and to take the place "usurped" by Napoleon in the domination of the Continent, revenge for his armies, vengeance for the insults he had suffered. His persistent thought was to carry the struggle to its final end, to prosecute the war relentlessly, not to show moderation toward a perfidious enemy, but to destroy his army and overthrow his power. . . . He would dominate France, this Latin Poland, give to the country of Montesquieu new institutions, and a king to the Revolution. The destiny coveted by him since Tilsit was being fulfilled, the hour had struck to reveal his genius, the hour when the unknown politician, hidden under the cover of a dreamer and a Utopian . . . was about to come out and reveal himself.[30]

Whether this analysis be correct or not, Alexander stood for the continuation of the war; furthermore, he had given encouragement to Bernadotte in his dreams of regaining the throne of France; lastly, he had encouraged the revolutionary movement in Germany. Metternich, and behind him Emperor Francis, had been horrified at the manifesto of Kutuzov and Alexander's Jacobinism; they feared his growing power, and above all they disliked the combinations he proposed for the future of France, the candidature of Bernadotte, acting in France as "viceroy or lieutenant-general of Russia."[31] Metternich on the other hand envisaged a peace in which Napoleon's power would be destroyed and Napoleon constrained to accept the dictates

[30] Sorel, *op. cit.*, VIII, 185-186.

[31] *Ibid.*, VIII, 200.

of the allies, but France would not be too much weakened. Should Napoleon be forced to abdicate in favor of his wife or son, such a regency, through family ties with the Hapsburgs, would place Austria and not Russia in a dominating position in Europe. He judged that time was bringing nearer precisely such a situation, and that therefore it was time to open negotiations before a defeated Napoleon was completely crushed.

An opportunity offered itself, and Metternich was quick to seize it. The Austrian General Meerveldt, captured by the French at Leipzig, had been released by Napoleon and returned to the allied headquarters with an indirect offer for peace. Indeed, Napoleon in an interview with Meerveldt had complained bitterly that the allies had not been sincere at the Congress of Prague, and he asked, "Why not accept a proposal to negotiate?" Metternich—who had said to Lord Aberdeen, "It is necessary to limit the power of France, but why refuse all negotiations; . . . a good peace is the goal of this war"[32]—responded with alacrity. A captured French diplomat, Baron de Saint Aignan, who was a brother-in-law of Caulaincourt, was the man at hand to be the unofficial intermediary. Saint Aignan was invited to the allied councils in Frankfurt and authorized to take down in an unofficial note the verbal proposals made by Metternich in the name of the allies. These proposals, which became known as the "bases of Frankfurt," offered as frontiers for France the "natural limits" of the Rhine, the Alps, and the Pyrenees. Both the Prussians and Alexander had opposed the scheme, but Metternich succeeded in wresting their consent from them with the argument that Napoleon would refuse and would thus have to bear the odium for the continuation of the war. Saint Aignan arrived in Paris on November 14; and two days later Maret, Napoleon's Minister of Foreign Affairs, replied, virtually rejecting these terms by demanding a new congress. But Caulaincourt convinced the Emperor of the folly of such an act, and Napoleon appointed Caulaincourt in the place of Maret as Minister of Foreign Affairs. Caulaincourt sent a note in a more conciliatory vein, and Metternich in turn replied to him on December 10, declaring he was gratified at the French acceptance of his terms as a base for further negotiations,

[32] *Ibid.*, VIII, 199.

but that he had to consult with his allies. In the meanwhile the allied sovereigns issued a proclamation to the French people declaring they were not fighting France but the power of Napoleon, that they wanted to see France great, powerful, and happy, and were ready to concede her territories which she had not possessed under her kings. Here matters stood for over a month pending the outcome of military operations, but these negotiations formed the background for the forthcoming Congress of Châtillon.

CHAPTER IX

The Campaign of 1814

I

As NAPOLEON fell back to the Rhine, his position from the military point of view was absolutely critical—he had a mere sixty thousand men left, and he wrote Marmont, "We are not at the present moment in a position to do anything."[1] Accordingly Alexander, supported by Blücher, Gneisenau, and Stein, advocated the immediate invasion of France and the crushing of Napoleon while the tremendous preponderance of allied forces was favorable for it. But Emperor Francis and Metternich, while seeking the defeat of Napoleon, were not anxious to ruin him and the Bonapartes, who were now linked with the Hapsburgs; Bernadotte was waiting for an internal explosion in France which would relieve him of the unpleasant prospect of fighting Frenchmen on French soil, and at the same time facilitate his accession to the French throne. Therefore a delay of over a month occurred before an agreement between the allies could be reached.

The crossing of the Rhine by the Bohemian Army started on December 20, followed by the crossing of the Silesian Army on January 1 and 2. On Christmas Day Alexander issued an order to his army from Freiberg, in which he exhorted his soldiers to show good behavior on enemy territory and to respect the unarmed. "That a country should fare well under its own government and laws," he wrote, "that faith, the language, the sciences, arts, and trades should flourish in each land to the advantage of all nations—such is our intent, and not the continuance of strife and destruction."[2] While Schwarzenberg's army was crossing the Rhine, Wittgenstein's corps was left to block Kehl and to maintain a liaison with Blücher.

[1] Bogdanovich, *Istoria Tsarstvovania Imperatora Aleksandra I,* IV, 338.
[2] *Ibid.,* IV, 349.

The latter, crossing at the confluence of the Neckar, pushed Marmont, who attempted to stop him at Kaiserslautern, back to Metz and the Meuse. While Yorck was left to invest the fortresses of Metz, Thionville, and Verdun, the Russian corps of Sacken and Olsufiev marched on Nancy, which fell on January 17. The keys of the city were submitted by Sacken to the Czar, who expressed his pleasure that the first important city on French soil was captured by Russians. Thereafter, crossing the Meuse, Sacken and Olsufiev marched towards Thoinville and Gondrécourt to establish contact with Schwarzenberg's army at Chaumont. Schwarzenberg in the meanwhile was marching farther to the south on a broad front stretching from Epinal to Geneva, and reached Dijon, Langres, and Bar-sur-Aube, while Blücher advanced on Vassy, St. Dizier, and Brienne. The French offered virtually no resistance, falling back ahead of the enemy, for the corps of Marmont, Macdonald, Victor, and Ney, after deduction of fortress troops, had merely 46,000 men among them. By January 26 the allied armies had completed their concentration between the Marne and the source of the Seine, and the campaign of France was about to begin in earnest.

The superiority of the allied forces in numbers was now overwhelming. Schwarzenberg had 200,100 men and Blücher 46,657, giving a total of 246,757 men. In addition three divisions totaling 20,930 men were to rejoin the Bohemian Army in February, and two corps of Bernadotte's Northern Army (Bülow and Winzingerode), totaling 42,800, entered France the same month. The distribution of the Russian armies at this point was as follows: At the moment of the crossing of the Rhine the Bohemian Army of Schwarzenberg totaled 61,400 Russian troops with 210 guns (38,000 infantry, 20,400 cavalry, 3,000 artillery), as compared with 92,000 Austrians with 372 guns, and 5,900 Prussians with 8 guns; the rest of the army was composed of Bavarians and Württembergers. As for the Silesian Army, the Russian contingent under Blücher was composed of 38,405 infantry, 12,886 cavalry, 4,589 artillery and engineers, totaling 55,880 men and 232 guns, as compared to 19,560 Prussians with 100 guns. Thus Blücher's army was nearly two thirds Russian.[3] These forces were at the time under the command

Reports of Barclay de Tolly, Langeron, and Sacken, Arkhiv Glavnago Shtaba No. 22854 and 22860 (*Ibid.*, Vol. IV, nn. 13; 14).

of Barclay de Tolly attached to the Bohemian Army, and of Langeron and Sacken attached to the Silesian Army. The corps of Langeron remained in reserve on the Rhine, except for the division of General Olsufiev and the cavalry of Korff (7,697 men), which were in the vanguard of Blücher's army. In addition Winzingerode's corps (about 20,000 men) was attached to Bernadotte's army, but participated in the invasion, as we shall see, during Blücher's advances in February.

Napoleon, seeing the exposed position of Blücher at Brienne, advanced on January 29 against Sacken, who was in the van, and approached the city. The corps of Ney and Victor attacked the castle, while the Russian cavalry of Pahlen counterattacked and captured five cannon from Victor. The French, however, after their first unsuccessful attacks, renewed their assault on the city and reached the castle, where they very nearly captured Blücher, Sacken, and their staffs. The Russians succeeded in driving the French out of the city but not out of the castle, which remained in French hands; and the battle ended at midnight with Blücher's army retreating to Trannes and to La Rothière, while Schwarzenberg advanced to come nearer to him. The losses on both sides numbered about 3,000 each. Blücher, having now been reinforced with the corps of Giulay and the Crown Prince of Württemberg, stopped his retreat and fell upon the enemy at La Rothière (February 1), engaging his whole army of 72,000 men, of whom 27,000 were Russians, against Napoleon's 80,000 men. The Russians (Sacken, Olsufiev, and the cavalry of Wassilchikov) attacked in the center, with Giulay on the left wing and the Crown Prince of Württemberg on the right. The reserves were also composed of Russian units under Grand Duke Constantine and Miloradovich. While Giulay succeeded in throwing the enemy back to Dionville, without, however, capturing the city, the Russian center was directed against La Rothière itself, Blücher himself leading the Russian column with mixed German-Russian shouts of encouragement: *"Vorwärts, Kinder Pashol!"* The attack of massed Russian cavalry was beaten back, but the second wave, composed of infantry with cavalry, broke through the French front, capturing a battery of 24 guns. By 7:00 P.M., with another Russian attack developing farther east, the city of La Rothière was captured, and Napoleon ordered a general retreat. The French losses were very heavy, numbering over 6,000 men and 63 guns (of which 24 were taken by the Russians). The allies lost 4,600 men, of whom 3,000 were Russians. Thus the first general battle on French soil was a brilliant victory for the allies.

After this battle it was decided, at the allied council of war on February 2 at Brienne, to advance on Paris—Schwarzenberg along the valley of the Aube and Seine and Blücher along the Marne, with the corps of Wittgenstein serving as liaison between the two armies. But Schwarzenberg moved so slowly and so hesitantly that Napoleon had time to concentrate 40,000 men at Troyes, which he evacuated only on February 6, falling back to Nogent. Blücher, on the contrary, moved with his customary impetuosity, passing Goudron on the sixth and pushing Yorck and Sacken on to Château-Thierry, the rest of the army following at two days' interval. Thus once more the rhythm of the joint advance of the two armies was broken, and Blücher's army was strung out along a road circling Napoleon's positions on the north. Napoleon was quick to see his chance for a flank attack and made his dispositions accordingly. While Victor and Oudinot were to remain at Nogent to block Schwarzenberg's advance, Marmont with the Guards and Grouchy's cavalry, striking north through Sézanne, was to fall on the Silesian Army, which was strung out in the arc formed by the Marne between Châlons and Château-Thierry. Leaving Nogent on February 9, Napoleon took charge of the operation himself and struck at Olsufiev's corps in the center of Blücher's marching line, just as it was engaging itself in the defile of St. Gond. Fifteen cannon and all the baggage were captured, and Olsufiev himself, two generals, and 2,000 men were taken prisoner; only 1,500 men succeeded in escaping to Champaubert. This success cut Blücher's army in two and separated Blücher himself from Sacken and Yorck. These two, unaware of what had happened in their rear, continued to push Macdonald back towards Meaux, and Sacken occupied La Ferté-sous-Jouarre on February 10, capturing three guns.[4] Upon receiving intelligence of the real state of affairs, Sacken fell back to Montmirail; Yorck followed, but too late to be of any use. Napoleon had reached Montmirail first and attacked the retreating Sacken from the rear. After the village of

[4] According to Bogdanovich, Olsufiev had 3,690 men with 24 guns and no cavalry. He held out until late at night using up his ammunition, and after his capture General Kornilov with 1,486 men and 15 guns succeeded in rejoining the Russian army.

Marché had passed back and forth four times, the main French attack (Mortier) at 2:00 P.M. succeeded in breaking through the Russian lines. Sacken, however, threw in his two reserve divisions and was aided by the van of Yorck's approaching corps. Not being able to capture Marché, where the battle raged till evening, Napoleon by a vast flanking movement around the Russian left flank succeeded in trapping four Russian infantry regiments. These, however, formed squares, broke through the enemy lines, and rejoined Sacken, who had retreated to Château-Thierry.

This stubbornly fought contest cost the Russians 2,800 men and thirteen guns, the French 2,000, and the Prussians 900 men.[5] Napoleon followed up his victory by pursuing Yorck and Sacken to Château-Thierry, and in this engagement Sacken lost 1,500 men and three guns and Yorck 1,300 men and six guns. The remnants of these two corps were in a pitiful condition, exhausted from marches and countermarches over roads rendered impassable by thaw, with their supplies exhausted and the French population against them. Accordingly Napoleon left Mortier to finish them off and turned against Blücher, who was pursuing his advance, pressing on Marmont. Blücher had reached Champaubert, but lacking cavalry, did not know what had happened to Sacken and Yorck. On the fourteenth Napoleon ordered Marmont to stop his retreat and block Blücher, while he himself attacked the latter at Beauchamps. Blücher was forced to form squares of his regiments, and fell back in good order, only to be attacked in turn by Grouchy with three divisions and the Guards Cavalry. Blücher's infantry squares were completely overwhelmed, and two Russian regiments were cut off. Only darkness saved the allies, at a cost of 4,000 Prussians and seven guns, 2,000 Russians and eight guns, whereas the French lost not more than 600 men. Blücher retreated to Châlons, where he was rejoined by Sacken and Yorck. His losses during the whole operation of the Marne amounted to 15,000 to 16,000 men and 40 guns. Napoleon, having decided that Blücher was finished, turned against Schwarzenberg.

The Bohemian Army in the meanwhile had been advancing very slowly, pushing Victor and Oudinot back toward Provins, Montereau, and Fontainebleau. In so doing Schwarzenberg was

[5] Report of Sacken, Arkhiv Glavnago Shtaba No. 16643 (Bogdanovich, *op. cit.*, IV, 387).

now in a position similar to the one in which Blücher had found himself, with his columns extended and offering a target for a flank attack by Napoleon. Moreover, with council divided at the allied headquarters and Jomini alone, supported by Alexander, advocating the continuation of the march on Paris, Schwarzenberg remained immobile from the fifteenth to the seventeenth of February, giving Napoleon a chance to complete his preparations. Schwarzenberg tried to gain time by informing Napoleon through his aide-de-camp, Count Paar, that the preliminaries of peace were about to be signed at Châtillon, and therefore demanding the suspension of movements of troops. But this ruse based on false news failed to impress Napoleon, who, continuing his offensive, forced Wrede back from Bray, Wittgenstein from Nogent, and the Prince of Württemberg from Montereau. Schwarzenberg stopped at Troyes and took up a battle position between St. Germain and the Seine. Once more the Czar, supported by the King of Prussia and General Knesebeck, wanted to give battle here, whereas Schwarzenberg, supported by Castlereagh and Nesselrode, was advocating the continuation of direct negotiations with Napoleon. The latter view having prevailed, Schwarzenberg ordered a general retreat back of the line of the Aube (February 22-23). At the same time a new negotiator, Prince Lichtenstein, was sent to Napoleon's headquarters to demand the suspension of hostilities.

On February 25 the three allied sovereigns met in a council of war at Bar-sur-Aube to discuss the next step. Present at the council were Schwarzenberg, Metternich, Castlereagh, Nesselrode, Hardenberg, and the generals Radetzky, Diebitch, Prince Volkonsky, and Knesebeck. The discussions were extremely violent and revealed the deep dissensions existing among the allies. The Czar insisted that battle should be given with Schwarzenberg holding the line of the Aube, while Blücher was to attack from the flank. But since the council was for continuing the retreat, the Czar yielded, on condition, however, that the order to retreat should not apply to the Silesian Army, which would be left free to act according to Blücher's own judgment and discretion. Meeting with British and Austrian opposition on this point, Alexander lost his temper and threatened to withdraw immediately all the Russian troops from the Bohemian Army and transfer them to the command of Blücher. The King of

Prussia, who, according to the observations of an inhabitant of Troyes, gave the impression of being Alexander's first aide-de-camp,[6] immediately said he would do the same with the Prussian contingents under Schwarzenberg. Threatened with this wholesale desertion from his forces, Schwarzenberg had to give in and declared he would stop his retreat at Langres, where he would take up a battle position, while Blücher would be left free to advance if he deemed it necessary. Upon further insistence from the Czar, the council decided to detach from Bernadotte's army the corps of Bülow stationed in Belgium, and that of Winzingerode stationed on the Rhine. These forces, numbering over 40,000 men, were to strengthen Blücher's army, while Bernadotte was to be given British, Dutch, and Hanoverian contingents. Following this council Barclay de Tolly retired from Bar-sur-Aube to Langres, Wittgenstein to Colombey, the Crown Prince of Württemberg to Blessonville, and Giulay to Arc-en-Barrois, leaving Napoleon with his 74,000 men and 350 cannon concentrated menacingly between the Seine and the Aube. Blücher at once started an offensive which opened a new phase of the war. Before studying it, it is necessary to say a few words about the peace negotiations which were proceeding in the meantime at Châtillon.

II

While the tide of war was turning against the allies so dramatically, the allied cause was further suffering from the increasing discord among the great powers, which revealed deep-rooted and growing opposition of views. Out of these antagonisms grew the attempts to make peace with Napoleon in the abortive Congress of Châtillon. The move came from England and was warmly supported by Austria; both these powers were now more concerned that the balance of power should not tip too much in favor of Russia than that the French Empire should be destroyed. England, which so steadfastly had been the enemy of Napoleon, was now for a conciliatory policy; and Austria, hoping to maintain the hold she had on France through Marie Louise, intended to capitalize on the dynastic ties with the Bonapartes even though she wanted the defeat of Napoleon himself. Consequently, both Castlereagh and Metternich put pressure on the recalcitrant Czar to follow up the allied Declaration of Frankfurt of December 1 by negotiations for peace.

[6] Henry Houssaye, *1814* (Paris, 1888), p. 81.

The Czar finally consented on January 20, but insisted that the military operation should not thereby be hindered or slowed down. At the same time he gave secret instructions to the Russian plenipotentiary at the coming conference to do all in his power to prolong matters and hinder the reaching of an agreement with France, while the military operations remained inconclusive. Though Napoleon did not believe in the sincerity of the allies, he had appointed Caulaincourt as his delegate, and the latter, after waiting three weeks at the allied outposts, was informed that the Congress was to meet at Châtillon. Thus two of the five participants had mental reservations, with Prussia hesitant and following Russia. The peace-at-any-price party was reduced to England and Austria. Furthermore the delegates selected—Sir Charles Stewart, Count Stadion, Baron Humboldt, and Count Razumovsky—were personally bitterly opposed to Napoleon. Under these conditions, chances for success were reduced considerably from the outset.

The Congress opened on February 4, and immediately, in accordance with his instructions, Razumovsky demanded an adjournment, declaring his powers were not in order. On February 6 Razumovsky received a letter from Nesselrode stating: "His Majesty completely approves the dilatory method you have followed since the beginning of the negotiations. He wishes that you should continue this procedure. Since the victory of La Rothière temporization is becoming more and more necessary."[7] The matter of the powers of the Russian delegate finally having been ironed out, the Congress settled down to work. Caulaincourt was quick to sense that his best chance was to act through the Austrians; consequently, he wrote a letter asking Metternich to act as mediator for the conclusion of an armistice, offering as basis for peace negotiations the frontiers of 1789 and the relinquishing of all fortified cities on the left bank of the Rhine (February 9). Both Metternich and Castlereagh were prepared to accept these terms, but Alexander objected with the tenacity of purpose he always showed when he had made up his mind. A letter stating that the Emperor of Russia found it necessary to confer with the allied sovereigns with regard to the objects pursued by the conference[8] had been drawn up previously, precisely in the event that it should be found necessary to postpone the nego-

[7] *Ibid.*, p. 96.

[8] *Ibid.*, p. 98.

tiations. Razumovsky accordingly insisted that unless this letter were sent in reply to Caulaincourt's communication, he would withdraw from the conference. Thus the negotiations were suspended indefinitely.

Castlereagh then took upon himself the task of overcoming the resistance of the Czar, but the latter replied that there was only one necessity, that of pursuing the war with the utmost energy. Castlereagh did not give up and wrote a lengthy communication to Alexander stressing his points, in reply to which Nesselrode wrote on behalf of the Czar that the latter regretted seeing the British incline toward the Austrian view of advocating peace and of slowing down the conduct of military operations—"disastrous tactics as shown by the misfortunes of Blücher's army."[9] Meanwhile Alexander made his view clear in an autograph note replying to a questionnaire of Metternich on the course of policies to be followed in the event of victory. The Czar declared that the proposals for an armistice should be declined and the war continued, but that the French people should be left free to choose the regime they wanted. The Bourbons should not be supported by the allies. As for Paris, the mood of the capital when it fell into allied hands should determine the attitude the powers would take toward the city, but members of the different governmental bodies as well as the most influential citizens should be convened under allied sponsorship to decide the choice of a head for the government. Should Paris remain faithful to Napoleon, the Czar thought it wiser to make a treaty of peace with Napoleon. All municipal governmental bodies and authorities should remain functioning under a governor-general appointed by the allies. The Czar expressed his desire that this governor-general should be a Russian, because "Russia was the power which had fought the common enemy longest."[10] Castlereagh and Hardenberg in reply to the same questionnaire advocated acceptance of Caulaincourt's offer and the immediate conclusion of peace. Alexander sent a second note in which he declared that he was persuaded that the allies had the same chances of success as before. "A lost battle does not destroy in one day the fruits of all our victories. . . . The Czar does not

[9] General Modest Ivanovich Bogdanovich, *Geschichte des Krieges 1814 im Frankreich und des Sturzes Napoleon's I* (Leipzig, 1866), II, 70.

[10] *Ibid.*, II, 308-309.

share the opinion of the allies that the fall of Napoleon is no longer necessary. On the contrary he thinks that never has the situation been more favorable for bringing peace to Europe and France. . . ."[11]

In the face of this obstinacy of Alexander, Hardenberg, hesitant, took the side of Russia; but Castlereagh remained as determined for immediate peace as before and on February 14 had a violent personal interview on the matter with the Czar at Pont-sur-Seine. The Czar had gone there to escape the diplomatic intrigues and to see that Schwarzenberg's army should advance more rapidly. Castlereagh in this meeting gloomily told the Czar that it was necessary to make peace immediately if the allies were to avoid being forced to retreat beyond the Rhine. Alexander angrily replied, "My Lord, it would not be a peace but an armistice which would merely give us a few days' respite. Understand once and for all that I shall not always be ready to have my troops make marches of four hundred leagues to come to your aid. I will not make peace so long as Napoleon remains on the throne."[12] However, the Czar did yield on one point—he did not object to the reconvening of the Congress of Châtillon on February 17; though once more Razumovsky was instructed to carry on his dilatory tactics.

In the meanwhile the military commissioners who had met at Lusigny on February 24 to work out the technicalities of the cessation of hostilities could not agree, and the conference was broken off. Under these circumstances the Congress of Châtillon stiffened its stand, and on February 28 Caulaincourt was summoned to give a categorical answer to the allied proposals of peace. But Napoleon, engaged against Blücher, was in no hurry to give the answer; and after waiting vainly till March 19 the Congress closed without any results. Castlereagh, under the influence of this failure on the armistice negotiations, changed his attitude and now advocated an adamant fight to the finish, even though the allies should be forced back across the Rhine. Accordingly, when the allied headquarters moved from Bar-sur-Aube to Chaumont, he raised the issue of British subsidies to the allied armies and under pretense of clarifying the financial questions pertaining to these subsidies suggested the signing of a four-power treaty effective for twenty years, whereby in return for the British subsidy each of the Continental powers (Austria,

[11] *Ibid.*, II, 309-313.

[12] *Ibid.*, II, 74.

Russia, Prussia) was to continue fighting without a separate peace with France. This treaty, signed on March 1, was obviously directed at the hesitancy of Austria, who now remained the sole advocate of peace and appeasement. Although the Treaty of Chaumont did consolidate the alliance of the four powers, the deep divergencies and animosities revealed by the Congress of Châtillon were to have a most dangerous effect on the conduct of military operations, and were in a great measure responsible for the subsequent allied defeats.

III

Blücher, supported by the Czar and his king, was impetuous; whereas Schwarzenberg, backed by Emperor Francis, Metternich, and Castlereagh, was all for caution. Following the council of war at Bar-sur-Aube, where Alexander had threatened to transfer his forces to Blücher, the elderly Prussian field marshal decided to march on Paris, but Schwarzenberg was permitted to continue his withdrawal so long as Napoleon was pursuing him. Should Napoleon turn with his main forces against Blücher, Schwarzenberg was to turn about and come to the aid of the Silesian Army by a counter-offensive of his own. Blücher in his impetuosity started his advance the day before the council of Bar-sur-Aube on February 24, and his columns began crossing the Aube at Baudemont, Angleure, and Plancy. He received a most encouraging letter from Alexander, who had also placed under his command the Russian corps of Winzingerode, which had captured Reims. The corps of Langeron had been ordered to leave Mainz on February 2 and had by this time reached Vitry-le-François. This corps could serve to cover Blücher's communications; from it were detached the divisions of Kapzevich, Rudzevich, and Baron Korff, totaling 11,000 men, and these were merged with the advancing army. With Sacken's corps of 13,700 men and Winzingerode's 26,000, Blücher had 50,000 Russians under him, compared with 40,000 Prussians (Yorck, Kleist, Bülow).[13] It is true that neither Bülow at Laon nor Winzingerode at Reims was immediately accessible, and the important French fortress of Soissons barred their way to Paris. Nevertheless, Blücher had ordered both of them to advance and rejoin him, Bülow toward Villers-Coteret and Winzingerode toward Oulchy-sur-Ourcq. At the same time, to

[13] Journal of Langeron, Archives Topographiques de St. Petersbourg No. 29103 (Houssaye, *op. cit.*, p. 125 n.).

induce Schwarzenberg to stop his panicky retreat and pin down as many French troops as possible, Blücher informed the Austrian that Napoleon was marching against the Silesian Army. This message sent by Blücher on February 26 was somewhat premature, for Napoleon left Troyes only the following day, but it did give both King Friedrich Wilhelm and the Czar an opportunity to insist that the Austrians should fulfil their part of the bargain, and Schwarzenberg, much against his will, was obliged to stop and turn about. At the news of Blücher's advance Napoleon had decided to leave Macdonald and Oudinot with 40,000 men to cope with the slow-moving Schwarzenberg, and himself march against Blücher.

The Army of Bohemia therefore started its counteroffensive against the two French marshals with a crushing superiority in numbers. On February 26 the Bavarians of Wrede attacked Bar-sur-Aube, while the main forces faced Oudinot, who had deployed his troops along the river Aube. Here on the morning of February 27 the Cossacks of Count Pahlen appeared on Oudinot's left flank, driving back French cavalry patrols. Oudinot realized the danger, particularly since overlooking his position on his left flank were the heights of Vernonfays, which he had not previously occupied. He therefore ordered the division of Leval to take possession of these heights, but was too late. As the French infantry proceeded to scale the slope, it clashed with the heads of the Russian columns advancing on the same heights, and the charges of Russian cuirassiers drove the French infantry back. Moreover, a battery of forty-eight Russian guns opened fire upon the French, who had little artillery. In vain did the French infantry make three bloody attacks on the heights, while Kellerman's cavalry, crossing the river, attempted to charge the great Russian battery at Vernonfays; this key position remained firmly in the hands of the Russians. Toward 4:00 P.M. Count Pahlen's cavalry succeeded in turning Oudinot's left, while the Russian infantry pressed hard frontally. The marshal, failing to obtain aid from Gérard, who was defending Bar-sur-Aube from the Bavarians, gave order to retreat and fell back to the line of the Seine. The precipitate retreat of Oudinot exposed Macdonald, marching to his aid toward La Ferté-sur-Aube, and the latter had to retreat hurriedly to Troyes. Thus the whole line of the Aube was abandoned by the French. This victory was essentially a Russian victory if we consider that against 21,000 French the allies had put into the field 26,000 men, of whom 21,000 were Russians under Wittgenstein, plus 1,700 Russian cavalry. Napoleon was not unduly worried at the news of this defeat—he estimated that the slow-moving Army of Bohemia would take at least a week to reach the Seine, and by this time he would have had time to finish off Blücher. Hence he continued, unruffled, his march against the Army of Silesia.

Blücher in the meanwhile was advancing rapidly. He crushed the weak corps of Marmont near Sézanne, and Marmont was forced to fall back to La Ferté-sous-Jouarre, where he was reinforced by Mortier, called up urgently from Soissons. By February 27 both marshals had been forced to fall back to the line of the Marne, at Meaux, where they decided to hold the right bank of the river. But Blücher, crossing the river at La Ferté-sous-Jouarre on the night of February 27-28, marched toward the Ourcq, while the Russians of Sacken attacked Meaux in a feint to keep the French busy. Marmont, seeing through this maneuver, fell back to Lizzy-sur-Ourcq, followed by Mortier, but the enemy had already succeeded in gaining a foothold on the right bank of the river and all French efforts to dislodge them had failed. By March 1 the whole Silesian Army had been assembled on the Ourcq.

Preparatory to the crossing of the river, Sacken made an attack and dislodged the French from Lizzy while Kleist and Kapzevich, marching along both banks, fell upon Marmont. The crossing of the river by the main body of the army had been set for the next day, but during the night Blücher received a message informing him of Napoleon's advance. Indeed, Napoleon with 35,000 men had passed Sézanne and reached La Ferté-sous-Jouarre; that is, he was placing himself squarely on Blücher's communications. There was nothing for Blücher to do but cancel the advance and get out of the trap into which he had fallen, with Marmont ahead of him and Napoleon at his back. To make matters worse, he had no idea where Bülow and Winzingerode were, and immediately to the north he was menaced by the strong French fortress of Soissons blocking all roads leading in that direction. Blücher thus found himself in an extremely critical position. With Napoleon at his back he could not think of attempting to force the Ourcq, for his retreat was cut; the way south was made impossible by the contact Napoleon had established with Marmont, and the way north was closed by Soissons. Nevertheless, the danger was least in going north, for he could try to skirt Soissons by crossing the Aisne further down stream, and he would also be closer to Bülow and Winzingerode. He therefore decided upon this course and proceeded northward to Buzancy, a few miles south of Soissons. From Soissons forked two main highways—one due north to Laon, the other east to Reims. Just as Blücher started this movement he received news of the sudden fall of Soissons, which came to him as a miraculous aid in his predicament.

Having received their marching orders from Blücher, Bülow and Winzingerode had set out for a rendezvous before Soissons. On March 2 at 9:00 A.M. with admirable precision the Prussian corps of Bülow and the Russian corps of Winzingerode came within sight of each other under the walls of Soissons, marching on the highways from Laon and Reims respectively. Forthwith the Russian batteries opened fire on the fortress, and Winzingerode sent his infantry in waves to attack the forts. For twelve hours the French garrison resisted bravely, but both Bülow and Winzingerode succeeded in getting their emissaries, Captain Mertens and Colonel Baron Löwenstern, into the city. The latter succeeded in persuading General Moreau, commander of the garrison, that with Blücher near and Napoleon far away he had no chance. Demoralized after a stormy council of war, Moreau signed a capitulation of the fortress the following day, March 3. The same day the city was occupied by both Russian and Prussian forces. Though it may be an exaggeration to say with Thiers that the fall of Soissons was, next to Waterloo, the greatest disaster in French history,[14] is is nevertheless true that it permitted Blücher to escape a nearly certain disaster. Napoleon was so incensed by the news that he ordered General Moreau and his staff to be court-martialed and shot, a fate which they escaped only because of the length of the trial, which outlived the Empire. Blücher stopped his retreat, whereupon Napoleon changed his plans and decided by forcing the passage of the Aisne at Berry-au-Bac to cut Blücher off from Reims and, by gaining upon him in speed, to reach Laon first. This in turn made Blücher conceive the idea of striking on Napoleon's flank while the latter's forces were extended during this march. For this purpose he selected the high plateau

[14] Thiers, *op. cit.,* XVII, 444.

of Craonne overlooking the road to be followed by Napoleon's army. Thereupon Napoleon, forced to give up his plan of marching toward Laon, decided to give battle to Blücher at Craonne. The result was one of the bloodiest engagements of the war, fought on the allied side almost entirely by the Russian army.

According to the plan for the battle worked out by Blücher, the Russian corps of Count Vorontsov with 16,300 infantry, 2,200 cavalry, and 96 cannon was to defend the plateau and keep the French engaged, while the combined cavalry of Winzingerode, Langeron, and Yorck (all told 10,000 sabers and 60 guns), supported by the infantry of Kleist, was to cross the Ailette River and following the Reims road come out in the rear of the French army. Sacken's corps (13,500 men) was to serve as general reserve back of Vorontsov. Napoleon decided to attack the flanks of the Russian army lined up on the plateau, concentrating his main effort on the Russian left flank, where Ney was to scale the plateau and come out back of the key Russian position of Hurtebise; Nansouty with cavalry and artillery was to hold the Russian center and the flank around Hurtebise. During the day of March 6 both sides took up their positions for the battle, and the French made some preliminary thrusts. Two Russian battalions were driven back from the village of Craonne, but a charge of the Russian Pavlograd Hussars drove the French back in turn. With one division Ney captured the abbey of Vauclerc and made his way up the slope to capture the key position of Hurtebise, but a Russian counterattack drove him back. Three times during the day Hurtebise changed hands, and finally remained with the Russians, Ney falling back to cover the abbey. The next morning the Russians had taken up a battle position on the plateau in three lines: a first line of fourteen battalions just back of Hurtebise, a second line of seven battalions half a mile back, and, at an equal distance, a third line composed of nine battalions. To the right of the first line the Pavlograd Hussars and four regiments of cossacks massed, preparing to charge the assailants. A battery of thirty-six guns was ahead of the first line, a second battery of twelve guns on the right flank faced the path of Les Dames, which Ney was to ascend, and a battery of eighteen guns overlooked the valley of the Ailette on the left flank. Sacken's corps and his massed cavalry of

4,200 sabres were stationed a couple of miles back of Vorontsov's third line.

Ney started the attack early in the morning with two divisions and a brigade which managed to gain a foothold on the plateau, but met with such a withering fire that he was forced to fall back. To support him Napoleon threw in the corps of Victor and the division of the Young Guards (Boyer de Rebeval), which attacked the farm of Hurtebise. Vorontsov, seeing the danger, ordered his advance units to abandon the farm and under pressure from Ney withdrew his left flank a little; it now formed a slight angle with the main line. Encouraged, Victor ordered his division to advance, but the result was that the Young Guards found themselves on the open plateau under a Russian cross fire which in one regiment killed thirty out of thirty-three officers. Seeing the predicament of this division, Grouchy brought up his cavalry, while two divisions of French Guard Cavalry under Nansouty pressed the Pavlograd Hussars on the right flank in a charge which was broken up by Russian artillery. At this point Vorontsov unleashed his counterattack, using Sacken's reserves. A brigade attacked Grouchy's cavalry, which broke in disorder and fell back upon Boyer de Rebeval's division, which in turn fled in disorder. The panic gained Ney's corps, which broke in turn, and the French were driven in utter confusion into the ravine. The plateau was now freed from the enemy. Since Vorontsov had brilliantly fulfilled his part in the battle, if at this moment Winzingerode had come out in the French rear, the crushing of the army of Napoleon would have been complete.

Unfortunately Winzingerode was late in starting and was further delayed by the terrible condition of the roads, a thaw having transformed them into quagmires. Just as Napoleon was throwing in his last reserves, which rallied Ney's troops to a counterattack, Blücher realized that Winzingerode's encircling movement had hopelessly miscarried and ordered Sacken and Vorontsov to abandon the plateau. The order reached the Russian commanders at 1:30 P.M., and Vorontsov refused to retreat, declaring he had held out for five hours and a retreat would be more costly than to hold on. But Blücher, who had decided to make his next stand at Laon, insisted; and Vorontsov had to obey. "The Russians, taking with them their cannon and a certain number of their wounded, retired step by step with an imposing calm, in battalions of chequered squares. The Navaginsk and Tula regiments gave up the ground only upon reiterated orders."[15] But as the plateau narrowed in the rear, Sacken's cavalry had to carry out eight successive charges to hold back the enemy while Vorontsov's infantry passed this bottleneck. The battle ceased at nightfall when the Russians succeeded in coming out on the main Laon highway. The losses on both sides were about even—5,000 for the Russians and 5,400 for the French, but the fierceness of the struggle may be gauged by the fact that nine French generals, including Victor, Grouchy, Boyer de Rebeval, and Cambronne, were wounded. Like Pultusk and Eylau, this was an indecisive battle which revealed the capacity of resistance of the Russian infantry, but also the lack of aggressiveness in carrying out wide offensive maneuvers.

Following this battle Napoleon was anxious to press his advance in such a way as not to give Blücher time to consolidate his defensive positions at Laon. Accordingly, the French marched in two columns, the main army along the road from Soissons and the corps of Marmont along the Reims road. The Guards Cavalry in the van of the main army presently came upon the division of Chernyshev (four infantry regiments and twelve guns) holding the defile of Etouvelles, and was thrown back. Ney came to the rescue of the cavalry and attempted to force the defile, but was thrown back in turn. All attempts to get through having failed, Napoleon, acting upon information furnished by a local inhabitant, sent two battalions of infantry and the Guards Cavalry around the defile through a path not known to the Russians. This forced Chernyshev to abandon the defile, and though he suffered severe losses, he managed to regain the army at Laon. This rear-guard engagement took away all chances of a surprise attack on Blücher, for it not only gave him warning of Napoleon's approach, but furthermore it gave him time to occupy a battle line. This line, as at Craonne, centered around a high plateau upon which the city of Laon is built. At the foot of it flows the river Ardon, on the banks of which are the suburbs of the city. The plateau with its steep slopes forms a kind of natural fortress. Bülow with 17,000 men was assigned to defend it. On his right to the west of Laon, facing the village of Clacy, were the

[15] Houssaye, *op. cit.*, p. 188.

Russians of Winzingerode; and on his left facing Athies and the Reims road, the Prussians of Yorck and Kleist. Sacken and Langeron were in reserve. Historians have disagreed on the size of the contending armies, German and Russian writers putting Blücher's forces between 97,000 and 110,000, and Napoleon's at 60,000. The French historian Houssaye, as a result of calculations which appear trustworthy, scales the figures down to 84,000 for Blücher and 36,000 for Napoleon.[16] In any event the disproportion of the respective forces made Napoleon overcautious. The first day (March 9) he merely deployed for battle and carried on local assaults. Ney, followed by Mortier, approaching Laon by the Soissons road, started to attack the suburbs held by Bülow, and these suburbs changed hands several times during the day. Blücher then decided to attempt to crush the French left flank deployed before the suburb of Semilly, and ordered Winzingerode to extend his line by engaging his whole artillery and a Russian division. Seeing this and fearing for his communications, General Boyer de Rebeval abandoned his attempts to capture Semilly and fell back, whereupon Ney came to his rescue with a cavalry charge which drove the Russians back toward Clacy. At this point Marmont's corps, six hours behind schedule, appeared on the Reims road and engaged Yorck at Athies. The latter withdrew his advance units from the village after setting fire to it. In the meanwhile Napoleon, unaware of Marmont's arrival, engaged the newly arrived Victor with two divisions against Winzingerode at Clacy, while Ney attempted to go around a marsh which covered the Russian position. At first the Russians, taken by surprise, lost 250 prisoners, but presently Ney came under the cross fire of Russian batteries and had to fall back. At the same time the Prussians succeeded in ejecting the French from the suburbs. The battle came to an end between five and six in the afternoon, with both sides holding their positions. The only one who had succeeded in gaining ground was Marmont, who then very imprudently ordered his troops to pass the night at Athies in an exposed and isolated position. Blücher saw his chance and, by a brilliant attack carried out in the darkness of the night by Yorck, virtually destroyed Marmont's corps. In utter confusion remnants trickled back to the safety of Napoleon's main army. This victory, a terrible blow to Napoleon, greatly en-

[16] *Ibid.*, p. 302 n.

couraged the allies. Blücher issued orders for the next day instructing Yorck and Kleist to pursue the defeated Marmont, and Winzingerode and Bülow to push Napoleon back to Soissons. Langeron and Sacken were to march via Craonne and make their way around to the rear of Napoleon's army. Napoleon, with the loss of Marmont's corps, had to give up any idea of an offensive battle; he decided merely to hold on and act according to circumstances.

The following morning, however, Blücher, ill with fever, had to relinquish his command to Gneisenau, who, more cautious by temperament, canceled the ambitious plans of the preceding night and merely ordered Winzingerode to drive the French out of Clacy. Clacy, which had been occupied during the night by the French, was held by the division of Charpentier supported by two divisions of Ney in reserve. Hence the whole battle resolved itself into a succession of Russian attacks against Clacy. Toward evening, after the ninth assault, the Russians were growing exhausted, and Gneisenau moved the corps of Bülow to their aid. Seeing this, Napoleon ordered a counterattack along the whole front, but this attack was repulsed. The failure of this maneuver and the heavy losses sustained finally made Napoleon decide to retreat toward Soissons, and victory remained with the allies. In the two days of battle the French had lost 6,000 men, whereas the allied losses did not exceed 3,500 men. Chernyshev with his Cossacks and 1,500 infantry harassed the French retreating toward Soissons.

Arrived at Soissons, Napoleon received further bad news. While he was fighting Bülow, the units of the Eighth Russian Corps (Langeron) under the command of the Count of Saint Priest, a French *émigré*, had captured Reims by a bold maneuver and thereby re-established the contact between the Bohemian and Silesian armies. This was a bad blow for Napoleon, but his genius was equal to the emergency. He ordered Marmont, and Ney with the Guards Cavalry and the division of Friant, to march to the recapture of that all-important city. In the meanwhile Saint Priest, having received from Blücher the news of the victory of Laon, which in the words of the Field Marshal had resulted in the destruction of Napoleon's army, felt himself sufficiently secure to quarter his men around Reims over a radius of twenty miles, without taking defensive measures. Marmont, eager to avenge the disaster of Athies, fell upon the unsuspecting Russians at night, and in one village the men were awakened to fight in their night attire. Desperate confusion prevailed, and only a part of the division of Panchulidsev and the detachment of Prussian Landwehr under General Yagow escaped. After this first success Marmont stopped within two miles of the city walls to await the arrival of Napoleon. Even under these circumstances Saint Priest refused to believe he was facing Napoleon and refused to evacuate the city before greatly superior forces; it was only after a general French attack had driven the Russians from the suburbs into the city proper that Saint Priest understood his error. But at this point he was mortally wounded, and with Panchulidsev having been wounded earlier, the command passed to the Prussian Yagow, who lost his head. Confused and fierce street fighting went on up to 2:00 A.M., when finally the city fell into French hands. The Russo-Prussians lost 2,300 killed and about the same number of prisoners, plus twelve guns, while the French losses amounted to only 700 men; it was an Athies in reverse—Napoleon had avenged his defeat at Laon.

IV

The capture of Reims not only once more severed the communications between the allied armies, but gave Napoleon an excellent base for operations against Schwarzenberg. Had Schwarzenberg profited by the success of Blücher to push on vigorously, he would have placed Napoleon in a critical position and might even have ended the campaign. But receiving secret instructions from Metternich to delay his advance, he followed these orders and moved as slowly as he could in the face of the increasing irritation of the Czar and the Russian Staff. Opposing the Bohemian Army were the corps of Macdonald and Oudinot with thirty thousand men, and farther to the south, on the Swiss border, Augereau with twenty thousand men who had been ordered by Napoleon to advance on Geneva. But left to themselves by Napoleon's march against Blücher, these marshals retreated speedily. Macdonald, feebly supported by Oudinot, first abandoned the line of the Aube, then that of the Seine; on March 4 he evacuated Troyes, on March 6 Nogent, and by March 7 he had established his headquarters at Provins. As for Augereau, instead of crossing the Swiss border he fell back to Lyons, which he reached on March 9. Schwarzenberg followed this retreat so slowly that it was not until March 14 that he ordered his van, the Russian corps of Rayevsky, to start crossing the Seine in the direction of Provins. But on receiving the news of the recapture of Reims by the French, he immediately stopped his advance and took up a defensive position. Napoleon in the meanwhile remained three days in Reims, from March 14 to March 17, hesitating which course to take. Since Schwarzenberg had stopped, he was free to march to a junction with Macdonald and face the Bohemian Army frontally, or more daringly, to march toward Troyes and strike a flanking blow at Schwarzenberg. He decided upon the latter move and issued his orders accordingly.

It is impossible to understand this last and all-important maneuver of Napoleon without visualizing the topography of the country he covered. Running in a straight line north-south was a highway from Reims via Châlons to the river Aube, which it crossed at Arcis-sur-Aube, and then continued south to the Seine, crossing it at Troyes, where the allied headquarters were located. The two rivers, the Aube and the Seine, flowing roughly east-west, join their waters west of Arcis and Troyes, near Nogent and Pont-sur-Seine. Thus an equilateral triangle was formed, its base being the highway from Arcis to Troyes and its apex the point of junction of the two rivers. Within this triangle and on the rivers we have to note a few towns: Mercy on the Seine and Plancy on the Aube slightly east of the junction, and Boulages slightly west of Plancy, therefore north of Mercy. Farther to the east, that is to say beyond the Arcis-Troyes highway, was the important highway junction of St. Dizier, and still farther in Lorraine toward the German frontier the great fortress of Metz, still held by the French. East of Arcis the Aube curves to flow southeastward toward Bar-sur-Aube, and two little cities, Pouby and Trannes, are situated there.

Leaving Marmont and Mortier with twenty thousand men to hold back Blücher as long as they could, Napoleon marched against Schwarzenberg in two columns. Ney followed the main highway from Châlons to Arcis, while the Emperor himself with the rest of the army paralleled his march on the west, passing through Epernay. This brought Napoleon nearer to the apex of the triangle; hence he selected Plancy and Boulages as the places where he would cross the Aube, and Mercy as the place where he would cross the Seine. In so doing he would have the additional advantage of coming closer to Macdonald and being able to strike at the allied forces which had advanced in this direction. On receiving intelligence of Napoleon's advance, Schwarzenberg showed the utmost irresolution, showering orders and counterorders. He finally withdrew his advance corps, ordering Rayevsky to return to Mercy, the Prince of Württemberg to hold the junction of the two rivers between Nogent and Pont-sur-Seine, Wrede to march north beyond the Aube at Arcis, and his reserves (Barclay de Tolly) to concentrate around Pougy. His plan apparently was to hold Macdonald back beyond the junction of the rivers, but to meet the oncoming Napoleon north of the Aube. In attempting to do this he stretched out his army in a huge semicircle and exposed it to the danger of Napoleon's falling upon and crushing its isolated sectors while his other units would be too far away to be of effective aid.

It was Alexander who first saw the danger of the position. He sent an aide-de-camp to ask urgently that Schwarzenberg come to see him, but, the latter being ill, the Czar himself went to the Austrian Headquarters, where he conferred with Baron Toll, the Russian representative with the Bohemian Army. Toll suggested a plan fully approved by the Czar whereby the units on the Seine and the Aube should be recalled and the whole army concentrated between Troyes and Pougy. Wrede's corps was to recross the Aube and hold the bridges at Arcis. After much persuasion on the part of both the Czar and Toll, Schwarzenberg agreed to modify his disposition in this sense. It is interesting to notice that the roles were now reversed, Alexander urgently advocating the retreat from the Seine. The result of these counterorders was that when Napoleon reached the Aube he found merely a screen of Cossacks covering Plancy and Boulages, and had no difficulty in securing the crossings there. Faced with this rapid retreat of the enemy, Napoleon once more modified his plans and decided to follow the Aube eastward along both its banks in such a way as to threaten and immobilize Schwarzenberg around Troyes. He therefore ordered that on March 20 Sebastiani and Ney should proceed to Arcis along the left bank, while the divisions of Friant, Defrance, Drouot, and Dulauloy should move along the right bank. Macdonald was to follow these divisions along the right bank.

For once Schwarzenberg, acting on his own initiative, showed a spirit of decision. Seeing a unique chance of falling upon the enemy while it was engaged in a perilous flanking march with its columns separated by a river, Schwarzenberg on March 19 ordered the army to prepare for battle the next day. The following morning, according to the schedule laid down by Napoleon, Sebastiani arrived at Arcis about 11:00 A.M., followed shortly by Ney. The scouting parties sent out towards Troyes revealed nothing abnormal, but cautiously Sebastiani decided to investigate for himself. As he made his way up a ridge he saw suddenly the whole Cossack corps of General Kaissarov and fifty-six squadrons of General Frimont's Austrian cavalry lined up for battle. Sebastiani had had time only to reach Arcis and bring out the two divisions of Guards Cavalry (Colbert and Exelmans) when the allies opened their attack. The Cossacks fell upon the right flank of Colbert's division while the Austrians charged frontally. The French divisions broke in a wild panic and fell back upon the division of Exelmans, which broke in turn. Pursued by Cossacks, the panic-stricken French cavalry surged in confusion into the narrow streets of Arcis just as Napoleon arrived there. Making his way through the flow of running men and seeing the danger of being swept into the river, Napoleon succeeded in stemming the panic and restoring a semblance of order. Ney in the meanwhile was at grips with Wrede's corps at Torcy and was still holding out there at nightfall, when at 10:00 P.M. Sebastiani at Arcis, anxious to avenge his defeat of the morning, launched a massed cavalry charge which for a moment endangered Wrede's corps by driving back the Cossacks and the Austrians of Frimont. But the withering fire of Russian grenadiers, supported by a countercharge of Russian cuirassiers and Prussian Life Guards, drove the French back; and the battle came to an end toward midnight.

The Russian losses for the day amounted to about 500 men, compared to an allied total of some 2,000, and to French losses of the same amount. Having received 14,000 men in reinforcements and still assuming that Schwarzenberg was retreating, Napoleon decided to take the offensive the next morning. He ordered Ney and Sebastiani to attack the enemy at 10:00 A.M., but as they set out they saw the allied army nearly 100,000 strong in battle formation. At the appearance of the French, Count Pahlen's cavalry started to charge, whereupon both Ney and Sebastiani decided to retreat. Napoleon, advised of the situation, approved the decision of his marshals; and during the rest of the day the French army recrossed the Aube, while the French rear guard desperately held back the powerful attacks unleashed by Schwarzenberg upon Arcis. Toward evening the French destroyed the bridges and slipped away in an unknown direction under cover of the night.

While these events were taking place on the Aube, Blücher started advancing from Laon (March 17), marching toward the Aisne in three columns. Mortier and Marmont, following the earlier instructions received from Napoleon, fell back on the road to Paris. Blücher, leaving Yorck and Kleist to deal with them, moved Winzingerode from Reims to Châlons, the Russians capturing Epernay. Thus with Schwarzenberg at Arcis the two armies had come close to each other. The Austrians captured Lyons on March 20—Augereau, demoralized, abandoning the city without combat. Under these circumstances what could Napoleon do? The obvious move after the battle of Arcis would have been to fall back toward Paris and rejoin Mortier and Marmont. Instead, Napoleon devised one of the most daring schemes of his career. He decided, instead of retreating westward, to go east toward St. Dizier and place himself squarely across Schwarzenberg's lines of communication. Indeed, at St. Dizier he would cut the road to Strassburg over which Blücher had advanced into France, and the road to Basel which was used by the Bohemian Army. Furthermore, he argued that Schwarzenberg would never dare to advance on Paris with the enemy at his rear, and he hoped that the Bohemian Army would therefore be induced to turn around and follow him eastward into Lorraine. There, beyond St. Dizier, was the great fortress of Metz, from which, as a base, Napoleon could offer battle to Schwarzenberg, and in which as a last resort he could take refuge. The scheme was well thought out, and it very nearly succeeded. Napoleon reached St. Dizier on March 23, passing Sommepuis and Vitry. Vitry was held by a Russo-Prussian garrison of five thousand men under a Colonel Shurshov. Ney approached the city and summoned him to surrender. The situation was identical with the one in which General Moreau had found himself at Soissons when summoned to surrender by Winzingerode and Bülow, and it held for Shurshov the same element of surprise at finding the enemy so far in the rear of the allied forces. But Shurshov refused to surrender and offered such stiff resistance that Ney deemed it prudent to go around the city without losing men for its capture.

Schwarzenberg had been perplexed by the sudden disappearance of Napoleon after the battle of Arcis, the more so in that he was receiving conflicting reports from his lieutenants as to the direction the French Army had taken. Under these circumstances he decided prudently to come nearer to Blücher's army by moving toward Châlons. It was during the course of this march that, as the Bohemian Army was crossing the Aube, it stumbled against Macdonald's corps, which was following in Napoleon's rear guard. The Russian Guards Cavalry Division under General Ozharovsky, all told 1,770 sabers, was thrown against Macdonald's transports and captured a number of prisoners and fourteen guns and, even more important, a courier carrying instructions from Napoleon which revealed where the Emperor was. On receiving this intelligence, Schwarzenberg called a council of war at Pougy, and here it was decided to abandon the line of communications toward Switzerland now cut by Napoleon, and to attempt to reopen a new one based on Holland by way of Châlons, Reims, and Mons. This would entail, first, a march to join Blücher, after which the united armies would turn east and by way of Vitry march against Napoleon. This rerouting of the operation made necessary the abandoning of Bar-sur-Aube, where Emperor Francis and his Court were in residence. Hence a courier was dispatched immediately to advise the Austrian Emperor to proceed to the safety of Austrian-occupied Lyons. Francis left Bar-sur-Aube early the next morning, March 24, avoiding the French by a bare twenty-four hours.

Following the council of war which decided on the march to Châlons, Alexander, Friedrich Wilhelm, and Schwarzenberg left Pougy on March 23. The decision taken at this council was exactly the one which Napoleon had hoped for—the allies were moving away from Paris and marching toward the fortresses in Lorraine, with the aid of which he hoped to crush them once more. Heretofore we have seen that Alexander had been directly intruding in Schwarzenberg's functions and more than once had forced a change in the latter's conduct of the war. Only once, at Arcis, had Schwarzenberg shown independent initiative, and here he had acted contrary to the advice of the Czar, who, more timorous in this case, had been against giving battle. Now, however, at this all-important point of the war, with the army marching on Châlons and Vitry, it was once more Alexander who by his initiative changed the course of the war and with it the course of history.

As the two sovereigns and Schwarzenberg were on their way to Châlons, they halted at Dampierre on the Aube. Here the Czar received a pouch of letters which had been captured from a French courier by the Cossacks of Chernyshev. This courier was proceeding from Paris to St. Dizier, and the contents of the messages he was carrying not only revealed discouragement and misery in Paris, but included a secret police report on the rapidly rising discontent against Napoleon. The Czar showed the letters to Schwarzenberg, who paid little attention to them. The sovereigns arrived for the night at Sommepuis, and here Schwarzenberg was informed that Winzingerode had occupied Châlons, Yorck and Kleist were at Château-Thierry, while Blücher, along with Langeron and Sacken, was approaching. The two armies had in effect made their junction, and the march of the Bohemian Army on Châlons was rendered unnecessary. Orders were therefore issued to cross the Marne at Vitry and to march directly on St. Dizier the next day (March 24). King Friedrich Wilhelm and Schwarzenberg left Sommepuis early in the morning to supervise this operation, whereas Alexander remained there a few hours longer. During the night he had been mulling over in his mind the contents of the letters captured by the Cossacks, and he had come to a decision. In the morning he called a council of his own generals, Barclay de Tolly, Diebitch, Prince Volkonsky, and Toll, and bluntly asked them their opinion on marching on Paris instead of going east. Barclay was for the pursuance of the march on St. Dizier, Diebitch suggested splitting the army in two, one part going east and the other west, while Toll wholeheartedly supported the Czar's suggestion. Barclay finally yielded, and forthwith the Czar and his staff left Sommepuis to communicate their decision to the King of Prussia and to Schwarzenberg. They caught up with the latter on the road to Vitry, and a halt was made. Sitting at the side of the highway with maps unfolded,

Alexander presented his arguments. The King of Prussia was won over immediately, but the Austrians strenuously opposed the change. After protracted discussions Schwarzenberg allowed himself to be convinced. It was decided that Winzingerode's corps should proceed to St. Dizier to keep Napoleon occupied, while the rest of the allied forces would turn about and start their march on Paris the following day. The troops were accordingly ordered to halt. As the news of this new decision spread, it was met with the utmost enthusiasm in both the Silesian and Bohemian armies.

Early the next morning, March 25, Schwarzenberg's army started its advance in two parallel columns which were to unite at Fère Champenoise, while Blücher was to march to Meaux and effect a junction there with Schwarzenberg. Since the Russian cavalry of Count Pahlen was marching in the van of the Bohemian Army, it soon came into contact with the units of Marmont's and Mortier's corps, which were hurriedly retreating toward Fère Champenoise. Here, however, both marshals decided to attempt to make a stand at the junction of the Châlons and Vitry roads, an attempt which met with the most disastrous results.

A charge of Russian hussars against the cuirassiers of Bordesoulle caused them to break in confusion. Marmont then sent Roussel's division, which collided with the second wave of Pahlen's cavalry and broke in turn. The French infantry was then drawn up in squares, whereupon Barclay threw in the Russian Guards Cavalry, which passed between these squares; and Marmont himself had to seek refuge in the middle of one of them. When presently the French infantry found itself with its back to a ravine and a force of Cossacks on its flank, the wildest panic broke out, the soldiers throwing down their rifles and abandoning the artillery. The whole brigade of General Jamin surrendered, while the rest streamed through Fère Champenoise in disorderly flight. Several thousand men fled in disorder until they reached Meaux the next afternoon at four o'clock. According to the report of Marmont, his corps lost 50 guns out of 60, 5,000 men, and 50 munitions carriages.[17] While all this was taking place, Blücher's cavalry (1,500 Cossacks supported by 2,500 Russian hussars and dragoons) fell upon two divi-

[17] *Ibid.*, p. 372.

sions of Macdonald's corps (Pacthod and Amey) a few miles away from Fère Champenoise. The two sovereigns, Alexander and Friedrich Wilhelm, hearing the gunfire, brought up the Russian and Prussian Guards—the result was the virtually complete destruction of the two French divisions and the loss of Macdonald's main transport. After these disasters Marmont and Mortier decided to abandon any further attempts to block the enemy and fell back to Provins, from which place they could regain Paris by a circuitous route.

The road to the capital was now open, and on March 28 the Bohemian and Silesian armies reached the Marne at Meaux. At a council of war in Quincy it was decided to attack Paris from the north in three columns: the right column (the Silesian Army) to march on St. Denis, the center (Rayevsky and Barclay de Tolly with the Guards and reserves) to march toward Bondy, the left (Giulay and the Crown Prince of Württemberg) to advance toward Neuilly, while Sacken and Wrede were to remain at Meaux to block any possible return of Napoleon's army. These movements were started at dawn on March 29, and about 5:00 P.M. the Czar and the King of Prussia, riding in the midst of their troops, came out on the heights of Clichy and saw Paris spread out before them. According to the memoirs of Danilevsky, the Czar's aide-de-camp, the enthusiasm of the Russians was indescribable. The Czar put up for the night at Schwarzenberg's headquarters at the castle of Bondy, and here orders were issued for a general assault on the city to start the following morning (March 30) at dawn. The right column was to attack the heights of Montmartre; the center, the suburb of Belleville; and the left, Vincennes.

While these events were occurring, Napoleon was scoring an utterly useless victory over Winzingerode at St. Dizier. The approach of Winzingerode with 8,140 men on March 26 had puzzled Napoleon very considerably. He could not understand why a corps belonging to Blücher's army, rather than one belonging to Schwarzenberg's, had come up. He decided that whatever the reason, it must be the van, with the main army following behind; therefore he resolved to crush it with all his might before dealing with the more powerful enemy. He attacked Winzingerode the next morning, and after a two-hour battle Winzingerode fell back to Vitry, having lost 2,500 men and eighteen guns. Napoleon followed him to Vitry, and only here did he learn the real state of affairs. Schwarzenberg by now had gained an advance over him of three marching days along the road to Paris. It was too late to save the capital. He therefore ordered his army to fall back by way of Troyes to Fontainebleau, south of Paris. At Troyes on March 30, as the final assault on Paris had already begun, he abandoned the command of the army to Berthier and made a futile dash toward Paris in the hope of reaching it before its fall, but it was already too late.

Chapter X

Paris to Vienna

I

Alexander had never had much liking for the Bourbons and particularly for the future King Louis XVIII. The latter wrote the Czar in 1813 putting forward his claims to the French throne. Alexander did not reply. In February the future king, then the Count of Lille, sent a secret emissary with a letter to Alexander dated February 2 proposing that the Czar address a proclamation to the French nation in which Louis would be named the legitimate sovereign of France, in order to help start a Royalist movement in Normandy, Brittany, and the Vendée. As Alexander did not reply to this letter, Louis wrote again on April 7 somewhat obsequiously, notwithstanding the previous snubs: "Events have advanced with an incredible rapidity, if anything could be incredible for the Russian nation ruled by Alexander I. Germany is free and soon the colors of Your Majesty will be floating on the Rhine, and you can easily understand the emotions aroused by such a thought in the soul of the descendants of Henry IV."[1] Alexander replied to this letter from Dresden on April 24, 1813, but the tone of his letter was reserved and dry. Whereas Louis addressed his message to "*Monsieur Mon Frère et Cousin*" and signed "*Votre bon frère et cousin,*" as is customary between sovereigns, the Czar addressed Louis merely as "*Monsieur le Comte*" and terminated his letter by the casual "*Recevez Monsieur le Comte les assurances de tous mes sentiments.*" Nevertheless Louis persevered, and in November once more wrote the Czar, suggesting that the way to turn the people of France away from Napoleon was to proclaim him (Louis) King of France. This one-sided correspondence resulted in a deep grudge which the elderly Bourbon pretender was to nourish against the

[1]Martens, *op. cit.*, XIV, 235-236.

Czar and which he was to express openly and in a somewhat boorish way after he ascended the throne. On Alexander's side the obvious flattery and lack of pride merely increased his contempt for the Bourbons.

When Talleyrand, after much hesitation, decided to abandon Napoleon and secretly throw in his lot with the Royalists, he dispatched a confidential Royalist emissary to the allied headquarters, Baron de Vitrolles, in an effort to ascertain the sympathies of the allied sovereigns toward the Bourbons. Vitrolles left Paris on March 6, and on March 17, through the agency of Nesselrode, he had an audience with the Czar. Alexander stated that the obstacles separating the Bourbons from the French throne were insurmountable, and that the army and the Protestants in France would not tolerate such a move.

> We have studied well what would be suitable for France [he added] if Napoleon were to disappear. We thought for a while of Bernadotte; his influence on the army, the favor he enjoyed with the friends of the Revolution have made our thoughts turn toward him, but several reasons made us change our mind. Eugene Beauharnais has been spoken of: he is esteemed in France, loved by the army; descended from the nobility, would he not have numerous followers? Otherwise, perhaps a well organized republic would best suit the French spirit. It is not for naught that ideas of liberty have so long germinated in a country such as yours.[2]

These remarkable words reveal the breadth of the political thought of Alexander, who terminated the talk, however, with a half hint: "Monsieur de Vitrolles, the day I shall be in Paris I will have no other ally but the French nation. I am leaving this evening for Prince Schwarzenberg's headquarters, and I promise that this conversation will have important results."[3]

Two weeks later, on March 29, Alexander had reached the gates of the French capital and had taken up residence at the Château de Bondy. Before making any further decisions as to the future of France, he was determined to take Paris without further delay. "Paris must surrender tomorrow," he said. At the same time he took military measures for the coming attack, and also to cover himself against a possible flank movement by Napoleon and to keep his

[2] Charles Dupuis, *Le Ministère de Talleyrand en 1814* (Paris, 1919), I, 112.
[3] *Ibid.*

communications open should the operation fail. The allies had 100,000 men assembled against the 40,000 men defending Paris, under Joseph Bonaparte, of whom 12,000 were the National Guard. The Russian army alone, 63,000 strong, far surpassed the enemy in size—the issue seemed certain, and the general assault was set for the next day. On the thirtieth at six in the morning a French emissary appeared unexpectedly at the Château de Bondy, a captain of the fire department of Paris by the name of Peyre, sent by the Governor of Paris, General Hulin. Alexander, wishing to establish communications with the city, received him immediately, and sent him back to King Joseph's headquarters to ask for the surrender of the city. "We will always be ready to negotiate," he said, "even if the fighting is taking place in the suburbs; but if we are forced to break through the fortified line it will be impossible for us to stop our troops and keep them from looting."[4] He ordered his aide-de-camp, Colonel Count Orlov, to accompany Peyre to Paris, and gave him powers to issue the order to cease firing, if he judged it necessary. Somewhat dramatically he told Orlov:

> You can stop a decisive attack and even a victory to save Paris. When God gave power and success to my arms, He wished me to secure the peace of the world. If we can achieve this end without spilling more blood, we will have reason to congratulate ourselves; otherwise we will pursue the struggle to the end. In a palace or in ruins, Europe will sleep tonight in Paris.[5]

Early in the afternoon, as the allies carried the French defense lines, Joseph lost courage, and leaving Marmont and Mortier in charge of the defense, went to Rambouillet. He had authorized Marmont to open negotiations with Schwarzenberg or Alexander, and to withdraw the troops toward the Loire. By five in the afternoon Montmartre alone was holding out, and a fierce battle was raging in the streets of the suburbs of Belleville. An emissary was sent by Marmont to the Czar to ask for an armistice. Alexander refused, but sent Orlov back with him to negotiate. As the Russian colonel approached the enemy lines, a French general came up: it was Marmont himself. "The desire of His Majesty is to save Paris for France and for the world," said Orlov. "That is also our hope;

[4] Houssaye, *op. cit.*, p. 491; Schilder, *Imperator Aleksandr Pervyi,* III, 203.
[5] Dupuis, *op. cit.*, I, 135.

what are your conditions?" asked Marmont. The Russian set forth the following conditions: Firing was to cease immediately, the French troops were to retreat beyond the fortified line, and a military commission was to discuss the conditions of the capitulation. Marmont accepted. Upon second thought Orlov came back and asked whether Montmartre, the hub of the defense, would be evacuated as well. Marmont consented to this also. In the meanwhile Montmartre had been captured by the troops of Langeron and thus the issue had been settled. The day had been a costly one, with a total of 8,400 casualties for the allies, of whom 6,000 were Russian; but for Russia it marked the end of a fifteen-year-old struggle; and for Alexander, the pinnacle of his destiny.

The commissioners appointed were Nesselrode and Orlov for Russia, and Count Paar, aide-de-camp of Schwarzenberg, for Austria. They met Marmont at his house, where most of the notables of Paris had assembled. The discussions lasted until 2:00 A.M., when the capitulation was finally signed. The French forces were to evacuate Paris by 7:00 A.M. and retire toward Brittany, leaving the city of Paris "commended to the generosity of the high allied powers."

While the deliberations were proceeding, Talleyrand came up to Orlov and said, "Would you kindly place at the feet of His Majesty, the Emperor of Russia, the expression of the profound respect of the Prince of Benevent?"—thus renewing the direct contact he had had with the Czar at Erfurt. Orlov replied with a smile, "Prince, you may be assured that I will bring these full powers [*blanc-seing*] to the knowledge of His Majesty."[6] Alexander, on hearing of this incident, observed, "It is still only an anecdote, but it might become history." At dawn that same morning a delegation from the city of Paris composed of the Prefect of the Seine, the Prefect of Police of Paris, eight mayors and municipal councilors, and the Chief of Staff and officers of the National Guard, presented themselves at the Château de Bondy to work out conditions regulating the occupation of the city, as the capitulation had covered only the status of the armed forces. Nesselrode introduced the delegation to Alexander, who thereupon made a second important pronouncement:

I have but one enemy in France and that enemy is the man who has

[6] Houssaye, *op. cit.*, p. 531; Schilder, *Imperator Aleksandr Pervyi*, III, 203-208.

cheated me, abused my confidence and broken all his oaths to me, and carried an odious and iniquitous war into my possessions. . . . I esteem France and the French, and I hope they will give me the opportunity to do good for them. Please tell the Parisians, Gentlemen, that I am not entering their walls as an enemy, and it is for them to accept me as a friend; also, that I have but one enemy in France and with that one I am irreconcilable.[7]

Alexander further promised that the policing of the city would be left to the National Guard, that the allied troops would not be lodged in private residences, and that nothing would be taken from the inhabitants.

Then Nesselrode was dispatched into the city, accompanied by a Cossack, and made his way to the home of Talleyrand, whom he found still only half-dressed. Embracing him effusively, Talleyrand immediately called the leading Royalists—Duke Dahlberg, Abbé Pradt, and Baron Louis—to a meeting with the Russian diplomat. The latter told them that the Czar had decided not to permit Napoleon to remain on the throne of France, but was prepared to decide what regime was to be given to France only after obtaining the advice of the leading men of the country.[8]

It will be observed that thus far the conduct of the negotiations solely with and by the Russians, with the exception of the minor role played by the Austrian representative Paar, had placed Alexander in a position of complete leadership. Rather ostentatiously, both Emperor Francis and Metternich were away at the Austrian General Headquarters in Dijon, while the King of Prussia was quite ready to play second fiddle to Alexander—a role which the Austrian Emperor was anxious to avoid. Lord Castlereagh was also in Dijon with Metternich. Shortly after the departure of the French delegation from Bondy, Caulaincourt arrived with a mission from Napoleon. The Czar saw him only a few moments and informed him that no further negotiations could take place with the defeated Emperor.

Now everything was ready for the triumphal entry of Alexander and the allies into the French capital.

At eleven o'clock on March 31 began the solemn entry into

[7] Schilder, *Imperator Aleksandr Pervyi,* III, 208.
[8] Nesselrode, *op. cit.,* II, 114-115.

Paris of the victorious armies through the gates of the Pantin suburb. First came the trumpeters, then the red-uniformed Cossacks of the Guard riding fifteen abreast, then the Prussian Guard Cavalry, then the Dragoons and Hussars of the Russian Guards. Following this array of cavalry came Alexander on a white horse, with Prince Schwarzenberg on his right and the King of Prussia on his left; behind them came Platov, the Hetman of the Cossacks, Lord Cathcart and Sir Charles Stewart, followed by over a thousand officers of the allied staffs. Now came the infantry, two regiments of Austrian Grenadiers, the Russian Grenadiers Corps, the Prussian Guards, two divisions of the Russian Guards, and, bringing up the rear, the Russian Chevalier Guards and forty-seven squadrons of Russian cuirassiers. The Parisians crowding the great boulevards were impressed by the superb appearance of these troops in their immaculate uniforms, and soon the few timid cries of "*Vive les alliés*," "*Vive Alexandre*," and "*Vive la paix*" became more and more general as the parade reached the main thoroughfares. While Alexander was riding in the parade he turned to General Yermolov and pointing discreetly to Schwarzenberg, riding next to him, said in Russian, "Thanks to this fatty, more than once have I tossed my head on my pillow"; then abruptly, "I wonder what they are saying now in St. Petersburg. There was a time when, in glorifying Napoleon, they considered me a simpleton." Observing some French girls who were being hoisted on Cossack horses to see the parade, he laughingly observed, "Provided this does not lead to the rape of the Sabines."[9] Meanwhile his aide-de-camp, Mikhailovsky-Danilevsky, suddenly observed a man in the crowd pointing a gun at the Czar. The officer fell upon the Frenchman and a scuffle ensued, but Alexander said "Leave the man alone, leave him alone." Then again, another Frenchman stepped up to Danilevsky and handed him a note which warned that the Palais de l'Elysée, where the Emperor was going to stay, had been mined. Talleyrand, hearing of this, immediately offered the hospitality of his own house instead of the palace. To what extent this whole incident was prepared by Talleyrand himself in order that the Czar should become his guest it is impossible to say.

The parade lasted five hours and broke up on the Champs-

[9] Schilder, *Imperator Aleksandr Pervyi,* III, 212.

Elysées, the Russian cavalry and Cossacks camping in the gardens adjoining this famous street. Alexander proceeded on foot to the house of Talleyrand, having accepted his hospitality. In the meanwhile Royalists were busy attempting to pull down the statue of Napoleon on the Vendôme column, and a riot started. A detachment of Russian Guards was called out to quell the disturbance. At nightfall other regiments of the Russian and allied forces whose appearance was not so brilliant entered the city quietly and took up garrisons in the suburbs.

Upon reaching Talleyrand's house, Alexander found there the King of Prussia, Nesselrode, and Pozzo di Borgo, with Talleyrand and Dahlberg prepared to start a conference. In an opening speech Alexander suggested that there were three possible courses: to make peace with Napoleon, leaving him on the throne; to establish a regency with Marie Louise as regent; or to recall the Bourbons. The first course was unanimously rejected by the assembly, Dahlberg suggesting the regency of Marie Louise with the King of Rome on the throne as a possibility; but Pozzo di Borgo fought this suggestion heatedly, and Alexander was obviously against it. Talleyrand said tartly that a republic was impossible, the Regency or Bernadotte an intrigue, and the Bourbons alone represented a principle. Somewhat hesitatingly Alexander accepted this, but asked, "How do I know that France wishes the Bourbons back?" To vindicate his point Talleyrand introduced as evidence the Royalist leaders, Baron Louis and Abbé de Pradt, and pledged the opinion of the Senate. Alexander then rather timidly raised the candidature of Bernadotte, but Talleyrand said that if a general was to be on the throne, then Napoleon was the first soldier in the universe. Next, since Alexander declared that it was not for a foreigner to dethrone Napoleon, Talleyrand undertook to do it, on condition that the powers should help him by issuing a declaration stating their resolution to recognize Napoleon no longer. Nesselrode, together with Dahlberg, was commissioned to write this declaration, which was published under the signatures of Alexander and Nesselrode alone, the Czar acting as chief of the European coalition. This declaration stipulated that the allied sovereigns would have no further dealings with Napoleon or his family, that they would respect the integrity of France as it existed under the kings, that is to say within the borders of January 1,

1792, and that they would recognize and guarantee the constitution which the French nation should select.

The Senate was therefore invited to form a provisional government, to prepare this new constitution, and to carry on the administration. On April 2 this provisional government was formed, with the acquiescence of the Senate, under the leadership of Talleyrand, and took up its duties on the ground floor of Talleyrand's house, the upper floors being reserved for the Czar and his suite. Soldiers of the Russian Guards stood as sentries around the house and in the street. Alexander received the Senate the same day and made another speech in which he said: "It is fair and reasonable to give France strong and liberal institutions which will be in keeping with the degree of enlightenment of the present times. My allies and I are determined to leave you the freedom of your decisions."[10] In token of good will he promised the return of all French prisoners in Russia. In pursuance of the pledge given the senators, Pozzo di Borgo and Nesselrode the next day attended a meeting of the provisional government to discuss the constitution to be given France. By April 6 the plan of this constitution was ready and was passed unanimously by the Senate and, with some later alterations, was given the name of *La Charte Constitutionnelle.* By this constitution France was proclaimed a monarchy, with the King enjoying extensive rights as chief executive. The legislative powers were divided between the King, the Senate, and the *Corps Législatif;* the old nobility was re-established, but the liberties acquired during the Revolution were maintained, and by Article II "the people of their free will called to the throne Louis Stanislas Xavier, the brother of the late King, and after him, the other members of the House of Bourbons, in order of seniority."[11] Though opposed by the more ardent Royalists and particularly by Vitrolles, the constitution was reasonable and fairly liberal, and was to become the charter of France until the Revolution of 1848. In spite of defects, it nevertheless provided the necessary stability for France after the great turmoil.

The next step was to prepare for the return of the Bourbons: this was to be carried out in two stages. First, the Count of Artois, the brother of the future king, was to come to Paris to assume the function of Lieutenant General of the Kingdom and pave the way

[10] *Ibid.*, III, 216.

[11] Dupuis, *op. cit.*, I, 199.

for the return of Louis XVIII, who was at the time in England. Knowing the character and the political sympathies of the Count of Artois, Alexander was worried. In an interview with Vitrolles the Czar strongly urged that the latter impress the Count with the necessity of sacrificing his political views to the spirit of the times, and of realizing that it would be fatal to attempt to restore the old order.[12] But when the Count of Artois arrived in Paris on April 12 and was solemnly and heartily welcomed by the population, he felt himself secure enough to express his intense dislike of the Senate, while extreme Royalists went so far as publicly to burn copies of the *Charte*. But, "in its role of protector and guarantor of French liberties, the Senate always had the solid backing of Alexander."[13] Thus a conflict broke out between the Senate, backed by the Czar, and the new Regent, with the senators refusing to recognize the Count of Artois until he changed his attitude. Once more Alexander acted, aided by Talleyrand, who tried to smooth things out by a compromise. While Nesselrode was persuading Vitrolles, Alexander undertook to put pressure on the Count of Artois by reminding him of the role which the Senate had played in overthrowing Napoleon and thereby rendering service to the Bourbons; he bluntly told him that the allies had guaranteed the new constitution and that even if the Bourbons were prepared to overlook the services rendered by the Senate, the allied sovereigns were determined to keep their pledges. This peremptory language produced the desired effect, and on April 14 the Senate officially requested the Count of Artois to take charge of the government of the country. But the Count, in his reply of acceptance, made it clear that he had not been empowered by his brother to accept the new constitution, and thereby left this issue still open.

Alexander's feelings toward the Royalists, never very favorable, were presently to be put to the test by an incident which justly incensed him. The Queen of Württemberg, who had been visiting in Paris, while on her way back to Germany was stopped at the village of Frossard by a detachment of Royalist troops and, after some indignities, was forced to return to Paris, after being deprived of her money and jewels. The troops were under the command of a Marquis de Maubreuil, who had formerly been in the service of

[12] *Ibid.*, I, 216.

[13] *Ibid.*, I, 226.

the Queen and who had a personal grudge against her. This outrage was clearly the vengeance of Royalists whose newly acquired sense of power was running riot. Alexander, who was first cousin to the Queen, acted swiftly. A letter from Nesselrode to Vitrolles, to be handed to the Lieutenant General, demanded immediate satisfaction and return of the stolen property. Though ultimately the leaders of this escapade were arrested and after some bickering the jewels and money returned, the Royalist Government took these measures tardily and did not show the zeal which the Czar expected. Thus Alexander felt a bitterness and irritation which presaged ill for future relations with the Royalists.

The clumsy handling of the situation by the Count of Artois made the arrival of the new King all the more imperative, and Talleyrand, sensing the danger, pressed him not to delay his arrival any longer, for the King had been detained at Hartwell in England by an attack of gout. Upon hearing of the King's rather alarming attitude toward the Senate and the new constitution, Alexander dispatched Pozzo di Borgo to England, ostensibly to compliment the King upon his accession to the throne, but, in reality, to impress upon him a more liberal attitude. Couched in strictly courteous and official language and addressed as from sovereign to sovereign, with full recognition of Louis's new rank, his letter, dated April 17, nevertheless was very specific in stating that only moderation in the face of the definite will of the people would avoid new calamities. "Your Majesty will win all hearts if you manifest liberal ideas tending to maintain and reaffirm the organic institutions of France."[14] But this letter, even though it fully recognized the King's new title, did not alleviate his grudge against Alexander, and resulted in an undiplomatic step on his part. Indeed, while passing through London on his way to France and in reply to a speech of welcome by the Prince Regent, Louis made statements calculated to hurt Alexander and to alienate the support of the Continental allies.

Furthermore, he pointedly gave all credit for his having regained the throne to England alone. "It is to the advice of Your Royal Highness to this glorious country and to the confidence expressed by its inhabitants that, after Divine Providence, I shall always at-

[14] Aleksandr Aleksandrovich Polovtsov (ed.), *Correspondance diplomatique des ambassadeurs et ministres de Russie en France et de France en Russie de 1814 à 1830 avec leurs gouvernements* (St. Petersburg, 1902); also *Sbornik*, CXII, 1-2.

tribute the re-establishment of my family on the throne of its ancestors."[15] Upon arriving at Compiègne, the King received Pozzo di Borgo once more on April 30 and "was given a lesson in constitutional law," to which the King replied that he was preparing a declaration which would be "communicated to His Imperial Majesty in the hope of obtaining his approbation."[16] When Alexander visited him the following day, however, the old King received him with a coldness that bordered on ill manners. Seating himself in an armchair, he offered Alexander a stool, and to Alexander's exhortations to be liberal he merely spoke of Divine Providence and of the fact that he represented the principles of law and order. Commenting to Prince Volkonsky on this visit, Alexander remarked, "It was to be expected that the King, old and ill, should sit in a chair; but I would have ordered another to be given my guest."[17] Again, after his entry into Paris on May 3, at a state dinner given in honor of the Czar and the King of Prussia, Louis walked into the dining room first, and when at table Alexander was served first as the guest of honor, the King observed sharply to the servants, *"A moi, s'il vous plait."* Alexander observed on this occasion, "We northern barbarians are more polite in our homes," and again, "One would think that he had returned me my lost throne."[18] Alexander found real pleasure in visiting Empress Josephine at Malmaison, and enjoyed the company of the attractive Queen Hortense. He expressed there freely his dislike for the Bourbons, stating that "those people will never be able to maintain themselves." To Madame de Staël, Alexander observed, "The Bourbons are incorrigible and will never be otherwise, they are full of the prejudices of the old regime. The Duke of Orleans alone is liberal, there is no hope for the others."[19] These remarks, reported to the King, further infuriated him against the Czar.

In the meanwhile Alexander's stay in Paris was coming to an end, and he was anxious to have the constitutional issues settled before his departure. In pursuance of his pledge, the King had issued a declaration at St. Ouen prior to his entry into Paris. In this declaration the King accepted the constitution, provided some of its clauses were modified. A commission was set up within the

[15] Dupuis, *op. cit.*, I, 309.
[16] Polovtsov, *op. cit.*, pp. 2-3.
[17] Schilder, *Imperator Aleksandr Pervyi*, III, 227.
[18] *Ibid.*, III, 228.
[19] *Ibid.*, III, 231.

two houses to work on the draft of this new version of the *Charte*, but on May 6 a royal ordinance convoked the assembly of the *corps législatif* for May 31 instead of June 10, as originally stated in the declaration of St. Ouen. Pasquier writes, "This measure was principally due, though the public was ignorant of it, to the insistence of Emperor Alexander. He felt the necessity of leaving France soon and did not wish to leave the capital before having assurances that the pledges given would be respected and that the nation would enjoy a constitution in which all interests would be protected and defended."[20] Indeed, Alexander left Paris on June 3, and the following day in a solemn session of the Chambers the King proclaimed the final version of the *Charte*, timing this ceremony after the departure of the allied sovereigns so as to make it a purely French affair.

Two more problems had to be settled, parallel to the question of giving France a stable government: one was the fate of Napoleon and the other a peace treaty with France, ending the war. It will be recalled that, prior to his entry into Paris, Alexander had refused to negotiate with Napoleon through the agency of Caulaincourt. Obviously, however, so long as Napoleon was at Fontainebleau in possession of a part of his army, no real peace or stability could come to the newly established government. But Caulaincourt had not given up hope. At Bondy he had obtained permission to see Alexander in Paris, where he had two audiences with the Czar, on March 31 and April 1. Alexander, now strengthened by the establishment of the provisional government which he affected to consider the legal government of France, told Caulaincourt bluntly that any negotiations with the object of conserving the crown for his master were henceforth useless and impossible, and he advised, in the name of peace, that Napoleon should select some place for himself and his family where he could reside quietly and where his security would be guaranteed. But Alexander dropped a hint that a regency for Marie Louise and the King of Rome might be considered if Napoleon abdicated quickly. On returning to Fontainebleau, Caulaincourt, acting upon this hint, tried to persuade the Emperor to to abdicate, though the latter was still thinking of marching on Paris. But Ney and several other marshals refused to follow and

[20] Dupuis, *op. cit.*, II, 30.

flatly declared that the army would not march on Paris. Faced with this rebellion, Napoleon fell back on Caulaincourt's arguments in favor of immediate abdication, and wrote an act of abdication in which he reserved the regency for his son and wife. He ordered Caulaincourt and the marshals remaining faithful to him to proceed immediately to Paris to submit this act for the consideration of Alexander. Thus on the evening of April 4, Talleyrand and his government were informed of the arrival of this delegation, composed of Caulaincourt and the Marshals Ney and Macdonald, demanding an audience with the Czar. Against the advice of Talleyrand, who wanted the meeting postponed, Alexander announced he would receive the delegation forthwith at midnight, but confronted them not only with Nesselrode and Pozzo di Borgo, but with all the members of the provisional government as well. The Czar, by advising the delegation to start negotiations with the provisional government, showed that he was attempting to leave the decision of the matter to the French people and the Senate. But as might be expected, the Marshals refused; and Alexander had to mediate. He first listened to them for half an hour, then asked them to retire, and calling in the members of the provisional government, argued the advantages that the abdication of Napoleon would give to France and Europe. But Talleyrand objected strenuously to the regency as being merely a temporary measure permitting Napoleon to regain his power. Once more Alexander spoke to the Marshals, then to the provisional government, reporting to each side what the other had said. By 2:00 A.M. it had become clear that no compromise was possible. Alexander had to arbitrate and was in a cruel dilemma, as he esteemed the Marshals and Caulaincourt and disliked the Bourbons. Moreover, the regency had great political advantages, for though it increased the influence of Austria, it diminished that of England. He hesitated. A fortuitous incident caused him to make up his mind.

In the evening of the preceding day Napoleon had issued an order to Marmont to bring his corps to Fontainebleau. Some of Marmont's officers, fearing their fate, mutinied and marched the corps to Versailles instead. This news was communicated to Alexander at dawn, just as he was hesitating what decision to take. He said to Pozzo di Borgo, "This is Providence manifesting Its will;

no more doubt, no more hesitations,"[21] and rendered the following decision to the Marshals when they came to ask for the final reply of the Czar: "Only an unconditional abdication of Napoleon for himself and for his whole family can be the means of suspending hostilities, which otherwise will be carried out with the utmost activity, profiting by the advantages of the positions previously occupied and abandoned by the corps [of Marmont] which has deserted its cause."[22] Thus the fate of Napoleon was sealed. The mutiny of Marmont's troops gave him no further chance, and he finally abdicated unconditionally on April 6.

The day before, on April 5, Alexander had said to Caulaincourt and the Marshals, speaking of Napoleon:

> He is unhappy today—I am becoming his friend and will forget the past. He will have the island of Elba as sovereign or for any other purpose he may desire; he will keep his title by which he is recognized and his family will have a pension. Tell him that if he does not want that sovereignty and finds no asylum anywhere, he can come to my country. He will be received like a sovereign; he can count on the word of Alexander.

The news of this pledge given unilaterally for Europe, as well as all the developments in Paris, reached Dijon and brought Emperor Francis, Metternich, Castlereagh, and Hardenberg post haste to Paris to counterbalance the dictatorship of Alexander. On arriving in Paris on the tenth, they went immediately into conference with Nesselrode, to try to rescind what they considered a disastrous decision on the part of the Czar. Metternich suggested an island off America for Napoleon; and Sir Charles Stewart, writing on these events to Castlereagh, expressed his profound misgivings, considering the proximity of Elba to Italy, whence Eugene Beauharnais and Murat might help him, and to France, where he still had so many adherents.[23] But neither Metternich nor Castlereagh could do anything. Alexander remained adamant, and Ney and Macdonald officially worked out the terms of the treaty concerning the fate of the Emperor. Metternich and the allied ministers went over the treaty on the evening of their arrival in Paris and suggested some alterations concerning the assignment of the Duchies of Parma, Piacenza, and Guastalla to Marie Louise. Castlereagh raised objec-

[21] *Ibid.*, I, 187.
[22] *Ibid.*
[23] Metternich, *op. cit.*, IX, 450-451.

tions to certain features of the treaty, declaring, however, that he did not wish to endanger thereby the internal peace of France or to counter the pledges given by the Emperor of Russia. The next day, April 11, the plenipotentiaries of Napoleon on one side and Nesselrode, Metternich, and Hardenberg on the other signed the treaty, which took the name of the Treaty of Fontainebleau. The French provisional government confirmed the treaty the same day; Castlereagh, however, refused to sign it, but promised to report the contents to his government and to give all assistance in the execution of its clauses.

So far Alexander had had his way in France. The King of Prussia had tacitly endorsed every one of his moves, and Emperor Francis and the allied statesmen had remained away from Paris. Thus Alexander

> had appeared in Paris in triumph as the chief, the guide and the arbiter of Europe, dominating in victory and magnanimity; his allies, absent or effaced. He appeared to have decided everything, settled everything, appeased everything. . . . He had the glory of having terminated the war and established peace in liberating both Europe and France. He had shown his power and his moderation. . . .[24]

But the cost of this was the increasing and bitter jealousies of both England and Austria. Though the problem of getting Napoleon out of the way had been settled by Alexander without consulting the coalition or the provisional government, the question of the establishment of normal relations with France was a matter for all the allied powers concerned, the more so that the armistice had been concluded with Napoleon and not with the provisional government. Accordingly, in a series of meetings between Talleyrand and the allied statesmen, the terms of a convention for the suspension of hostilities were discussed and on April 23 duly signed between France and each of the allies separately. By this convention hostilities were officially suspended and friendly relations re-established with France. The allied forces were to evacuate French territory included within the frontiers as of January 1, 1792, whereas the French forces were to abandon all fortresses or regions which they still held outside France. All military equipment and artillery in these fortresses and all vessels or other naval material in ports were

[24] Dupuis, *op. cit.*, I, 236.

to be ceded to the allies. Prisoners and hostages were to be exchanged or sent home.

This convention paved the way for the formal treaty of peace, and once more a series of conferences took place between the allies and Talleyrand, starting on May 10. During these negotiations the divergence of views and the jealousies among the allies became much more acute. Metternich had reassumed his position of chief minister, speaking for the coalition, and he considered as his main task the restraining of Russia in her friendship toward France, a friendship which had shown itself in a pledge given by Alexander in his declaration of March 31 stating that France would not be reduced beyond the frontiers of 1792 and that Russia would waive all claims to pecuniary indemnity. He complained that the sympathy shown by Russia for the French increased their haughtiness and that the French were adopting a tone customary to the members of the Napoleonic government. Metternich and, to some extent, Castlereagh were also worried by the evidence of Russia's pretensions to Poland and by the fact that notwithstanding these pretensions Prussia continued to remain in the wake of Russia's policy. Thus the lines of cleavage which were to become so evident at the Congress of Vienna and were to split the coalition in two were already becoming visible. Though no minutes of the conferences have been kept to tell us the inside story of these negotiations, it is apparent that Alexander did not play the dominant part he had played earlier, preferring to leave much latitude to the official Russian delegates, Nesselrode and Count Razumovsky.

Thus the treaty of peace, which was signed on May 30, known to history as the First Treaty of Paris, represented a compromise of the views and the interests of the various allies, based, however, on the Russian declaration of March 31. Though the French were disappointed in some respects, it was an extremely moderate peace, leaving to France her borders as they had been at the beginning of the revolutionary wars in 1792, and exonerating her from any indemnities. France was now provided with a stable government and was at peace with the allies; Napoleon's fate had been settled, and all this in two months—a remarkable record of diplomatic efficiency, due in great part, as we have seen, to the energy and resolution shown by Alexander. There remained the problem of disposal of the territories of the former French Empire outside the boundaries of France proper—a problem which would have to be solved at the Congress of Vienna.

During his stay in Paris, Alexander had made himself much liked by the French people. Chancellor Pasquier, then Prefect of Police of the capital, wrote in his *Mémoires*, "Emperor Alexander was becoming very popular. One could see that everything revolved around him. His ally, the King of Prussia, passed unnoticed."[25] The Czar deliberately courted this popularity even at the risk of losing his popularity with his own troops. He appointed General Sacken as Military Governor of Paris and his aide-de-camp, a French *émigré* in Russian service, Rochechouart, as military commandant of the city. The latter in particular was accused by Russian officers of giving preference to the French, and bitter resentment was felt in the army over an order permitting the French National Guard to arrest Russian soldiers for disorderly conduct. This led to numerous cases of desertion. The Russian garrison in the city was subjected to the most stringent discipline, and during Holy Week an order was issued forbidding Russians to appear in any theaters or places of amusement. With heavy guard duty all over the city, the troops were given little rest and complained that their lot was now harder than during the campaign. It was only on the eve of the Czar's departure from Paris that the Russians relinquished their guard duty to the French National Guard and evacuated the city.[26] General Sacken resigned as military governor and received from the Municipality of Paris, in memory of his benign administration, a rifle, two pistols, and a sword with the inscription "*La Ville de Paris au Général Sacken.*"

Before Alexander left Paris he made one more rather unexpected attempt to restore good relations with the French Bourbons. He raised the issue of a marriage to be arranged between his sister the Grand Duchess Ann and the Duc de Berri, son of the Count of Artois. But Louis XVIII did not intend to be under any obligations to Russia, and the suggestion fell flat. Without refusing, the King showed so little enthusiasm for the project that Alexander discreetly dropped it, storing up further resentment against the Bour-

[25] *Mémoires du Chancellier Pasquier*, II, 279, as quoted in Schilder, *Imperator Aleksandr Pervyi*, III, 230.

[26] Schilder, *Imperator Aleksandr Pervyi*, III, 223-224.

bons. Louis XVIII also refused to have Caulaincourt appointed as his ambassador to Russia, and as Alexander had retained a feeling of friendliness for him, this in turn increased the Czar's irritation. It was in this mood that Alexander, accompanied by the King of Prussia, took his way toward England.

II

The Czar had previously expressed to Sir Charles Stewart his desire to visit England, and the result was an official invitation by the British Government to the three allied monarchs; however, Emperor Francis declined, wishing to get back to Vienna. Alexander was accompanied by a large suite including Nesselrode, Prince Leopold Coburg (the future king of Belgium, then in Russian service), Barclay de Tolly, Prince Volkonsky, and Hetman Platov, to mention the most important. On June 7 he sailed from Boulogne on a British royal yacht and reached Dover the same evening. The next morning the allied rulers left for London at 4:00 A.M. to escape the crowds which they expected, but the news of their departure had spread, and as they approached London they were slowed down by the cheering people. Alexander then changed to the private carriage of Count Lieven, the Russian ambassador, and drove into the city unrecognized to take up residence at Pulteney House, where his sister, the Grand Duchess Catherine, was living. The Czar remained in England for nearly three weeks, during which time, as guest of the Prince Regent, he was shown the sights of London and received the constant acclaim of the people. Notwithstanding the whirl of official and social engagements, Alexander's visit to London must be considered a complete failure, and he was in part to blame for this. Again, as in Paris, he met with popular acclaim, but with coolness and hostility from the Court as a result of unfortunate circumstances.

The Grand Duchess Catherine had preceded him to London, arriving on March 31. She was to pave the way for Alexander's visit, but turned out to be his worst ambassador. According to Princess Lieven's *Memoirs,* which give us the inside story of this visit, she was a woman of considerable charm and personality, but her domineering and haughty attitude displeased the British. "She surprised and astounded the English more than she pleased them."[27] She did not get along with the Prince Regent, finding his conversa-

[27] Dupuis, *op. cit.,* I, 104.

tion ribald and vulgar. In short, she did not please London; and, having taken a dislike to the Prince Regent, instead of creating a favorable atmosphere for the forthcoming visit of the Czar, she produced the exact reverse. A comedy of errors, a certain lack of personal tact on the part of Alexander, and a clash of prides and mentalities did the rest. The Regent, informed of the arrival of the Czar, announced he would call upon him; but the Emperor waited in vain for three hours, becoming very impatient. The Regent did not come, and later explained that he was afraid to face the huge crowds which had assembled before Alexander's residence and were wildly cheering the Russian ruler, forcing him to come out again and again on the balcony. The Emperor then called on the Regent, a visit which was the only official meeting between the two. The visit was short and the Regent was cold, feeling hurt that Alexander had refused his invitation to reside in St. James Palace in order to stay at the home of Grand Duchess Catherine. The contrast between the wild acclaim and cheering which greeted Alexander and his own personal unpopularity further embittered the Regent. Alexander in turn became cold and haughty toward the Regent, whom he termed to Lieven "*un pauvre sire*." He assumed a strictly formal politeness toward the cabinet ministers, but was very friendly toward the opposition, particularly toward Lord Holland and the other Whigs and Princess Charlotte. He wanted to call on the Regent's estranged wife and was dissuaded with great difficulty by his ambassador. However, during a gala performance at the opera, when he observed the Princess of Wales occupying a box opposite the one in which he was sitting with the Regent, he immediately got up and bowed, forcing the Regent to do the same. Once more the whole house cheered; once more the Regent was hurt. Alexander took the stand that these matrimonial difficulties did not concern him, but nevertheless he had antagonized the Regent, not without malicious joy. At the great military review held in his honor Alexander punctilously arrived on time, but the Regent was an hour late, excusing himself perfunctorily, after which the review started. Alexander, at the next court reception, which was scheduled to start at 9:00 P.M., arrived at 11:30, excusing himself by saying that he had been visiting Lord Grey. Both the Regent and Alexander had taken a violent dislike to each other and showed it in this petty way;

but once more, as in Paris, if the Czar was unpopular with the sovereign he made up for it by his popularity with the masses, which never waned throughout his stay.

A very different reception was to meet him in Holland, where he was the guest of his future brother-in-law, the Prince of Orange-Nassau, the future King William II of Holland. Here the acclaim and warmth of reception—as well as official hospitality—came from both the Court and the people, and were sincere and genuine. As he made his entry into Antwerp, Alexander passed under an arch of triumph with the inscription "*Alexandram Benedicto Liberavit orbem, Nobis reddidit patriam*" (To Alexander the Blessed, who liberated the world and gave us back our country).[28] His stay in Holland was marked by a visit to Saardam, where Peter the Great had worked as carpenter on the Dutch East India wharves. Here, as was to be expected, Alexander was given a particularly warm reception. Like Peter the Great, Alexander passed his time inspecting everything of importance, showing particular interest in the Dutch naval establishment, where he visited the naval school and remained for hours chatting informally with the cadets. After a ten-day stay in Holland, Alexander went home through Germany and arrived in St. Petersburg to savor the fruits of his triumphs among his own people. Although he had ordered the canceling of all official celebrations in his honor, there was no mistaking the enthusiasm of the people: he had reached the peak of his popularity—a popularity which, however, was to vanish thereafter.

Meanwhile, and throughout this entire period, the allied powers were busily engaged in negotiating among themselves to prepare the ground for the coming great congress, which was to be held at Vienna. The allies had shown great wisdom in avoiding jealousies and quarrels until victory was achieved, but these were merely smoldering; and, now that Napoleon was safely out of the way, they threatened to burst into flame. Metternich was viewing with increased misgivings the prominent role played by Russia, and Castlereagh shared these sentiments. Hardenberg, forced to follow in the wake of his king in his dependence on Russia, was anxious to weaken France and to prevent the mediation of any third party in the dealings between Prussia and France, particularly any of the

[28] Bogdanovich, *Istoria Tsarstvovania Imperatora Aleksandra I*, IV, 551.

small states of Europe. These views permitted Metternich to sketch out a general program of action for the coming congress which would make for closer co-operation among what he deemed to be the conservative powers—namely, Austria, England, and Prussia —against the ambitions of France on the one hand and of Russia on the other. Indeed, with Austrian control secured over parts of Italy and parts of Germany, Metternich should have had nothing more to desire; England, having assured her naval and economic supremacy through the downfall of France, should also have been content to leave things as they were. But with a France on the one hand anxious to regain her lost ground and an expansionist Russia on the other, he saw a definite danger to the stabilization of the new order, the more so since Prussia remained blindly attached to Russia. There was no use in destroying the Napoleonic Empire if a powerful Russian Empire were to menace Austria from the north and the east, extending its influence through Prussia into the heart of Germany. Alexander's ambition to take possession of Poland seemed to justify Metternich's alarm.

Alexander's plan for the creation of a united Poland under his crown had leaked out sufficiently to produce feelings of friendliness toward him among the Polish refugees in France. Prince Adam Czartoryski, in Paris, resumed the cordiality and the friendly attitude which had characterized his earlier relations with the Czar. More important, the remnants of the Polish corps of Poniatovski, which had followed Napoleon in his retreat, now turned to Alexander for support, and were treated with special benevolence by the latter. About five thousand strong, under the command of General Dombrovski, these troops in May, 1815, were placed under the command of Grand Duke Constantine in Paris. Rumors that the Grand Duchy of Warsaw would not be given back to Prussia but would be given to Russia, to be united with Lithuania in a separate Polish kingdom under Russian rule, had gained wide credence among these Polish contingents and could not escape the vigilant attention of Metternich.

This became a matter for serious discussion in conferences among the allied ministers held daily at noon in Metternich's home. Prussia was to be compensated for the loss of her share of Poland by Saxony, and Austria was to receive similar compensations in Northern Italy. If Prussia appeared to be pleased by such a transaction, Austria was not, and the struggle was on. Sir Charles Stewart noted that Alexander had assumed a tone of superiority in the alliance which made him authoritative and commanding; the negotiations were therefore not carried out on an equitable and friendly basis, and he complained that both Austria and Prussia, for the purpose of furthering their own aims, conceded to Russia a Polish frontier up to Kalish. But they refused to give away Cracow and Thorn, and thought that the new Poland should not be ruled by a member of the Russian dynasty.[29] Alexander retorted sharply that he had an army of 480,000 men, and that he needed Thorn and was not prepared to concede a single village to Austria.

A crisis had been reached which threatened to split the alliance. Austria began speaking of resistance to Russia, but, faced with the superior armed might of Russia and Prussia, she realized that only an alliance with France would give her a chance for victory. But the fear of seeing the French armies once more in Germany overshadowed her fear of Russia. England put pressure on Russia to tone down her demands and threatened to form a coalition against her by winning over Prussia. Negotiations to this effect started, and Hardenberg seemed cordial but demurred at the last moment—the influence of Russia over Prussia, or more exactly, that of the Czar over King Friedrich Wilhelm, was still very strong. Alexander finally showed himself more conciliatory and suggested that Thorn and Cracow, with their surrounding territory, should be neutralized, but insisted that the whole of Saxony must be ceded to Prussia. England then suggested an armed mediation by Great Britain, Holland, and France, to which other powers might accede, to settle the issue between Austria, Russia, and Prussia; but Metternich turned down the idea out of fear of France. Hardenberg then proposed that Thorn and the territory up to the river Wartha, and Cracow with the district of Zamosci up to the Nidda River, should be given to Prussia and Austria respectively. To this proposal Alexander countered with the suggestion that if the Grand Duchy of Warsaw were given to Russia, Saxony given to Prussia, and Mainz made a city within the Germanic Confederation garrisoned by the troops of the Confederation, he would agree to see both Cracow and Thorn made independent cities. The question of

[29] Dupuis, *op. cit.*, II, 55.

Mainz thus became an important secondary issue. This strategically important city was claimed by Bavaria, her claim being supported by Metternich—and by Prussia, supported by Russia. The fear of seeing Russian and Prussian troops occupy the city made the allies finally accept a temporary solution, embodied in a protocol of May 31, specifying that the city be temporarily garrisoned by Austrian and Prussian troops.

Thus these negotiations in Paris showed the deep divergence existing among the allies, and led to no postive results. It was owing to this situation that Castlereagh, at the news of Alexander's intention to visit London, had insisted that the Emperor Francis and King Friedrich Wilhelm should be invited at the same time, so as to keep Alexander from playing the part of sole victor in London. Castlereagh also expressed the view to Lord Liverpool that the presence of the three sovereigns and their ministers in England would permit the continuation of the arduous negotiations and would place the Prince Regent in the position of arbiter. But in going to England Alexander was not seeking the mediation of the powers but merely relaxation and acclaim, and the chilly reception accorded him did not make the atmosphere propitious for successful negotiations. Nevertheless, having failed in Paris, the negotiations were taken up again in London upon the arrival of Metternich, representing Emperor Francis; but again the atmosphere was so unpropitious that nothing of importance was accomplished except the working out of technical modalities for the coming Congress of Vienna. Out of special deference to the Czar, who was returning first to Russia, the conference, which had originally been scheduled for August 15, was postponed until October 1. In the interim the powers were solemnly obligated not to change in any way the existing *status quo*, and to consider all present distribution of territories and occupation by armed forces as merely temporary. Metternich, however, profited by his stay and, capitalizing on the friction between the Regent and the Czar, insinuated himself into the good graces of the Regent. As for Castlereagh, he had already been won over to the Austrian cause. Thus, with Alexander back in Russia, a temporary lull settled over the tense international situation while the lines were being drawn for the coming great diplomatic struggle at Vienna.

III

Although official negotiations had ceased after the conference in London, undercover negotiations were proceeding apace, and of these the most important were the discreet overtures made by England to France. Talleyrand, anxious to see any possible breach in the alliance of Chaumont, was quick to see his chance and responded with alacrity. Upon Castlereagh's expressing a desire to know the views of France, Talleyrand wrote him a letter which Castlereagh forwarded to the Duke of Wellington with a covering note indicating that Russia was taking the place of France in the fears of the British Government. Castlereagh in this message openly expressed his concern over the possibility of Russia's and Sweden's jointly dismembering Denmark, in view of the presence of Bennigsen's army in Holstein, and said that he wished to clarify the French position with regard to Poland.[30] Talleyrand became increasingly frank and friendly with Sir Charles Stewart, and the Duc de Berry made an official visit to London. A rumor of a possible alliance between France, England, and Spain spread over Europe. Castlereagh decided to make a stop in Paris on his way to Vienna. There he discussed the Polish question with the Austrian ambassador, Meerveldt, and suggested a way of offsetting the ambitions of Alexander by proposing the creation of an independent Poland under the guarantee of all the powers. These ideas met with the complete approval of France and foreshadowed the inevitability of close co-operation between England and France. Thus a situation was rapidly developing whereby at the coming Congress it was no longer France but Russia that was to be regarded as the common danger and the common enemy. This attitude is well illustrated by an incident which occurred in Paris on September 6. Talleyrand, at a diplomatic dinner, asked Wellington what were the prospects for peace. "You will have peace," observed Wellington, upon which Talleyrand replied, "Yes, if the Emperor Alexander is willing to give it to us."[31]

Absent in Russia, Alexander was not well aware of this changing attitude of his allies; the discovery of it was to embitter him and accounts for the stand taken by Russia at the Congress.

[30] Robert Stewart [Viscount Castlereagh], *Letters and Despatches of Viscount Castlereagh* (London, 1853), X, 76-77.

[31] Dupuis, *op. cit.*, II, 330.

The famous saying of the Prince de Ligne, "*Le Congrès danse mais ne marche pas,*" has somewhat obscured to posterity the real aspect of the Congress of Vienna. With nearly all the sovereigns and statesmen of Europe settled in the beautiful Austrian capital for six months, the city inevitably attracted the leading lights of the world of society and the arts, and assumed an aspect of frivolity; a social life of festivities and dances seems to have been the main preoccupation of those present at the Congress, and both political and social intrigue thrived. "Society is more inconsequential and more monotonous than ever," wrote the Prussian delegate Baron Humboldt. "The endless bickerings between the two northern women [the Duchess of Sagan and Princess Bagration] is the lofty and worthy subject about which all thoughts and conversations turn."[32] Speaking of this celebrated Russian beauty whose salon in Vienna played such a role, Baron Nostitz wrote, "Princess Bagration still maintains a salon where people meet on certain days. A beautiful, cultivated woman who loves life can always give her charms new brilliance in such a manner."[33] Countess Bernstorff, wife of the Danish envoy, complained, "The Russians obtruded their presence everywhere with their characteristic boldness, especially General Tchernitscheff, who placed emphasis upon playing an important role, and he succeeded ably."[34]

Alexander was thoroughly at home in this atmosphere of social frivolity and intrigue. His discreet flirtation with the lovely Countess Auerspeg attracted wide attention, and stories went round of his simplicity and informality: how he dropped in at a Viennese tavern alone, drank some beer, paid for it, and slipped out unnoticed; or, to the delight of the social gossips, of a wager which he made at Count Zichy's house with Countess Vrbna as to who would be able to dress more quickly. The Czar and the Countess were to change from ordinary dress to full court attire, which the Countess did in a minute and a half, whereas the Czar took a minute longer. Many eyebrows were lifted at his solitary walks with Prince Eugene Beauharnais, for whom Alexander developed a real feeling of friendship,

[32] Frederick Freksa (comp.), *A Peace Congress of Intrigues (Vienna, 1815): A Vivid, Intimate Account of the Congress of Vienna Composed of the Personal Memoirs of Its Important Participants* (New York, 1919), p. 160.

[33] *Ibid.*, p. 126, from the memoirs of Baron Nostitz.

[34] *Ibid.*, p. 24.

and it was whispered that on one occasion a Viennese fruit vendor who looked askance at this friendship with a member of the Napoleonic family had pelted the Czar with rotten apples. But, as Stein points out in his diary, the Czar with his easy manners, ingratiating smile, and perfect mastery of German made himself popular with the Viennese. As in Paris and in London, Alexander had the knack of winning the people.

However, the record of the business sessions of the Congress shows a very different Alexander, headstrong and tenacious, fighting grimly and single-handedly the assembled powers of virtually the whole of Europe. For Talleyrand and Metternich were responsible for placing Russia in the position France had formerly held at the bar of assembled Europe. For Russia, the main issue was Poland. Poland became the focal point of the negotiations around which all other questions gravitated.

Alexander arrived in Vienna on September 25, together with the King of Prussia. Emperor Francis went out to meet them, and the three monarchs made a solemn entry into the city on horseback. The Kings of Denmark and Württemberg had preceded them on September 22, while the Empress of Russia and the King of Bavaria arrived on the twenty-seventh and twenty-eighth respectively. Most of the diplomatic delegations having preceded their sovereigns, the Congress was completely assembled by the end of the month. The Czar immediately took the center of the stage, and a secret police report of the *Polizei Hofstelle* states rather amusingly that "the foreign sovereigns now residing in Vienna and their retinues cannot hide their resentment at seeing all the honors going by preference to the Emperor of Russia, who is only a barbarian."[35] But Talleyrand expressed the situation more correctly when he said: "Judging by the pretensions of Russia, it would appear that a war had been waged more against the success of Bonaparte than against his principles, for it was not worth destroying one colossus to re-establish another."[36]

Talleyrand's policy, as the representative of a defeated power aspiring to regain its lost status, was clear and was carried out with incomparable genius. His objects were, first, to shift the moral blame

[35] Maurice Henri Weil, *Les Dessous du Congrès de Vienne . . .* (Paris, 1917), I, 225.
[36] Löwenhielm to Engestrom, October 26, 1814 (*ibid.*, I, 394).

from France to Russia, which he made out to be the new ruthless aggressor aiming at doing now to Europe what Napoleon had done previously. Second, to prevent the coalition of victorious powers from monopolizing the decisions and keeping France out. This he could best achieve by assuming the championship of the interests of the smaller powers, and by posing as the defender of the principles of legitimacy and rights as against the greed of the great powers —particularly of Russia with regard to Poland and of Prussia with regard to Saxony. Third, to attempt to break up the unity of the great powers by making Russian and Prussian aspirations appear dangerous to both England and Austria. As Prussia remained in effect a satellite of Russia and as the Saxon issue was bound irretrievably with the Polish issue, ultimately the whole thing boiled down to a struggle against Russia alone. Though the first official meeting was not held until December 24, there was plenty of scope for opening this attack in the informal preliminary gatherings. We have seen how carefully Talleyrand had prepared his ground by a *rapprochement* with both Metternich and Castlereagh prior to the opening of the Congress, and with both these statesmen increasingly concurring in his anti-Russian views he was able to play his game with brilliant success.

The delegations of the four allied powers had assembled by September 13; the very large Russian delegation was composed of Nesselrode, Capo d'Istria, Pozzo di Borgo, Count Razumovsky, and Baron Stackelberg (the Russian ambassador to Vienna), with Czartoryski, Stein, and Laharpe acting as advisors on the Polish, German, and Swiss questions. However, the conduct of affairs was to be vested entirely in Alexander, and the whole delegation may be regarded as merely an advisory body. Informal meetings between the representatives of the four powers began on September 15, to discuss the procedure of the conference. It was decided "that the conduct of the business must practically rest with the leading powers,"[37] and these included both France and Spain. But in reality the initiative—actually, the power of decision—was to be retained in the hands of the four allied powers, which therefore would form a secret committee within the official directing committee of six powers. However, the arrival of Talleyrand on September 23 made this

[37] Charles Kingsley Webster, *The Congress of Vienna, 1814-1815* (London, 1919), p. 61.

decision meaningless, for by September 30 he had demanded a committee of the eight signatory powers to the Treaty of Paris, that is to say, the addition of France, Spain, Portugal, and Sweden to the original four. The bickering after Talleyrand's action resulted in the postponement of the official Congress for a month until, on October 30, the full committee of eight assembled to attempt once more to reorganize the work, but still could not come to an agreement. However, with negotiations on the issues at stake proceeding apace, if informally, the Congress finally shaped itself into an official directing committee of eight powers, with the decisions in the hands of a secret committee of five powers, which eventually broke into two blocs: France, England, and Austria on one side, with Russia and Prussia on the other. The committee of five remained the center of the Congress and carried on its work through a number of specialized committees, such as the committee on Switzerland, the committee on international rivers, etc. Separate and working independently, another committee was to draw up a constitution for Germany.

As has already been stated, the Polish-Saxon question was the central issue upon which all the other questions depended for their settlement. In the preliminary instructions given by Alexander to Nesselrode in St. Petersburg on August 14 the following claims were to be put forward by Russia at the coming Congress: "The conservation of the Duchy of Warsaw is what I am asking for," writes the Czar, "and at this price I am ready to uphold Austria and Prussia in all demands they may make to indemnify themselves for the portions of the Duchy which belonged to them." He goes on to say that having promised through the Treaty of Kalish a territory which would connect Prussia with Silesia, he would not object if Prussia recovered the province of Posen and the region of Kulm, and he would endorse the cession to Prussia of the whole of Saxony up to the river Elster and the frontier of Bohemia. With regard to Austria, Alexander declared that he could leave to her only that part of the Duchy of Warsaw which included the salt mines of Wieliczka and the circle of Podgorcie, in such a way that the Vistula should become here the frontier between the two empires. Austria should therefore compensate herself by asking the whole of Northern

Italy, the Tyrol, Salzburg, Innviertel, the Illyrian provinces, and Dalmatia.[38]

The attack against Alexander's scheme was initiated by Castlereagh. On October 4 he sent his first memorandum to the Czar, declaring that the Russian demands violated Russia's engagements under the Treaty of Kalish, which stipulated that Prussia should get back all her territories as of 1806, and also the Austro-Prusso-Russian Treaty of June 27, 1813, in which it was agreed to dissolve the Duchy of Warsaw and partition it between the three powers, to evacuate all troops from the Duchy, and to give Danzig back to Prussia. "Now the Emperor of Russia considers it his right [wrote Castlereagh] to dispose of the entire Duchy of Warsaw under the pretense that his troops had taken possession of the Duchy first. This is in direct opposition to previous treaty engagements, and if Russia considers it a moral duty to better the lot of the Poles she should do that to the Poles in her own provinces and not embark on experiments which would create unrest among the Poles remaining in the neighbouring states." The note terminated with the threat that so long as the Czar insisted on this "unfortunate project" it would be impossible for the Congress to convene formally to discuss the arrangements. A second memorandum by Castlereagh on October 14 proposed that Poland should be made independent with the boundaries of 1791 and with the constitution of that time. If Russia should refuse such independence, the Vistula up to Sandomir should become the frontier (along its right or eastern bank); and if the Czar insisted on retaining the city of Warsaw on the left bank, Thorn should go to Prussia.

In reply to this memorandum, a Russian memorandum accompanying a personal letter of the Czar to Castlereagh sharply pointed out that the reference to previous treaties no longer applied in view of the changed situation. It mentioned the enormous sacrifices made by Russia for the common cause, the fact that the demands for compensation by other powers had so greatly increased as to make Russian demands modest, and finally that the western powers had not objected to the occupation of Poland by Napoleon and the acquisitions of Polish territory made by Austria and Prussia as allies of

[38] Karol Lutostánski (ed.), *Les Partages de la Pologne et la lutte pour l'independance* (Lausanne, 1918), pp. 345-346.

Napoleon (October 20). Castlereagh had hoped to line up both Austria and Prussia on his side by working out a military alliance between them, but, though Metternich was willing and Hardenberg somewhat hesitant, the King of Prussia steadfastly maintained his loyalty to Alexander. Hardenberg was ready to bargain, and on October 9 asked the assent of Austria and England to the annexation of Saxony by Prussia. Metternich agreed on condition that Bavaria should receive Mainz. Castlereagh was working to obtain from the powers a refusal to recognize any acquisitions made by Russia in Poland. Such a declaration was to be made to Alexander by the Emperor of Austria and the King of Prussia while the three allied sovereigns were making a visit to Hungary in November, but Alexander took the initiative by complaining to both sovereigns about the anti-Russian attitude assumed by both Metternich and Hardenberg. Thus the whole of Castlereagh's maneuver collapsed. The King of Prussia refused to listen to any further anti-Russian moves, and with Saxony meanwhile creating an increasing strain between Austria and Prussia, Metternich withdrew from the joint action against Russia. Castlereagh lamented that "unless the Emperor of Russia can be brought to a more moderate and sound course of public conduct, the peace which we have so dearly purchased will be of short duration."[39]

In view of failure to obtain any success with Alexander in regard to Poland, on December 19 Austria, France, and England decided to renounce their attack against Russia on the Polish issue and concentrate against Prussia on the Saxon issue. Hardenberg, apparently frightened, asked Stein's advice whether it was wise to advocate war with Russia. Stein replied that it was not, in view of the presence of 250,000 Russians plus 38,000 Polish troops between the Vistula and the Wartha, and with Bennigsen's Russian army in a position to menace Prussia from Holstein; whereas Austrian and Prussian forces were entirely scattered. On November 19 Grand Duke Constantine announced that the Polish Army had been raised to 70,000 men, and Stein in his diary complained that "through the Polish matter the business of the Congress has become disrupted and weakened and the seed of envy scattered among the nations."[40] Prussia then

[39] Castlereagh to Liverpool, November 11, 1814 (Webster, *The Congress of Vienna*, p. 104).

[40] Freksa, *op. cit.*, p. 377.

offered Russia the cession of Poland with the line of the rivers Wartha and Nida as frontier. Thus Thorn would remain Prussian and Cracow Austrian. Alexander replied that he was prepared to grant the status of a free city to both Thorn and Cracow, provided Saxony were given to Prussia, and Mainz made a fortress of the Germanic Confederation. At the same time Prince Repnin was ordered to issue a proclamation in Saxony transferring the occupation of that country to Prussian troops. These maneuvers had the desired effect. Prussian allegiance to Russia was made complete, and a deadlock was reached in the opposing camp. Alexander had outplayed his enemies. He remained adamant, refusing to budge an inch and assuming a menacing tone to Talleyrand, who had been gleefully watching the rift between the allies while playing his own game. Alexander declared: "I have two hundred thousand soldiers in the Duchy of Warsaw; let them try to drive me from it."

Meanwhile the increasing coldness between the Czar and Metternich developed into an open quarrel. Alexander pointedly ceased to appear at Metternich's functions, and finally challenged him to a duel. Upon the advice of Emperor Francis, Metternich did not take up the challenge. Here was Talleyrand's chance, and he made the best use of it. During the earlier period he had remained very quiet, but now he began discreetly to maneuver for a *rapprochement* with both Metternich and Castlereagh. On December 16 Metternich made formal overtures to Talleyrand and proposed joint action. Castlereagh, more cautious, endeavored to "treat him with all proper regard and to keep him generally informed of our endeavors to promote common objects."

The first inkling Alexander had of these maneuvers was when he proposed a formal conference to settle the Polish-Saxon question, which duly met on December 29. Both Austria and England demanded Talleyrand's participation in the discussion. At this point the Saxon issue overshadowed the Polish one. Hardenberg demanded an immediate recognition of Prussia's rights over Saxony, declaring that he would consider a refusal tantamount to a declaration of war. Five days later, on January 3, in a secret meeting Castlereagh offered Metternich and Talleyrand the draft of a treaty which he had written out with his own hand. It provided for a military alliance against Russia and Prussia and, ironically, was modeled on the provisions of the Treaty of Chaumont against France. Furthermore, Bavaria, Hanover, and Holland were invited to join it, and expressed their willingness to do so. With a duplicity which does little credit to its signatories, the treaty was kept secret and the pretense of the four-power alliance with Russia and Prussia was maintained. Alexander was not aware of the existence of the treaty until Napoleon's return, but he noticed the solidarity of action and hardening of the attitudes of Castlereagh, Metternich, and Talleyrand at the subsequent meetings of the Congress. Bitter haggling continued, though some small concessions were made on both sides.

The news of Napoleon's return from Elba produced such a sobering effect as to make the Congress forget all its bitter divergences and quickly seek a compromise solution of the various problems, so as to make possible once more a united stand of the allied powers against Napoleon. The Machiavellian work of Talleyrand was undone in a few hours. On March 11 Alexander, at the special request of Emperor Francis, agreed to a reconciliation with Metternich, declaring that unforgivingness was not Christian. The Council met and decided on joint measures against Napoleon. Suddenly the importance of Russia as a military factor loomed once more so great that Capo d'Istria, who attended this meeting, had his little revenge. He purposely arrived late at the Council, to find all the delegates of the powers anxiously awaiting the decision of Russia.

> A number of faces had already become long and drawn when the Count finally arrived, with a cheerful composed disposition, carrying his portfolio under his arm. With a quick glance he took in the situation and by keeping intentionally silent he celebrated a small triumph. He described this to me with smiles several days later. Then he spoke, and declared with fiery words that the Czar placed all his strength at the disposal of the coalition against the common enemy. In a moment the expression of those present became normal again.[41]

The eight powers issued a joint declaration denouncing Napoleon as a public enemy, and on March 25 the coalition between Austria, England, Prussia, and Russia was renewed, with an agreement to put 450,000 men in the field. Armies were set in motion. However, Alexander was to get one more bitter shock. The flight of Louis

[41] *Ibid.*, p. 153, from the memoirs of the Countess Lulu Thurnheim.

XVIII had been so swift that he left behind the text of the treaty of January 3, and the secret military alliance against Russia was revealed. Napoleon ordered the Duke of Bassano to hand it over to the Russian agent in Paris, Butiakin, who forwarded it to the Czar in Vienna. Alexander had a violent explosion of temper, but later calmed down and declared that notwithstanding the treaty he would continue to oppose Napoleon.

He insisted, however, that in view of the coming war the German and Polish issues should be settled first. An agreement on the Polish issue signed between Austria and Prussia on May 5 made possible an understanding with Russia. The question was settled on a compromise basis. Posnan and Danzig remained with Prussia, and Galicia with Austria, while Cracow was made a free city. The rest of Poland became a kingdom in Russian hands, endowed with a constitution as promised by Alexander. As for Prussia, she obtained two fifths of Saxony, containing 850,000 subjects. The other settlements do not directly concern us. Alexander did not wait for these conditions to be embodied in the final treaty, but left for the front on the twenty-fifth of May, making for the Rhine.

A few of the side issues must be mentioned. Through Stein, Alexander kept a close watch over the committee on German states, which was composed solely of representatives of those states. This committee met in the early days of the Congress, then recessed to meet again in May. It was largely through Alexander's influence that it came to a successful conclusion, as Alexander demanded that it should finish its work before he left. The committee on Switzerland was also under the special patronage of the Czar, who appointed both Capo d'Istria and Laharpe as members, partly because of his friendship toward Laharpe, and also because of his irritation at the violation of the neutrality of Switzerland by Austria. Thus the Czar took a special interest in the work of this committee, whose importance was consequently out of proportion to the size of the issue at stake. Switzerland, accordingly, fared particularly well, with a liberal constitution based on the Act of Mediation of Napoleon of 1803, and with the addition of Valais, Geneva, and Neufchâtel to its confederation.

Another issue in which the action of Alexander was decisive was the fate of the Empress Marie Louise, whom Alexander chivalrously took under his protection. It was at his insistence that Marie Louise was given the Duchy of Parma for the duration of her life.

Lastly, there were matrimonial issues. In the early days of the Congress, when the relations between Russia and Austria had not yet been impaired, steps were taken to arrange a marriage between the Grand Duchess Catherine and Archduke Karl of Austria. However, Karl opposed the idea, and it was dropped, with the result that the Grand Duchess was engaged to the Crown Prince of Württemberg.

The final act was signed on June 9, only nine days before Waterloo. Russia obtained by this settlement 2,100 square miles of territory with a population of over 3,000,000, as compared with Austria's gain of 2,300 square miles with a population of 10,000,000, and Prussia's 2,217 square miles with a population of 5,360,000. Considering the respective shares of the three powers in the struggle against Napoleon, Russia's acquisitions were relatively modest.

IV

When the news of the return of Napoleon was received and a new war appeared inevitable, it was decided in Vienna that the Russian Army, two hundred thousand strong, which had been wintering along the Nieman, would march to Nüremberg, where it would form the general reserve of the allied armies. Later these plans were modified, and it was decided that the Anglo-Prussian forces were to concentrate in Belgium, the Austrian Army to occupy the line of the upper Rhine so as to link up with the Austrian forces operating in Italy, and the Russian Army to hold the middle Rhine, concentrating between Mainz and Mannheim. It was in pursuance of this plan that Alexander, upon leaving Vienna, proceeded through Munich and Stuttgart to Heilbronn, where the Russian General Headquarters were established. On June 6 he moved his headquarters to Heidelberg; and on June 20, upon receiving the alarming news of Blücher's defeat at Ligny, he called a council of war which decided to concentrate the Russian and Austrian forces between Basel and Mainz for a joint advance on Nancy. But upon receipt of the news of the Battle of Waterloo, the urgency for this advance disappeared, and the Russians proceeded to cross the Rhine more leisurely at Mannheim; after which they captured or laid seige to those French fortresses on the eastern border which were still holding out.

Châlons was taken by assault, and Chernyshev captured six guns in addition. The corps of Langeron was diverted in order to lay siege to Metz, Thionville, Verdun, and Saarlouis. The rest of the army proceeded by slow stages to advance on Paris, ruthlessly putting down any French attempts at guerilla warfare.

Alexander accompanied his troops as far as St. Dizier, where he received a courier from Wellington stating that his presence in Paris was imperative. Hence, accompanied by Emperor Francis and King Friedrich Wilhelm, the Czar rode ahead of his troops and reached Paris on July 10. A month later a Russian grenadier and a cuirassier division entered the city for the second Russian occupation of the capital, and the bulk of the Russian Army, under the command of Barclay de Tolly, now given the title of prince, was quartered in Champagne. Here on September 11, in the presence of the two allied sovereigns, the Duke of Wellington, and representatives of the minor nations of Europe, Alexander held the last great pageant which he was to stage for the benefit of Europe, and which was the final climax to the Russian participation in the sanguinary wars of the preceding twenty years.

After a few days of maneuvers, the entire Russian Army, 150,000 men and 540 cannon, with the exception of Langeron's corps, which was still besieging the French fortresses, passed in review before the Czar under the critical but impressed eyes of the military observers of Europe. This review did more to further Alexander's diplomacy than anything else had done, for the Czar knew how to make the best use of such publicity.

During his stay in Paris the negotiations for peace with France dragged on without making headway, because of the excessive demands of Austria and Prussia, who now insisted upon partitioning France. Alexander remained consistent in his policy of maintaining the territorial integrity of France; and it was also through his influence, with the aid, in this instance, of the Duke of Wellington, that Blücher was restrained from retaliatory acts of destruction which the Prussian Field Marshal wanted to inflict upon Paris. This pro-French policy of the Czar once more brought on acute strain between him and his allies. Losing patience and desiring to get the issue settled, Alexander suggested that Louis XVIII should write him a personal letter in which the King would bitterly denounce the territorial demands of the allies and solemnly declare that he would renounce his throne rather than cede any further territory. By showing this letter to his allies, Alexander placed them in the dilemma of abandoning their claims or facing a dangerous revival of anarchy in France, and thus he won his point.

On November 20 was signed the Second Treaty of Paris, by which France retained her frontiers of 1790, abandoning merely a few frontier fortresses. She had to pay a contribution of 700,000,000 francs, of which the share falling to Russia was 100,000,000 and to submit to be garrisoned for five years by an army of occupation of 150,000 men under the command of the Duke of Wellington. The Russian corps of occupation in this army was fixed at 27,000 men with 84 guns, and was placed under the command of Count Vorontsov, assigned to the Champagne region with headquarters at Maubeuge. Alexander did not wait for the details of these terms to be worked out, but left Paris at the end of September immediately after the proclamation of the Holy Alliance. He went home by way of Berlin, and the bethrothal of his brother Nicholas to the daughter of King Friedrich Wilhelm was announced during his stay there. Then he went to Warsaw, where he made a solemn entrance as the new King of Poland. After a protracted stay in Poland, where he concerned himself with the organization of the new kingdom, he finally returned to St. Petersburg on December 14.

Throughout this period, and as the most important development both for Russia's internal affairs and for the role she was to play in Europe, Alexander was undergoing a remarkable mental and moral evolution which was climaxed by the proclamation in Paris of the Holy Alliance. This development must now be discussed in more detail.

V

The Congress of Vienna, with the disclosure of the gigantic intrigue against Russia hatched by England, France, and Austria in their secret alliance of January, 1815, left an indelible mark of bitterness on the supersensitive soul of Alexander. Owing in part to the influence of a woman, Baroness Krüdener, his bitterness was to be transmuted into a form of religious mysticism which resulted in the much publicized Holy Alliance. But the origin of this striking evolution in the Czar's character went further back and was in fact consistent with his whole mental and political outlook of earlier days. The roots of the Holy Alliance reached back to the Novossiltsev memorandum of 1803, just as they were to be reflected in the future at the congresses of Aix-la-Chapelle and Verona. What was new was merely the religious overtone which was given to a political philosophy held consistently by the Czar throughout his reign—the philosophy of a federation of the nations of Europe into an organized society of nations motivated by law, order, and the brotherhood of sovereigns. Reared in the spirit of the atheistic eighteenth century, Alexander had merely paid the lip service to religion he felt was required of a monarch; hence, at first, religious ideals had little to do with his political ideas. The change seems to have taken place in the middle of 1812, when he suddenly asked Empress Elizabeth for a Bible. After a search of the palace, a King James version of the Bible was found, and Alexander plunged into the reading of it with obvious delight.

If we consider the span of his destiny which within two years, from the burning of Moscow to his trumphant entry into Paris, took him from the depths of disaster to the pinnacle of glory as arbiter of the destinies of Europe, we can well understand how strained and unbalanced his nervous temperament might have become. It was in this frame of mind, coupled with the lassitude produced by the intrigues of the Congress of Vienna, that he came under the spell of Baroness Krüdener. But her influence did not generate anything—it merely echoed and strengthened an already existing trend; hence it was short lived, if intense at the time.

The great-granddaughter of Field Marshal Munich and the wife of the former Russian ambassador to Venice, Copenhagen, and Berlin, Baroness Krüdener became a French novelist in her own right by the publication of a novel, *Valerie,* which made a considerable sensation in literary circles. The tragic death of a friend was responsible for her conversion, first to the creed of the Moravian brethren and then to chiliasm, fashionable at the time in Europe, and she became a prominent member of the cosmopolitan occult and pietistic circles of Europe, preaching the gospel of the return of Christ in the body for a thousand years. Her wanderings over

Europe in preaching this gospel brought her to Baden while Empress Elizabeth was sojourning at Karlsruhe. It was under the sponsorship of Alexander's consort, anxious to give the Emperor spiritual consolation, and through the agency of her lady in waiting, Mlle Stourdza, that an interview was arranged with the Czar at Heilbronn on June 4, 1815. Alexander considered this interview providential, since it came in dramatic response to a particularly acute stage of religious brooding he was going through at the time. In a three-hour conversation he was won over to her views, and at his request she went with him to Paris, where she took up residence at the Hotel Montchenu, next door to the Elysée Palace.

She and her co-worker, Empeytaz, conducted the religious meetings which attracted such notables as Chateaubriand, Benjamin Constant, and Madame Récamier—her fame having spread through the rumors concerning the conversion of the Czar. Alexander attended these meetings assiduously and was brought into touch with a solitary and embittered philosopher, Bergasse, who liked to discuss the problem of the betterment of humanity. At these informal meetings with Bergasse and Baroness Krüdener germinated the ideas which formed the basis of the Holy Alliance.

The declaration of this alliance was officially signed on September 26 by Alexander, Emperor Francis, and King Friedrich Wilhelm, and made public to a startled world during a review of the allied forces of occupation near Paris the same day. Couched in biblical language, the covenant solemly declared that it had no purpose other than:

> To publish in the face of the whole world their [the sovereigns'] fixed resolution both in the administration of their respective states and in their political relations with every other government to take for their sole guide the precepts of that Holy Religion; namely, the precepts of justice, Christian charity, and peace, which, far from being applicable only to private concerns, must have an immediate influence on the council of princes and guide all their steps, as being the only means of consolidating the human institutions and remedying its imperfections.

Accordingly, in conformity with the words of the Scriptures, the sovereigns pledged themselves to remain united in the spirit of true fraternity, which involved the lending of mutual assistance and the governing of their peoples in a paternal spirit. "As fathers of families, they will lead them . . . to further Religion, Peace, and Justice." Force was to be used solely for such reciprocal service:

> . . . the three allied princes looking on themselves as merely delegated by Providence to govern three branches of the one family, namely Austria, Russia, and Prussia, thus confessing that the Christian world . . . has in reality no other sovereign than Him to whom alone power belongs, because in Him alone are found all the treasures of love, science, and infinite wisdom; that is to say, God, our Divine Saviour, the word of the Most High, the word of Life. . . . (Article III)[42]

The alliance was to be open to adherence of any power subscribing to its doctrine. The fact that all the powers of Europe did sign it, with the exception of England, the Pope, and Moslem Turkey, was the most striking evidence of the influence wielded by Alexander.

The Prince Regent of England, engrossed in his marital troubles and having a personal dislike for Alexander, left the decision on this matter to Castlereagh, who termed it "a piece of sublime mysticism and nonsense." The Prince Regent refused to sign it on the ground that all acts of the British Crown required the countersignature of a minister. The very vagueness of the principles enunciated in the Holy Alliance made it possible to interpret it in whatever sense necessary, and Metternich was quick to see the use he could make of it for the purpose of combating the resurgent revolutionary tide. On the other hand, the renewal of the clauses of the Treaty of Chaumont at the same time as the signing of the Second Treaty of Paris gave the Alliance a body and a practical instrument of power it had not formerly possessed. Thus the combined treaties were to serve as the skeleton of the grand alliance of European nations, an alliance which in the mind of Alexander was to restore peace to embattled Europe and lay the foundation for a real brotherhood of nations.

[42] Translation given in *Encyclopaedia Britannica*, 11th ed.

Chapter XI

France and the Congress of Aix-la-Chapelle

I

It is no exaggeration to state that from the time of the return of the Czar from Paris up to the Congress of Aix-la-Chapelle, St. Petersburg became the diplomatic capital of Europe. Reporting to his government, the French chargé d'affaires Comte de la Moussaye wrote: "All the monarchs are seeking today an alliance with Emperor Alexander. They are, so to say, present at his court through the presence of princes of their blood and by sending brilliant or well-selected embassies."[1] And again:

> Nothing is more remarkable than the resignation with which the powers of the Continent submit themselves at this time to the decisions of Russia. Their ambassadors in St. Petersburg assume the attitude of people who are soliciting and not negotiating. Emperor Alexander dictates his decisions, which are not contested, and the general disarmament of Europe is going to make them even more absolute. His armies remain as numerous and as fine as ever. The weak representations addressed to him by Austria and England have not produced up to the present any results.[2]

The bethrothal of Grand Duke Nicholas Pavlovitch (the future Nicholas I) to Princess Charlotte of Prussia, and the marriage of Alexander's sister with the Prince of Orange, the heir to the Dutch throne, in February, 1816, further cemented the already numerous dynastic ties Russia had with Continental powers; but aside from these, Russian diplomacy showed extraordinary activity all over Europe from Madrid to Stockholm and Constantinople and, as De la Moussaye points out, couriers from the various cabinets of Europe arrived and departed every day.

[1] De la Moussaye to the Duc de Richlieu, March 24, 1816 (Polovtsov, *op. cit.*, I, 453; also *Sbornik*, vol. 112).

[2] Same to same, April 13, 1816 (Polovtsov, *op. cit.*, I, 467-468).

A perusal of some of the minor issues dealt with by Russian diplomacy in 1816, taken at random, will give an idea of the scope and range of Russia's activity. Bavaria applied for Russia's mediation in a quarrel with Austria over the territory of Salzburg. Similarly Sardinia appealed for protection against Austrian claims on Alexandria, the region of Novara, and the Simplon road. The Austrian delegate, Count Paar, sent to St. Petersburg to negotiate this issue, returned to Vienna empty-handed because of an adverse decision of Alexander; and Austria had to abandon her claims on Sardinian territory. Contrariwise, the Grand Duchy of Baden had to give up some of its territory and the Count of Hochberg, its representative, left St. Petersburg without obtaining redress. The King of Spain appealed to Russia for aid when Brazilians invaded the region of the Rio de la Plata. The Bonapartist Duchesse de Saint Leu appealed to Alexander for protection when France demanded her extradition from Austria, where she had taken refuge; through the agency of the Czar she was permitted to remain in Gratz. A quarrel between the French Government and Prince Borghese of Italy over the possession of some pieces of statuary was similarly brought to the attention of the Czar. The Duc de Richelieu in a personal letter to the Czar complained that French Bonapartist and republican refugees settled in Brussels were conducting a campaign to overthrow the Bourbon dynasty in France, and were advocating putting on the French throne the Prince of Orange, as had been done with William I of England in 1688. All French remonstrances to the Dutch Government remained unheeded, and Richelieu wrote:

> I have hope only in the powerful intervention of your Majesty. . . . With the mobility of the French people and the facility with which they give credence to the most absurd rumors everything is to be feared and nothing must be neglected. I therefore dare to beg Your Majesty to deign to give orders to your ministers here, at the Hague, and in London to support the demands we are going to make on the King of the Netherlands.[3]

By order of the Czar the Conference of Ambassadors in Paris took up and settled the issue with the Dutch Government.

These examples suffice, and they come in addition to the major issues of European diplomacy which were handled by the Czar and his ministers. Of these by far the most important, and the one that

[3] *Sbornik*, LIV, 475.

drew the constant and vigilant attention of Alexander, was the increasingly alarming internal condition of France, closely tied up with the problem of the liquidation of France's obligations under the Treaty of Paris. Before turning to France, however, it is necessary to mention that at this time, with Pozzo di Borgo serving as ambassador in Paris and the star of Capo d'Istria beginning to set, the industrious and experienced Count Nesselrode was assuming the direction of Russia's foreign affairs. First as Vice-Chancellor, then as Chancellor, Nesselrode was to have a diplomatic career nearly as lengthy as that of Metternich, though his retiring and somewhat self-effacing personality made him merely a Secretary of Foreign Affairs in the hands of the czars and not an all-powerful chancellor like Metternich.

II

It was during the negotiations for the second Treaty of Paris—that is, while Emperor Alexander was still in Paris—that there occurred a shift in the French Government which very markedly influenced its relations with Russia. Since the discovery of the document relating to the signing of the secret alliance between France, Austria, and England at the Congress of Vienna, Alexander had developed a passionate hatred for Talleyrand. He had never had a high opinion of his character, but now he spoke openly of him as a traitor. King Louis XVIII had no liking for him either, and the Royalists now in power could not forgive Talleyrand his stormy and shifty past. However, so long as Talleyrand was useful to his country, the King tolerated him; but now it became apparent that Talleyrand was becoming a liability to France because of the Czar's changed attitude toward him.

> Louis XVIII felt that the support of the Emperor would be lacking so long as the Presidency of the Council [of French Ministers] was in the hands of someone who had mortally offended the Czar. . . . The successor to M. de Talleyrand was designated naturally by the very course of the events which had brought on the latter's fall: the promoter of the British Alliance had to give his place to the devoted servant of Russia and her Emperor.[4]

Indeed, this "devoted servant," the Duc de Richelieu, who was

[4] Léon de Crousaz-Crétet, *Le Duc de Richelieu en Russie et en France, 1766-1822* (Paris [illegible]39), 141.

appointed to head the French Government after the fall of Talleyrand, belonged as much to Russian history as to French history. As a very young man this descendant of the Great Cardinal and heir to one of the greatest fortunes of France was visiting Vienna in 1790. There at a dinner party at the house of the Prince de Ligne he met a courier from Russia who gave him news of the Russian armies that were fighting the Turks. Forthwith, eager for adventure, Richelieu, together with Prince Charles de Ligne and Count de Langeron, decided to enroll in the Russian Army as a volunteer. The three young men were well received at Prince Potëmkin's headquarters. Richelieu and de Ligne were appointed to the brigade of General Markov, belonging to the corps which under Suvorov carried out the storming and capturing of the fortress of Ismail. In this attack Richelieu distinguished himself sufficiently to be rewarded with the Sword of St. George. After the fall of Ismail he returned to France and inherited an immense fortune, but after the flight of the King to Varennes he considered it unsafe to remain in France and in August, 1791, decided to return to Russia. He was careful, however, to ask for a passport from the National Assembly so as not to be listed as an *émigré,* and gave as reason for his going back to Russia the desire to acquire more military experience in the Turkish War in order to be more useful to France later.

Arriving at St. Petersburg, he got in touch with Prince Nassau, a colorful adventurer who, in the words of Langeron, was "a Spanish general, a German colonel, a Russian admiral, and a Polish seigneur, without speaking a word of Spanish, German, Russian, or Polish." Nassau introduced him at court, and Empress Catherine admitted him into her private circle, which met at the Hermitage. In 1792 Catherine entrusted him with a mission to the headquarters of the Royalist forces of Prince Condé at Coblenz. After the Prussian defeat at Valmy, which turned the tide of the Wars of the Revolution, the Austrian High Command announced that it was disbanding this *émigré* force. Catherine then gave Richelieu sixty thousand rubles with which to provide for the expenses of any French *émigrés* desirous of settling in Russia in the newly conquered regions along the Sea of Azov, where they were to be provided with land and given very favorable terms. They would retain their religious freedom and would be given rights of Russian nobility if they belonged to the French nobility; six thousand of them were to form two infantry regiments receiving two years' salary under war conditions, and thereafter peacetime salaries. All expenses were to be paid in advance. But most of the *émigrés* preferred to keep on fighting the Revolution, the more so because Austria had renewed the payment of their salaries. Richelieu stayed with them and participated in the campaigns of 1793-1794 as observer for the Russian General Staff. For this participation in the military operations of the *émigrés* he was listed as an *émigré* and his property in France was confiscated.

In 1795 he returned to Russia and through the patronage of the elderly Field Marshal Count Rumiantsev was appointed colonel in second of the St. George Cuirassier Regiment, his friend Langeron receiving a similar appointment in another regiment. Two years later he was made a major general and took over the command of the Cuirassiers of the Emperor. However, he did not get along with Czar Paul I, who insisted on petty matters of drill to which Richelieu was not suited temperamentally. Accordingly, after a few snubs from the Czar he retired, living in Poland and trying to obtain a a passport for France. When the relations between Russia and France became friendly again, he managed to go back to Paris through the agency of the Russian embassy; through the influence of Count Morkov the First Consul was persuaded, in 1802, to strike his name off the list of *émigrés.*

Later, in Vienna, Richelieu suddenly received a personal letter from Alexander I inviting him back to Russia, where the Czar showered him with signs of benevolence. He received, in addition to a personal gift of ten thousand francs from the Emperor for immediate expenses, an estate in Courland which brought him a large revenue, and the following year he was appointed Military Governor of Odessa. By this time he had completely mastered the Russian language and could carry on his administrative work in that tongue. Subsequently he was made Governor-General of the whole of Novorossia, a region extending along the Black Sea from the Don to the Pruth and as far north as the governments of Kiev and Poltava. There he showed the most remarkable administrative ability and set himself enthusiastically to the task of developing this empire recently wrested from Turkey and practically untouched. His devotion to his task came from a true love of Russia, but at the same time he saw a chance to help his fellow-countrymen in distress, and many French *émigrés* were given jobs under him.

Whatever his motives, the results were brilliant. In ten years under his administration Odessa grew from a city of 8,000 inhabitants to 35,000, and the population of Novorossia from 300,000 to 2,000,000. In Odessa he enlarged the port facilities by building a large mole and creating two ports, one for vessels coming down the Dnieper and plying the coast, the other for vessels coming from abroad by way of Constantinople. He created an exchange, established banks and trade courts, and lowered the tariff, with the result that the rich produce of the Ukraine and the Crimea which used to pass through Danzig and other Baltic ports now went through Odessa. The trade of Moldavia and Wallachia began passing through this port, and vessels carried merchandise to and from Odessa to all the Mediterranean ports as far as Marseilles. Thus the number of vessels entering the port rose from 300 in 1802 to 1,000 in 1813, and the total trade turnover from 2,000,000 to 25,000,000 rubles. Furthermore, he embellished the city with boulevards and parks, and founded a theater, primary schools, and finally a high school which took the name of the Richelieu Lyceum and became one of the most important educational institutions in Russia under the able guidance of a French *émigré*, Abbé Nicolle. Odessa rapidly grew to become an important cosmopolitan center; and England, France, Austria, and Spain opened consulates there, England even sending a consul-general. In 1813 Queen Marie Caroline of Naples, exiled from her kingdom since 1806, made a prolonged stay in Odessa with her son Prince Leopold, and enjoyed the brilliant social life which centered around Richelieu.

The Duke was equally instrumental in developing the back country. Already Catherine had sent agents to the Rhineland to enroll colonists under very favorable conditions, and fifteen thousand Germans were settled in thirty villages around Odessa and in northern Crimea. Richelieu carried on this policy by bringing in Alsatians, Germans, Greeks, Bulgarians, and Armenians, and was successful in settling on the land the last of the nomad Tartar bands by building villages for them. He paid special attention to the Crimea, where, under the supervision of another French *émigré*, the Marquis de Traversay, were laid the foundations for the growth of Sebastopol as the great military port of the Black Sea. The Russian naval establishment on the Black Sea grew to become a powerful fleet of 12 vessels of the line, 4 frigates, 25 brigs, and 40 smaller vessels, with a total complement of 25,000 men, and with arsenals at Nikolaev and Sebastopol. Small wonder that Alexander remarked: "The French Revolution has done a great deal of harm, but I have to be grateful to it for giving me such men as Richelieu, Langeron, and Traversay."[5]

In 1814 with the return of monarchy in France Richelieu obtained from Czar Alexander leave to go back to Paris to try to recover his lost estates. Having settled his affairs in France, he was on the point of leaving that country to resume his duties in Russia when he was called to power by Louis XVIII. He now enters the history of France.

Talleyrand spoke of Richelieu sarcastically as the man in France who knew the most about the Crimea, but though there was some truth in this quip, he nevertheless had at this point an inestimable advantage over his more experienced predecessor in that he possessed

> the confidence and the esteem of him who made himself in a way the protector of defeated and spoliated France: he had been for twelve years the faithful servant of the Emperor of Russia . . . and could hope for everything from the gratitude and benevolence of Alexander, and that was an inestimable factor (*titre*) at the time when the good offices of Russia alone could preserve us [France] from a new dismemberment.[6]

Richelieu, however, did not want to assume such responsibilities, and it was only the joint and persistent entreaties of both Louis XVIII and the Czar which finally overcame his reluctance. But even then he considered his appointment as a personal misfortune, and in a tone akin to despair he wrote to Langeron, his successor in Odessa: "You have already learned what has happened to me. The King and the Emperor have forced me to take the place of Talleyrand. . . ."[7] And again, to the Abbé Nicolle: "Pray to the good Lord for me; I have never been so much in need of his help. Poor France, poor Odessa, poor Crimea."[8]

Indeed, Richelieu was to face a superhuman task in trying to keep France united. The Chamber of Deputies elected in August, 1815, had a strong Royalist majority composed of 350 members, but their

[5] *Ibid.*, p. 96. *Ibid.*, p. 144. [7] *Ibid.*, p. 142. [8] *Ibid.*, p. 143.

leanings were growing more and more extreme. Headed by the brother of the King, the Count of Artois, the so-called "Ultras" were anxious not only to restore the old order, but to seek vengeance on anyone connected with the previous regime; and the moderate Richelieu could not but see that such a policy would lead to anarchy, civil war, and possibly another revolution. It is interesting to notice that during his tenure of office Richelieu dutifully notified Alexander of every step taken in his handling of the internal affairs of France, sometimes writing the Czar at intervals of merely a few days. These letters and the lengthy reports Pozzo di Borgo sent to Nesselrode kept Alexander as well informed of the developments in France as if he had remained in Paris, and in the replies of Alexander to Richelieu we see the Emperor giving advice and guiding him very much as if had still been in Russian service. Too, the relations between Pozzo di Borgo and Richelieu became so cordial that the Ambassador carried to him by word of mouth suggestions which the Czar did not deem advisable to put on paper. Thus the influence of Alexander on the internal affairs of France remained constant, ever present, and powerful.

The first serious crisis which revealed the spirit of vengeance animating the Chamber arose over the so-called Law of Amnesty. Richelieu rightly saw that the "white terror" and the persecution of the former Bonapartists were leading to a civil war and possibly a new revolution, and he wrote despondently to Langeron in Odessa, "You would have pity if you could see the life I am leading. In Odessa a new village, new trees planted, would warm my heart and console me for my troubles; here is no consolation of any kind. . . ."[9] Pozzo di Borgo reported that the Ultras were becoming more and more aggressive and that the King himself had remarked to the Russian ambassador that he would become their first victim if the Ultras gained full liberty. Under these circumstances Richelieu considered the passage of the Law of Amnesty by the Chamber to be a great victory for the government, and he wrote to Alexander jubilantly in this vein. The Czar in his reply congratulating Richelieu hinted strongly that such a recalcitrant Chamber should be dissolved. Scarcely had the Law of Amnesty passed when a new crisis arose over the revision of the electoral law which revealed the grow-

[9] December 10, 1815 (*Sbornik,* LIV, 457).

ing power of Ultra opinion and the increasing prestige of the Count of Artois. Both Russia and England became increasingly alarmed, fearing that the intransigent attitude of the brother of the King would produce an explosion in France if the Ultras came into power. While Wellington wrote a letter to the King pointing out the danger of the situation, Alexander in his turn issued a rescript to Nesselrode for communication to Richelieu stressing the same ideas. In a private letter to Pozzo di Borgo dated February 7, Nesselrode was very much more explicit: "Please make him [the Count of Artois] understand that the Powers are not there to uphold his foolishness and to support his attempt to win the throne through a reactionary system so completely nonsensical."[10] At the same time Alexander drew the attention of the French Ambassador in St. Petersburg, the Comte de Noailles, to the conduct of the Chamber, whose counterrevolutionary tendencies were endangering the unity of France. In April, just as the Chamber recessed till October, Alexander wrote openly to Richelieu that the only way to calm the anxiety of the Powers and to put an end to the pretensions of the Ultras was to have a new Chamber, or to bring it under control in such a way that it should act in conformity with the constitution. The idea of dissolving the Chamber was already gaining ground, but Richelieu hesitated a long time.

Meanwhile the situation in the French provinces was rapidly drifting toward anarchy. Alexander issued a new warning pointing out that the acts of the Chamber were in contradiction to the treaty of November, 1815, of which the main purpose was the maintenance of the *Charte* and of the royal authority. Richelieu yielded and persuaded the hesitant King to issue a decree on September 5 to prorogue the Chamber and call for new elections. It is interesting to notice that the very same day, and two days before the royal ordinance had been published, Richelieu wrote to Alexander informing him of this measure. The Czar was much pleased by the news, and the measure received full support in Berlin and Vienna as well. In London it led to a violent press campaign against Richelieu's government, which oddly was accused of being Jacobin and revolutionary. The English newspapers unanimously supported

[10] Charles Pozzo di Borgo, *Correspondance diplomatique du Cte Pozzo di Borgo et du Cte de Nesselrode* (Paris, 1890), I, 313.

the Count of Artois and his ultraroyalist party. Crousaz-Crétet comments:

It is to be believed that these rather singular tactics on their part were due less to sincere convictions than to their jealousy of Russia, whom they had already been accusing for a long while of directing everything in France. The dissolution of the Chamber appeared to them as a concession made to the demands of Emperor Alexander, and they were nearly unanimous in criticizing it.[11]

Such indeed was to be the interpretation given to Richelieu's policy by the infuriated Ultras, who took advantage of the convening of the new Chamber on November 4 to open their attack. They found two powerful if unexpected allies in Talleyrand and in Canning. Talleyrand, anxious to get back into power, began to associate with the members of the parliament which had ousted him, and to spread rumors that Richelieu had made France a vassal of Russia and was himself so weak in character as to be unable to uphold the dignity and independence of France in the face of the Great Powers. Canning, visiting Paris at the time, gave full support to the Ultras. He openly stated that the Bourbons would never be permitted to throw themselves at the feet of Russia.[12]

But Richelieu, undaunted, stuck to his course, and in return for his concessions in matters of internal policy obtained Alexander's support on the outstanding questions of foreign policy, all-important to France. Two interlocked issues were the main concern of Richelieu—the evacuation of France by the allied forces of occupation, and the alleviation of her financial burden due to the maintenance of the army of occupation and to her obligations under the Treaty of Paris. Since France had had a bad harvest, Richelieu was forced to import foodstuffs and grains from abroad, particularly from Odessa, and thereby incurred further accusations of pro-Russian sympathies. Richelieu set out as early as May, 1816, to obtain from Alexander the settlement of both issues in question, and writing confidentially to the Czar he appealed for a reduction in the army of occupation. On July 4 he wrote again:

The more I think of it, the more this measure appears to me indispensable in the very interest of the allies whose aim is that France should be quiet.

[11] *Op. cit.*, p. 220.

[12] Pozzo di Borgo, *op. cit.*, I, 449-457.

I am persuaded that nothing will give us such an ascendancy over the Chamber of Deputies, which we never have had, as to be able to announce at its opening the advantages we have been able to obtain for France.[13]

He goes on to say that the Duke of Wellington had been approached on the matter, but though not averse to the idea had replied evasively; hence he requested the Czar to put pressure on his allies. Here it should be said that the Duke of Wellington as commander in chief of the forces of occupation had the supreme decision on technical matters pertaining to the military situation. The political relations had been entrusted to the Conference of Ambassadors of the Allied Powers in Paris, which, after the departure of the sovereigns from Paris, was instructed by the latter to meet weekly for the study of questions raised by the foreign occupation of France. "In these conferences it was, without doubt, the Russian Ambassador General Pozzo di Borgo who occupied the predominant place. . . . The envoys of the other powers, Baron Vincent, Count Goltz, Sir Charles Stewart, took only a secondary part in the deliberations of the conference."[14] Thus it was that though Richelieu could deal directly with Pozzo di Borgo in matters relating to the Conference, he had to work through Alexander to obtain results from the Duke of Wellington. The latter replied after a long delay that the issue of reducing the allied contingents depended on the measures taken by France to meet her financial obligations under the Treaty of Paris. Thus both issues were tied into one. Richelieu then negotiated a loan from two British banking houses, Messrs. Baring and Hope, and met this objection in such a way that on February 10, 1817, the allied ambassadors officially notified the French Government that in view of the fact that France had fulfilled her financial obligations, the army of occupation was to be reduced in the fall of the same year by thirty thousand men.

But there was still a thorny question to be settled—that of the liquidation of debts contracted before 1814 and amounting to over a billion francs. Richelieu had proposed that by eliminating all doubtful debts claimed by individual foreigners, the sum would be reduced to 200,000,000. This proposal was immediately accepted and supported by Russia, but met with the most resolute opposition from Prussia. Because of this the question dragged on for nearly a

[13] Crousaz-Crétet, *op. cit.*, p. 212. [14] *Ibid.*, p. 160.

year. Finally, Alexander wrote to Wellington asking him to examine a possible settlement of the affair with the Conference of Ambassadors; this led to the final settlement on April 23, 1818, when three conventions were concluded, scaling the debt down to 240,000,000 francs. Louis XVIII wrote a letter to Alexander thanking him effusively: "*Monsieur mon frère*, owing to the friendship of Your Majesty, your generous intervention, and I may say, the wisdom of your councils, the important question of liquidations has been terminated in a manner as advantageous to France as might be hoped for under the circumstances."[15]

It was during these negotiations that Russia first suggested the calling of a conference of sovereigns in the spirit of the agreement of 1815. Richelieu now raised the demand for the termination of foreign occupation in France, and Capo d'Istria told the French ambassador in St. Petersburg, Comte de Noailles, in June, 1817, of the Russian project, according to which the proposed meeting of the sovereigns would become a congress in which the small states of Europe would be represented as well, thus putting an end to the domination of Europe by the four major powers. A city of secondary importance between Austria and Russia and France would be selected as the place of meeting. Subsequently Capo d'Istria informed Noailles that the congress would be held in September, 1818, and would discuss the issue of the evacuation of France by the allied forces. He declared emphatically that the occupation of France should not be prolonged beyond the three-year limit, and deemed it regrettable that an idea should have gained ground that France could not enjoy tranquillity without the presence of allied troops. In an interview which Alexander had with Noailles as early as March, 1818, the Czar mentioned his forthcoming journey to the conference somewhere on the Rhine in the fall and declared emphatically that he would overcome all obstacles to "liberate France from the foreign yoke." France having met the demands previously, there was no more reason for refusing to discuss the question of the evacuation of foreign troops, and it was decided that the congress should meet at Aix-la-Chapelle. Writing to Alexander on May 5, 1818, Richelieu said: "We dare hope that Your Imperial Majesty will terminate your labor *(achevera son ouvrage)* and by giving back

[15] King Louis XVIII to Emperor Alexander, Paris, May 16, 1818 (*ibid.*, p. 267).

France to herself will complete the great work of the confederation of Europe. . . ."[16]

III

A circular in the form of a "Confidential Memoir" written under the direction of Alexander was then dispatched by Russia to all the powers. In this remarkable document Alexander stressed that the troubles of humanity during the great revolutionary period had been due essentially to "individualism and partial or exclusive political combinations," and went on to say that the association of states under the Holy Alliance

> has assured the inestimable advantages of civil order and the inviolability of persons and institutions. It has consecrated and guaranteed everywhere legitimacy, *ab antiqua*, and recognized by the treaties now in force the territorial possessions of every state. In order to maintain this end, the principle of a general coalition must be established and developed by further eventual action.

In the mind of the Czar, therefore, the settlement of the French problem was merely a corollary of a greater problem of European solidarity, and for this purpose he wanted the conference to include all signatories of the Holy Alliance. But this was precisely what Metternich was seeking to avoid, and in this he was supported by the British Government. "It was the Tsar's contention that the Treaty of Alliance of November 20, 1815, had provided (article VI) the machinery for a real European government. In a series of congresses wherein the representatives of the Powers might deliberate in common upon all matters concerning the general welfare he saw the inception of a European legislature."[17] But neither England nor Austria wanted to see Spain receive a hearing in the Congress, or France regain her lost power and prestige as a result of her participation on an equal footing with the Allies. Accordingly Metternich proposed to eliminate from the field of discussion at the coming meeting any issues not pertaining to the relations of the Allies with France—this step supported by England would give England a monopoly over the South American issue and Austria a similar monopoly in Germany and Italy, by keeping both Russia and France from having a voice in these issues. Prussia somewhat hesitantly gave her support to Austria on this question, and Russia had to yield,

[16] *Sbornik*, LIV, 575.

[17] Cresson, *op. cit.*, p. 71.

accepting the idea that the conference should be limited to the four powers and France.

Nevertheless, when the Congress actually met in Aix-la-Chapelle, Alexander, who arrived there accompanied by Nesselrode and Capo d'Istria, had once more the illusion of being the all-powerful arbitrator of the destinies of Europe. As Gentz avowed to the German writer Warnhagen von Ense: "It was not Austria and Metternich, nor England, to say nothing of Prussia, but Emperor Alexander and Capo d'Istria who were directing the Congress. Capo d'Istria gained a predominant influence."[18] Perhaps no better illustration can be found of the influence attributed to Alexander at the time than the fantastic plot hatched during the Congress by French Bonapartists to kidnap the Czar. The Russian secret police discovered a conspiracy headed by a group of leading Bonapartists including Laborde, Piget, Dietrich, Pouillot, and others, whereby Alexander was to be taken into custody by them and forced to issue the following proclamation to the French nation:

In the name of the Fatherland and the Emperor Alexander:

Art I. We decree, in accordance with the decisions taken at our Congress of Aix-la-Chapelle, that the army of occupation shall be evacuated during the last days of the present month and be returned within its own frontiers.

Art II. We proclaim, according to the deliberations of the Congress held in a secret session of the sovereigns, that, in the name of France, Napoleon shall be transferred back to France and that Prince Francis Charles Napoleon [the King of Rome] shall be proclaimed Emperor of the French and Marie Louise Empress Regent.

Signed at our Congress of Aix-la-Chapelle
in date of our Assembly.......... 1818[19]

The discovery of this plot produced a stir but did not deter Alexander from subsequently going to Brussels, where the kidnapping was to have taken place.

Even though the allied sovereigns insisted this was merely a reunion and not a congress, the Congress of Aix-la-Chapelle had much of the brilliance of the Congress of Vienna. With the three allied sovereigns were Metternich, Gentz, Hardenberg, Bernstorff, Nesselrode, and Capo d'Istria. France had sent Richelieu and

[18] Schilder, *Imperator Aleksandr Pervyi*, IV, 119.

[19] *Ibid.*, IV, 119 n.

Rayneval; and England, Wellington, Castlereagh, and George Canning. Outside the official Congress but watching it closely were the bankers—Baring, Bethmans, and the Rothschilds; journalists such as Perry, the editor of the *Morning Post;* singers such as Catalani, and seeresses such as the celebrated Mme Lenormand. Finally, the wives of the diplomats enjoyed both the social whirl and the political intrigues. The Russian delegation had two outstanding women, Countess Shuvalov and Countess Lieven. It was there that the latter was to embark on her celebrated romance with Metternich, which not only made her the willing agent of the Austrian Chancellor, but was to make history later. All the smaller courts of Europe excluded from the deliberations had their observers, and Alexander enjoyed this mixed atmosphere of social grace and politics in which he felt so at home. "Once more he saw the whole of Europe surrounding him and watching every one of his movements."[20]

By September 20 all the delegations were present, and the Congress was ready to open. Two questions were considered. Throughout the conference the Russian delegates kept attempting to bring Spain into the conference, or at least to initiate some form of mediation in the Spanish question; these moves Castlereagh viewed as an attempt to create a union of Russia, France, and Spain prejudicial to England, and therefore they met with the determined opposition of Great Britain. This left the other question, the relations with France, as the prime issue of debate; here two matters had to be settled—the evacuation of the forces of occupation and the liquidation of the French indemnity resulting from the Treaty of Paris. As France had to date discharged her obligations punctually, the financial issue was settled by consolidating the outstanding debt into one payment within a year, of a total of 265,000,000 francs, part in cash and part in interest-bearing *rentes*. In return for this settlement the Allies agreed to withdraw the forces of occupation by November 30. These decisions were embodied in a collective note dated October 9 in which the Allies declared that they regarded this solemn act as a final completion of the General Peace and invited the King of France to unite henceforth his councils and his efforts with those of the allied powers.[21]

[20] Waliszewski, *Le Règne d'Alexandre Ier*, III, 34.

[21] Robert Balmain Mowat, *A History of European Diplomacy 1815-1914* (London, 1927), p. 30.

It was, however, on this last point that Russia was pursuing a policy distinct from that of her allies. Indeed, if Alexander had made himself the ardent champion of France, it was not for France's sake. Once, during the Congress, he observed to his aide-de-camp Colonel Danilevsky that he could not tolerate the French. He added, however, that it was good that the French had given the world a universal language—better to speak this one than invent a new one.[22] In his mind the re-entrance of France into the community of nations on an equal footing was to be merely a step in the direction of forming that European federation or directorate which was to complement the Holy Alliance. To this policy he clung tenaciously throughout the conference; and, amplifying the contents of his memorandum on April, 1818, he presented the Congress on October 8 with a second memorandum, written by Pozzo di Borgo. In this memorandum a complete scheme of European federation was presented in a somewhat verbose and confused way, veiled in the intricacies of the diplomatic language of the day.[23] Pozzo di Borgo proposed that, even though the quadruple alliance should remain as a guarantee against France, a general alliance should be formed of all the signatories of the Treaty of Vienna with the object of guaranteeing the *status quo*, both political and territorial, of the powers of Europe. This alliance would aim at giving every nation the same protection against aggression that an individual possesses in a well-organized society; and since this protection is given to an individual through the agency of a police force, an international police force would have to be created, of which the Russian Army would form the nucleus. The Czar further suggested the formation of an international general staff, but this idea met with the strenuous opposition of Wellington. The striking resemblance of these proposals to the ideas in the covenant of the League of Nations is too obvious to require comment.

The proposal produced consternation and near panic. Castlereagh, believing that it was time for England to resume her isolation, declared that such a scheme would infringe upon the independence of nations, the recognition of which was a fundamental principle of British foreign policy. Metternich saw in the scheme a veiled at-

[22] Schilder, *Imperator Aleksandr Pervyi,* IV, 130.
[23] *Sbornik,* CXIX, 802.

tempt at Russian hegemony, and even Prussia was worried over the fate of her acquisitions on the Rhine. Castlereagh suggested a compromise solution, which would give some satisfaction to the Czar, whereby Europe, by the inclusion of France in the concert of powers, should be ruled by the five Great Powers. Indeed, a secret protocol dated November 15 stipulated that "the five Powers have decided not to depart, either in their relations with each other or with other states, from the principles of union which until now have presided over the common interests, a union become more strong and indissoluble from the bonds of Christian brotherhood which join them."[24] Richelieu, enthusiastic, attributed this advantage for France to Alexander, and writing to Descazes, said, "One ought to kiss his footsteps."[25] Indeed, the very language of the Holy Alliance used in the framing of the above quotation, with its reference to the bonds of Christian brotherhood, indicated that the Allies, in an attempt to placate the Czar, had met him on a compromise solution.

On October 28, acting upon the advice of Wellington, Alexander paid a visit to King Louis XVIII in Paris; and this visit, preceded by a military review of the Russian forces of occupation at Maubeuge, did a great deal to lift the heavy veil of mutual antipathy which had previously existed between the two sovereigns. After the closing of the Congress, Alexander proceeded by way of Brussels, Karlsruhe, and Vienna back to Russia. He was well pleased with the results obtained and observed, "Here this Congress, of which so much has been said, which was represented as so mysterious, is over, and peace established. We have pledged ourselves to meet once more in three years."[26]

Summing up the position of Russia at this Congress the famous Russian historian Soloviev writes: "A close union was observed between the governments of Vienna and London, a union caused by the jealousy and fear of the immense power of Russia and by its interference in all European problems."[27]

[24] Cresson, *op. cit.*, p. 74 n. 1.

[25] Waliszewski, *Le Règne d'Alexandre Ier*, III, 40.

[26] Schilder, *Imperator Aleksandr Pervyi*, IV, 167 n.

[27] Soloviev, *Foreign Policy of Emperor Alexander I* (St. Petersburg, 1877) (in Russian), as quoted in Nicholas [Mikhailovich], *L'Empereur Alexandre Ier* (St. Petersburg, 1912), I, 200.

Chapter XII

Congresses of Carlsbad, Troppau, and Verona

I

Scarcely had the powers settled the delicate question of their relations with France when their attention was turned to the growing revolutionary agitation in Germany. Metternich in particular was genuinely alarmed, but he also saw a chance to use this revolutionary menace for the purpose of strengthening Austria's hold over the Germanic Confederation. For these reasons he exaggerated the importance of the agitation, confined mostly to students and secret societies of the Carbonari type, and was extremely anxious to impress Alexander with the gravity of the menace. The letters of Emperor Francis to the Czar, as well as the messages of Metternich to Nesselrode and Capo d'Istria, invariably dwelt upon the seriousness of the revolutionary disease spreading in Europe. "Germany," said Metternich, "is much more ill than any other state in Europe." Metternich intensely disapproved of Alexander's policy in Germany and was anxious to bring him over to his point of view.

In March, 1816, the Duke of Saxe-Weimar granted a liberal constitution to his subjects; the following year the King of Württemberg consulted his people with regard to the granting of a constitution; and on August 29, 1817, the Grand Duke of Baden accorded the most liberal constitution of the three. All these rulers were closely related to the Czar, and all three had consulted him concerning their reforms. It was known that it was at the instigation of Alexander that the young King of Württemberg had started his reign with this liberal measure. Metternich had vainly tried to block these liberal trends at Aix-la-Chapelle. But presently an event occurred which gave Metternich his chance—the assassination in March, 1819, of the noted German writer, Kotzebue. Kotzebue had entered the Russian service, had been since 1792 president of the

Court of Justice in Esthonia, and under Paul I had even been exiled to Siberia for writing certain pamphlets. Afterwards he had been the director of the German theater in St. Petersburg, had been attached to the staff of the army in 1812 as official writer, and in 1813 had entered Prussia with the Russians and taken a prominent part in awakening the enthusiasm of the Prussians for the war of liberation. He was Russian Consul-General in Prussia in 1814-1816, and at the time of his death was Alexander's confidential agent whose task was to report on the state of mind in Germany. For having written against the liberal movement among the students of the universities, he was stabbed to death by a student of theology at the University of Erlangen, Karl Sand, whose trial revealed that he had acted in accordance with the orders of a secret society. This death, as well as an attempt on the life of a second Russian agent, Stourdza, shocked Alexander greatly, for the Czar had always made a distinction between liberalism and revolutionary anarchy, which he feared. Metternich was exultant. Writing to Gentz on April 9 he said sarcastically, "We will see what the Emperor of Russia will say about the amiable way in which his Councilors of State are treated in Germany. Yet while in Germany Russian agents are being secretly murdered, other Russian agents preside over Carbonari Clubs in Italy."[1] Metternich had contended that these liberal tendencies of Alexander were merely attempts on his part to stir up trouble for Austria. He hinted darkly that inflammatory articles in the German press originated in Russian embassies, and he accused Russia of intriguing in Italy as well. He wrote to Gentz from Naples on May 7, "If there had not always been Russian agents covering Italy in all directions and seeking to inflame the hopes of the [revolutionary] parties in speaking of the liberalism of Emperor Alexander, there would not be any permanent agitation in the minds [of the people]. . . ."[2]

But Italy could wait; Metternich was anxious to settle the German issue first. Under his sponsorship the Conference of Carlsbad took place between the representatives of major German states and passed a series of repressive measures establishing a censorship, bringing the universities under surveillance, dissolving all secret societies, and establishing at Mainz a committee with inquisitorial

[1] Metternich, *op. cit.*, III, 236.

[2] *Ibid.*, III, 254-255.

powers. Alexander was not present at this meeting, though he watched its proceedings from afar. Metternich attributed his success to the absence of the Czar. ". . . What I have been wanting to do since 1813, and what that terrible Emperor Alexander has always spoiled, I have done because he was not there. At last I have been able to follow my whole thought, to affirm all my principles of public law. . . ."[3] But he found it necessary, notwithstanding his success, to obtain the approbation of Alexander for the measures passed at Carlsbad. On September 22 the Russian ambassador, Golovkin, wrote from Vienna that "the Austrian government appreciates the stand taken by Emperor Alexander not to interfere in the internal affairs of Germany, but it considers that for once an open approbation given to the declarations of Carlsbad would be not only opportune but very desirable."[4] But Alexander saw through the maneuver—however much he was impressed by the assassination of Kotzebue, he was not prepared to endorse this attempt on the part of Metternich to gain a complete hegemony over Germany. Accordingly in his letter to Emperor Francis on October 16, 1819, he merely expressed his wishes that "the temporary and transitory measures taken by Austria should achieve their purpose." He followed this emphasis on the temporary nature of the repressive measures of Carlsbad by one more important document—namely, instructions to all the Russian ambassadors, in the shape of "a survey of the ideas of the Emperor on the affairs of Germany" dated November 21, 1819. In this document he elaborated general principles of policy, in accordance with the transition of his ideas from liberalism to Metternichian conservatism, making a clear distinction between revolution and liberalism.

Alexander stressed the point that governments had lost prestige and that their power could be derived only from liberal institutions granted to their people. But he insisted: ". . . in speaking of liberal institutions we did not have in view any arrangements ceded through weakness or terms enforced on the sovereigns by demagogic leaders, nor constitutions granted under the stress of difficulties, to avoid the coming storm. . . . Liberty is and has to be circumscribed in proper limits . . . and those limits are the principles of order."[5] Accordingly,

[3] Pierre Rain, *Un Tsar idéologue, Alexandre Ier (1775-1825)* (Paris, 1913), p. 385.
[4] Martens, *op. cit.*, IV, 268.
[5] *Ibid.*, IV, 269-270.

the Czar acknowledged the right of every individual German state to take such measures as necessary to maintain order, and urged noninterference by governments outside of Germany; these should merely approve such measures in the name of the solidarity of European governments against the forces of revolution. This remarkable document showed the distance separating Alexander from Metternich. The Austrian Chancellor, however, did not see it as a question of divergence of political views, but fatuously reduced it to a matter of his personal influence over the vacillating Czar. He saw it merely as a duel between himself and the liberal Capo d'Istria, whom he hated. On July 29 he wrote gleefully, "I have good news from St. Petersburg. Capo d'Istria feels he has been beaten completely *(à plate couture)*; that is evident. The Emperor Alexander and I, we will decide many issues by ourselves. . . ."[6] Again on August 8 he wrote that Alexander had said, "Since 1814 I have been mistaken about the spirit of the people: what I considered right, now I find wrong. I have done a great deal of harm; I will try to repair it."[7]

In the meanwhile Russia's policy on German affairs was coming closer to the policy of England rather than to that of Austria. When Castlereagh declared to Count Lieven that Great Britain could not approve of the decrees of Carlsbad because there could not exist an alliance of governments against their peoples which would not eventually endanger the governments, Russia concurred, and the Russian Government by a circular letter dated January 27, 1820, expressed very much the same views. This letter asserted that the German states must be left free to establish relations among themselves and that foreign intervention would be harmful, particularly if resulting in "a league with the sole aim of maintaining the absurd claims of absolutism."[8] The circular went even further and declared that should the German states wish to organize a federated state in the place of a confederation of states, thereby invalidating the act of the Treaty of Vienna concerning Germany, Russia not only would not oppose the move, but would "welcome it without reserve."[9] Such views were sheer heresy in the eyes of Metternich, and it required a great deal of effort on his part to express his satisfaction to

[6] Metternich, *op. cit.*, III, 363.
[7] *Ibid.*, III, 365.
[8] Martens, *op. cit.*, IV, 270.
[9] *Ibid.*, IV, 271.

the Russian ambassador, Count Golovkin, stating that Russia's policy was "excellent, perfect." Privately, however, he complained that Russia was inconsistent in supporting liberalism and fighting revolution at the same time.

Indeed, even after Carlsbad, Alexander was still giving active support to the liberal cause in Germany. In October his brother-in-law, the King of Württemberg, visited him in Warsaw and complained bitterly about the interference of Austria in the internal affairs of German states as a result of the decrees of Carlsbad, and demanded the protection of Russia in the name of the principles of the Holy Alliance or, as the King himself put it, "in the name of liberty and the free exercise of the monarchial principles, guaranteed by the Holy Alliance."[10] Alexander put forward the principle that although an insurrection against a sovereign was unacceptable, it was nevertheless the sovereign's right and privilege to grant liberal measures to his people, if he so desired. Accordingly, he not only acceded to the demand of the King of Württemberg, but, solicited by the other small German states, took up their cause against Prussia and Austria and began massing Russian troops in Poland in the fall of 1819, a measure which worried Metternich considerably. In December, 1819, a circular note of Nesselrode invited the South German states to maintain their opposition toward Austria. The King of Württemberg, now feeling secure under the wing of Alexander, suggested that the whole issue be submitted to the Diet of Frankfurt and afterwards submitted to the sanction of the powers comprising the Holy Alliance. Frightened by the prospects of a conflict with Russia, Metternich made concessions both to Württemberg and to the other South German states, on condition that they should refrain from any such appeal.

But when in January, 1820, a revolution broke out in Spain, followed in July by a revolution in Sicily against the King of Naples, and in August by a similar insurrection in Portugal, Metternich saw his chance to regain the lost ground, and his arguments gained weight with Alexander.

II

The Italian cause had evoked considerable sympathy in Russia even in high diplomatic circles. Count Golovkin, writing from

[10] Cresson, *op. cit.*, p. 97.

Vienna to Nesselrode on July 27, 1820, said: "Napoleon gave Italy three things for which people give their life: i.e., nationality, glory, and a constitution," and he accused Austria of taking these three things away and of attempting to Germanize the Italian people. But for Alexander the revolution in Naples meant merely the spreading of the revolutionary conflagration endangering Europe. Writing to him in this vein, Emperor Francis declared that the events in Naples could not leave Russia indifferent, and proposed a meeting with the Czar at Pest. The King of Prussia was invited too, though Metternich told Golovkin that his absence would be fully understandable because of the condition of affairs in Prussia. England was not asked, as being too indifferent. Metternich obviously wanted to keep the interview strictly limited to the two emperors. But Russia in reply to the invitation put forth a proposal for a congress of powers to include France and England which would discuss all the outstanding issues, including the revolutions in Spain and Portugal. After much hesitation Metternich accepted, though he strove to limit the scope of this congress, which he insisted would be dangerous if not confined to a specific object. To meet Alexander's wishes it was agreed that the congress would convene in October at Troppau in Silesia, this city being approximately halfway between the two capitals. Having yielded on the point of convening a congress, Metternich remained determined to circumscribe it as much as possible, being interested only in obtaining a free hand in Italy. He suggested taking as a basis for the program of discussions the instructions given to Count Lebzeltern for confidential communication to the Russian Government. These clauses were accepted by Russia as the basis for discussion at the congress, and it is interesting to note how closely they parallel the famous declaration of Troppau, revealing thereby the dominant role played by Metternich. This was to be Metternich's congress, and not Alexander's, as Aix-la-Chapelle had been.

The British Government indicated its disapproval of Metternich's memorandum and of the whole idea of the congress by declaring that it would adhere to its own course of action "at the risk of seeing the alliance move away from us without having quitted it,"[11] and pointedly refused to send a plenipotentiary to the coming

[11] *Cambridge Modern History,* X, 27.

meeting, merely appointing Sir Charles Stewart, ambassador in Vienna, as an observer without power to make decisions. France similarly restricted the power of her delegates, and to the disappointment of Alexander did not send the Duc de Richelieu but merely appointed La Ferronnays and the Marquis de Caraman, ambassadors respectively to St. Petersburg and Vienna. This once more played into the hands of Metternich, who had been anxious to limit the congress to deliberations with Russia alone, or possibly with Prussia as well.

The Congress opened on October 20 with the Emperors Alexander and Francis present, and the Crown Prince Friedrich Wilhelm representing Prussia pending the arrival of the King. The Russian delegation was composed of Nesselrode, Capo d'Istria, and the Russian ambassador to Vienna—Count Golovkin; the Austrian was headed by Metternich and Gentz, and the Prussian by Hardenberg and Count Bernstorff. Under the pretext that the delegates of England and France were empowered only to "report" and not to make decisions, they were not invited into the informal meetings of the three sovereigns where the important decisions of the congress were made.

In these meetings the Austrian memorandum was discussed, and the issue soon resolved itself into an open duel between Metternich and Capo d'Istria, since Alexander was now completely attuned to Metternich's views. Writing in his diary, Metternich before the opening of the conference said somewhat fatuously: "Nesselrode will come too; Emperor Alexander does not want to face me alone"; but on November 10 he noted, "The benevolence of Emperor Alexander toward me is still lasting. It is a return to the year 1813. If he had been in 1815 what he was in 1813 there would not have been the year 1820."[12] On November 29, he said, "He is today actually at the point where I was thirty years ago." Capo d'Istria had taken a clear-cut stand against the Austrian memorandum, and at the private conference of October 26 he bitterly attacked the conduct of the King of Naples: "On the one hand," he declared, "he gives his solemn oath to acts which call a number of his subjects around the throne, and on the other he attempts to punish these same people by bringing foreign troops into his country. And why does he wish

[12] Metternich, *op. cit.*, III, 377.

to punish them? Because they gave their oath, like himself, to acts sanctioned . . . by his own authority."[13] But Capo d'Istria, supported in his stand by La Ferronnays, was alone in his struggle against Austria. Both Alexander and the docile, "self-effacing" Nesselrode were anxious to give their full co-operation to Metternich in his struggle against the revolutionary menace. Thus even though the Czar would have liked to place the action of the powers on the former basis of the Holy Alliance, and though Capo d'Istria presented a memorandum to the congress in this sense, nevertheless Russia adhered fully to the Austrian demands, including the right to occupy Naples militarily. The Prussian delegation, instructed to co-operate with Austria, also gave its adherence.

Thus in the meetings held by the sovereigns of the three northern powers there gradually evolved the points which were incorporated into the "Preliminary Protocol" of November 19, written by Capo d'Istria and signed by the delegates of Austria, Prussia, and Russia. The introductory clause of this famous document stresses the danger to which Europe was exposed as a result of the outbreak of revolutions, and the determination of the signatory powers to respect their obligations as well as to assure the development of civilization. In Article I these powers declare that states which had been subjected to internal changes as a result of revolution would cease to be a part of the European alliance until their internal situation gave guarantee of order and stability. The Allied Powers would therefore refuse to recognize any such changes (Article III). In the event that these changes should endanger neighboring countries, the signatory powers would attempt to bring the offending country back into the alliance "first by friendly pressure and secondly by coercive force, should the use of such a force become indispensable."[14] Having enunciated these general principles, the protocol goes on to seek their application to the specific case of Naples, with the sole purpose of giving back to the King of the Two Sicilies his freedom of action and the power to re-establish order with specific guarantees as to the existence and the integrity of the Kingdom (Article IV). Consequently the Austrian Army, acting in the name of the signatory powers, was authorized to proceed to a temporary occupation of Naples, and special commissioners were to be appointed by each power to carry on nego-

[13] Martens, *op. cit.*, IV, 279.

[14] *Ibid.*, IV, 283.

tiations under the chairmanship of the Austrian plenipotentiary with the Government of Naples (Articles V and VI). Article VII stipulates that the Congress would carry on its work along these lines until the attitude of the King of Naples and of the governments of London and Paris became known.

It was further decided to issue an invitation to King Ferdinand to come to Laybach, where the Congress was to reconvene. Czar Alexander and Emperor Francis agreed to appeal individually to the Pope to serve as mediator with the Neapolitan revolutionaries. On December 12 Alexander wrote an eloquent letter to the Pope as head of the Catholic Church, apostle of morality and religion, and sovereign of parts of Italy, requesting him to influence the peoples of the Two Sicilies.

The reaction in London to the protocol of November 19 was one of unmitigated irritation. Castlereagh complained bitterly to the French ambassador, Descazes, that to him it was unbelievable that "the three courts, without consulting previously or agreeing with the two courts which they had solicited to aid them, should discuss and work out a code of international policy, thereby making themselves the regulators of all the states." He declared that this was the establishment of a universal monarchy by the very powers which had enslaved and partitioned Poland.[15] At the same time Castlereagh was somewhat perplexed, for he disapproved of the events in Naples and secretly was in favor of Austrian military intervention. Moreover, the British Fleet had put into Naples for the same purpose. He therefore wrote to his brother that he wished to leave Austria unembarrassed in her course, provided Britain had the same freedom of action. Accordingly, on December 19 Lord Stewart presented to the congress a memorandum which stated that Lord Castlereagh disapproved of the events which had taken place in Naples and admitted that a state might find it necessary to interfere in the affairs of a neighboring state if its interests were threatened, but that he could not accept that such a case should be converted into a principle, as had been done in the protocol. This veiled support of his cause delighted Metternich, who was not anxious about principles provided he had his way, but the Russians were profoundly irritated and complained that there was a contra-

[15] Crousaz-Crétet, *op. cit.*, p. 407.

diction between the official stand taken by the British and their underhand support of Metternich. Over a month later, when the conference was already sitting at Laybach, there arrived the official reply of Castlereagh to the invitation to adhere to the protocol. "He should not have felt it necessary," he wrote, "to have made communications to the British representatives at foreign courts had it not been for a circular communication by the Courts of Austria, Prussia, and Russia to their several missions, which if not adverted to might convey very erroneous impressions of the past as well as of the present sentiments of the British Government," and he goes on to say that the clauses of the protocol were "in direct repugnance to the fundamental laws of the United Kingdom"; that the British Government, though disapproving of the Neapolitan revolution, had declared to the allied courts "that they should not consider themselves called upon or justified to advise an interference on the part of this country."[16]

In France the news of the signing of the protocol was received with the utmost perplexity. The Duc de Richelieu was anxious not to alienate England or Russia, and yet was afraid that the principle of intervention might be applied to Spain as well. After much hesitation he finally instructed his delegates at Troppau to refuse to accede to the protocol even though France, he declared, accepted certain articles in it and was anxious not to break up the alliance.

But by this double refusal of England and France the alliance was irreparably broken, and in the last meeting of the Congress held on December 24, the British representatives were conspicuously absent. Thus Europe was divided into two groups of great powers holding irreconcilably opposed policies and principles, and this cleavage was to become deeper and deeper throughout the nineteenth century. Therein lies the great historical significance of the Congress of Troppau. And such a shift in the balance of power in Europe was inevitably to produce ramifications and widespread effects far beyond the scope of the objects pursued at the Congress.

France came closer to England, and Russia to Austria, with Prussia as the satellite of the latter. In the opinion of the French writer Crousaz-Crétet: "The alienation of Russia was for our coun-

[16] Spencer Walpole, *A History of England from the Conclusion of the Great War in 1815* (London, 1878-1886), II, 318-321.

try a calamity; at least so judged M. de Richelieu and, as we shall see, the negotiations which will be carried on at Laybach will endeavor to avoid the consequences of it."[17] But in the main France and Russia from now on were moving toward opposite poles, and this irreconcilability became even more pronounced in the case of England. Analyzing the policy of Castlereagh, the British historian Sir Archibald Alison writes:

> It was observed that the Character of England was unchanged and unchangeable, that self-interest was in every situation the ruling principle of her action. She was very conservative, and spared neither blood nor her treasure and was very urgent to get foreign governments to join her when the danger was at her own door and her own institutions threatened by the contagion of French principles, but she became very liberal and systematically stood aloof when other countries were threatened by a similar peril.[18]

Right or wrong, this view of England dominated Russian diplomacy from now on and led to the growth of rivalry and hostility between the two nations. The days when every good Englishman was a Russian and vice versa were definitely over. Also over was the great dream of a Europe united in the Grand Alliance promulgated by Alexander; it had received a death blow from which it never recovered. Viewed from this angle the subsequent Congress of Laybach becomes merely a postscript to the all-important happenings at Troppau.

It was at Troppau that Alexander received the news of the mutiny of the Guards Semenovsky Regiment. The issue in itself was unimportant, being merely the protest of the men against the harsh treatment inflicted upon them by their colonel. It was quickly settled and had no political implication, but thc mere fact that such a thing could happen in the highly disciplined Russian Guards was an ominous sign which Alexander interpreted as one more evidence of revolutionary danger.

Having recessed at Troppau, the Congress met again, as agreed, in January at Laybach. The Emperor of Austria arrived there on January 4, Alexander on the seventh, and King Ferdinand of Naples on the eighth. The King of Prussia was absent, having returned to

[17] *Op. cit.*, p. 414.

[18] Sir Archibald Alison, *Lives of Lord Castlereagh and Sir Charles Stewart, the Second and Third Marquesses of Londonderry* (Edinburgh, 1861), II, 146.

his capital, but in soul and spirit he was with the allies. Pozzo di Borgo, who had been called to Troppau in December, joined the Russian delegation and participated in its work. The French also added de Blacas to their staff. Otherwise the conference remained unchanged except for the representatives of various Italian states who had been invited to attend. We are not concerned here with the pitiful role played at the Congress by King Ferdinand. The important thing is that the Congress worked out the definite modalities of the Austrian intervention and set the machinery in motion. The British representatives, Sir Charles Stewart and his aide Gordon, alternated at the meetings but continued strictly in their role of observers. When Stewart discovered that the action against Naples was to be carried out in the name of the Allied sovereigns, he protested loudly and insisted that a statement should be inserted in the journal of the conference to the effect that "in spite of the presence of a British representative at the conferences which are being held at Laybach he is not authorized to associate himself directly in the 'procès-verbal' of the conferences, that the King his master has not judged it to be in accordance with the attitude in which he is placed towards the questions there treated to appoint a Plenipotentiary to these Conferences."[19] This and the increasingly violent outbursts in the British Parliament against the policies of the allies made the British position clear.

The French carried on their hesitant policy of following weakly in the footsteps of the British, thereby further alienating Alexander, and the efforts of Richelieu to win him back without changing France's course were of no avail. However, the Western Powers did not show sufficient energy to hinder in any way the action of Metternich, who was supported by Russia. On February 2 Austria, Prussia, and Russia signed an agreement pledging themselves not to recognize the government of Naples until the full restoration of royal authority as it had been before the revolution. Previously, on January 31, Nesselrode had issued a circular making the stand of Russia clear:

The revolution in Naples has given the world an example . . . of what nations gain when they attempt political reforms along the way of rebel-

[19] Charles Kingsley Webster, *The Foreign Policy of Castlereagh, 1815-1822, Britain and the European Alliance* (London, 1925), II, 316.

lion. This revolution has only produced anarchy and . . . has created a monstrous regime incapable of serving as the foundation for a government compatible with public order and the primary requirements of society. The Allied Sovereigns . . . decided immediately not to consider legal what the revolutionaries and usurpers have established in the Kingdom of Naples and this decision has been accepted by nearly all the governments of Europe.[20]

At the same time an ultimatum of the three powers was issued predicting the direst consequences if the revolutionaries refused to submit to the authority of the King, and on February 9 the Neapolitan Government was officially informed of the advance of the Austrian army of General Frimont, which would be supported by a Russian army if necessary. Following this the ministers of Russia, Prussia, and Austria left Naples.

But scarcely had these events taken place when a revolution broke out in Sardinia early in March. This new evidence of revolutionary agitation so impressed Alexander that he immediately offered an army of one hundred thousand men to move against Sardinia jointly with the Austrian forces, which would be diverted from the conquest of Naples. This offer was not wholly welcome to Metternich, as seen by his remark to the British delegate Gordon: "A hundred thousand Russians are eating up Italy, I am intensely sorry *(désolé)*, but still the cinders are better than the flame."[21] Alexander saw the main danger to be in France and warned La Ferronnays:

Maintain if it is necessary your strict neutrality but watch yourselves; watch carefully because it is in Paris, in the midst of you, that the dangerous center of these terrible and frequent revolutionary outbreaks is located. It is the directing committee [in Paris] which gives the signal for the revolutions in countries which have been carefully prepared by intrigues and agitation.[22]

In Paris, however, the news of Alexander's offer to move his army produced a reaction of fear lest the Russian armies, after subduing Sardinia, should invade France on their way to Spain. La Ferronnays was instructed to sound out the Czar in this respect, and Alexander promised formally to respect his treaty obligations to

[20] Nesselrode to Count Stackelberg, Russian minister in Naples (Alison, *op. cit.*, III, 145 n.).

[21] Webster, *The Foreign Policy of Castlereagh*, II, 329.

[22] Crousaz-Crétet, *op. cit.*, p. 441.

France. But the defeats inflicted by the Austrian armies both on Naples and on Sardinia were so crushing and so swift that there was no need for any Russian military moves.

Scarcely had the Italian issues been thus settled by force of arms when the news of Ypsilanti's incursion into Rumania and the beginning of the Greek Revolution reached Alexander. These events will be dealt with fully in Chapter XIII, but from the preceding pages it becomes evident why Alexander was so averse to supporting Ypsilanti, contrary to the latter's expectation.

On May 12 a joint declaration in the name of the three sovereigns was issued, elaborating and explaining the principles which had guided them during the Congress and reaffirming their decision never to depart from these principles; the following day the two emperors left Laybach, Alexander making his way home through Hungary and Galicia after an absence of eleven months. His constant meetings with Emperor Francis had produced a feeling of intimacy and friendship between the two sovereigns which delighted Metternich. To what extent in the mind of the Czar the cause of Russia and Austria were merged in the greater concept of a European alliance may be seen by a letter written by Prince Menshikov to Count Golovkin in Vienna. The Czar had granted a subsidy to the Austrian General Radetzky, later Field Marshal and the hero of the revolutionary wars of 1848 in Italy; Menshikov expressed the hope in the name of the Czar that Radetzky would not be hurt by this gift, for "His Majesty is interested in the fate of a general of an army which he considers to be, just like his own army, one of the divisions of the great army of the good cause."[23]

III

The decade following Waterloo saw Russia and Spain closely associated. Those two countries, so remote geographically but with destinies in some respects strikingly parallel, now saw their paths cross, and for a while Russian influence in Spain became preponderant. This development was already apparent in the year preceding the Napoleonic invasion of Russia, when it became obvious that Spain, in its desperate struggle against the French, was a natural ally of Russia, about to start her great fight with the same foe. Hence the unofficial agent of the Spanish insurrectionists in St.

[23] Schilder, *Imperator Aleksandr Pervyi,* IV, 250 n.

Petersburg, Zea Bermudez, not only was recognized by Russia but was instrumental in the signing of a treaty of amity between the two nations. However, it was in the period of the Holy Alliance that Spain began to loom as an increasingly important factor in the eyes of Alexander I in pursuance of his ideal of the Grand European Antirevolutionary Alliance, and this because Spain, at that time, became a pivotal point in the struggle between liberalism and conservatism, and therefore a diplomatic battlefield for England on one side and the conservative powers on the other. True, this great battle was being fought elsewhere, particularly in Italy, but Italy was Metternich's preserve; and, furthermore, from Spain the revolutionary movement radiated to Latin America as well. When Ferdinand VII was restored to the throne of Spain by the Treaty of Valençay (December 11, 1813), the Spanish colonies had already declared their independence and the question was rapidly becoming acute. Although Miranda had been well received at the court of Catherine II and showered with presents by the Empress when he came to Russia to advocate the cause of the independence of Spanish America, Alexander I was determined to help reinstate the dominion of Spain over her colonies in an effort to stem the tide of revolution, which he rightly feared would eventually reach Spain proper. Spain in turn looked to Russia for support when the Portuguese from Brazil invaded the Banda Oriental (the La Plata region) in 1816 and captured Montevideo the following year. This request for support came after Spain had turned down an English offer of mediation under terms Ferdinand was not prepared to accept.

Thus an obscure struggle, developing in far-off Uruguay, served to draw the lines in Europe between the two great powers pitted against each other in the name of opposing political principles. It was natural under these circumstances that the Russian minister to Madrid, Tatischtchev, anti-British by sentiment and upholding the principles of the Holy Alliance against liberalism, should have become *persona grata* not only with the King but with the Queen and the conservative circles known as the Camarilla. Tatischtchev was called the virtual foreign minister of Spain, and it was he who suggested the appeal to Russia in Spain's quarrel with Portugal. Alexander upheld Spain to the point of advocating a military expedition of the Holy Alliance powers into Portugal as punishment for her invasion of Montevideo. But as might be expected, England opposed the scheme, and Tatischtchev then proposed an official appeal to the Holy Alliance. At the same time the Spanish Government asked Russia to permit the use of Russian shipyards for building up the naval forces about to be used for the reconquest of colonies. Russia suggested instead the outright sale of some Russian warships to Spain. Negotiations were conducted secretly between Equia, the Spanish war minister, and Tatischtchev, and were concluded in July, 1817, without the knowledge of Pizarro, Minister of State, or Figueroa, Minister of Marine. Russia was to send to Spain five ships of the line and three frigates at a price of 54,400,000 pesetas (15,000,000 francs),[24] and the squadron left Russia in September of the same year. It was not until February, 1818, that the ships reached Cadiz, delayed partly by storms and partly by a long stay in England due to disagreements about the payment. By the time they reached Spain the ships were not in seaworthy condition, and Pizarro complained bitterly that their bottoms were worm-eaten and their sails torn.[25] Alexander, upon hearing about the condition of his vessels, suggested replacing the two ships of the line which were particularly damaged with three frigates, but King Ferdinand refused this offer and kept the ships.

At the same time, in March, 1817, Russia was negotiating for the cession by Spain of Port Mahon on the island of Minorca, to be converted into a Russian naval base. The importance of such a base in the Mediterranean was so obvious that when the news of these negotiations reached London it produced a great stir. Castlereagh approached Metternich with a view to drawing up the project of an alliance which would include Prussia as well and thus isolate Russia. It was possibly this development which induced Alexander to abandon the idea at the last moment even though a convention had already been signed with Spain to that effect.

This incident forms one of the most obscure pages in Russian diplomatic history. What was Alexander's motive in trying to secure Port Mahon? To some extent it was probably the continuation of Russia's Mediterranean policy, which in the previous decade had centered around the Russian base at Corfu. But Corfu, by its geo-

[24] *Cambridge Modern History*, X, 209.

[25] José García de Léon y Pizarro, *Memorias de la Vida del Excmo. Señor D. José García de Léon y Pizarro* (Madrid, 1894), III, 453.

graphical position, had a vital bearing on the Eastern Question and Turkey, whereas the Balearic Islands were too remote for such a purpose. On the other hand, located close to the coast of France, next to that of Spain, and in relative proximity to Gibraltar, Port Mahon offered an ideal base for direct pressure on Spain and was a menace both to France and to Britain. This move must be viewed therefore as a part of Alexander's policy, which put the interests of the European Alliance ahead of the Russian interests proper; as leader of this alliance Alexander was eager to secure an instrument of direct coercion against the liberal powers, which he was opposing all over the map of Europe. But Port Mahon was not worth the sacrifice of Russia's general position in Europe in the face of a threat of isolation, just as Corfu was not worth the loss of the advantages secured at Tilsit. The suggestion sometimes put forward that Alexander wanted this base to stamp out piracy in the Mediterranean may be dismissed as implausible.

It nevertheless remained true that there existed a discrepancy in Russia's diplomatic action at this juncture (1817), which exasperated Metternich intensely, in that whereas Russia was adamantly conservative in her action in Spain she was still liberal in France and in Germany. There may be several explanations for this: in the first place we are still in the period of transition in Alexander's policy from liberalism to conservatism, and there appeared still to be a struggle in his mind between the two opposing trends. Very soon this flux and hesitation were to give way to a uniformly conservative policy. Secondly, it appears that Tatischtchev, in Madrid, was carrying out a more determined and clear-cut policy than his master. Indeed, up to the time of the Congress of Aix-la-Chapelle the Czar showed hesitation in responding too readily to the Spanish appeals for aid, made at the instigation of his own ambassador. Lastly, there was the influence of Pozzo di Borgo in Paris, who was playing his own intricate game. In June, 1817, Pozzo wrote a memorandum advocating that Spain grant to her colonies local autonomy, some liberal concessions, and better administration if she wished to avoid seeing these colonies come under the domination of petty local despots. He further suggested, somewhat later, that Spain should abandon hope of regaining her colonies and devote her efforts to retaining those which still remained loyal to her by concentrating her forces in Mexico and Cuba. Probably at the instigation of Pozzo in July, 1817, Fernan Nuñez, the Spanish minister to France, presented a note to the Conference of Ambassadors in Paris concerning the relations of Spain and her colonies with Portugal, and suggesting indirectly that the matter should be taken up and settled by the conference. The conference split on the issue: the Russian and Austrian ambassadors supported the move, whereas Wellington acidly called the note a concoction of Pozzo di Borgo, Tatischtchev, and Fernan Nuñez;[26] and Sir Charles Stewart refused to act upon it. Castlereagh in his turn issued a memorandum in August suggesting a mediation of powers, with negotiations to be held in London, conditional on a more liberal policy on the part of Spain and a pledge of nonuse of force. This memorandum was warmly supported by Richelieu and Metternich, but Capo d'Istria, in his reply to a letter of Pozzo's, took the stand that Russia's policy was to bring Spain actively into the Holy Alliance, but without being forced to go so far as to send military aid to that country.[27]

Thus the question of mediation in Spanish affairs showed once more a disparity of views between the powers, and now it was Alexander's turn to offer his solution. On November 17 the Czar issued a memorandum on the colonial question and suggested that the colonies should be returned to Spain through the agency of the Grand European Alliance and that, barring the use of military force, an economic boycott should be applied to the colonies to coerce them back into the fold of the mother country.[28] The suggestion met with no response, Castlereagh declaring it "too vague for comprehension." Actually the reverse was true—it was too explicit in its suggestion of applying a method harmful to British trade interests in South America. As for Gentz, he declared it to be a "bad joke."

Thus the Spanish appeal to the powers for aid was getting nowhere. In the meanwhile the rebels in South America, particularly in Argentina, were making alarming headway; and although Spain was marshaling her forces to send them overseas, the condition of her army and finances was such as to make it necessary for her to try once more to obtain aid from the outside—the more so since the Con-

[26] Arthur Wellesley, First Duke of Wellington, *Supplementary Despatches and Memoranda of Field Marshal Arthur, Duke of Wellington, K. G.* (London, 1858-1872), XI (1864), 735; XII (1865), 3.

[27] *Sbornik*, CXIX, 359-392.

[28] *Ibid.*, CXIX, 474-482.

gress of Aix-la-Chapelle was about to meet. The Spanish ministers at the courts of Russia and France made simultaneous moves to obtain the accrediting of a Spanish representative to the forthcoming conference. Both courts replied affirmatively, but with the reservation that the other powers should consent. As might be expected, Castlereagh opposed his veto to the scheme, and the combined *démarches* in Paris of Richelieu, Pozzo, and Fernan Nuñez failed to move either Stewart or Wellington. Castlereagh saw in this move, once more, the intriguing hand of Tatistchtchev, and once more came out with a countersuggestion. He proposed that the Duke of Wellington should be appointed mediator in the name of the five powers and that the negotiations should be transferred to London. No force was to be used, and the colonies were to enjoy whatever trading advantages the mother country had. In substance it was the same suggestion as had been made previously by Castlereagh. Both France and Russia objected to this proposal, and counterproposals were put forth by both Richelieu and Capo d'Istria. Capo d'Istria suggested that Spain should be left to work out her own problems, even to the point of military intervention, but that the United States should be invited to send a representative to the conference table, for no mediation on this question could be complete without the presence of an American delegate. Castlereagh in turn declared this plan to be "unsatisfactory and objectionable";[29] once more the powers were getting nowhere in handling the Spanish question. Seeing this, after an audience granted to Castlereagh upon his arrival at the Congress, Alexander came around to the British plan and instructed Tatischtchev to co-operate with Wellesley, the British minister to Spain, in persuading the King to accept the Duke of Wellington's mediation. However, Ferdinand, hurt at the refusal to admit a Spanish envoy to the Congress, refused to accept the mediation, and this led in turn to the recall of Tatischtchev from Madrid (October, 1819). Thus once more, as much as Alexander was interested in Spain, he would not go to the point of endangering or disrupting the European alliance.

But three months later, on January 1, 1820, the long pent-up revolution broke out in Spain among the troops assembled on the island of León awaiting departure to South America, and the Con-

[29] Webster, *The Foreign Policy of Castlereagh,* II, 419-420.

stitution of 1812 was proclaimed in effect. The revolt spread rapidly to Ferrol, to Galicia, and finally reached Madrid in March, forcing the King to give his oath to the liberal constitution. A provisional junta took charge of affairs, pending the convening of a new Cortes. The revolutionary movement spread to Naples and Sicily in July, and to Portugal in August. Thus Spain came into the limelight as the fountainhead of a great movement against the legitimacy of the Holy Alliance powers. In the midst of these events Capo d'Istria wrote on July 27 to Richelieu concerning both the Spanish and the Neapolitan revolutions: "On one side we see a consoling prospect of a real fraternity between the states and the gradual perfecting of social institutions; on the other there appears the formidable empire of anarchy and revolutionary despotism."[30] Richelieu in reply advocated a conference on Spanish affairs, but the idea, as was to be expected, was immediately vetoed by both Austria and England. Richelieu, however, persisted in claiming that if France and Russia maintained a firm attitude the conference would be called. But it was not until the year 1822 that such a conference could be convened to deal with the Spanish question.

Indeed, in the meantime the situation in Spain had become so grave that it was urgent that something be done about it. The events in Spain proper completely overshadowed, as far as Russia was concerned, the question of the South American colonies. These virtually dropped out of the scheme of Russian diplomacy, but not until one curious move had been made to enlist Russia's support in one of the many plots which were being hatched at the time with the idea of establishing monarchies in South America. This particular one originated in Buenos Aires and was sponsored by France. It aimed at putting Prince Charles Luis Bourbon-Lucca on the throne of the Spanish colony of Buenos Aires. An agent sent from that city, Gomez, arrived in France in 1819 and won the support of Dessolle, Prime Minister in the interval between the two terms of Richelieu's administration. Dessolle sent an emissary, Hulot d'Osery, to St. Petersburg, whose task was not only to obtain the support of Russia for this candidature but also to induce Russia to put pressure on Ferdinand VII to consent to the idea. But Alexander refused, on the grounds that he did not want to be a party to anything harmful

[30] Martens, *op. cit.*, XIV, 4.

to Spain at this time. Thus the scheme fell through. In the meanwhile, by 1822, the Spanish colonies had virtually achieved their independence and Spain had lost the entire empire which provided her with her greatest resources; this caused increased financial distress, which in turn increased the revolutionary agitation in the country. Cadiz, Cartagena, and Seville acted as independent republics; and the Bourbon sympathizers set up their own government in the north. In Madrid the King was a virtual prisoner in his palace, and he wrote to Louis XVIII stating that his crown was in danger. Civil war, which was raging over the country, threatened to cross the border into France, where the agitation of the Carbonari likewise endangered the French throne; the French Government, alarmed, had set up the famous *cordon sanitaire* on its Spanish border, ostensibly to keep out yellow fever, but in reality to limit the spread of revolutionary contagion. The new French Prime Minister, Villèle, who succeeded Richelieu in December, 1821, was moderate and opposed to any military venture in Spain. Neither he nor his foreign minister, the Duc de Montmorency, had the confidence of Pozzo, and Villèle tried sincerely to win the friendship of Russia by instructing La Ferronnays to state in St. Petersburg that the new government would "follow the same principles of moderation and the same political course as the council presided over by the Duc de Richelieu, and therefore requested the Emperor to accord it the same confidence."[31] But a newcomer in diplomacy, the Vicomte de Chateaubriand, ambassador in London, had different views, and was most ardently advocating a war in Spain to crush the revolutionists—a view which met with increasing favor in Russia. It was under these circumstances that the Congress of Verona met to discuss the Spanish problem.

Alexander left his capital to attend the Congress on August 15, 1822, on what was to be his last trip to Western Europe. His mother, the dowager Empress Marie, worried by the leanings the Czar showed toward Catholicism, exacted a special pledge from him that while in Italy he would not visit Rome. How far this fear was justified—a fear due to the mystical and religious mood in which Alexander was at the time—it is difficult to say, but apparently there was a rumor of such a visit circulating in St. Petersburg. Indeed,

[31] *Ibid.*, XIV, 12.

the Count de Laskarene, Sardinian envoy in Russia, wrote confidentially to Charles Albert of Sardinia, "The tendency of the Emperor toward Catholicism was suspected in the Imperial family. The Empress Mother, fearing that an interview with the Holy Father might make her son decide to re-enter the bosom of the church, has insistently requested him not to go to Rome."[32] Stopping in Vienna on his way to the Congress, Alexander was greatly impressed by the abbot Prince Hohenlohe, who told him he had been selected as the instrument of Providence to give peace and quietude to the peoples of Europe. On the other hand he passed a whole evening conversing with the Quaker, Allen, who had come to Vienna specially for that purpose.

Alexander's stay in Vienna lasted three weeks, during which time he remained at the Hofburg and held a series of preliminary conferences with Emperor Francis and Metternich, preparatory to the meeting of the Congress, with the idea of establishing a common front. During these negotiations he pledged himself to renew diplomatic relations with Turkey, if Turkey were willing to give guarantees with regard to the Orthodox Christians and the future of the Greeks. After he had disposed of the Greek problem Alexander turned his attention to the Spanish situation, and declared himself willing to send an army to Spain if necessary, though only if the other powers were willing to support him. But he thought France, by her geographical position, was the logical power to intervene in Spain, and hence he was willing to leave the initiative to her.[33] Thus Alexander, with his religious ideology on the one hand and the removal of Capo d'Istria's influence on the other, had definitely turned his back on the selfish interests of Russia proper for the sake of the ideal of the pacification of Europe. He expressed his political philosophy in striking words in a conversation at Verona with Chateaubriand:

> There can be no more question of British, French, Russian, Prussian, Austrian policies; there is now only one general policy, which in the name of the salvation of all has to be accepted by peoples and kings alike. It is for me to show myself as supporting the principles upon which I founded the Alliance. An occasion offered itself in the Greek insurrection.

[32] Nicholas Mikhailovich, *op. cit.*, I, 268.

[33] K. Waliszewski, *Le Règne d'Alexandre Ier*, III, 97.

Nothing would have appeared to be more in the interests of my people, of the public opinion of my country, than a religious war against Turkey. But I detected in the troubles in the Peloponnesus the signs of revolution and immediately I abstained. . . . Providence did not place at my orders eight hundred thousand soldiers to satisfy my own ambitions, but for the purpose of protecting religion, morality, and justice and to establish the principles of order upon which rests human society.[34]

It was in this state of mind that Alexander arrived in Verona on October 16 and took up his residence in the magnificent castle of the Marchese de Canossa. He found waiting for him Emperor Francis, King Friedrich Wilhelm of Prussia, the former Empress Marie Louise (now Duchess of Parma), the Grand Duke of Tuscany, the Duke of Modena, the kings of Naples and Sardinia. In the diplomatic delegations were: for Austria, Metternich, Gentz, and the Austrian ambassadors in London, St. Petersburg, and Berlin; for England, the Duke of Wellington, the Marquis of Londonderry, brother of the late Castlereagh, and others; for France, the Duc de Montmorency and the French ambassadors in Vienna, St. Petersburg, Berlin, and London, the latter being Chateaubriand. In the suite of Alexander and forming the Russian delegation were the generals Prince Volkonsky and Prince Menshikov, Chief of the General Staff, with Nesselrode, and the ambassadors to London and Paris, Lieven and Pozzo di Borgo.

Of these various personalities the most colorful and to some extent the most influential in shaping the course of events was the Vicomte de Chateaubriand, who had arrived in Verona preceded by his tremendous literary reputation. His affiliations with Russia were important and dated some time back. He was well known in Russia, where his romantic novels were extremely popular. He had been for a number of years in literary correspondence with Empress Elizabeth, the wife of Alexander, and she had defrayed the expenses of his famous voyage to Jerusalem which resulted in the publication of his *Itinéraire à Jerusalem*. He had more than once expressed his desire, in moments of discouragement, to retire and finish his days in Russia. In coming to Verona, Chateaubriand knew exactly what he wanted: he wanted to involve France in a war with Spain in order

[34] Vicomte François René de Chateaubriand, *Le Congrès de Vérone, Oeuvres complètes* (Paris, 1861), X, 114-115.

to stamp out the revolution which he as a Royalist deemed dangerous to his country, and above all he hoped that victory would give France the military prestige lost at Waterloo and would consolidate the French throne. Thus his views were in accordance with Alexander's, at least to a certain extent, and somewhat fatuously he wrote about his meeting with the Czar, "We had seen each other only a quarter of an hour when we liked each other."

The Congress of Verona was the most brilliant international meeting since Vienna; and, like the Congress of Vienna, it was accompanied by a round of festivities and an unending social whirl. In this atmosphere women were destined to play an important part in behind-the-stage intrigues. The Russian delegation had three ladies who were prominent in these intrigues. These were the Princess Zenaïde Volkonsky, whose social graces attracted a wide circle of admirers, and, even better known, Countess Lieven and Countess Tolstoy. Countess Lieven, the wife of the ambassador to London, had already played a prominent part at Aix-la-Chapelle. Apparently she did not get along well with Chateaubriand, for he gives a very unfavorable and unfair picture of her. "Madame de Lieven, with a sharp and unattractive face, is a common woman, tiresome and dry, who has only one type of conversation—vulgar politics; besides, she knows nothing and hides her paucity of ideas under an abundance of words."[35]

Countess Tolstoy, the widow of the Grand Marshal of the Court, had lived in Paris and was the go-between for Chateaubriand and the Empress, sending unofficial reports on French politics which Alexander read assiduously. Her salon was frequented by the extreme monarchists belonging to the "Ultras," and, through her recent marriage to a Frenchman, de Vernegues, former French monarchist and agent in Russia, her influence on French political circles was considerable. Waliszewski considered it not improbable that she arranged, with the support of Pozzo, the appointment of Chateaubriand to Verona.[36]

The Congress of Verona discussed five outstanding issues: piracy in the Central American waters, treatment of the Negroes, Italian affairs, relations between Russia and Turkey, and, finally, the Spanish

[35] Vicomte François René de Chateaubriand, *Mémoires d'outre tombe* (Paris, n.d.), IV, 249.

[36] Waliszewski, *Le Règne d'Alexandre Ier*, III, 103.

question. In addition the questions of the navigation of the Rhine, of the regency of Urgel, and of the affairs of Greece were touched upon. Of all these questions Russia was interested only in the Turkish, Greek, and Spanish issues. The Greek delegation, at the instigation of Metternich, was not admitted to the Congress; and the Turkish question was taken up in a special committee composed of the British, Prussian, Russian, and Austrian delegates, with the Marquis de Caraman as French observer. The very fact that Russia participated in such a committee was a great concession on her part, but few results, if any, were achieved. Similarly, the affairs of Italy were discussed in a second special committee composed of delegations from the Italian states. In the question of piracy, Russia declared that she could not take any decision which would force her to make up her mind in regard to the independence of the Latin American states. Thus, by a process of exclusion, we come to the one issue which was important for Russia and which was discussed by the general Congress, and that is the question of Spain.

The issue was raised officially by a communication of the Duc de Montmorency in the meeting of September 20 when he asked for a clarification of the position of the powers in the following instances: (1) If France were obliged to recall her ambassador from Spain, would the four powers follow suit? (2) In the event of a war between France and Spain, would the powers give France moral support? (3) In the event that circumstances made necessary the intervention of all the powers, what aid would they offer to France? Austria and Prussia replied that any effective aid, aside from moral support, would necessitate the convocation of a new congress. "Prince Metternich, pretending to be pro-Russian, while detesting Russia, talked about the war without wanting it. . . . Jealous of Russia and a friend of England, the Vienna cabinet considered it a courteous way of giving a negative reply."[37] Russia, "more loyal and daring," replied with a categorical affirmative to the three questions: She would recall her ambassador and would give to France all material and moral aid without any restrictions or conditions of any kind. England, for her part, refused to countenance any intervention in the affairs of Spain and reserved her rights. The Duke of Wellington refused to sign the minutes of the meetings of October 20 and

[37] Chateaubriand, *Le Congrès de Vérone, Oeuvres complètes,* X, 57.

November 17, the latter being the meeting in which the powers gave their reply. Thus there was once more a clear-cut break between the stand taken by England on one side and France and Russia on the other, with Austria and Prussia hesitating. The conference was deadlocked, and to cover up the impasse a solution was found in the sending of notes to the respective ambassadors in Madrid, to be forwarded to the Spanish Government, expressing the fears and regrets of the powers at the course of events in Spain. Should the Spanish Government reject these notes, the ambassadors would be free to demand their passports. Prussia and Austria sent their notes on November 22. The Russian note was sent to Bulgary, who had replaced Tatischtchev, four days later on November 26. It merely expressed the fear that the situation in Spain would lead to grave complications between France and Spain which Russia was anxious to avoid, and insisted that the desire to see a sane administration in Spain did not constitute on the part of Russia any wish to intervene in Spain or to interfere with her independence.

England abstained from sending any note. Upon this the conference adjourned; the notes sent to Spain were a diplomatic verbiage of no import used merely to camouflage the impossibility of establishing a common front of action. Viewed from this angle, the Congress was a complete failure. But it gave France the unconditional support of Russia for the coming invasion of Spain and the tacit acquiescence of Prussia and Austria. Writing to Metternich from Pilsen on January 4, 1823, on his way home, Alexander stated:

> The alliance is in full power. The union of the three monarchs which forms its base was never closer. . . . Thus the means which the alliance has at its disposal are immense and the question is merely to keep them ready and to use them at the right time and in the proper instance. . . . Returning home I will busy myself assiduously getting everything ready to come to the aid of the alliance at the opportune moment.[38]

This zeal of Alexander for the cause was embarrassing to France. In the same letter to Metternich, Alexander complained bitterly about the "weak and uncertain course of France and the lack of sincerity of England." Indeed, in Paris the council was divided: Villèle stood for peace, Montmorency was hesitant, and Chateaubriand was for action. Pozzo was instructed to put pressure on

[38] Schilder, *Imperator Aleksandr Pervyi,* IV, 551-552.

Villèle, and in a secret meeting with him in December insisted that France should follow the course suggested at Verona and send an expedition to Spain. Giving in finally, Villèle declared that he must have a pretext for the war through recall of ambassadors from Madrid. He denied any intention on the part of France to leave the alliance and added, "I know where France can find a sincere ally, and of all the powers in Europe, Russia alone is placed by us in this category."[39] Accordingly, in January, under the pretext that Spain had given no satisfactory reply to the collective notes of Verona, the allied ambassadors were recalled from Madrid.

In the meanwhile the resignation of the Duc de Montmorency brought the appointment of Chateaubriand to the Ministry of Foreign Affairs (January 1, 1823). Immediately the new minister proceeded diligently to prepare the campaign, but once more Alexander embarrassed him by his excessive zeal. Chateaubriand, who wanted this war to be a purely French affair, was alarmed when the Czar offered the formation of a reserve Russian army in Poland sixty thousand strong, to be placed at the disposal of France and to be used for the alliance, which army was to be called the Army of the Alliance. "It is difficult for us," wrote Chateaubriand, "to say that we accept your services as long as they are reduced to words, but the moment they are converted into action we do not want them any more."[40] But when England showed signs of attempting to block the French plans, Alexander took an adamant stand and declared that if England attacked France during the war, Russia would consider this a declaration of war against the allies and would act in accordance. "This strong language helped to restrain Mr. Canning."[41]

Similarly, Alexander blocked a complicated intrigue of Metternich, as much directed against France as motivated by jealousy of Russia. Austria suggested that King Ferdinand of Naples, as relative and heir to Ferdinand VII, should be made regent of Spain; and he persuaded the Neapolitan Government to ask that the commander in chief of the French army operating in Spain, the Duc d'Angoulême, should accordingly be placed under the orders of the Neapolitan Prince of Castel-Cicala; the latter, as representative of the King of Naples, was to proceed to the French headquarters. Russia

[39] Pozzo di Borgo's report, dated December 31, 1822 (Martens, *op. cit.*, XIV, 16).
[40] Chateaubriand, *La Guerre d'Espagne, Oeuvres complètes*, X, 195.
[41] *Ibid.*

sharply warned the King of Naples to remain in his own kingdom and to attend to the business of governing it, and nothing more was heard of the scheme. Thus by his energetic diplomacy, if not by the military measures which Chateaubriand feared, Alexander very effectively aided the French cause.

The French Army entered Spain on April 7, 1823, and by August 31 the campaign came to an end with the capture of Trocadéro. In October the Cortes restored the King to his rights, and Ferdinand returned to Madrid in triumph. In November, 1824, Alexander rewarded Chateaubriand with the highest Russian decoration, the Grand Cross of St. Andrew, and pointedly avoided giving one to Villèle. It was only after Chateaubriand, through the French ambassador in Russia, asked for the same distinction for his chief that the latter received it. Well might Alexander be pleased: he had achieved, through the agency of France, what he wanted in Spain.

There still remained the colonial question. At the instigation of Pozzo two secret conferences were called in Paris in October, 1823, between the allied ambassadors and Chateaubriand, and again in the summer of 1824, but nothing came of them except much gratuitous advice to Spain to put her house in order, to grant free trade to the colonies as a bait to England (which Spain did in December, 1823), and even to attempt to reconquer the colonies, starting with Mexico. A suggestion to call a conference on the Latin American situation was turned down by Canning, and Alexander for his part told La Ferronnays that he was much too busy with Greece to worry about the Spanish colonies.

The Spanish issue was the last important issue in which Alexander was involved in the field of international politics. With only two years to live, tired and disillusioned, more and more the prey of pietism and mysticism, Alexander longed for peace. Hence his attention from now on was given only to matters directly pertaining to Russia, and in the interest of avoiding war. Of these, the most important and the most menacing was to be the situation in Turkey with regard to Greece and the Principalities. Thus Russian diplomacy was now to be concentrated almost entirely on the Near Eastern question.

Chapter XIII

The Eastern Question

I

In the first half of the nineteenth century Russia's action and interests in the Balkans centered upon Serbia and Rumania, just as in the latter half of the century they were to be focused upon Bulgaria. The reason for this was that Serbia and the Danubian Principalities were the first to raise the standard of rebellion against Turkish domination, and Russia encouraged the tide of nationalism in those provinces of Turkey merely as a part of the pattern of the great struggle between Russia and Turkey for the domination of the Black Sea, Constantinople, and the Straits. Also, with Slavonic Serbia there were ties of blood, religion, and language, while the non-Slav Rumanians were Russia's immediate Balkan neighbors and were linked to her through the community of religion and certain cultural factors, such as the use at that time by the Rumanians of the common Cyrillic alphabet. There was of course also Greece, but, though Russia played a powerful role in her destiny, Greece by her geographical and maritime position was subject to the influence of such western countries as France and Britain, and therefore could not become the virtually exclusive preserve of Russia, as the other two countries were to become for a quarter of a century. During the Napoleonic period we have seen that the Danubian Principalities, and to a lesser extent Serbia, had been important figures in the great game of chess played by Napoleon and Alexander I. To understand the subsequent developments of Russia's policy in these regions it is necessary to review once more the main developments during the momentous first fifteen years of the nineteenth century, but this time from the point of view of the effect of Russia's policies on the Rumanian and Serbian people on the one hand, and on Russo-Turkish relations on the other; in other words, to narrow the problem down to the Eastern question alone, as outside the wider field of general European diplomacy.

Russia first acquired the right to interefere in Turkish affairs on behalf of the Balkan Christians by the Treaty of Kuchuk Kainardji, imposed upon Turkey in 1774 by Catherine the Great after victory in her first Russo-Turkish War. By Article VII of this treaty Russia was "permitted" to protect the Christian religion in Turkey, and Turkey pledged that henceforth the Christians would not be persecuted. This somewhat vague clause was the basis for all further Russian action in the Balkans and most particularly in the Danubian Principalities. Russia further received permission to have a permanent embassy in Constantinople and to establish consulates wherever she saw fit. She also obtained for Russian subjects the right of navigation and free trade on the Black Sea and the Danube and within the territory of the Turkish Empire, on the basis of the most-favored-nation clause. Lastly, the Russian troops which had occupied the Danubian Principalities were to restore them to Turkish authority conditional on better administration and the granting to the people of certain privileges in matters of taxation, religious freedom, and representation. The treaty was sufficiently vague to permit a very wide margin of interpretation of its clauses, and as Thugut, the Austrian statesman, said, it was "a model of cleverness *(habileté)* on the part of Russian diplomats and a rare example of imbecility on the part of the Turkish negotiators."[1]

When in 1798 Russia joined the anti-French coalition and found herself the ally of Turkey, a force of ten thousand Russian troops under General Hermann reoccupied Moldavia, preparatory to an advance into Albania in conjunction with Suvorov's march into Italy; but this operation never materialized, and the troops were withdrawn. Three years later, in 1802, the bands of Pasvanoglou, the famous Pasha of Vidin, which had been operating in Serbia, crossed into Wallachia and by their depredations forced many Rumanians to flee into Transylvania. Russia intervened and reminded Turkey of her rights under the Treaty of Kuchuk Kainardji. This intervention resulted in the appointment of Prince Constantine Ypsilanti, a client of Russia, as Hospodar of Wallachia, and of Prince Muruzi as Hos-

[1] Sir John Arthur Ransome Marriott, *The Eastern Question: An Historical Study in European Diplomacy* (Oxford, 1918), p. 153.

podar of Moldavia. The Russian consul in Yassy, Bolkunov, drew up a list of complaints against the abuses of the former hospodars and of the Turkish authorities, and Turkey confirmed the privileges conferred by the treaty of 1774. However, Russia demanded and obtained the addition of some new clauses, making more concrete her right to intercede on behalf of the Rumanians: thus the Hospodars would be elected for seven years and could be deposed only if charges against them were endorsed by the Russian ambassador in Constantinople. During their administration the hospodars were "to take into consideration" the representations of the Russian consular agents; the Rumanian boyars (nobles) were to have a voice in fixing the expenditures, as well as in administering the funds for cultural purposes such as establishing and maintaining hospitals, schools, etc.; the taxes were to remain as of the year 1783; and the owners of estates whose lands had been confiscated for military purposes by the Turks were to have their lands restored to them. These demands were drawn up by the Rumanian boyars themselves and Russia merely endorsed them.

Of the two hospodars, Ypsilanti remained a faithful friend to Russia and supported Karageorg's revolt in Serbia, whereas Muruzi turned pro-French, thereby incurring the hostility of the Government of St. Petersburg. But when the French ambassador in Constantinople urged the Porte in 1806 to depose both hospodars as nominees of Russia, Russia protested this measure as a direct attack "on the dignity, interests, and rights of Russia" and threatened Turkey with war.[2] A powerful Russian army had been assembled around Odessa in preparation for a possible French invasion of Morea. As for England, she put pressure on Turkey, and, on October 17, the Porte announced the re-establishment of the deposed hospodars. But six days later Russia sent an ultimatum to Turkey announcing that on October 16 General Michelson had been ordered to occupy the Principalities as a precautionary measure, and stipulated that the army would be withdrawn only upon Turkey's guaranteeing the maintenance of law and order along the Russian border. In addition Russia demanded the free passage of the Straits for Russian vessels, as agreed in the treaty of 1805, as well as the renewal of the Anglo-Turkish Treaty. In reply Turkey declared war upon Russia. This

[2] Nicolai Iorga, *Histoire des relations russo-roumaines* (Jassy, 1917), p. 226.

war, with its inconclusive hostilities, lasted until 1812, and was fought on Rumanian soil. General Michelson conquered Moldavia while Admiral Seniavin was taking possession of the islands of the Archipelago, and the Porte was informed by the Russian commander in chief that Russia was willing to evacuate the Principalities if the Porte would abide by the former treaties, renew the British Alliance, and ask General Sebastiani, the French ambassador, to leave Constantinople.

But with the signing of the Treaty of Tilsit, Michelson received the order to negotiate an armistice with the Turks and to prepare for the withdrawal of Russian troops from the Principalities. The negotiations between the Russian delegate Lashkarev and Said Mehmed Effendi took place at Slobodzie, with the French Commandant Guilleminot acting as mediator. The armistice was duly signed in August, 1807. According to its terms both parties were to withdraw troops from Moldavia within thirty-five days. In addition, Russia was to return to Turkey the island of Tenedos, as well as the ships captured by Seniavin. But the armistice convention was not ratified by the Czar. Peace negotiations were again opened at Yassy and continued for two years, but without much result, for the Turks, spurred on by Austria, adopted dilatory tactics. Michelson, whose death had occurred in the meanwhile, was replaced by Prince Prozorovsky, and the latter in turn by General Kamensky, as commander in chief of the Russian forces in Moldavia and Wallachia. In 1809, in view of the cooling relations between France and Russia, the Turks were encouraged to break off the negotiations and redeclare war. Russia's demand for the possession of Moldavia and Wallachia had met with the open refusal of Austria—a refusal instigated by France; and Russia now reduced her conditions of peace, this time demanding Moldavia alone. Negotiations were renewed in Bucharest between Italinsky, the Russian ambassador in Contantinople, and Hamid Effendi, the Turkish negotiator, who, encouraged by French and Austrian support, remained adamant. When, however, the Turks sustained a crushing reverse at the hands of General Markov, they offered Bessarabia alone, in November, 1811; but the Russians under their new commander in chief, General Kutuzov, pressed on, and on December 14 Kutuzov made a triumphant entry into Bucharest, with church bells ringing in welcome. In February hostilities flared up anew, but the threat of war with Napoleon reduced the Russian effectives in Moldavia, and Alexander reduced his demands once more, specifying only Bessarabia and the delta of the Danube, which the Turks had insisted upon keeping.

We have already seen the diplomatic negotiations which were going on behind the scenes during the months preceding the invasion by Napoleon, and how the sending of Admiral Chichagov to Moldavia helped to influence the attitude of Austria. With the danger of the Napoleonic invasion becoming more and more imminent, Kutuzov was instructed to speed up the negotiations with Turkey, and, acting on his own initiative, he finally signed the preliminaries of peace on May 28, 1812, along the lines of the Turkish offers made in November. Peace was finally concluded at Bucharest in July. By the Treaty of Bucharest all previous treaties concerning the status of the Rumanians were confirmed, but Bessarabia and the delta of the Danube were transferred to Russia. The boundaries were "henceforth to be the Pruth to its entrance into the Danube, and from that point, the left bank of the Danube down to its entrance into the Black Sea by the Kilia mouth."[3] Thus the Pruth became for the Rumanians "the accursed river," and the thorny Bessarabian question came into existence.

However, the Russian Government catered to the Moldavian majority in the newly acquired province by the appointment of Rumanians to administrative offices. The first governor was Scarlati-Stourdza, and other members of the Rumanian nobility, Ghica and Stourdza-Varnav, were put in charge of districts. In 1818 Alexander granted a constitution to Bessarabia, written in Russian and Rumanian and based on the ancient usages and customs of Moldavia. The church services and all judiciary and legislative acts, as well as private transactions and civil suits, were to be conducted in the Rumanian language. Thus Russia attempted to protect the interests of the Rumanians and acknowledged their nationality; but, by a curious contradiction, the foreign office in St. Petersburg used Greeks in Russian service as consuls and diplomatic agents in the Principalities. Pini and Pisani were appointed to Yassy and Bucharest, and were succeeded by Minciaky. Similarly, following Stourdza, a Greek, Katakatzi, was made Governor of Bessarabia. Most of these officials

[3] Marriott, *op. cit.*, p. 189.

were either members of, or in sympathy with, the Greek secret society known as the "Hetairia," and were working to further the cause of the revival of Greece. Thus a conflict of interests between Greeks and Rumanians was bound to develop, and very soon it came to a head with dramatic consequences.

II

Scarcely had Alexander arrived at the Congress of Laybach when he received the unwelcome news of Prince Ypsilanti's incursion into Rumania, which was the first overt act of rebellion against Turkey in the coming Greek revolution. Metternich immediately used this incident to discredit Capo d'Istria in the eyes of the Czar; and, indeed, nothing could have been more contrary to the mood of the Czar at that time than this outbreak of a revolution in the Balkans with such great inflammatory possibilities. Hence Alexander immediately instructed Baron Stroganov, his ambassador in Constantinople, to inform the Porte that the policy of Russia was directed against any attempts "violating the internal peace of any country," and that his only desire was to maintain a strict fulfilment of the existing treaties between the two countries. At the same time Prince Wittgenstein, the Commander in Chief of the Second Army, was ordered to maintain the strictest neutrality along the border of Moldavia.[4]

But these measures could not offset the fact that Russia was incurring a heavy responsibility by permitting the Greek revolutionary societies to be organized on her territory. Indeed, two Greek societies contributed to the uprising of their countrymen: the Philomuse Society, founded at Athens in 1812; and the Philike Hetairia, first organized in Odessa in 1814. Although the first was a kind of literary and intellectual club, the Philike Hetairia was a political organization, and as such actually organized and directed the general movement. The large Greek colony in Odessa, composed of bankers, merchants, and priests, some of them refugees from Constantinople, was a breeding place for ideas of Greek liberty and nationalism, and the center of the struggle of the Greek Orthodox Church against the secular oppression of the Moslems. The men who founded the Society were imbued with definite ideas that Turkey was on the point of dissolution and that Russia would come into possession of Constantinople. Hence, in the event of a rebellion of the Greeks,

[4] Schilder, *Imperator Aleksandr Pervyi*, IV, 198.

Russia's assistance would be certain, and rumors were assiduously spread that the Society enjoyed the secret protection of the Czar. The Society was patterned after the Carbonari and was divided into seven classes, ranging from the "Vlamides," or brethren, to the "Chiefs of the Initiated" and the secret "Supreme Authority." Money poured into the organization, for the Greek merchants in Odessa were very wealthy, and the numerous officers of Greek extraction serving in the Russian Army offered their enthusiasm and their belief in direct action. The organization spread over the whole of Turkey wherever there were Greek colonies, yet the Turkish Government seems to have been unaware of its activities. The Russian secret police discovered its existence in 1818.[5] Up to 1820 the Hetairia merely organized itself and did missionary work, its "apostles" going all over the Greek world fanning discontent; as in all revolutions, the Greek Revolution was the outcome of a complex set of intellectual, political, social, and economic factors, and the Hetairists did their best to exploit these for their own ends.

The question of a supreme leader for the movement was of paramount importance. The supreme direction of the Hetairia was offered to Capo d'Istria, but for obvious political and diplomatic reasons he found it prudent to refuse. The next offer went to Prince Alexander Ypsilanti (or Hypsilantes), eldest son of the Hospodar of Wallachia, whose deposition in 1806 brought on the war between Russia and Turkey. A major-general in the Russian Army and an aide-de-camp to the Emperor, Ypsilanti was well qualified by his social position for such a task. He not only immediately accepted the offer, but assumed dictatorial control of the whole movement. An event not directly concerned with Russian history gave him the opportunity of striking at once—the rebellion of the powerful Ali Pasha of Jannina, who was wresting the Epirus from Turkish rule and promising independence to the Greeks.

While the Turkish Army under the energetic Khurshid Pasha struck at Ali and succeeded in defeating him in Jannina after severe fighting, Ypsilanti swung into action. On March 6, 1821, he crossed the Pruth and invaded Moldavia. The reigning hospodar, Michael Soutzos, and the leading officials, themselves members of the Hetairia, gave him full support and placed the military and financial

[5] George Finlay, *History of the Greek Revolution* (London, 1861), I, 120-121.

resources of the Principality at his disposal. In a proclamation to the people of Moldavia Ypsilanti stated that Russia was behind the insurrection and would come to his assistance. But the insurrection did not produce the expected results—Russia, it soon became known, was holding aloof, and this demoralized the rebellion; Ypsilanti lost valuable time at Yassy and reached Bucharest only on April 9, thus giving time for the Turkish resistance to be organized; but above all, the Moldavians and Wallachs did not support the movement, for they felt no sympathy for the Greeks who had ruled them for a century as agents of Turkish despotism.

Hence a parallel national Rumanian movement developed under the leadership of a minor Rumanian boyar, Todor Vladimirescu. A former lieutenant colonel in the Russian Army, Vladimirescu had been decorated with the Russian Cross of St. Vladimir, from which he derived his name. He hated Turks and Greeks alike and started an insurrection of his own in Little Wallachia. At first the ally of the Hetairists, he soon turned against Ypsilanti and issued to the Rumanian people a proclamation imbued with an ardent spirit of nationalism. When the decision of Czar Alexander reprobating Ypsilanti was made official in Bucharest and Yassy, and when this was followed by the assassination of Vladimirescu by order of Ypsilanti, the latter's prestige collapsed completely. His disorganized forces became the easy prey of the Turks, and there was nothing left for him to do but cross the Austrian border, where by order of Metternich he was interned in Munkacz until 1827. Released, he died the following year. After some fighting in which the remnants of Ypsilanti's force defended themselves with desperate bravery, Turkish authority was re-established in the Principalities. However, Ypsilanti's adventure in Rumania was the beginning of the nationalist movement there, thanks to Vladimirescu, and touched off a revolution in Greece which was to lead to important historical developments. As such it deeply involved Russian interests in both the Danubian region and in Greece, and was therefore to become an important historical event.

The reoccupation of the Principalities by the Turks led to a new protest to Turkey by Russia, followed by a recall of the Russian ambassador and consuls. The Moldavian and Wallachian boyars presented an appeal to Russia to deliver them once more from the

Turkish yoke, and a movement was started among the Rumanian refugees in Transylvania and Bukovina to work out a national constitution for the Principalities. A delegation of sixteen members arrived in St. Petersburg from Bucharest asking for a reorganization of Wallachia and the appointment of native hospodars. The Porte yielded, and by the firman of the following year two Rumanians, Gregory Ghica and Jonitza Stourdza, were appointed hospodars for Moldavia and Wallachia respectively. In the meanwhile the Rumanian refugees returning from exile started to agitate against the two hospodars, and worked out a new constitution creating a hereditary dynasty which would take the power from the boyars. This constitution was vetoed by Russia; however, it showed that the Rumanian nationalist movement was gaining such strength that some further reforms would have to be granted. Accordingly, the new Russian consul-general in Bucharest, Minciaky, who was appointed in 1822, went to Constantinople in 1825 to discuss the Rumanian problem. He obtained the evacuation of the Principalities by the Turkish forces and canceled the vexatious measures introduced as a result of the Ypsilanti rebellion. By 1826 the left bank of the Danube was once more devoid of Turkish soldiers.

However, under the energetic impulse of Nicholas I the Russian attitude toward Turkey on all the outstanding problems, including the Greek, Serbian, and Rumanian questions, became so threatening that in June Turkey consented to send delegates to a conference at Akkerman in Bessarabia. This conference, at which the Russian delegates were Counts Vorontsov and Ribeaupierre, opened in August; and on October 7 the Convention of Akkerman was signed, eliminating the danger of war. The Turks under this convention confirmed all privileges previously granted, as well as the *Hatti Sherif* of 1802. The hospodars were to be elected by the divans and the boyars for a period of seven years, with the consent of Russia in the choice of the candidates. Similarly, dismissals and abdications of the hospodars could become effective only by joint permission of Russia and Turkey. In addition, the hospodars were to take into consideration the representations of the Russian ministers and consuls on the subject of privileges enjoyed by the Principalities;[6] among

[6] William Miller, *The Balkans: Roumania, Bulgaria, Servia and Montenegro* (London, 1923), pp. 91-92.

the new privileges granted were to be the restitution of territories under Turkish occupation, the exemption from taxes for two years, and the establishment of free trade.[7] Thus Russian diplomacy had supported the Rumanian national aspirations; and in fact it was said that this conference had given the Rumanian people more than they would have obtained by a victorious war. Summing up the results, we may say that the rule of the Phanariots definitely came to an end, and the Rumanians were to become masters of their own destiny under the protectorate of Russia. However, an oligarchy of boyars had been established, and in Moldavia special privileges in matters of taxation were granted to them by a "Golden Bull." This led to agitation for a constitution which started with renewed vigor, even though peace and order had been re-established. But when the Russian ambassador Ribeaupierre passed through Yassy and Bucharest on his way from Akkerman back to Constantinople, "ambitions knelt very humbly at the feet of his influence."[8] The decisions at Akkerman, however, produced merely a temporary lull, and two years later the long-delayed Russo-Turkish War broke out, leading to the sixth invasion of Rumanian soil by the Russian armies. But it was not so much the events in Rumania as those which were developing in Greece which were the cause of the war. Yet if we consider that the Greek Revolution was set off by the Ypsilanti rebellion in Rumania, it becomes evident how closely interlocked were the destinies of the Balkan nations. This is vividly illustrated by the similarity in the pattern of events in Serbia to those in Rumania, though Serbia gained autonomy earlier and the Russian influence there was less pronounced.

III

At the turn of the century, although Serbia was garrisoned by the fierce Janizaries, the Turkish governor, Pasha Hadju Mustapha, governed the province wisely and benignly and was popular with the Christian raia. The reforms of Sultan Selim III aroused the Janizaries to rebellion, and the latter occupied Belgrade jointly with the celebrated brigand Pasvanoglu. Killing Hadji Mustapha, they divided Serbia among their four *dahis*, or chiefs, and proceeded to massacre the Christian population (1804). The survivors among the Serbs armed themselves and found a leader, the son of a peasant

[7] Iorga, *op. cit.*, p. 207.

[8] *Ibid.*, p. 269.

known as Karageorg (Black George); the latter, after assembling a considerable armed force, joined with the neighboring Pasha of Bosnia, who had been instructed to crush the rebellion of the Janizaries. Belgrade was retaken by the combined forces, and the leader of the Janizaries was killed. Although the Serbs at the start of the fighting had been in support of the Turkish Government, during the struggle the idea of emancipation from Turkish rule began to gain ground, and Karageorg sent a delegation to St. Petersburg to ask for the support of Russia. Encouraged by the promise of the Czar to take up their cause in Constantinople, the Serbs demanded that the Turks evacuate their fortresses within Serbia; this demand led to a war with Turkey, which coincided with the war which Russia had declared upon Turkey in 1806. Karageorg established communications with the Russian headquarters, and a Russian force was sent to Serbia to co-operate with the Serbian insurrectionists. This combined force defeated the Turkish Army at Shtoubik in 1807, but, with the Treaty of Tilsit and the subsequent armistice in the Balkans, the Russians withdrew and left the Serbs to fight on alone.

In the meanwhile Karageorg had organized a Serbian government, creating a Soviet of twelve senators and a national assembly, the Skuptchina. With the resumption of hostilities between Russia and Turkey, once more the Serbs joined the Russians. A Serbian division under Milenko Stoykovich advanced down the Danube and, capturing Brza-Palanka, established contact with the Russians across the river. But the Russians were slow to move, and a Serbian division was crushed by the main Turkish army near Kamenitza on May 19, 1809. The subsequent Russian invasion of Bulgaria relieved the pressure on the Serbs, who counterattacked, and by the end of the year had regained all the territory they had lost.[9] During the following year Karageorg complained bitterly of the desultory support he was receiving from the Russians, and began looking toward Austria for support. It will be remembered that the Moldavian campaign was conducted without much vigor by Field Marshal Kamensky, even though he had issued a proclamation calling on the Serbs to unite with the Russians in the name of their common faith, blood, and tongue. The truth was that Russia at the time had merely an

[9] Prince Stephan Lazar Eugene Lazarovich-Hrebelianovich, *The Servian People, Their Past Glory and Their Destiny* (New York, 1910), II, 651.

academic interest in the fate of Serbia; it will be recalled that, during the negotiations in St. Petersburg over Napoleon's scheme for the partition of Turkey, Russia was willing to give Serbia to Austria. Thus, at this early period, we see appearing a constant source of potential trouble in the Balkans—the swinging of Serbia alternately between Austrian and Russian influences.

In the meanwhile, responding to Kamensky's appeal, the Serbs once more joined forces with the Russians, and they captured Negotin and Brza-Palanka and for the second time laid siege to Kladovo. A Turkish army thirty thousand strong under Kroushid Pasha invaded Serbia in retaliation and, working its way up the Morava, captured Krushevatz, while a second army of forty thousand came from Bosnia. With the aid of a Russian corps of thirty thousand Karageorg inflicted a smashing defeat upon Krushid Pasha at Varvarinsko Pole, and the army invading from Bosnia was driven back into that province. After these successes the Serbs in their turn invaded South Serbia, while the Russian corps, having fulfilled its mission, regained the main Russian army in Bulgaria. The Turks asked for an armistice (December, 1810).

Turkey's war with the Russians was resumed in 1811, but not her war with the Serbs. The Sultan proposed to Karageorg the recognition of Serbian autonomy within the territory occupied by the Serbian forces, the recognition of Karageorg as ruler of Serbia on an equal footing with hospodars of Moldavia and Wallachia, with Serbia remaining a vassal to Turkey and paying tribute. The Serbs replied that since they were the allies of Russia they would leave the negotiations concerning their fate to Russia. Accordingly the Treaty of Bucharest, which put an end to the Russo-Turkish War, embodied most of the above clauses—namely, full autonomy for Serbia, full amnesty to the insurgents, payment of tribute by Serbia to Turkey, and retention of Turkish garrisons in the main fortresses of the province.

But the Napoleonic invasion of Russia and the withdrawal of the Moldavian Army of Kutuzov from the Balkans left the Serbs at the mercy of Turkish vengeance. The Turks invaded and reconquered Serbia, driving Karageorg in flight first to the mountains and then as a refugee into Russian Bessarabia. His place was taken by Milosh Obrenovic, a former farm hand, who was acceptable to the Turks because of his extreme servility and subservience to them. The change was not unwelcome to Russia, for by this time there were definitely two parties in Serbia—the pro-Russian and the pro-Austrian—and although most of the Serb military leaders were pro-Russian, Karageorg had wanted to place Serbia under an Austrian protectorate. Milosh's subservience, however, was more apparent than real; and after the fall of Napoleon, when Russia was once more powerful, he deemed it safe to start a rebellion against the Turks. He also sent a mission to the Congress of Vienna which was received there by Alexander I. Having listened to the complaints of the Serbs, the Czar lodged a protest through his ambassador in Constantinople against the nonobservance of the clauses concerning Serbia in the Treaty of Bucharest. In the meanwhile the Turks had assembled two powerful armies under Marashli Pasha and Kurshid Pasha for a simultaneous invasion of Serbia from Bulgaria and Bosnia, but the arrival of the Russian note and the fear of Russian armed intervention made the Porte issue an order for the armies to stop at the border, and for the commanders to open negotiations with Milosh. Marashli Pasha conceded to Milosh local self-government in the form of a revival of the old Skuptchina, the creation of mixed courts, and the right of the Serbs to carry arms; but the issues had to be endorsed by the Porte, and the latter allowed the confirmation of these rights by a Sultanic firman to be postponed indefinitely. Meanwhile, an attempt by Karageorg to return to Serbia and regain his leadership resulted in his assassination by order of Milosh. In November, 1817, freed of his rival, Milosh decided to proclaim himself Prince of Serbia. Turkey refused to acknowledge this change, but the speedy recognition of Milosh's title by Russia overrode the Porte's decision and placed the new semi-independent state on the map.

All these issues remained outstanding with the Porte up to 1820, though in the negotiations concerning the revision of the Treaty of Bucharest they were officially sponsored by the Russian embassy in Constantinople. As a result of the Russian pressure the Porte finally consented to receive a Serbian mission which had arrived in Constantinople to settle the issues. However, the outbreak of the Greek Revolution, with the resulting conflict between Russia and Turkey, gave an excuse for the Porte to break off these negotiations, and the

Serbian envoys were jailed as hostages. Not until the Conference of Akkerman did the Serbian question come up again, but here Russian diplomacy finally succeeded in obtaining from Turkey an acknowledgement of the new status of the Serbs. By the Convention of Akkerman the Russian protectorate over Serbia was recognized and Article VIII of the Treaty of Bucharest concerning Serbia was redefined. The Porte promised a *Hatti-Sherif* within a year and a half, granting self-government and the recognition of Prince Milosh as hereditary Prince within the borders of 1813, although Serbia was to remain under Ottoman suzerainty. Furthermore, Serbia was to be given back six disputed districts, a single tax was to replace all the duties and taxes within the province, and the Serbs were to be given religious freedom as well as the right to travel throughout the Ottoman Empire. But the Turks profited by the outbreak of the Russo-Turkish War to postpone the fulfilment of these pledges, and the matter had to be taken up anew after the war.

IV

Ypsilanti's rebellion in Rumania produced very grave repercussions both in Turkey and in her Greek provinces, and, notwithstanding Czar Alexander's desire to keep his country aloof, finally involved Russia. Indeed, an insurrection in Morea followed one month after Ypsilanti's invasion of Moldavia, and the Turks were virtually driven out of the peninsula. At the news of this double insurrection the fury of Sultan Mahmoud II knew no bounds. He ordered the arrest of Greek notables in the Phanar suspected of participation in the Hetairia, and had them put to death. The Grand Vizier was discharged on the ground of weakness, and in the *Hatti-Sherif* appointing his successor the Sultan made an appeal to the Moslems to defend their faith. Thus religious fanaticism was aroused with ominous results. In April more members of the Greek aristocracy in the Phanar were put to death, and this was followed by mob violence; Greek villages on the Bosporus and the Greek quarter in Constantinople were mobbed, and hundreds of Greeks were massacred. Finally on Easter night as the eighty-four-year-old Patriarch of the Greek Church, Gregory, was officiating at the midnight service, a band of Janizaries broke into the church, dragged him out, and after tearing off his sacrificial robes, hanged him on the gates of the church. Two archbishops, ten members of the Holy

Synod, eight priests, and nearly all the members of the congregation were put to death. Following this, a general massacre of the Greeks occurred, and in Constantinople alone ten thousand were said to have perished after submitting to horrible indignities and tortures administered with no regard for innocence, sex, or age. The body of the murdered Patriarch was delivered to a band of Jews who dragged it through the streets (April 24) and finally threw it into the sea, but the body was recovered and smuggled out to Odessa. By order of the Czar great honors were accorded the murdered Patriarch, and after three days of prayer in all the churches his body was buried in the Cathedral of the Transfiguration. At the news of these events the whole Greek nation took to arms and began fighting with desperate courage.

As for Russia, though she could disavow Ypsilanti, she could not allow to go unheeded the assassination of the head of the Orthodox Church and the horrors which had followed, especially since, in their blind fury, the Turks had also killed some Russian sailors and insulted the Russian flag. In the face of this situation the first move of the Russian ambassador in Constantinople, Baron Stroganov, was to consult his colleagues in an endeavor to create a united diplomatic front of Christian nations. At his request a meeting of ambassadors took place on April 25, and Stroganov suggested that a collective note by all the powers should be addressed to the Porte protesting the massacres, and that each power should send a man-of-war to Constantinople, ostensibly for the protection of its nationals. But neither the French nor the British ambassadors were prepared to commit themselves to such measures, fearing that Turkey would see in them an assault on her sovereignty. The next meeting took place on the sixteenth, and in the interval Lord Strangford had received a letter from the Reiss Effendi giving assurances that these events would not be repeated. Pointing out that British policy was based on the principle of noninterference in internal affairs of other nations, Lord Strangford declared at this meeting that Turkey had given sufficient reassurances, and he was warmly seconded by the French chargé d'affaires, Vicomte de Viella. In vain did Stroganov point out that Turkey never abided by her promises relating to nonoppression of Christian minorities and that the Reiss Effendi's promises did not mean anything; the British and the French ministers carried their point, and no collective note was sent. Turkey learned that there was no solidarity among Christian powers on behalf of Christians.

Only a week later a Greek bishop and six members of the Greek colony in Constantinople were put to death, and this was followed by riots and massacres of Greeks in the Phanar district as well as in the suburbs and villages along the Bosporus. The new Patriarch, Eugene, had to flee for safety. Stroganov called for a warship from Odessa, and presented a letter of protest to the Grand Vizier to be forwarded to the Sultan. The Grand Vizier refused to accept the letter. As the disorders continued, Stroganov broke off relations with the Porte and remained in seclusion in his embassy awaiting instructions from St. Petersburg. But the Turks struck back. With the Austrian embassy acting as intermediary, the Porte forwarded a letter on June 27 to Nesselrode complaining of the activities of Stroganov, as well as of the protection given by Russia to the Greek rebels. It further justified the killing of the Patriarch on the ground that he was a traitor, and drew a caustic parallel to the death of the last Patriarch in Russia, supposedly killed by Peter the Great in 1715. In writing this the Grand Vizier was in error, for the Patriarch Adrian died a natural death and was not murdered by Peter the Great, but the reference was so obviously insulting as to provoke a violent Russian reaction to the note. This came in the form of an ultimatum of eight days, presented by Stroganov to the Porte on July 18, demanding that Turkey should pledge herself to rebuild the destroyed Christian churches, to protect the Christians from further persecution, and, in the case of the Danubian Principalities, to re-establish the dispossessed hospodars and remove her troops under the clauses of the Treaty of Bucharest. On July 26 Stroganov sent his dragoman to the Porte to ask for an answer; the Turkish Government requested an extension of time to study the document, but Stroganov, adamant, demanded his passports and left Constantinople on August 10. War seemed imminent; indeed, military preparations were being undertaken in Russia. But Alexander, not wanting war, contented himself with this rupture of diplomatic relations and did not press the point further. The British, French, and Austrian diplomats busied themselves trying to patch up the quarrel, but the issue dragged on, and as long as the Turks refused to comply with the ultimatum the stalemate continued. It was not until the reign of Nicholas I that the issue was settled.

In order to carry on their struggle against the Turks, the Greeks were in need of money and seagoing vessels. They hoped to obtain both of these from Russia, even though Alexander's support of their cause had been hesitant and lukewarm. For this purpose they dispatched a delegation under Metaxas to the Congress of Verona in the hope of gaining Russia's support, by which they might obtain credits either directly from Russia or, through Russia's influence, from France and England. But their hopes were not fulfilled. Alexander, at first willing to raise the Greek issue at the Congress, later (apparently under pressure from Metternich) avoided doing so, and the Greek delegation never got beyond Ancona. "Not a voice was raised in favor of the Greeks," wrote Gentz.[10] Thus disappointed in the matter of support from Russia, the Greeks turned to England.

Castlereagh had already been approached in this connection in 1820, but had expressed his doubts as to the chance of success for the revolution. He had stated to Metternich that providence alone could help Greece, and to Sir Charles Bagot, British minister in St. Petersburg, he wrote that he was not convinced that the expulsion of the Turks from Greece would be beneficial to the Greeks.[11] Canning, on his side, was lukewarm toward the idea of getting Britain entangled in a Continental issue, but he was also anxious not to allow Russia to gain further influence in the Eastern Mediterranean. Thus he refused all open support of the Greek revolution, "for fear lest England, using force in Greece, would be accused of joining the Holy Alliance";[12] but he was prepared to undermine Russian influence with the Greeks by helping them indirectly. This help took the form, in 1823, of recognizing the Greeks as belligerents, a move which permitted them to attack any ship entering Turkish harbors or carrying munitions to the Turks. In 1824 a loan of £3,000,000 at 13⅓ per cent interest was granted by a consortium of British bankers, followed by a loan of £800,000 at 5 per cent. These

[10] Friedrich von Gentz, *Dépêches inédites du chevalier de Gentz aux hospodars de Valachie . . .* (Paris, 1876-1877), I, 157.

[11] Edouard Driault et Michel Lhéritier, *Histoire diplomatique de la Grèce de 1821 à nos jours* (Paris, 1925-1926), I, 160-161.

[12] Stanley Lane-Pool, *The Life of Lord Stratford de Redcliffe, K. G.* (London and New York, 1890), p. 116.

were followed by a series of loans which resulted in the virtual financing of the revolution by the City of London. Furthermore, the publicity given the Greek cause by the death of Lord Byron and the appointment of Lord Cochrane to the command of the Greek naval forces were factors which made the Greeks turn to England for protection. Thus Russia once more met England as a rival, even in this corner of the Near East. France also extended some aid to the Greeks, but her main interests were in Egypt, so that her competition for the time being was not to be taken seriously.

Notwithstanding the British inroads into the Russian sphere of influence, Alexander remained firm in his decision not to allow Russia to become involved in a war over Greece. War fever was rising in Russia, and Alexander alone opposed it, though for a moment at the time of the recall of Stroganov he seems to have wavered. In 1819 Count Kankrin presented a secret memorandum on the expulsion of the Turks from Europe and the military measures to be taken for this purpose. In July, 1821, Diebitch presented a report concerning the military preparations for a war with Turkey, and at the moment Alexander thought of rallying France to his cause. Speaking to LaFerronays, the French ambassador in St. Petersburg, he said, "With the aid of France everything would become easy, even if Austria and England side with the Porte . . ."; and he added that the best solution would be that "nobody should take anything [from Turkey], and that we should give good governments to those countries."[13] He made a bid for an alliance: "Your old policy ties you to the Turks. Their alliance would give you few advantages today. It is Russia that France should have for ally today." But this mood seems to have vanished quickly, and the true nature of Alexander's thought appeared when he said, "If we answer Turkey with war, it would be the triumph of the Paris Central Committee [a revolutionary body believed to co-ordinate revolutionary movements all over Europe] and not one government would remain standing on its feet."[14] It was this consideration above all, and his war weariness after such a stormy career, that made Alexander stubbornly maintain his attitude in the face of opposition all around him.

Inevitably on this issue he came to the parting of the ways with Capo d'Istria, who, listening more and more to the call of his Greek

[13] Schilder, *Imperator Aleksandr Pervyi,* IV, 269. [14] *Ibid.,* IV, 225.

blood, was pleading with him not to negotiate but to act *(ne plus négocier mais âgir)*. When early in 1822 Metternich suggested a meeting of allied foreign ministers at Vienna, preliminary to the calling of a congress to discuss Greek affairs, Alexander accepted, thereby abandoning a principle of Russian diplomacy observed since the time of Catherine II—the principle of not permitting the interference of foreign powers in the relations between Russia and Turkey. Capo d'Istria thereupon presented his resignation, which Alexander accepted. In August Capo d'Istria left Russia to live in Geneva, and Alexander in parting said: "We will see each other . . . you can be assured that my feelings toward you will not be altered."[15] Commenting on this departure, the historian Karamzin wrote to a friend at the time: "It is a pity that the amiable and intelligent Count Capo d'Istria is leaving us. There are few such people. Europe has buried the Greeks; God grant the resurrection of the dead."

Indeed, the triumph of the reactionary elements in Russia and of Metternich, who had so long been intriguing against Capo d'Istria, was great, but Russia had not "buried the Greeks." What this step meant was that Russia was not going to war for them. Alexander was prepared, nevertheless, to keep on using diplomatic pressure, and, in his mind, the Greek question was to be integrated into the much more complex problem of the general relations between Russia and Turkey. It must also be borne in mind that up to this point there was no urgency in providing military aid to the Greeks, because thus far they were defeating the Turks. Indeed, the Turks had been driven out of Morea, and on January 13, 1822, the so-called Constitution of Epidauros had been proclaimed—the first attempt to give the whole of Greece a centralized government under Greek rule; and on June 21 the Turkish garrison holding the Acropolis at Athens capitulated. Much graver from the point of view of the traditions of Russian diplomacy was the accusation, as stated by Grand Duke Nicholas, that "the affairs of Turkey, directed since the time of Catherine II by the Emperors of Russia communicating directly with Stamboul, passed under the control of Europe."[16] To some extent this interference of other powers in Russo-Turkish affairs was due to the very nature of the situation which developed after the recall of Stroganov. Indeed, since Russia had broken off relations

[15] *Ibid.*, IV, 231.

[16] Nicholas Mikhailovich, *op. cit.*, I, 267.

with Turkey, she had to use the mediation of the British and Austrian legations in Constantinople to deal with the Porte, and her interests in Turkey were placed in the hands of the British minister.

Metternich and Canning had taken very much the same position —both were working for a Russo-Turkish reconciliation because of distrust of Alexander's pacific intentions in the crisis. Seeing in Alexander's sympathy toward the Greeks a revival of his old dreaded spirit of liberalism, a trend which would break up the Holy Alliance and endanger the struggle against the revolutionary spirit elsewhere, Metternich suspected Alexander of using the Greek Revolution as a pretext for further dismemberment of Turkey. He was not convinced by Tatishtchev's declaration in Vienna that the Czar "wanted nothing but peace, the integrity of Turkey, and an amnesty for all rebels."[17] He conceded the right of Russia to claim the fulfilment of the treaty obligations which the Porte had signed, but, together with Stratford-Canning in Constantinople, he refused to admit that these treaty obligations in any way involved Greece. With these considerations in mind British diplomacy was working for the restoration of diplomatic relations between Russia and Turkey, as a tangible sign of reconciliation and a base for further settlement of the outstanding issues. But Alexander remained adamant: Turkey must first comply with the terms of the Russian ultimatum of 1821 before a minister would be appointed to Constantinople. Failing to obtain any results from Russia, the British tried to persuade the Turks to yield, but without success; a complete deadlock ensued, both in the Greek situation and in the thorny question of the evacuation of the Danubian Principalities. The Anglo-Turkish negotiations broke down completely in October, 1823; and Strangford, writing to Wellesley, complained that "this worse than Turkish obstinacy in refusing to listen to reason on this point [the evacuation of the Principalities] is very discouraging and very vexatious."[18]

The next attempt to break the deadlock came, however, from Russia. In January, 1823, Alexander arranged for a secret meeting with Emperor Francis at Czernovitz to discuss the Oriental situation and to obtain a community of action with Austria. Metternich, feigning a diplomatic illness, according to Gentz, was not present;

[17] *Mémoires du Prince de Metternich . . .*, III, 573.

[18] Harold William Vazeille Temperley, *The Foreign Policy of Canning, 1822-1827; England, the Neo-Holy Alliance and the New World* (London, 1925), p. 330.

the two emperors passed a week together in October, that is, just at the time of the breakdown of the British efforts in Turkey. It was here that Alexander first raised the question of holding a general conference at St. Petersburg. In January of the following year the great powers were officially invited to a conference to discuss a Russian plan for the settlement of the Balkan question. Accompanying the circular letter of invitation was a note dated January 9, 1824, written by Nesselrode, containing the outlines of the Russian plan. Aside from general provisions, such as forcing the Turks to guarantee the nonmolestation of Christian minorities in Turkey, and the establishment of autonomous principalities in the Balkans, it offered a suggestion for settling the Greek question by the setting up of three principalities, in East, West, and South Greece; the first to include Thessaly, Boeotia, and Attica; the second, Epirus, Acarnania, and the former Venetian colonies; the third, Morea and Crete. These states were to be autonomous and enjoy freedom of trade, but remain vassals of Turkey and pay an annual tribute to the Sultan.[19] It was probable that this plan was prompted by a twofold desire—to limit the spread of British influence in Greece, and to meet the conditions existing at the time in Greece proper, where rival governments were quarreling between themselves. But when through an indiscretion, probably intentional, of the British Government, the plan was published in the *Constitutionnel* of Paris on May 31, it produced a storm of indignation in Greece. In a note to Canning, Rhodias, Secretary of the Executive Council of Greece, declared grandiloquently that the Greeks would prefer a glorious death to having such a shameful fate imposed upon them. Mavrocordatos went even further and, denouncing the "hospodarization of Greece," offered Morea to England as a protectorate in return for British aid.[20] Thus the net result of this move of Nesselrode was to throw Greece still further into the arms of Britain. As for Turkey, she flatly rejected the proposal as an interference in her internal affairs.

It was under these auspices that the conference opened in St. Petersburg in June with all the powers present, but recessed without results and did not actually get under way until it met again on February 24. Metternich, who disliked the idea of the conference,

[19] Theodor Schiemann, *Geschichte Russlands unter Kaiser Nikolaus I* (Berlin, 1904-1919), I, 334-335.

[20] Temperley, *op. cit.*, p. 333.

continued to delay the appointment of his delegate, Lebzeltern. France, with her eyes on Spain, was lukewarm, and England refused to participate, merely ordering Stratford-Canning to proceed to St. Petersburg as unofficial observer. Alexander himself was not pressing matters very strongly, and confessed to LaFerronays with regard to the Greeks, "I do not want their independence or their complete triumph, but there exists there a center *(foyer)* of conflagration which it is necessary to stamp out."[21] Under these circumstances and in this atmosphere the conference was doomed to failure from the start. Russia put forward insistently the demand that force be applied if necessary. Metternich opposed this, though finally on March 13 a protocol was drawn up embodying the results of the conference to date, forming a compromise between the Austrian and Russian views. According to this protocol Turkey would be invited to recognize the right of European powers to intervene in Near Eastern affairs, and an armistice was to be imposed in the Greco-Turkish conflict under threat of intervention by the powers; but Austria, France, and Prussia took the teeth out of the proposal by eliminating any element of compulsion or threat of action by the powers.

Thus the conference had failed to achieve anything, and though Russia was given the initiative to send the note at her discretion and finally delivered it on June 7, it merely produced an effect, in the words of the Austrian internuncio in Constantinople, Baron Ottenfels, of the four powers "discharging their little popgun at the Porte." Indeed, Turkey, interpreting the absence of England at the conference as a sign of division between the powers, and furthermore having received secret encouragement from Metternich, not only refused to comply with the Russian note but declined any further dealings with the powers on the Greek question. The importance of the conference lay, not in the direct results achieved, but in its indirect consequences. Alexander, informed of Metternich's intrigues with Turkey, was so incensed that on August 18 he ordered a circular letter sent to the Russian envoys abroad notifying them that Russia could no longer work with Austria on the Eastern question. This move brought to an end the Neo-Holy Alliance. Changing her course, Russia turned to England once more for support, and the conference in which England had refused to participate thus para-

[21] Waliszewski, *Le Règne d'Alexandre Ier*, III, 115.

doxically opened the way for a *rapprochement* between these two countries.

It will be recalled that the British ambassador in St. Petersburg had attended the opening of the conference in June, but England had refused any official participation when the work was resumed in February. However, the arrival in January of Sir Stratford-Canning in St. Petersburg as observer obviously could be used as an occasion for direct negotiations between the countries. Neither side wanted to make the first move, although George Canning had instructed his cousin to use any opportunity for a direct arrangement of the outstanding issues, without, however, making any advances in that direction. Thus in the first meeting between Nesselrode and Canning the discussion concerned the Anglo-Russian difficulties in the Pacific Ocean, while both sides studiously avoided mentioning Greece, until in leaving Canning made a passing reference to that country. This permitted Nesselrode to consider that the British had taken the first step, and the ice was broken.

It was, however, the clever and intriguing Countess Lieven who was really responsible for bringing the two countries closer together. Arriving in St. Petersburg from London at this time, she met Nesselrode and impressed upon him the fact that Canning was seeking an understanding with Russia concerning the Greek situation, that he had dreamed in his youth of the liberation of Greece, and that he was not so radical in his views as was generally supposed. Nesselrode mentioned these things to the Czar, who granted an audience to Countess Lieven on the eve of her departure for London in September, and was favorably impressed by all she said. She thus became the unofficial intermediary between Nesselrode and Canning, and upon her return to London she hinted to Canning that though Russia would not take the initiative in the matter, the government in St. Petersburg would welcome an agreement with England, considering that the Holy Alliance was virtually dead. Canning in turn was impressed, and began considering the possibility of joint action with Russia to impose an armistice in the Balkans, and even dropped a hint to Sir George Cockburn touching the strength of the Mediterranean fleet.

Meanwhile the Turks, under pressure from Britain, had accepted the clause in the Russian ultimatum dealing with the evacuation of the Principalities, and Russia appointed Minciaky, her consul-general in Moldavia, as chargé d'affaires in Constantinople, to prepare the way for the re-establishment of diplomatic relations. Nevertheless, she delayed sending Ribeaupierre, who was to succeed Stroganov, pending the full acceptance of the ultimatum. Matters stood at this point when three important developments ushered in a new phase in the situation. These were the death of Louis XVIII in 1824 and the advent of Charles X, which prepared the way for closer co-operation between Russia and France; the death of Alexander I in 1825, which brought the energetic and aggressive Nicholas I to power; and, finally, the appearance in Greece of the Egyptian army under Ibrahim Pasha.

At the time of his death Alexander was still in the prime of life, in the middle forties, but his health had been undermined by the struggles and strains of his stormy career. He was mentally and morally exhausted, and his mystical tendencies had developed to a point where he had more than once hinted that he dreamed of finishing his days in the seclusion of a monastery. In the late fall of 1825 he accompanied his wife, Empress Elizabeth, who had been ailing, to Taganrog in southern Russia, where it was hoped the warmer climate would help her recover. Here, during an inspection of the southern provinces, he caught a chill which developed into the illness from which he never recovered. A persistent legend has it that he did not actually die at this time, but went to reside in a monastery in Siberia under the name of Fedor Kuzmich, and lived there for more than thirty years longer, and that the body of a soldier had been interred in his place in the Cathedral of St. Peter and St. Paul in St. Petersburg, the burial place of the Czars of Russia. Much research has been carried on in an effort to solve this question, but to this day the mystery of his death still remains. Be that as it may, the disappearance of Emperor Alexander from the political scene of Europe came just when all the immediate issues in the field of international relations resulting from the French Revolution and the Napoleonic Wars had been settled. Viewed from this angle it may be stated that the death of Alexander marks the end of an era, at least in so far as the influence of Russia on European affairs was concerned.

But life of course cannot stand still, and though Europe had settled down to a relative peace which was to last for over a quarter of a century, the Eastern Question was rapidly approaching a climax. Under the energetic impulse of Alexander's successor, his young and ambitious brother, Nicholas I, Russia was to be plunged into a new war with Turkey only three years hence. But the very fact that from now on the attention of all the European powers was to be riveted on the Balkans and Greece showed that there was no other issue of primary importance in Europe itself and that a state of temporary equilibrium had been reached. The all-important role played by Russia in maintaining this equilibrium has, the writer hopes, been demonstrated in the preceding pages. Even though Alexander for only a short while dominated the scene of European diplomacy, his genius consisted in never losing sight of Europe as a whole. He was bitterly criticized in Russia for sacrificing the interests of Russia proper on occasion to the wider concept of peace and the maintenance of order in Europe. That his dream of European federation did not work out, that he himself in the course of his career evolved from liberalism to the reactionary conservatisms of the Holy Alliance, does not detract from the fact that in the main he pursued his course with unflinching determination and steadfastness. But if on the other hand we compare the place occupied by Russia in European affairs at the beginning of his reign and at the time of his death, the legacy of accumulated power and prestige he left to his successor makes a most impressive record which should have offset the complaints of his critics in Russia.

The results of the reign of Alexander I may be summed up as comprising two main threads which were to be closely woven by his successor into the fabric of future Russian history: on one side the immensely enhanced power and prestige of Russia, on the other the quest for permanent stability and order in the whole of Europe. But therein lay the danger, for an impetus once given does not stop, and the precarious equilibrium established in Europe was to be jeopardized by the continuing rise of Russia herself in the middle of the nineteenth century, just as it was to be imperiled at the turn of the twentieth century by the rise of Germany. The strong-willed, determined, but less brilliant Nicholas I was to associate himself even more actively than his brother with what has come to be known—not entirely correctly in view of the role played by Russia—as the

Metternich System. For though the ideas which have gained in history the luster of the accepted creed of conservatism are associated with this Austrian statesman, it was Nicholas I who made himself the real leader of the conservative alliance in Europe. Thus the rift which first appeared in the concert of European powers at the congresses of Troppau and Verona gradually developed into a clear-cut contest between the liberals and the conservatives, with England and France on one side and Russia on the other, flanked once more by a self-effacing Prussia and at times a wavering Austria. If this had not been so, the next great conflict in European history would have involved Austria or Prussia instead of Russia, and there would have been no Crimean War. But the position of predominance achieved by Nicholas I as well as his sponsorship of conservative principles was viewed by the powers as a menace to European equilibrium, and resulted in the lining up of England, France, Austria, Sardinia, and Turkey—a veritable league of European nations—against Russia, supported hesitantly by a friendly but neutral Prussia. With Russia's defeat in the Crimean War the equilibrium in Europe was restored once more; Russia resumed her place in Europe on the same level as the other great powers, and a historical trend begun by Catherine the Great and so notably developed by the genius of Alexander I came to an end.

Bibliography

Alison, Sir Archibald. *Lives of Lord Castlereagh and Sir Charles Stewart, the Second and Third Marquesses of Londonderry*. Edinburgh, 1861. 3 vols.

Blease, Walter Lyon. *Suvorof*. New York, 1920.

Bogdanovich, General Modest Ivanovich. *Geschichte des Krieges 1814 in Frankreich und des Sturzes Napoleon's I., nach den zuverlässigsten Quellen*. . . . Aus dem Russischen von G. Baumgarten. Leipzig, 1866. 2 vols.

———. *Istoria Tsarstvovania Imperatora Aleksandra I i Rossia v ego Vremia*. St. Petersburg, 1869-1871. 6 vols.

Bourdeau, Colonel Emile-Hippolyte. *Campagnes modernes*. Paris, 1916. 3 vols.

Cambridge Modern History, Vol. X. Edited by A. W. Ward, G. W. Prothero, Stanley Leathes. New York, 1911.

Camon, Commandant Hubert. *La Guerre napoléonienne. Précis des campagnes*. Paris, 1903. 2 vols.

Castlereagh: *see* Stewart, Robert.

Caulaincourt, Marquis Armand Augustin Louis de. *With Napoleon in Russia: The Memoirs of General de Caulaincourt, Duke of Vicenza*. Abridged, edited, and with an introduction by George Libaire. New York, 1935.

Chateaubriand, Vicomte François René de. *Memoires d'outre tombe*. Paris, n.d.

———. *Oeuvres complètes de Chateaubriand*. Nouvelle édition . . . précédée d'une étude littéraire sur Chateaubriand, par M. Sainte-Beuve. Paris, 1861. 12 vols.

Clausewitz, General Carl von. *La Campagne de 1812 en Russie*. Traduit de l'allemand par M. Begouën. Paris, 1900.

Combe, Colonel Michel. *Mémoires de colonel Combe sur les campagnes*
1896.
de Russie, 1912; de Saxe, 1913; de France, 1814 et 1815. Paris,

Creasy, Sir Edward Shepherd. *History of the Ottoman Turks: From the Beginning of Their Empire to the Present Time.* New York, 1878.

Cresson, William Penn. *The Holy Alliance: The European Background of the Monroe Doctrine.* New York, 1922.

Crousaz-Crétet, Léon de. *Le Duc de Richelieu en Russie et en France, 1766-1822.* Paris, 1897.

Czartoryski, Le Prince Adam Jerzy. *Alexandre Ier et le prince Czartoryski, correspondance particulière et conversations.* 1801-1823, publiées par le prince Ladislas Czartoryski, avec une introduction par Charles de Mazade. Paris, 1865.

Driault, Edouard. *Napoléon et l'Europe. Austerlitz, la fin du Saint-empire (1804-1806).* Paris, 1897.

———, et Lhéritier, Michel. *Histoire diplomatique de la Grèce de 1821 à nos jours.* Paris, 1925-1926. 5 vols.

Dupuis, Charles. *Le Ministère de Talleyrand en 1814.* Paris, 1919. 2 vols.

Finlay, George. *History of the Greek Revolution.* London, 1861. 2 vols.

Fortescue, Sir John William. *A History of the British Army.* London and New York, 1899-1930. 13 vols.

Freksa, Friedrich (comp.). *A Peace Congress of Intrigues (Vienna, 1815): A Vivid, Intimate Account of the Congress of Vienna Composed of the Personal Memoirs of Its Important Participants.* Translated, and with introduction and notes, by Harry Hansen. New York, 1919.

García de Léon y Pizarro, José. *Memorias de la Vida del Excmo. Señor D. José García de Léon y Pizarro.* Madrid, 1894. 3 vols.

Gentz, Friedrich von. *Dépêches inédites du chevalier de Gentz aux hospodars de Valachie, pour servir à l'histoire de la politique européenne (1813-1818).* Paris, 1876-1877. 3 vols.

Haumant, Emile. *La Culture française en Russie (1700-1900).* Paris, 1910.

Hennequin, Captaine Louis. *Zurich. Masséna en Suisse, messidor an vii–brumaire an viii (juillet-octobre 1799).* Paris, 1911.

Houssaye, Henry. *1814.* Paris, 1888.

Iorga, Neculai. *Histoire des relations russo-roumaines.* Jassy, 1917.

Labaume, Eugène. *Relation circonstanciée de la campagne de Russie.* Paris, 1814.

Lafuente y Zamalloa, Modesto. *Histoiria general de España, desde los tiempos más remotos hasta nuestros días.* Madrid, 1840-1867. 30 vols.

Lane-Pool, Stanley. *The Life of Lord Stratford de Redcliffe, K. G.* London and New York, 1890.

Lazarovich-Hrebelianovich, Prince Stephen Lazar Eugene. *The Servian People, Their Past Glory and Their Destiny.* New York, 1910. 2 vols.

Leger, Louis Paul Marie. *Histoire de l'Autriche-Hongrie, depuis les origines jusqu'en 1918.* Paris, 1920.

Löwenhielm, Carl Gustaf. *Min lefvernes beskrifning.* Stockholm, 1923. 1923.

Lutostański, Karol (ed.). *Les Partages de la Pologne et la lutte pour l'indépendance.* Lausanne, 1918.

Maggiolo, Vicomte Adrien de. *Corse, France et Russie. Pozzo di Borgo, 1764-1842.* Paris, 1890.

Marriott, Sir John Arthur Ransome. *The Eastern Question: An Historical Study in European Diplomacy.* (2d edition, revised.) Oxford, 1918.

Martens, Fedor Fedorovitch. *Recueil des traités et conventions conclus par la Russie avec les puissances étrangères.* St. Petersburg, 1874-1909. 15 vols.

Metternich, Chevalier de. *Mémoires, documents et écrits divers laissés par le prince de Metternich, chancelier de cour et d'Etat.* Publiés par son fils le prince Richard de Metternich, classés et réunis par M. A. de Klinkowstroem. Paris, 1880-1884. 8 vols.

Miller, William. *The Balkans: Roumania, Bulgaria, Servia and Montenegro.* London, 1923.

Morfill, William Richard. *A History of Russia from the Birth of Peter the Great to Nicholas II.* London, 1902.

———. *Poland.* London, 1893.

Mowat, Robert Balmain. *A History of European Diplomacy 1815-1914.* London, 1927.

Nesselrode, Count Charles Robert Vasilievitch. *Lettres et papiers du chancelier Cte de Nesselrode, 1760-1850 [-1856], extraits de ses archives.* Publiés et annotés, avec une introduction, par le Cte A. de Nesselrode. Paris [1908-1912]. 11 vols.

Nicholas [Nikolai Mikhailovich], Grand Duke. *L'Empereur Alexandre Ier*. St. Petersburg, 1912. 2 vols.

Notovitch, Nicolai. *La Russie et l'alliance anglaise, étude historique et politique.* Paris, 1906.

Phipps, Colonel Ramsey Weston. *The Armies of the First French Republic and the Rise of the Marshals of Napoleon I.* London, 1939. 5 vols.

Pingaud, Léonce. *Bernadotte, Napoléon et les Bourbons (1797-1814).* Paris, 1901.

Pisani, Chanoine Paul. *La Dalmatie de 1797 à 1815, épisode des conquêtes napoléoniennes.* Paris, 1893.

Polovtsov, Aleksandr Aleksandrovitch (ed.). *Correspondance diplomatique des ambassadeurs et ministres de Russie en France et de France en Russie avec leurs gouvernements, de 1814 à 1830.* St. Petersburg, 1902-1907. 3 vols. Also *Sbornik,* Vol. CXII.

Pozzo di Borgo, Charles. *Correspondance diplomatique du Cte Pozzo di Borgo et du Cte de Nesselrode.* Paris, 1890. 2 vols.

Rain, Pierre. *Un Tsar idéologue, Alexandre Ier (1777-1825).* Paris, 1913.

Rambaud, Alfred Nicolas. *A Popular History of Russia, from the Earliest Times to 1880.* Translated by L. B. Lang. Edited and enlarged by Nathan Haskell Dole. Including a History of the Turko-Russian War of 1877-78, from the Best Authorities, by the editor. Boston, 1882. 3 vols.

Rodocanachi, Emmanuel-Pierre. *Bonaparte et les îles Ioniennes, un épisode des conquêtes de la République et du premier Empire (1797-1816).* Paris, 1899.

Rose, John Holland. *Life of William Pitt.* New York, 1924.

——— (ed.). *Select Despatches from the British Foreign Office Archives relating to the Formation of the Third Coalition against France, 1804-1805.* London, 1904.

Rostoptchin, Comte Feodor Vasilievitch. *La Vérité sur l'incendie de Moscou* . . . suivi de ses *Mémoires écrits en dix minutes; son mot sur Fouché, Talleyrand et Pothier; anecdote de la pelisse.* Paris, 1823.

Sbornik, Imperatorskago Russkago Istoricheskago Obchestva. St. Petersburg, 1864-1916. 148 vols.

Schiemann, Theodor. *Geschichte Russlands unter Kaiser Nikolaus I.* Berlin, 1904-1919. 4 vols.

Schilder, Nikolai Karlovich. *Imperator Aleksandr Pervyi, ego zhizn i tsarstvovanie.* St. Petersburg, 1897-1898. 4 vols.

———. *Imperator Nikolai Pervyi, ego zhizn i tsarstvovanie.* St. Petersburg, 1885-1886. 2 vols.

———. *Imperator Pavel Pervyi.* St. Petersburg, 1901.

Somberg, A. A. *A History of Sweden.* New York, 1931.

Sorel, Albert. *L'Europe et la révolution française.* Paris, 1885-1904. 8 vols.

Stewart, Robert [Viscount Castlereagh]. *Letters and Despatches of Viscount Castlereagh.* London, 1853. 12 vols.

Temperley, Harold William Vazeille. *The Foreign Policy of Canning, 1822-1827; England, the Neo-Holy Alliance, and the New World.* London, 1925.

Thiers, Adolphe. *Histoire du consulat et de l'empire,* faisant suite à *L'Histoire de la révolution française.* Paris, 1845-1884. 21 vols.

Vandal, Albert. *Napoléon et Alexandre Ier. L'Alliance russe sous le premier empire.* Paris, 1891-1896. 3 vols.

Waliszewski, Kazimierz. *Paul the First of Russia, the Son of Catherine the Great.* London, 1913.

———. *Le Règne d'Alexandre Ier.* Paris, 1925. 3 vols.

Walpole, Spencer. *A History of England from the Conclusion of the Great War in 1815.* London, 1878-1886. 6 vols.

Webster, Charles Kingsley. *The Foreign Policy of Castlereagh, 1815-1822, Britain and the European Alliance.* London, 1925.

———. *The Congress of Vienna, 1814-1815.* London, 1919.

Weil, Maurice Henri. *Les Dessous de Congrès de Vienne, d'après les documents originaux des archives du Ministère impérial et royal de l'intérieur à Vienne.* Paris, 1917. 2 vols.

Wellington, Arthur Wellesley, 1st Duke of. *Supplementary Despatches and Memoranda of Field Marshal Arthur, Duke of Wellington, K.G..* Edited by his son, the Duke of Wellington. London, 1858-1872. 15 vols.

Index